THEY TOLD
ME NOT
TO TAKE
THAT JOB

THEY TOLD ME NOT TO TAKE THAT JOB

Tumult, Betrayal, Heroics, *and*
The Transformation *of*
Lincoln Center

REYNOLD LEVY

PublicAffairs
New York

PublicAffairs books are available at special discounts for bulk purchases in the U.S. by corporations, institutions, and other organizations. For more information, please contact the Special Markets Department at the Perseus Books Group, 2300 Chestnut Street, Suite 200, Philadelphia, PA 19103, call (800) 810-4145, ext. 5000, or e-mail special.markets@perseusbooks.com.

Library of Congress Cataloging-in-Publication Data

Levy, Reynold.
  They told me not to take that job : tumult, betrayal, heroics, and the transformation of Lincoln Center / Reynold Levy.—First Edition.
     pages cm
  Includes bibliographical references and index.
  ISBN 978-1-61039-361-4 (hardback)—ISBN 978-1-61039-362-1 (ebook) 1. Performing arts—New York (State)—New York—Management. 2. Lincoln Center for the Performing Arts. 3. Levy, Reynold. I. Title.
  PN1588.N49L48 2015
  792.09747′1—dc23

                                                                              2014049065

First Edition

10 9 8 7 6 5 4 3 2 1

One of the longest journeys in the world is the journey from Brooklyn to Manhattan—or at least from certain neighborhoods in Brooklyn to certain parts of Manhattan. I have made that journey, but it is not from the experience of having made it that I know how very great the distance is, for I started on the road many years before I realized what I was doing, and by the time I did realize it, I was for all practical purposes already there.

NORMAN PODHORETZ, *Making It,* 1967

There are roughly three New Yorks. There is, first, the New York of the man and woman who was born here, who takes the city for granted and accepts its size and its turbulence as natural and inevitable. Second, there is the New York of the commuter— the city that is devoured by locusts each day and spat out each night. Third, there is the New York of the person who was born somewhere else and came to New York in quest of something.

Of these three trembling cities, the greatest is the last—the city of final destination, the city that is a goal. It is this third city that accounts for New York's high-strung disposition, its poetical deportment, its dedication to the arts and its incomparable achievements. Commuters give the city its tidal restlessness; natives give it solidity and continuity; but the settlers give it passion.

E. B. WHITE, *Here Is New York,* 1949

I look forward to an America which will reward achievement in the arts as we reward achievement in business or statecraft. I look forward to an America which will steadily raise the standards of artistic accomplishment and which will steadily enlarge cultural opportunities for all of our citizens. And I look forward to an America which commands respect throughout the world not only for its strength but for its civilization as well.

PRESIDENT JOHN F. KENNEDY,
Amherst College, October 26, 1963

To Elizabeth

For almost thirteen years, you were Lincoln Center's first lady.

I am very fortunate that you have been mine as well.

Thank you for reading, critiquing, and living through

the content of *They Told Me Not to Take That Job*.

I cannot imagine having been president of Lincoln Center

or an author without you at my side.

CONTENTS

A Photographic Ensemble between pages 166 and 167

ACKNOWLEDGMENTS

I've been working on my rewrite.
That's right
I'm gonna change the ending
Gonna throw away my title
And toss it in the trash
Every minute after midnight
All the time I'm spending
It's just for working on my rewrite
Gonna turn it into cash

—PAUL SIMON, "Rewrite," from
So Beautiful Or So What

Paul Simon is correct. Writing a book is mostly a solitary exercise. But I am very fortunate to have benefited from the guidance of good and gifted friends.

Those now noted read all or parts of the manuscript. They offered a combination of trenchant critiques and moral support. More than a few of their reactions caused me to reconsider a point of view or to deploy the English language more clearly and compellingly. I am exceedingly grateful for each reserving the time so that *They Told Me* could be a better book. Warm thanks are extended to Kara Medoff Barnett, Ed Bligh, Bart Friedman, Jennifer Homans, Winston Lord, Dick Martin, Nessa Rapoport, Dan Rubin, and Julie Sandorf.

I am particularly indebted to Jennifer, Kara, Ed, Winston, and Dick for the care and the discipline with which each offered me advice. They are extraordinary. Writers all, they knew precisely just how to convey criticism, leaving the product improved and the author's ego reasonably undamaged.

My son Justin gave every page of this memoir a close reading. Little can please a father more than to have a child, of whatever age, take such a keen interest in his work. I am the beneficiary of what can only be called a loving critique.

By contrast, being at the helm of an organization is very much a collective enterprise. Whatever accomplishments may have occurred during my tenures as executive director of the 92nd Street Y, president of the AT&T Foundation and a senior officer at the firm, president of the International Rescue Committee, and president of Lincoln Center can be attributed to extraordinarily gifted and driven staff and to resourceful, energetic, and influential boards of directors.

At Lincoln Center, a spirited expression of appreciation is extended to my chairpersons in chronological order of their service: Beverly Sills (since deceased), Bruce Crawford, Frank A. Bennack Jr., and Katherine Farley. Each was the embodiment of civic service at its best. Possessed of very different backgrounds, personalities, and operating styles, I admire them all. Lincoln Center is the stronger because they came to its side.

These extraordinary leaders symbolize the Lincoln Center trustees overall. Their generosity of spirit, time, and treasure keeps critical nonprofit institutions like Lincoln Center world class and vibrant. To serve with them, tackling problems (and sometimes people), was a rare privilege.

I am also indebted to my colleagues at Lincoln Center. The senior staff with whom I worked closely are a peerless group of professionals. They simply do not come any better than Ron Austin, Kara Medoff Barnett, Peter Duffin, Russell Granet, Jane Moss, Liza Parker, Tamar Podell, Nigel Redden, Lesley Rosenthal, Dan Rubin, and Betsy Vorce. Each in turn leads teams who brought to Lincoln Center uncommon energy, ideas, entrepreneurship, and managerial skill. While I am not given easily to superlatives, it comes naturally to state without fear of contradiction that the employee body of Lincoln Center knows no equal.

There was for me a professional life before Lincoln Center. Leading a singular organization, the International Rescue Committee, was a profoundly moving experience. It is not too much to say that it changed my life. I never think of a glass of clean water in the same way. It is precious and not to be taken for granted. To have been associated with an organization devoted to the relief of suffering of innocent victims of armed conflict was an extraordinary experience.

Not only was holding the post of president an honor, but I was truly blessed by my chairpersons, John Whitehead, Winston Lord, and Dr. James Strickler. All were conscious of the need for this CEO to enjoy considerable running room in an organization that itself required basic repair. Because of them, thousands of refugees are alive and thriving. But for them, the fate of thousands of others would be far less promising.

The Harvard Business School, the Peterson Institute for International Economics, the Nathan Cummings Foundation, and the Charles H. Revson Foundation, where I played supportive roles, and other organizations cited throughout the book, all helped to shape my view of leadership and to prepare me for its challenges. I am particularly grateful to Allen Grossman of HBS; Fred Bergsten, the founder and CEO of the Peterson Institute; and Julie Sandorf, the president of Revson Foundation. They have been exemplary colleagues in every way.

In writing this book, there are friends to whom I turned for help. There are colleagues at whose side I labored. There are mentors and role models from whom I learned much. And then there is someone who embodies all of these qualities. His name is Bart Friedman. We first met sixty years ago and for much of the time ever since we have kept in close touch. *They Told Me* benefited from his sage advice just as I have all of my adult life.

When my plans to leave Lincoln Center became news, Peter Osnos called to express keen interest in having PublicAffairs publish my book, if I intended to write one. His was a welcome gesture. Peter's introducing me to Clive Priddle, the publisher of PublicAffairs and my editor, was a gift. The team Clive assembled has handled all aspects of the magical transformation of a manuscript into what you now hold in your hands. They have done so with singular care and attention. At every turn, *They Told Me* is the beneficiary of Clive's high standards and those of his colleagues. I am one grateful author.

It is not for nothing that Andrew Wylie is a legendary agent. No e-mail to him failed to receive an almost instantaneous and thoughtful response. He is a man of few words, but it is worth weighing them carefully. I appreciate his tutelage.

For my final eighteen months at Lincoln Center, Rachel Moore was my executive assistant. Her efficiency, tact, graciousness, and sheer hard work made it possible for me to think about what this book might be like.

Annie Perretta worked conscientiously and skillfully to type the early drafts of this manuscript. She was a joy to be around. Apparently I was not, as she abandoned me for the Stern School of Business. I am grateful to her for assuming this accountability. It was an act of highly valued friendship.

She then passed on this responsibility to Henry Wainhouse. Henry, too, took on this assignment with consummate care, skill, and good humor. He did so at all hours, sometimes seven days a week, until it was complete.

I cannot imagine undertaking and completing this work without their collective assistance.

I am not sure whether it is easier or more difficult to live with an around-the-clock chief executive or a crazed writer. Somehow my wife Elizabeth has managed both with aplomb. She not only read *They Told Me*. She not only critiqued it. She lived it. Countless people have been introduced to Lincoln Center by her during my tenure as president. She was nothing less than Lincoln Center's first lady.

I am lucky that she has been mine, too.

PROLOGUE

Much of my professional life has been spent as the chief executive officer of three institutions: the 92nd Street Y, an internationally renowned community and cultural center; then the International Rescue Committee, a leading refugee relief and resettlement agency; and finally Lincoln Center, America's oldest and the world's largest and most prominent performing arts complex.

I have also served as the architect and first president of the AT&T Foundation, at its founding one of America's largest asset-based corporate philanthropic funds, and chairman of the board of two bellwether private foundations, Nathan Cummings and Charles H. Revson. The combination of leading top-notch public service organizations and directing over $1.5 billion of grants to hundreds of recipients left me with nothing short of a sense of reverence for what nonprofits and foundations can accomplish. The roles I played allowed me to encounter professionals and trustees at their very best: fully aligned, thoroughly committed, remarkably resourceful, and utterly devoted to the discharge of their missions.

The results? Countless lives saved, the sick healed, children educated, clients trained for jobs, and millions exposed to the very best in the performing and visual arts that our planet has to offer. Nonprofits can rescue refugees and displaced people and reunite children separated from their families. They can eliminate cholera, polio, malaria, and HIV-AIDS from the face of the earth. They can revolutionize the delivery of health, educational, social, and cultural services using the wonders of twenty-first-century technology. They can do all of these things and much more when leadership is encouraged and when vital energy is aimed directly at the client and the cause.

Sadly, I have also witnessed, up-close and personal, institutional disarray and dereliction of duty. It is very distressing to encounter professionals who do not measure up to the standard of conduct that those they serve have every right to expect. It is painful to observe trustees in positions of authority who permit such deficient behavior in those who report to them. When such trustees are themselves casual about the discharge of their own solemn responsibilities, I despair.

This memoir reveals the dynamics of some of these nongovernmental enterprises. Millions of employees and volunteers labor diligently to support them. They all deserve well-governed and well-led organizations, places in which to do their best work.

Those in positions of authority who fall well short of accomplishing what is reasonably expected of them are often not held accountable. How can that be? When customers and audiences are poorly served. When budgets are in deficit condition. When operations are off kilter. And when balance sheets are drained of assets. Such performance failures are hardly inevitable. They are the consequence of poorly monitored institutions and of inept management. They are examples of leadership gone astray.

Despite the lapses that I cite, I hope readers will come away from this volume with a palpable sense of why America's nonprofit institutions are so important. The challenges of discharging their mission well are easily as complicated as running a commercial or governmental entity, and no less significant for the welfare of our communities and for the competitive standing of our country.

I wrote this book wishing that professionals and volunteers might find useful lessons from my experience. It will be a source of pleasure if there are takeaways in these pages that can help others who are striving for superior programs, healthier balance sheets, sounder operating budgets, and excellent governance.

This is my account, and I do my best in good faith to accurately depict Lincoln Center's officials and other important figures, revealing their noble feats of leadership and their painful acts of omission and commission, the better to learn from them.

The three organizations with which I was privileged to be associated are highly regarded. Whatever their shortfalls, deficiencies, and blemishes, the 92nd Street Y, the IRC, and Lincoln Center continue to draw to themselves unparalleled levels of professional talent, voluntary expertise, and philanthropic resources.

The character, comportment, and competence of nonprofit organizations are not to be taken for granted. Eternal vigilance is the price we must pay for ensuring that valuable institutions like these will remain beacons of superlative service. America needs tens of thousands of public service agencies, each in its own way serving as a source of excellence and object of civic pride.

I hope my story assists and encourages those drawn to causes such as these.

Map of the Lincoln Center Campus

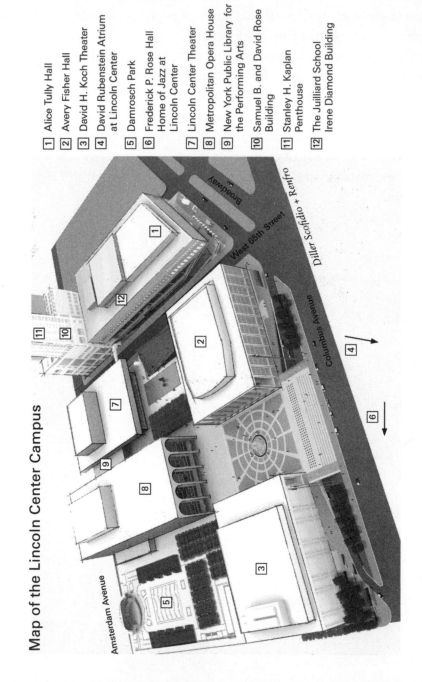

1. Alice Tully Hall
2. Avery Fisher Hall
3. David H. Koch Theater
4. David Rubenstein Atrium at Lincoln Center
5. Damrosch Park
6. Frederick P. Rose Hall Home of Jazz at Lincoln Center
7. Lincoln Center Theater
8. Metropolitan Opera House
9. New York Public Library for the Performing Arts
10. Samuel B. and David Rose Building
11. Stanley H. Kaplan Penthouse
12. The Juilliard School Irene Diamond Building

CHAPTER I

A Kid from Brooklyn Becomes a President (Again)

I was warned. They told me not to take that job.

"It's a freewheeling circus, Reynold. And there's no ringmaster."

"Why would you want to cope with so many self-reverential personalities run amok?"

"Only Darwin and Hobbes would fully understand what's really going on over there."

To compete to be the president of Lincoln Center was regarded by my friends and mentors as bordering on a self-destructive act.

The most recent incumbent, Gordon Davis, had lasted all of nine months. The board chair, Beverly Sills, was mired in controversy, exhausted after seven and a half years in that role, and eager to leave. Lincoln Center's much-touted redevelopment project was tied in a Gordian knot.

The widely admired developer Marshall Rose, who so successfully spearheaded the restoration of Bryant Park, had just resigned from his post as chair of Lincoln Center Redevelopment and was quoted on the way out as saying, "[I] was stabbed in the back."[1]

If that sounds Shakespearean, the allusion fits. Rivalries abounded. Personalities clashed. Egos reigned. Reputations were badly damaged. And the whole circus was reported on assiduously by a delighted press, analyzed to a fare-thee-well by the newspapers and weekly magazines:

First, its President of 17 years, Nathan Leventhal, stepped down just as the [redevelopment] effort was getting underway. Then, the Metropolitan Opera held the project hostage in a very public battle over management issues. Then, the economy took a dive, terrorists attacked New York, and now Lincoln Center's new President, Gordon J. Davis, has decided to resign after less than a year. Can the institution still hope to raise $1.5 billion to rebuild its complex over the next ten years? Some top cultural officials have said no, that the project was likely to be postponed or abandoned, perhaps simply because the Met and the other constituent arts groups still cannot agree on how to proceed.
— Robin Pogrebin, *New York Times*, September 29, 2001

. . . a study in the treacherous—some would say dysfunctional— politics of the city's largest and most fractious arts organization. Hamstrung by rivalries among the Center's warring constituent members; undercut by Ms. Sills, who seemed unwilling to cede power to her new President; and derided by staff members . . . a disillusioned Mr. Davis finally called it quits on September 27.
— Elisabeth Franck and Andrew Rice, *New York Observer*,
    October 8, 2001

Lincoln Center is a community in deep distress, riven by conflict over a grandiose $1 billion redevelopment plan . . . instead of uniting the Center's constituent arts organizations behind a common goal, the project has pitted them against one another in open warfare more reminiscent of the shoot-out at the OK Corral than of a night at the opera. "To say that it is a mess is putting it mildly," says Johanna Fiedler, the author and a former staff member at the Metropolitan Opera. "There is nobody running the show right now."
— Leslie Bennetts, *New York Magazine*, February 4, 2002

What is wrong with Lincoln Center? The problem goes deeper than the virtuoso bickering over redevelopment which, to judge from reports, fills the corridors of what is called "the world's largest cultural complex." The chief personalities of the place—Beverly Sills, Joe Volpe, Paul Kellogg, and the rest—make entertaining copy, and it would almost be a pity if the soap opera were to end.

—Alex Ross, *New Yorker*, April 1, 2002

The situation at Lincoln Center was in a state of disarray. Disagreements proliferated, and civility had all but disappeared. Relationships and processes that had bound constituent artistic organizations together were unraveling, very publicly. At stake was the very future of Lincoln Center as the leading performing arts institution in the world.

There were real challenges and threats to be managed. The nine performing arts organizations, two educational institutions, and one branch of the New York Public Library all confronted some combination of these realities: declining and aging audiences; a post-9/11 flagging economy; competition for consumer discretionary income; and significant reductions in government support—federal, state, and municipal—for annual operating requirements.

Yet the most pernicious dangers emanated from inside Lincoln Center, in the form of self-inflicted wounds. In the absence of forward-looking leadership, resident artistic forces behaved more like rivals and adversaries than partners and allies. Staff and trustees were highly unrealistic about the energy and determination needed to remedy decades of deferred maintenance, to fix a deteriorating infrastructure, and to enliven tired and uninviting public spaces. Instead of reimagining how cultural encounter and civic engagement might meet in the twenty-first century, Lincoln Center had become a nasty mixture of shortsightedness and pettiness.

Parochialism prevailed. Lincoln Center was a quarrelsome, unpleasant place. Its leaders seemed tired, bereft of ideas, and lacking in energy. The best years of the oldest American performing arts center, the largest and most prominent in the world, were increasingly described in the past tense by observers, commentators, and insiders.

Fortunately I was forearmed, because I chose to disregard the warnings.

After six years of traipsing through much of the Third World and many failed states as the president of the International Rescue Committee

(IRC), one of the world's leading refugee assistance organizations, somehow the stresses and strains of Lincoln Center, with its sixteen acres and twelve world-class arts institutions, struck me as manageable.

After having dealt with Laurent Kabila of the Democratic Republic of Congo, Paul Kagame of Rwanda, Slobodan Milošević of Serbia, and their followers, Joe Volpe, the volcanic general manager of the Metropolitan Opera, seemed to me if not a pleasure, well, hardly daunting.

And having ordered food drops from the air over Kosovo; rushed assistance to malnourished children in Burundi, Tanzania, and East Timor; and let the world know that the Eastern Congo and South Sudan are the planet's two most dangerous places, because I had witnessed human agony and depravity there with my own eyes, Lincoln Center and its key figures, with their bombast and betrayals, somehow fell into a proper context. Whatever the quarreling was about, surely life or death was not at stake.

Another motivation for me to compete for the job was that although I am a very well-traveled and a reasonably well-read guy, I am an unabashedly proud New Yorker. The events of 9/11 shook me and my seemingly impregnable, defiant city to our psychic foundations. Rather than "retreat" to the challenge of teaching and writing in a just-offered, tenured post at the Harvard Business School, I was haunted by a question: How could I help, even in a small way, recently elected Mayor Bloomberg to nurture my hometown back to recovery?

For much of my adult life I had watched JFK, LaGuardia, and Newark airports embarrassingly deteriorate. Second-tier American cities and third world countries had more modern transportation infrastructures. I had rooted in vain for New York City to once again compete for large trade shows and professional conventions by modernizing the utterly outmoded Javits Center. I also had seen little forward movement on converting the Farley Post Office at 34th Street between Eighth and Ninth Avenues into a new Moynihan Station, which has been on the drawing board as the much-desired *eventual* replacement for the deteriorating Penn Station. Few people believed that the Second Avenue tunnel would be completed, and certainly neither on time nor anywhere near budget. I watched sadly as major ideas for the development of Governor's Island moved from one stage of drift and indecision to another.

All of these and other projects critical to New York's economic future were stymied by political battles among mayors, governors, Assembly speakers, and Senate majority leaders. The projects were victims of what Senator Chuck Schumer politely called the culture of inertia.

Mayor Michael Bloomberg promised a different future. And I hoped that my professional habit of getting things done might be put to good use.

Ever since my stint as executive director of the 92nd Street Y from 1977 to 1984, I had been beguiled by the performing arts. I was, and remained, a Lincoln Center loyalist, enamored of its ten first-class resident arts organizations and two teaching academies. The opportunity to help them overcome their many self-imposed obstacles to progress and to lead in Lincoln Center's preparation for the next generation of artists and audiences was simply too tempting. And so was being in charge of the largest and most consequential presenter of arts in the world.

ORIGINALLY I THOUGHT the chances of my being selected by the search committee were even at best. True, my seven years with the 92nd Street Y had brought about a much-noticed revitalization of all the performing arts at that venerable organization. But the powers that be at Lincoln Center might have viewed the Y as modest in size, an upstart, a marginal player.

Their possible attitude reminded me of a story I used to tell as the Y's executive director whenever I needed an excuse for being late to an appointment downtown. Traffic traveling south on Lexington Avenue was often at a standstill. Hailing a taxi meant risking a delayed arrival. The subway was also notorious for equipment breakdown. I ran the risk of being held up in a train that would just not move. So, when seeking forgiveness, I would mention Isaac Stern, who performed at the Y for years.

Fairly early in his career, he was pacing up and down in his famous agent's office in a distressed state. Isaac was represented by the legendary impresario Sol Hurok. They were very close, and Sol treated Isaac like a son:

"Isaac, you look very upset. What is wrong?"

"Papa, each year you schedule me on the west coast at the start of the season. By the time I cross the country and reach New York in the late spring, my playing has improved, and I am ready for the tough-minded, demanding New York newspaper critics. But for some reason, this year, my very first solo recital is here in Manhattan."

"Isaac, I have forgotten. Where did I book you?"

"I am playing at the 92nd Street's Y Kaufmann Concert Hall."

"Oh, Isaac, quit worrying. That is an out of town engagement."

Would the search committee in 2002 dismiss my Y experience as not only "out of town," but also too far in the past to be relevant, as I had left that executive director post eighteen years earlier?

In my favor, I had been the architect of the AT&T Foundation, the largest corporate-asset-based philanthropic entity in America. The arts was one of its leading priorities. Together with Exxon and Philip Morris, the AT&T Foundation was the most generous corporate benefactor to the performing arts in the country. Most Lincoln Center artistic organizations regularly received handsome charitable gifts from the foundation during my tenure as president or chairman from 1984 to 1996.

But few institutional philanthropists contributed enough to loom large in the economic life of the ballet, the theater, the orchestra, and the opera, to name but four of the beneficiaries of AT&T support. My leadership there was nice, perhaps a plus, but hardly dispositive.

If that was the case for my time at the AT&T Foundation, it was even more so for my role as chair of the Nathan Cummings Foundation, a formidable family fund with a substantial performing arts program to its credit.

Even my business responsibilities at AT&T—helping to lead its media, public relations, advertising, and public affairs programs and assisting in charting a course for the company to conduct business overseas—might have been viewed as of marginal relevance to playing the role of the Lincoln Center's president.

Teaching, consulting, and writing seemed to gain me no credit in search committee deliberations. I was not asked a single question about these roles, except whether I expected to give them up entirely if I was offered the job.

My time as president of the largest refugee relief and resettlement agency (1997–2002) was regarded as somewhat exotic work, its applicability to Lincoln Center hard to fathom.

I had two opportunities to overcome any doubts, misperceptions, and reservations, at full search committee meetings. And although I had not previously met two of the most influential members—Frank A. Bennack Jr., president of the Hearst Corporation and vice chair of Lincoln Center, and Bruce Crawford, the chair of the Metropolitan Opera—and knew Beverly Sills, Lincoln Center's chair, only slightly, the interviews seemed to go smoothly.

When one of my primary rivals, a quintessential insider, Joseph Polisi, at that time the president of The Juilliard School for some thirteen years, publicly withdrew from contention, my prospects improved. Little did I know with how many job applicants I was actually competing, including former cabinet members in the Clinton administration and corporate leaders of some repute from around the country.

I described the forces at play to my wife Elizabeth, whose response was unforgettable.

"Reynold, you are a competitive guy. I am sure you will secure this offer, and the place will be lucky to have you.

"But are you sure you want this headache of a job, in view of all that you are learning about the poisonous environment at Lincoln Center?"

She was absolutely right to pose that question.

Why was I drawn to this post, notwithstanding all the warnings and the prevailing negativism?

Generally, I favor the underdog. When two sports teams play against one another, and I am a fan of neither, I routinely root for the club that comes from the town with the highest unemployment rate. The 92nd Street Y—dispirited, running an operating deficit, underutilized, talent deprived, and needing an infusion of energy and leadership—had been just the place for me.

In 1982 AT&T, at that time the largest company in the world, was just about to divest itself under court order of local telephone companies and compete in every American market for both services and equipment, as well as to conduct business abroad. Under such circumstances, it was turning to outsiders for help. I was flattered to be asked to be one of them. And what I knew about the business initially consisted of picking up a phone and waiting for a dial tone.

I, a New Yorker, was working in a firm dominated by midwesterners; a Democrat in a rock-solid Republican corporation; a fellow who preferred Beethoven to Willie Nelson, and tennis to golf. Four strikes against me, I was told. It was the perfect challenge.

The IRC had trouble meeting payroll and severe problems making financial ends meet. The nobility of its cause and the compelling need for its services threatened to be overwhelmed by a scarcity of revenue, the absence of cost controls and risk enterprise management tools, and a breakdown of management accountability. Institutional crisis was fast approaching. Maybe I could lead in the repair of a broken, but very worthy and much-admired, organization.

So the mission ahead at Lincoln Center appealed to me. I was drawn to the challenge of resolving conflict in its conspicuously failing physical transformation. It was mired in controversy. I was confident that I could solve the stalemate and help lead the organization out of a cul-de-sac.

But I hoped to do much more than break an impasse.

I wanted to associate with the glamour and the glitter, to be ultimately responsible for the production and presentation of classical performing arts and of the new, the fresh, and the innovative. I yearned to encourage gifted staff to bring to their indoor and outdoor stages the most daring, audacious, and ambitious work. I was drawn to the soaring wonder of the performing arts at their finest.

Really, though, what I longed for was to expand, and by a wide margin, the Lincoln Center practice of subsidized tickets and free performances that lowered the barriers to entry for working-class families. This is the Lincoln Center that welcomes all and invites New Yorkers and visitors from every economic class to come early and stay late. I yearned for it to remain or to become a destination in and of itself, an oasis of relaxation and greenery in a crowded and dense town, a mainstay contributor to the quality of life in New York City, and a very important source of civic pride.

At this book's opening I quote E. B. White, who described three kinds of New Yorkers: those who were born here; those who commute; and those from out of town or another country, who arrive in New

York City as their final destination. Lincoln Center must serve all three, but it needed to extend itself, with special attention, to welcome those first-generation New Yorkers, "the settlers," who give the city passion.

As a kid growing up in a poor and working-class neighborhood in Brooklyn during the 1950s and 1960s, I attended PS 100, situated between Brighton Beach and the edge of Coney Island, and Abraham Lincoln High School, located on Ocean Parkway. Both offered an excellent education for students willing and able to take advantage of a superb faculty and a tradition that highly prized excellence in teaching and learning. And both placed no small emphasis on the performing arts as a pathway to education; a method of transmitting national and universal values; a source of social cohesion; and a way for kids to develop self-confidence, poise, empathy, and a capacity to imagine.

The band, the symphony, the chorus, the chamber music group, and the annual musical theater competition; the class trips to Broadway and Off Broadway, and to museums: all these in-school and extracurricular activities were led by an inspiring faculty deeply committed to exposing their students to the joys of music, dance, theater, film, and visual art.

What existed in abundance for most school kids in those decades had largely disappeared from New York City's public school system by the end of the twentieth century. As I prepared to meet with Lincoln Center's search committee, I wondered whether its members would encourage a new president to take the lead in restoring the arts to school curriculum and exposing kids in unprecedented numbers to the treasures at Lincoln Center.

Lincoln Center should be devoted to the first-generation New York family, that Metro card–holding, brown-bag-carrying youngster, those children receiving one or more forms of public assistance. No kid should grow up in the cultural capital of the world without being exposed to the best in the performing and visual arts. Lincoln Center needed to show the way not just by enunciating that precept, but by practicing it. I was confident that our doing so would be neither unnoticed nor unemulated.

MUCH OF MY OWN enthusiasm for the performing arts and concern for their financial well-being originated in my childhood and late adolescence. Abraham Lincoln High School and the intellectually ambitious students drawn to it nurtured my exhilaration in learning. Lincoln was a very large public high school. There were about as many students in my senior class as there were in the total undergraduate enrollment at Hobart College, where I was destined to go. I remember looking around the college campus and asking, "Where is everybody?"

Hobart professed justifiable pride in an outstanding faculty that cared about teaching in small classes and in the pursuit of a liberal arts education as an intellectual adventure. I couldn't wait to partake of it.

My only major concern was money. Hobart offered a generous scholarship, but it was less than half of what I needed for tuition, room, and board. Some of the remainder I could borrow from the state and federal governments at a very low interest rate, but debt was a condition I hoped to avoid as much as possible.

From the beginning of my time in Geneva, New York, in 1962 until graduation in 1966, I took every job I could. I arrived two weeks early in my freshman year to work at the bookstore. There was no pay, but I received free books. I worked the food line in the cafeteria for $1 a meal and all I could eat. Later, when it became clear that I was a very good student, I served as a tutor to both members of fraternities and athletes, who needed all the assistance they could afford in swimming upstream intellectually to pass some fairly demanding required courses.

My dad offered to help, but we never discussed how much money would be involved or how often he could send it. Then, in my first week at school, a lovely letter from him arrived with a check for $7. He sent heartfelt wishes for success at Hobart and promised to forward the same sum every week. He wished it could be more.

Well, forty weeks of school times $7 per week equaled $280, about 5 percent of the some $4,000 I needed for tuition, room, and board. I knew that Dad was doing all he felt he could to support me.

Soon after receiving Dad's letter, I joined my newfound friends at a local pub and pizza hangout named after its owner, "Dutch." I signed over the check to Dutch to pay for a pizza and a Pepsi. As a kid from Brooklyn, I knew something about decent pizza, and what Dutch offered wasn't bad at all. Given how few culinary choices there were in Geneva, Dutch's affordable fare and friendly atmosphere made me feel very much at home.

A week later, on a break from studying, I made my way back to Dutch's. As I entered, he greeted me and led me over to a corner, asking how I was faring at school. We exchanged pleasantries, and then he put his arm around my shoulder and said, "Son, I am sorry to tell you, but your dad's check bounced."

I was mortified. Dutch said it was no problem, last week's food and drink would be his treat and not to worry, but he felt I ought to know.

When I returned to my dorm room, I wrote Dad a letter. I exaggerated the number of jobs I was able to manage and told him that while I appreciated very much receiving his weekly checks, really, they were not necessary.

He never sent another. The bounced check was never mentioned. He must have felt relieved by my freeing him of the obligation to send me something weekly. Finances at home were obviously much tighter than I had ever imagined.

I learned many lessons at college, and not all of them were in the classroom. Financially, I was on my own. And I have been ever since.

Really, I did not mind. In fact, it occurred to me that until my freshman year in college, I had never given much thought to our family's financial circumstances. True, sometimes my birthday gift as a child would come months late, whenever the household's cash trickle allowed. For me, sleeping in the living room next to my younger sister, Joyce, was quite natural.

My pleasures as a child were simple, and Dad had a knack for making them fun. For example, on Saturdays, on the rare occasions when we were alone, while my mom was at the beauty parlor, we would go up to the rooftop of our apartment building, where one of the tenants maintained a pigeon coop. On those occasions, Dad would remove his trumpet from its case and play tune after tune. I was totally absorbed, a joyful, admiring audience of one.

We'd then return to our fourth-floor apartment, where Dad would prepare lunch for just the two of us. His menu was consistent: scrambled eggs and my choice of either rye toast or an English muffin, with sliced tomato on the side, and Tropicana orange juice to drink.

We had no formal dining room, so usually as a family we ate together in a nook at the tail end of our tiny kitchen. But with Mom not home, we didn't need that much space, so Dad would open the oven door, which served as our table, and we both sat at footstools, happily conversing.

By the time I was nine years old, and my dad was thirty, in the afternoon, weather permitting, I was allowed to join my friends in the immediate vicinity of our apartment building. One of us—Johnny Rodriguez, Elliot Wienerman, Mark Feldman, or Allen Rome—would bring a pink rubber ball—the only kind worth using, a Spalding—and depending on how many friends gathered, we played street games to our heart's content: hit the penny, off the wall, curves, punch ball, stick ball, stoop ball, slap ball, kings, handball, paddle ball, running bases.

If the weather was inclement, then I was in for a real treat. Dad would roll up the throw rug in the living room and lay out brown butcher block paper. He would find a set of magic markers in a desk drawer and put a 78-rpm record on the Victrola to play Dizzy Gillespie, Dave Brubeck, Benny Goodman, Artie Shaw, or Vivaldi. He would ask me to imagine what the composer might have been thinking or what kind of mood he was trying to convey and then draw whatever came to mind.

It was an exercise in creativity, and we would discuss my earliest attempts to think about what the sounds I was hearing meant to me and how they moved me. Translating them into another form of art was always exciting. Dad made sure that the drawing was Scotch taped to the front door to greet Mom when she returned home.

If there was time left over, then came the really fun part. My dad was a skilled tap dancer. He greatly admired both Fred Astaire and Gene Kelly, but because he was five feet eight, like Mr. Kelly, he would impersonate him, putting on khakis, athletic socks, penny loafers with taps on them, and a pretty tight-fitting white T-shirt. Then he would dance a Kelly routine just like those made famous by the movie *Singin' in the Rain*.

At bar mitzvahs and weddings my father could be relied upon to tap a dance for the assembled guests.

One of my most memorable late birthday gifts was a certificate to attend classes at a tap dance school. To this day, it doesn't take much to coax me into a time step or a soft shoe. My upbringing provided an enticing exposure to music, dance, and visual art. It prepared me to appreciate the rich cultural inheritance we all can enjoy.

These childhood pleasures and the bliss that comes from economic ignorance faded as I grew older, replaced by a sense of financial insecurity. I pledged that my spouse, children, sister, niece, and granddaughter would not want for life's necessities or even occasional extravagances. What lured me away from the 92nd Street Y to AT&T was not just feeling that my work was complete at the world's largest community center. The opportunity to test my mettle in a for-profit firm entering competitive foreign and domestic markets was enticing. Could I prove my worth to senior executives for whom a profit and loss statement and the return on equity were all that mattered?

Taking that job would put me in an entirely new financial condition. A handsome salary, annual bonuses, and stock option awards would allow me to build a nest egg. Then, after a decent interval (which turned out to be a dozen years), I might return to public service, without worrying about whether I could afford to do so.

Although my twelve years with AT&T proved to be lucrative, at least by my own standards and expectations, they did not mitigate the impact of my encounter in early adulthood with the reality of debt and its consequences. I am sure that this experience is partly responsible for my ironclad commitment to deliver balanced or surplus budget results in all of the posts I have held, for all the years I have held them.

Living beyond one's means is unhealthy for families and institutions. Working hard to generate surplus capital is an admirable discipline, organizationally and personally. Special needs and rainy days are inevitable. Accumulated savings will help to manage them. That small pizza and Pepsi at Dutch's and that bounced check embarrassed an eighteen-year-old freshman. It was one source of distress that never again made an appearance in my life.

MY YEARS AT Lincoln Center were tumultuous and eventful. They began in March 2002 and ended on January 31, 2014.

During this period the New York Philharmonic publicly reversed itself, first triumphantly announcing a merger with Carnegie Hall, and then, five months later, abashedly declaring the merger a nullity, much to the embarrassment of all involved parties.

This fiasco was no surprise to those who had watched the New York Philharmonic closely. We sadly observed an orchestra adrift, lacking in managerial and trustee leadership. Its superb musicians, often perform-ing with astonishing virtuosity, deserved better.

During his seven-year tenure, its music director, Lorin Maazel, was arguably among the world's most technically able conductors, and surely *the* most handsomely paid. He was also, before and after con-certs, for all intents and purposes missing in action, a veritable mystery man. During his tenure, never once, unlike virtually all of his prede-cessors, did he deign to conduct The Juilliard Orchestra or any other private school ensemble. He never expressed interest in improving the state of music education in New York City's elementary and secondary schools. Indeed, he rarely appeared on local radio or television. The board of directors and staff seemed entirely comfortable with a music director largely unrelated to the city that surrounded him. The New York Philharmonic was in a sense a disembodied ensemble, led by a globe-trotting septuagenarian, more at ease on his Virginia farm or, apparently, in almost any European capital, than in Manhattan.

Concurrently, Gustavo Dudamel, Michael Tilson Thomas (MTM), and David Robertson, to name but three conductors, came to per-sonify the excitement and energy generated by the Los Angeles Phil-harmonic, the San Francisco Symphony, and the St. Louis Symphony, respectively. These are well-led institutions; they know what they are about. They have artistic profiles and stand for something musically. Audiences and critics flock to their performances. Other cities in Amer-ica and around the world invite them to perform, early and often. Each artistic leader embodies and personifies the town that engages him pro-fessionally. MTM and Gustavo are known to concertgoers and taxi drivers alike. That was not the case for their counterpart in New York City.

It is said that if you don't know where you are going, any road will take you there. The New York Philharmonic's detour to Carnegie Hall was paved with a reckless neglect of the interests of a precious artistic institution and the public it was bound to serve. For Lincoln Center's resident orchestra, maintaining robust audiences was a constant chal-lenge. The New York Philharmonic was stuck, year after year, with an alarming operating deficit. It was neither seasonal nor cyclical, but structural. Governance and management mediocrity became the norm. How could this condition be tolerated by respected trustees possessed of the capacity to express their views and, if necessary, part company with an organization that seemed to be just coasting along?

At the same time, the New York City Opera fought hard to leave what it described as a deficient New York State Theater in favor of becoming one of the resident artistic organizations at the 9/11 site, but without success. Twelve years later and counting, it remains a mystery as to which artistic organizations will occupy a piece of that hallowed ground.

As the New York City Opera searched for another home, there was an air of desperation about its odyssey. In a sense, the search was nothing more than an exercise in futility and escapism. There was simply never an adequate audience or fund-raising base to build a new opera house from the ground up on the island of Manhattan.

But once Paul Kellogg, the artistic director, declared the New York State Theater artistically unfit for the New York City Opera, the die was cast. Although the company had for more than forty years somehow been able to work reasonably well notwithstanding the venue's purported acoustic deficiencies, for unfathomable reasons Paul believed it could no longer do so. The audience, in effect, was told that staying away was entirely understandable.

Its members heeded that advice—in droves—with deleterious consequences for the company's finances, its morale, and its very future.

The entire board of directors and staff of the Opera were badly distracted by edifice wanderlust and allowed themselves not to notice as attendance eroded, seasons were contracted and curtailed, and the endowment became a piggy bank to finance consistent and alarmingly high operating deficits.

These were the years when Beverly Sills left the chair of Lincoln Center, sworn to retire, only to emerge ninety days later as the president of the Metropolitan Opera.

When the mayor, Mike Bloomberg, read me the riot act over an anonymous disclosure to the *New York Times* of a $15 million gift he had pledged to Lincoln Center two years before to launch redevelopment.

When Joe Volpe, the general manager of the Metropolitan Opera for sixteen years, did all within his power to stop the physical redevelopment of Lincoln Center. He often behaved boorishly, just as his reputation would lead one to expect. Volpe, joined by a small but powerful group of naysayers, failed to halt what would ultimately be a $1.2 billion-plus physical transformation of Lincoln Center, but not for want of trying. For many and varied reasons, Volpe's retirement was welcomed, and everyone looked forward eagerly to his successor.

Peter Gelb was greeted in 2006 by an inbox overflowing with challenges. His marketing innovations were lauded. The live transmission of opera to several thousand movie theaters in the United States and around the world was widely praised. His management of the challenge of music director James Levine's frequent illnesses and convalescence was much admired.

But his artistic direction of the Met was deemed highly uneven. It received very mixed reviews. In any event, whatever appeared on the Met's stage never wanted for attention.

For me, many of Gelb's artistic choices were brave and the results often memorable. However, there was far less to debate about the Met's economic fortunes under Gelb's leadership. They continued a decline that was well under way during Volpe's last years in office. During Gelb's tenure, the Met's annual budget, already in very shaky condition, climbed from roughly $215 to $330 million. Deficits also grew, or were closed by invading the corpus of a badly eroding endowment.

What was wrong with the Met's business plan? How could its operating statement and balance sheet have eroded so badly since 2006, even as record fund-raising occurred? Was anyone pressing Peter Gelb for a major course correction?

It was frustrating to run the risk of being held accountable for the travails of resident organizations like the New York Philharmonic, the New York City Opera, or the Metropolitan Opera, over which Lincoln Center had little control. In the case of the New York Philharmonic and the New York City Opera, Lincoln Center extended every effort to point the way to artistic and financial solvency, orally and in writing. We could propose, but only those proud, independent entities could choose whether to act on our recommendations. Many were airily dismissed, and others were simply ignored.

There were many bright spots during this period as well, artistic and otherwise.

Lincoln Center's geography was redefined by its newest constituent, the Wynton Marsalis–led Jazz at Lincoln Center. In 2004 it opened to critical acclaim three stunning, Rafael Vinoly–designed spaces on the fifth and sixth floors of the Time Warner Building at Columbus Circle.

Lincoln Center Theater's major challenge seemed to be finding adequate storage space to house its many Tony Awards. *Contact, Coast of Utopia, The Light in the Piazza, South Pacific, Other Desert Cities, War Horse,* and *Golden Boy* were just a few of its much-heralded productions during the tenure of Andre Bishop and Bernard Gersten.

The Chamber Music Society, under the fresh artistic leadership of Wu Han and David Finckel, acquired new energy and vitality. Its activities expanded to include many more performances in Alice Tully Hall, more touring, and residencies around the United States and the world. The Lincoln Center Film Society also became more ambitious in the number and kind of its offerings and in related educational programming. And Lincoln Center's own eclectic presentations of more than four hundred annual events were perhaps never as bold, creative, and award-winning as in the period from 2002 through 2014.

Leaders of the burgeoning, affluent hedge fund industry were persuaded to adopt Lincoln Center as their artistic cause, and the much-applauded, now consensus-blessed, ambitious physical transformation of Lincoln Center proceeded apace.

The entire city block, 65th Street from Broadway to Amsterdam Avenue, and all the artistic facilities that align it, were utterly transformed into a warm, receptive, and engaging boulevard of the arts. Never again could Lincoln Center be called forbidding, anonymous, or unwelcoming.

With the transformation of Alice Tully Hall, the expansion of The Juilliard School, the renovation of the New York State Theater (since renamed the David H. Koch Theater), the creation of a state-of-the-art third performance space for Lincoln Center Theater, two new screening rooms and an education center for the Film Society, and new dance studios for the School of American Ballet came a beautifully designed, graceful welcome to Lincoln Center's main campus, one filled with light and life. There are new green spaces, new restaurants, and a totally Wi-Fi'd campus. Twenty-first-century technology is displayed indoors and out. And there is a remodeled, utterly overhauled, privately owned public space called the David Rubenstein Atrium (named after its principal donor), a new Lincoln Center Commons, open free of charge to the public 365 days a year.

New board leadership took hold at Lincoln Center, the New York City Ballet, Lincoln Center Theater, the Chamber Music Society, the Film Society, and most recently, the New York Philharmonic.

This book reports on these events and their results, including both those who helped achieve progress and those who fell short. My administrative colleagues and the trustees to whom we report escape neither unscathed nor unpraised, as the case may be.

The donors are described with admiration and candor—from the generous who give willingly because they believe in their benefaction and derive pleasure from contributing to a cause beyond self, to the bargainers who treat philanthropy as another opportunity to extract advantage.

IN REFLECTING ON the forces and personalities at work in the world's largest performing arts center, much more is involved than an account of heroes and villains, winners and losers, who's up and who's down. Above all I hope to illuminate certain truths, not just about Lincoln Center, but also about the leadership and management of key institutions in our society.

Institutionally, America is supposed to run on a strong three-sector engine, monitored by a vigorous Fourth Estate. Each sector, prodded by a free press, is said to contribute significantly to the public welfare, in a division of labor virtually unique to our country. But the gap between the promise and performance of all of these sectors is growing, alarmingly so. And the faith of Americans in the proper execution of their respective responsibilities has badly eroded, perilously so.

The first sector is government at all levels: federal, state, and local. Each is divided into executive, legislative, and judicial branches, which share power with one another. And each is supposed to act ultimately in accordance with the will of the people, the consent of the governed as expressed through free and fair elections. The polity is the ultimate consummation of the will of the people. American democracy has no other master.

So I have been taught. By Madison, Jefferson, and other Founding Fathers, the authors of arguably America's only tract of political philosophy, the *Federalist Papers*.[2]

The second sector is free enterprise. It is composed of for-profit institutions presumed to act in the best interests of their shareholders by delighting customers, partnering with suppliers, and conducting themselves not only lawfully but in a socially responsible way. Such being the case, little regulation from government is said to be required. What is in the interest of General Motors and Goldman Sachs is in the interest of the United States. Ordinarily, capitalism triumphs where government treads lightly.

So I have learned. From Friedrich Hayek, Adam Smith, Milton Friedman, and Alan Greenspan.[3]

The third sector is the realm of nonprofit institutions. Accountable neither to voters nor to shareholders, eleemosynary organizations form when markets and governments fail to provide needed services at high enough levels of quality and at low enough cost. Exempt from taxes and eligible to receive tax-deductible gifts, these publicly subsidized nonprofits are intended to promote the general welfare.

The pluralism of this third sector allows for the coexistence of hundreds of thousands of organizations serving the commonweal, a critical component of the genius of America. Educating our kids, healing our sick, offering the visual and performing arts to a demanding and discerning public, ministering to our religious needs, providing social services of all kinds, generating ideas in think tanks and patents at research universities, and safeguarding our civil rights and liberties, these and other indispensable services are performed better in America than elsewhere because of our extensive voluntarism and philanthropy.

So I have gathered. Courtesy of Alexis de Tocqueville, Waldemar Nielsen, Lester Salamon, and Robert Putnam, among others.[4]

Politicians are accountable to citizens. The $4.5 trillion budgets they collectively wield each year, and the millions of workers the federal, state, and local governments employ, are intended to serve public needs. No more. No less. Answerable to the American people who choose to vote, politicians must face the public in regularly held elections, in which their performance will be judged.

Members of the boards of directors of for-profit institutions are supposed to govern them intelligently and prudently. Our $17.5 trillion economy depends on it. That means careful selection of a qualified chief executive officer and the constant monitoring of the chief executive

officer's (CEO's) performance, as well as that of the senior management team. It entails rigorous review of company strategy and close
examination of an organization's strategic risk profile. It suggests that
the director of a for-profit firm is responsible not to the CEO but to the
shareholders and the customers, first and foremost.

All around this nation, nonprofit organizations, private institutions
devoted to the public good, also struggle with the challenges of governance, the fast-changing marketplace, government relations, and leadership. The lessons I learned at Lincoln Center might be valuable not
only to those who labor in the country's fast-growing, nonprofit third
sector, but also to those employed by the government or in the private
sector.

On January 19, 2012, a Gallup study revealed that Americans' satisfaction with the size and power of the federal government was at a
record low of 29 percent. Their satisfaction with the size and influence
of major corporations remained near an all-time low of 30 percent.
Gallup concluded its report: "The results suggest that it's a case of 'pick
your poison' in the political arena when it comes to big business and
big government—Americans are quite dissatisfied with the size, power
and influence of both."[5]

This lack of confidence is widespread, and it characterizes the prevailing attitude of Americans. Citizens are losing trust in the US Senate,
the House of Representatives, the presidency, labor unions, the media,
religious organizations, and government as a whole. A Pew Research
Center poll taken in 2012 confirmed the Gallup study.[6]

When people lose faith in key institutions, they are less able to solve
common problems. As a candidate to run on the Republican ticket
for president in 2012, Jon Hunstman characterized our key national
challenge as a "trust deficit." It is serious and it is corrosive, he claimed.

The Edelman Trust Barometer, administered for fourteen consecutive years, also found that faith in government and business is in a very
severe downward trend. According to this study, published on January
19, 2012, government suffered the deepest trust decline in the history
of the poll, and business was not far behind in the public's loss of
confidence.[7]

By comparison, faith in nongovernment organizations has held
up reasonably well. But that level of credibility and confidence can

be squandered easily. Maintaining public approval is a constant challenge and requires high-quality governance and management. The public's trust must be earned every day. If proof were needed, for decades the US Supreme Court and houses of worship were exceptions to the sweeping tide of negativism depicted in well-regarded opinion surveys. This is no longer the case.

When government is not trusted, voter participation rates fall. Democracy languishes. Resistance to corrective action rises.

When business is distrusted, the demand for regulation escalates, and the expressed needs of corporations for lower taxation and trade liberalization fall on deaf ears.[8]

And when nonprofits falter, when confidence in them erodes, charitable contributions plummet, and faith in the voluntary sector diminishes.

The active consent of the governed, shareholder and customer satisfaction, and nonprofits that discharge their fiduciary responsibilities with care: these are the fundamental building blocks of a vibrant governmental sector; a healthy free enterprise economy; and an energetic, creative, and highly emulated nonprofit sector.

The disciplined reporting and commentary of journalists plays a critical role in holding all three sectors accountable. After all, they consist of institutions that are supported by the public. They are dependent on citizen, client, consumer, investor, and donor approval. The media are the independent source of information on which all of these constituencies depend to reach sound judgments.

Selected board chairs, trustees, and executives are criticized in these pages because those who enjoy a precious public trust should be called to account for acts of brazen omission or commission that occur on their watch. No one was held accountable by President George W. Bush for the intelligence failures that led to 9/11, or for the disaster that befell our country in Iraq, or for the utterly unnecessary damage to lives and property caused by the catastrophic failures to prepare for Hurricane Katrina and to deal with its consequences. Similarly, many at Lincoln Center who ran excessive operating deficits, deferred building maintenance inexcusably, allowed endowments to remain stagnant or deteriorate, or permitted artistic drift did so with impunity.

Not a single senior executive has been indicted for white-collar crimes associated with the disappearance of Lehman Brothers, Bear Stearns,

Countrywide, MF Global, or Arthur Andersen as independent entities. Nor have senior management or outside directors of the likes of Bank of America, Enron, WorldCom, Citibank, Merrill Lynch, Fannie Mae, and Freddie Mac been held accountable for stunning acts of omission and commission that betrayed the trust of shareholders and arguably violated the spirit, if not the letter, of dozens of laws and regulations.

Analogously, the CEOs and board chairs of some of the non-profits that comprise Lincoln Center were not held responsible for the weakened artistic and financial state of the organizations they were charged to protect. For this reason alone real-life situations are recounted in the pages ahead, no doubt to the embarrassment of some, but only with the intention of helping others cope with similar challenges.

This third sector of ours, nonprofit institutions, is hardly immune from the abuse and neglect of trustees and professionals. Lincoln Center's constituents were governed by some trustee leaders who did not hold their CEOs accountable for performance and who violated the trust invested in them to manage risk. Tales of organizations losing their way do not go untold here.

However, many with whom I worked took their responsibilities very seriously. These men and women were devoted to the common welfare, their egos in check, their energies unleashed, their resources generously offered. They accomplished nothing short of an institutional transformation. Prominent among them were the trustees of Lincoln Center, the parent body and the campus landlord, together with most of their constituent counterparts.

They comprised in total some 525 of New York City's most accomplished figures, drawn from all sectors of society. These trustees found in Lincoln Center and its resident organizations a cause worthy of their time and treasure. They, and the benefactors they helped attract, renewed Lincoln Center physically and programmatically for a new generation of artists and audiences. In the quest, they enjoyed the company of gifted and hardworking employees, driven to succeed.

This is their story, too.

MY DAILY LIFE at the Lincoln Center was filled with tension and beset by provocation.

The situation called to mind one of my favorite quotes from Machiavelli, who warned his Prince about the dangers of introducing change into an organization or a polity. His admonition, I discovered, was well worth heeding:

> There is nothing more difficult to take in hand, more perilous to conduct, or more uncertain in its success, than to take the lead in the introduction of a new order of things.
>
> For the reformer has enemies in all those who profit by the old order, and only lukewarm defenders in all those who would profit by the new order. The lukewarmness arising partly from fear of their adversaries . . . and partly from the incredulity of mankind, who do not truly believe in anything new until they have had actual experience of it.

Transforming Lincoln Center was not without blind alleys, strong-willed opponents, unexpected detours, speed bumps, and more than a few sleepless nights.

I was helped by more than my community center, Fortune 50, and refugee professional experience to put it all into proper perspective. I was also assisted by a sense of humor.

For example, when the members of the Lincoln Center search committee asked what I, as a candidate, would do to reduce embarrassing rivalries that ran rampant across campus, I replied that my prior position at the IRC and my friendship with Jean Marie Guéhenno, the undersecretary for UN peacekeeping, would enable me to borrow some of his troops to occupy Josie Robertson Plaza and separate the warring factions.

Or when Mayor Bloomberg asked me, "What's the difference between your job, Reynold, and Kofi Annan's, the Secretary-General of the United Nations?," I replied, "I don't know, Mr. Mayor."

"Well, then, what's the difference between the UN Security Council and Lincoln Center?"

I looked quizzical, and he continued: "The Secretary-General and the Security Council need only cope with five vetoes. You and Lincoln Center have twelve."

The mayor was referring to a decision reached before my arrival that all material actions about the physical redevelopment of Lincoln

Center had to be unanimously approved by every resident artistic organization.

The unintended consequence of such a rule is that it strongly predisposed the sixteen-acre campus and its artistic facilities to neglect and inattention. To be charitable, it promoted the perpetuation of the status quo. To be accurate, it caused the decay of many of the Center's buildings, its public spaces, and its physical infrastructure.

Allowing each constituent to wield a veto on virtually any and all matters, while self-destructive if pushed to its logical conclusion, was also consistent with the legal and governance framework of the Center. Each of the twelve constituents comprising Lincoln Center was its own independent 501(c)3 organization, fully equipped with a board of directors, an operating budget, a balance sheet, and a mission statement.

Lincoln Center, the organization I ran, sometimes referred to as "Linc. Inc.," performed important common functions. It operated one of the largest underground garages in New York City. It maintained all of the public spaces surrounding the artistic facilities: cleaning and repairing them; protecting them from inclement weather; policing them with a private security force; and offering contemplative, social, and performing arts activities throughout the Lincoln Center complex, along with extensive food and beverage service.

Lincoln Center was authorized to rent the public spaces to outside parties under a renewable five-year license from the Parks Department. It created the Lincoln Center Corporate Fund, raising from $4 to $6 million annually as general operating support for constituent use. It successfully sought funds for Live from Lincoln Center, a forty-year tradition of airing constituent performances across the syndicated stations of the public broadcasting network throughout the nation. And to round out the artistic diet offered to the public and use the constituent venues and ensembles when they were otherwise empty or idle, Lincoln Center offered what has become the most extensive arts presentation program in the world.

In addition to these regular activities, the services performed by Lincoln Center during the course of its mammoth physical redevelopment placed a premium on cooperation between and among constituents and reliance on a set of unprecedented Lincoln Center offers of service and revenue.

Beyond the formalities, the chair of Lincoln Center regularly held meetings with her counterparts at the twelve resident artistic organizations, as I did with mine. Likewise, my staff regularly convened meetings of professional communities across constituent boundaries in finance, public relations, marketing, fund-raising, and the like.

Such meetings conveyed information, shared best practices, and allowed colleagues to help one another. They built trust. Ultimately, my ability to get consequential things done depended on the exercise of leadership, devising solutions to problems, creating ways to seize major challenges, and convincing others of their wisdom. It was also immensely assisted by mobilizing the goodwill of influential trustees who wished to leave Lincoln Center stronger than they found it, who yearned to see it flourish. My calendar was filled with trustee meetings. One-on-one conversations not only with members of Lincoln Center's board, but also with constituent trustees, were frequent.

Gathering important figures, board members, and hired hands behind a common plan was essential. The diffusion of power at Lincoln Center, its factionalism, and its bias toward inaction, not to mention its flamboyant personalities, had to be overcome. Those powerful forces revealed in no small measure why friends and colleagues of mine told me not to take that job.

THIS BOOK EXPLAINS how transformational change, even in the face of such seemingly intractable obstacles, was realized. Architecturally. Artistically. Civically. Economically.

Such change is all about finding common ground, summoning the energy to propel Lincoln Center and its constituents forward, modernizing and enlivening the governing structure while almost nobody noticed, and leading by example. Exercising the power to persuade can regularly prevail over antiquated rules and regulations and over members of the "division of second guessing," Lincoln Center's largest department.[9]

For me, Lincoln Center's future was too important to ignore in favor of other pursuits, and too critical to the nation's cultural life to take lightly. So I immersed myself in the undertaking. But because of my full occupational history, I was able to maintain a critical distance, to be totally in, but never fully of, the place.

Totally in, but not entirely of, had been a recurring theme in my professional life.

From 1975 to 1977 I was the staff director of the Task Force on the New York City Fiscal Crisis, proposing revenue enhancements and budget cuts that would do far less damage to poor and working-class New Yorkers than those advanced by Mayor Beame and Governor Hugh Carey. But I had never worked for the City or State of New York. Who was I to offer sound public policy options?

I was the executive director of the 92nd Street Y, where being a Jewish civil servant and being a certified social worker were at that time regarded as necessary. I was neither.

I moved to AT&T with no experience in business whatsoever, save for a few solo practitioner consulting stints, speaking fees, and writing for publication. "You hired someone who ran a community center to help meet the challenges of divestiture and AT&T's entry into a competitive world?" my boss was often asked.

Of course, at the International Rescue Committee I was widely viewed as an interloper, a "corporate suit," devoid of the lifelong refugee experience seen as a prerequisite for its president.

And my situation was roughly the same at Lincoln Center. Sure, I had some legitimate connections to the arts, but none compared with the likes of Joseph Polisi, Joseph Volpe, Bernard Gersten, and Peter Martins, each of whom had spent more than two decades with The Juilliard School, the Metropolitan Opera, Lincoln Center Theater, and the New York City Ballet, respectively.

It has been observed that if you are swimming inside a bottle of fluid, you are likely to become familiar with its properties, but you are totally unable to detect, let alone describe, the shape of the bottle. Knowing the contours of the flask that holds the liquid, the institution that animates art, comes naturally to me.

Being totally in, but not entirely of, one's setting affords a measure of detachment and perspective often lacking in a professional too immersed in the details, too habituated to organizational routine, or simply too bored to break the mold, to engage in self-criticism, and to embrace change.

UNSURPRISINGLY, MY ADJUSTMENT to Lincoln Center was not entirely smooth, and my presence raised questions, gave rise to curiosity, and met with some resistance. These realities may have been exacerbated by my choice of automobile.

My father, a man of sweet temperament, solidly rooted values, and strong convictions, died in our home in Riverdale, a portion of which my wife, Liz, and I converted into a hospice after he endured a series of what were very tough bouts with cancer.

Dad didn't ask for much as mortal weakness set in and death approached. He was courageous and stoic. But of all things, he fervently requested that I drive his 1993 Mercury Marquis for as long as it would last. It was a giant of a car: four-door, maroon in color, light gray leather interior, fully air-conditioned, with terrific speakers and power everything (windows, seats). For him, its purchase was a point of pride and accomplishment, a step up in luxury and price, and I know he imagined driving it forever.

That car had 20,000 miles on it the year of his death. When it was finally retired, at eighteen years of age, it approached 165,000 miles. And whenever I drove that Mercury, we communed, my father and I. His presence was palpable. That compensated a lot for the ribbing I received when driving his monstrously oversized, ten-mile-a-gallon relic through New York City streets.

People have asked me what was best about being the president of Lincoln Center. I replied, as you would expect of any self-respecting New Yorker, "parking." The job came with its own space. Who could ask for anything more?

My hours of work at Lincoln Center were long. I often left Riverdale, about four miles north of the George Washington Bridge, bordering on the Hudson River, at 6:00 a.m. or earlier. At that hour, it took me only twenty-five minutes, door to door, to arrive at my office. I'd breeze down the Henry Hudson Parkway and connect to Riverside Drive, taking it to 96th Street, where I would hang a left, then a right onto West End Avenue. Even at that early hour, I'd see a substantial number of pedestrians, fifteen or twenty at least, standing in front of their co-ops, condominiums, and rental apartments, trying, often in vain, to hail a cab. West End Avenue was not a place taxis frequented, for reasons I never understood, because demand for them always seemed to exceed supply.

With the passing weeks, I began to notice that people on the street seemed to be waving at vehicles behind me. I looked in the rearview mirror but saw nothing. I checked my lights to see if I had left the brights on, and my seat belt to see if the door had closed with the belt caught in it, or whether the door itself was slammed shut.

One morning, in a light rain, while stopped for a red light at 87th and West End Avenue, I saw a man in his fifties waving right at me. He ran across the street and knocked on my window. I opened it warily. What, he wished to know, would I charge him for a "quick hop" to 48th Street and First Avenue?

It finally occurred to me that I was being hailed as a driver of a gypsy cab, one of New York City's many illegal vehicles, always large American sedans. Their drivers cruise the streets for fares at all hours, when Yellow Cabs are scarce and when many customers find radio cabs difficult to reserve or unaffordable.

Parents adversely affected by the Great Depression often encouraged their daughters to learn to type. Having acquired that skill, should unemployment ever loom, they would have a job to fall back on. My dad would have loved knowing that he had supplied me with an employment safety net. Should Lincoln Center not work out, I could do worse than cruise West End Avenue for readily available customers each weekday morning. To 48th Street and First, I'd charge $50.00. After all, that's way across town. It was raining, which by rights should carry a premium. And gypsy cab drivers are rarely tipped. It's best to build a gratuity into your base charge.

One Sunday morning, soon after I was appointed and before I was given a red plaque with my parking space, number 39, imprinted on it to put on my dashboard, I approached the entrance to the Lincoln Center parking lot where senior executives pull in.

A security guard I hadn't yet met stopped the car and asked for identification. I told him I was the new president of Lincoln Center. He looked very confused. Stepping back and taking in a full view of my (Dad's) car, he mentioned that Gordon Davis, my predecessor, drove a new convertible Audi. And Nat Leventhal, who held the job for seventeen years, always drove a new Lexus. The guard's look of consternation begged for an explanation, but I was speechless.

Suddenly his confusion turned to a smile. Ushering me into the garage with a sweeping hand gesture, he said, "I know. Your other car. The one you drive every day. It must be getting a tune-up and some repairs."

In this way, I learned early on that even a beat-up old Mercury Marquis could find its proper place at Lincoln Center.

And if it could, perhaps I could as well.

CHAPTER 2

Welcome to Lincoln Center

Toto, I have a feeling we're not in Kansas anymore.
—JUDY GARLAND, *The Wizard of Oz*, 1939

A ny new CEO must spend time becoming acquainted with the dynamics of the organization he or she is asked to lead. I believe strongly that leadership is a collective endeavor. It is well observed that there is no "I" in the word team. Winning the trust and confidence of my staff colleagues and the trustees at whose pleasure I served was therefore fundamental.

There were three other priorities to attend to in the early months of my tenure as president of Lincoln Center.

First, its governance structure had to be fixed. Lincoln Center consisted of twelve world-class, independent artistic and educational organizations, called constituents, and the parent body. Each possessed its own board of directors, mission, workforce, annual budget, balance sheet, and distinctive methods of operating. Each focused relentlessly on achieving excellence in its art form. Such close attention to perfecting craft works well. It explains why Lincoln Center's family of cultural organizations is world renowned for producing and presenting the highest quality of performing art and for unsurpassed teaching of the next generation of artists.

The common challenge was identifying ways and means for these proud organizations to work together to achieve objectives beneficial to all. Most often, the individual parts function admirably. But taking fullest advantage of the scope, scale, proximity, and potential synergy of the whole remains a tantalizing and arduous challenge. Collective action requires consensus. At Lincoln Center, there is no central command and control headquarters. The more consequential the issue, the more onerous the task of fashioning agreement.

Second, the economic model that drove Lincoln Center's operations was simply not adequate for the twenty-first century. Highly dependent on both ticket revenue and annual donations, it needed an overhaul. And the trustees and staff who could offer the necessary intellectual capital to help modernize it had to be identified, recruited, and mobilized.

Third, even as I engaged in my own extensive listening tour to replace suspicion with trust and confusion with clarity, I knew I needed to devise a formula that would jump-start redevelopment.

Assuming the mantle of professional leadership at Lincoln Center during a particularly tumultuous period was daunting. But hardly unique.

I invite those who think of Lincoln Center's incapacity to direct all of its parts to work together as singularly dysfunctional to consider university presidents. They cope daily with school deans; individual faculty; alumni committed more to a component part of the enterprise than to the whole; and the athletic department, its coaches, and its adherents. The strength of a school's divisions has its virtues, to be sure. But it also poses a major barrier to timely cooperation and collaboration.

The CEOs of many national organizations, such as the Audubon Society, Planned Parenthood, the Corporation for Public Broadcasting, the United Way of America, and the American Red Cross, must deal with extremely powerful chapters. Often they prefer to determine their own fate.

Hospital presidents are also beset by parochialism and a diffusion of authority. Ask them about the competition for space; research funds; and reward and recognition between and among the departments of, for example, medicine, surgery, radiology, and cancer.[1]

So Lincoln Center's aptitude for dysfunction was not unique, even if it was often on public display.

The heavy and lonely burden of responsibility for overcoming the powerful forces of the status quo helps to explain why so many candidates shy away from accepting tough jobs in forbidding environments. All large nonprofits, in the absence of energetic, purposeful, results-oriented leadership, run the risk of having the centrifugal forces that separate and divide overwhelm the centripetal forces that might pull the parts together. Is it any wonder, then, that nonprofit CEOs of sizable institutions complain of frustration and burnout, and that the average length of stay at the very top of these organizations is only six to seven years?

Changing institutions is hard work. Overcoming the status quo takes time. It requires persistence. The forces of resistance, both active and passive, are strong. Leaders must accumulate influence by understanding the interests of others, gaining their trust, and identifying the common ground that serves all parties. It is forming such a consensus that moves nonprofits (and corporations and nations) forward.

But my concern is not with the plight of the weary and wary CEO. It is with those who often get completely lost in day-to-day organizational struggles and preoccupations: the student, the patient, and the audience member.

The actual performance of private institutions intended to serve the public good often undermines their stated purpose. What in theory should fully deserve government subsidy and philanthropic support may be far less deserving in practice. Frequently, it is only the president and members of the board of directors who can insist on an institutional direction that draws its meaning from the outside in, not the inside out: student-centered learning, patient-centered care, audience-focused arts centers.

IF ACHIEVING FORWARD-LOOKING consensus is the end, the means is the organization, how it is composed, and how it operates.

At Lincoln Center, one important, sweeping reform that could propel progress was to expand the board of trustees numbering forty-three in 2002 and ultimately increasing to eighty over the next decade. The reasons to do so were compelling. Our agenda was ambitious. We aspired to physically transform Lincoln Center. To fix all that was broken. To replace all that was beyond its useful life. To renovate and build new public spaces and artistic facilities. To remove Lincoln Center from its pedestal and have it embrace the cityscape all around it. Concurrently, we wanted all of our programs to continue to flourish. And we hoped to attract many more first-generation Americans to enjoy what Lincoln Center has to offer.

Accomplishing all of this would not only be expensive, it would require expertise from many fields: real estate, finance, law, accounting, engineering, entertainment, hospitality, public relations, advertising, high-tech, and consulting, among others. By expanding the Lincoln Center Board of Directors/Trustees and raising expectations for giving funds and acquiring them from new recruits, we could take a giant step forward in successfully launching a capital campaign. Simultaneously, we could approach our trustees as partners in figuring out how best to address the dozens of challenges and opportunities generated by an enlarged and modernized campus.

By increasing the number of trustees, the board's nominating and governance committee could also recruit leading hedge fund, private equity, and money-centered bank businessmen and women. We could spread our geographic targets to include trustees hailing from Miami, Washington, Chicago, Los Angeles, and San Francisco, as well as from abroad—Switzerland and China, for example. This expansion would raise the metabolism of the board, diversifying its ranks by age, profession, gender, ethnicity, and location. As a result, the board's perspective on Lincoln Center would be fresh and holistic.

Of the forty-three trustees I inherited, fourteen were the designees of constituents. They generally viewed the trustee role as protecting and advancing the interests of the resident artistic organization each represented. The natural tendency of those trustees was not to think of Lincoln Center as a whole but about the piece each cared most about. As a consequence, an intense and vocal minority of the board were present to prevent any act that might adversely affect a particular constituent and to advance any act that could strengthen it.

By contrast, any new trustees we recruited would tend to view Lincoln Center as a whole, not just as a landlord and service provider to constituents, but also as an important civic actor in the life of New York City, the cultural capital of the world. Out of this broader view of Lincoln Center as a source of economic development, as a tourist attraction, as an agent for the community of artists and audiences, much would follow. Imaginations would be ignited. The time and attention of trustees and their colleagues would be tapped. And financial support would naturally flow.

The expansion of Lincoln Center's board enhanced its determination to make an important difference in the life of the city. The institution became less parochial and more broad minded, less narrow in its vision and more enthusiastic about what collectively we might all accomplish.

We could not change the basic structure of Lincoln Center. But we could revolutionize the way the parent body was composed, redefine what was expected of its members, and reconfigure how it operated. No single act did more to advance Lincoln Center's success during my tenure as president than the board's approval several times to expand its number, increase the opportunities for trustees to participate in its active governance, and raise the expectations of what new recruits were expected to accomplish.

LITTLE HAS CHANGED over the decades in the way performing arts centers and their component parts—like theaters, or opera companies, or jazz ensembles, or orchestras, or ballet troupes—are financed. While closely examining the operating budgets of Lincoln Center's constituents after my arrival, I began to wonder what century I was in. And the choice was not, in all respects, between the twentieth and the twenty-first! The famous Russian impresario Sol Hurok would have been completely comfortable with the operating budgets of all the entities of Lincoln Center. Even Wolfgang Amadeus Mozart would not find them unrecognizable, accustomed as he was to the need to seek out wealthy patrons and attract a fee-paying public.

In essence, the revenue base for these world-class artistic organizations is divided into three parts: ticket revenue, contributed income, and funds generated from endowments.

Given the competition for the discretionary expenditures of most New Yorkers and tourists, there is a limit to how much an institution can charge for a ticket, or as an economist would put it, a narrow range of price elasticity. The marketplace for contributed income is also highly competitive, and many arts organizations have neither the staff nor a board willing or able to raise the funds needed by their organizations. Walking on hot coals barefoot often seems preferable to asking friends and strangers for donations to a worthy cause.

Finally, endowment fund-raising is not frequently or robustly practiced, and the travails of the stock market throughout the decade of the 1990s and into the first few years of the twenty-first century were not kind to this source of revenue.

Meanwhile expenses rise. Unionized labor contracts with high levels of compensation and extraordinarily rigid and costly work rules prevail. Heating, air conditioning, and maintaining and securing public spaces and artistic facilities in a first-class fashion is extremely costly. So, too, are artistic expenses. And at Lincoln Center, it would be difficult to find an advocate for reduced rehearsal time, or skimpy sets, or less than ambitious productions mounted on our stages.

Moreover, in the arts, expecting productivity gains is highly unrealistic. One cannot play Beethoven faster. A chamber music quartet always requires four players.[2]

This collision between the constrained sources of revenue and spiraling expenses did not bode well for the future of Lincoln Center and its resident artistic organizations. Therefore, I wished to create a new economic model, one that would not only strictly contain administrative expenses, but would also identify and secure reliable new or enhanced sources of net revenue.

In fact, the Lincoln Center board's finance and new venture committees set as a goal that within three years, at least 50 percent of the $10–12 million of annual ticket revenue would be garnered from these novel or enriched initiatives. We set our minds to exceeding that target and accelerating that timetable.

Tackling this opportunity was a self-imposed challenge. It meant lifting our sights as an organization. It demanded different skills and new learning. Ambition and self-sacrifice were required. We wished to prove that Lincoln Center was neither complacent nor self-satisfied, but rather energetic, tenacious, and hungry.

First, we more than tripled our net revenue from food and beverages in the form of restaurants and catering.

Second, we took full advantage of our resplendent new campus by attracting Channel 13 as a tenant, yielding in excess of $1 million per year, and Mercedes-Benz Fashion Week, yielding $3.2 million annually, the latter to be divided among Lincoln Center's constituents.

Third, taking a cue from the transformation of marketing Broadway tickets, Lincoln Center engaged in yield management of its "inventory," or dynamic pricing. In essence, when demand is high for a given performance, we "rescale the house" to increase the number of high-priced tickets or simply raise prices, always leaving a critical minimum number at an accessible cost for a public that cannot afford the higher range. This practice has generated hundreds of thousands of dollars in incremental revenue each year.

Fourth, Lincoln Center introduced a facility fee: first $2.00, then $2.75, and then $3.50 per ticket. Unlike in other New York City venues that imposed such a charge but have in fact offered few if any improvements, the paying public could not fail to notice Lincoln Center's burgeoning physical transformation. Contrary to the fears of some, not a single objection was lodged. Within two years, virtually every constituent at Lincoln Center introduced its own facility fee on tickets as well.

Fifth, Lincoln Center's staff began modestly to sell its services to constituents and to lessees in the areas of marketing and sales, customer service, and information technology.

Sixth, Lincoln Center negotiated a contract with John Wiley & Sons for an imprint exclusively devoted to performing arts and carrying our institution's name and imprimatur. To date, twelve books have been published, and handsome royalties have been generated by them, simultaneously advancing and enriching our mission.[3]

Seventh, Lincoln Center operates one of the largest underground garages in all of New York City. Being president of Lincoln Center involves understanding how to manage the economics of a huge parking lot and the safety and comfort of tens of thousands of customers who use it. There are early-bird parkers. There are performance parkers. There are parkers who come during the day to shop. There are commuters who park at Lincoln Center and take the subway or a taxi downtown. There are monthly parkers who can't find a space, or are on a waiting list, at their nearby co-ops or condominiums. And there are employee parkers.

Figuring out the algorithm for how to differentially set prices given all of these uses of the garage was a challenge worth seizing. We needed to maximize revenue and remain consistent with our central mission:

to serve paying customers, members of Lincoln Center's audience. And we needed to leave ample room for my ancient Mercury.

Eighth, as part of Lincoln Center's physical redevelopment, we took a major risk and built the only freestanding restaurant in Manhattan since Central Park's Tavern on the Green, called Lincoln Ristorante. With Jonathan Benno, the former chef of Per Se, in the kitchen, and Nick Valenti, the president of the Patina Group, as our partner, this stunning glass structure with a lawn rooftop designed by Diller Scofidio + Renfro almost immediately became a campus hangout and watering hole. It serves not only pre- and post-theater diners, but also those who treat it as a destination for the evening. No fewer than one hundred thousand people enjoy lunch or dinner there annually.

The decision to build this restaurant, situated between Avery Fisher Hall and Lincoln Center Theater and facing the Paul Milstein Pool and Terrace, featuring an iconic Henry Moore sculpture, was opposed by many constituent trustees and executives. They dwelled on the restaurant's costs rather than its benefits and pointed to past failed attempts to create commercially viable dining facilities on the campus. Now they clamor for reservations and complain bitterly when their preferred time for lunch or supper, or their favorite table, or the private dining room, is unavailable.

Financially, the restaurant brings Lincoln Center a handsome six-figure annual rent guarantee, plus a percentage of gross sales above certain million-dollar thresholds.

Ninth, plenty of attention was paid to improving annual performance in contributed income. To cite only three of many examples, when I arrived at Lincoln Center in 2002, it held two galas, one in the fall and one in the spring. They typically raised a total of $2–3 million gross. During my years of service, Lincoln Center held ten or more fund-raisers each year, including the Mostly Mozart Gala, American Songbook Gala, David Rubenstein Atrium Gala, Midsummer Night Swing Gala, Fall and Spring Gala, and special events like a celebration in honor of Ralph Lauren featuring Oprah Winfrey.

By 2010 we expected to raise from $9 million to $14 million gross from these gatherings. How much each brings in depends on the nature of the occasion, its content, and the identity of the honoree. Beyond the funds raised from any given benefit, each offers Lincoln Center the chance to befriend guests invited by gala supporters. Many who have become significant individual benefactors to Lincoln Center were first introduced to our work at special celebratory events.

Not only did the board of directors increase in size, but each newcomer was required to contribute $250,000 per year personally or through a publicly held company or privately held firm. It was also expected that within six months to a year of service on the board, a leadership pledge of $3–5 million or more to our capital campaign will be forthcoming. Typically, such pledges are redeemed over three to five years.

In 2002 trustees were contributing an average of about $80,000 annually. In 2014 forty-three trustees gave at the $250,000 level, and the average for the rest was up to $140,000. The net effect of board expansion and raising expectations for trustee giving is an increase of annual support to $20 million each year, compared to $7.9 million in 2002, leaving aside the very generous trustee gifts to the capital and endowment campaign. More than $56 million was raised for the endowment.

A third lucrative source of recurring contributed income funds, Lincoln Center's largest, is called the Great Performers Circle (GPC). The GPC is ably led by four distinguished Lincoln Center trustees of long standing: Renee Belfer, Bart Friedman, Roy Furman, and Ann Ziff. They, together with staff, have attracted 104 members to this body of supporters. Each contributes $35,000 annually. This donation entitles members to attend three events that take place annually in spectacular private homes or very attractive public spaces.

A sumptuous meal is served. In the most intimate of settings, artists such as Lang Lang, Kelli O'Hara, Emanuel Ax, Laura Benanti, Joshua Bell, and Audra McDonald have performed and mixed and mingled with guests. It is a terrific way for generous supporters of Lincoln Center to become acquainted with great artists and with one another.

The GPC raises about $3.4 million annually. It is as if Lincoln Center enjoyed a 5 percent "draw" on a permanent endowment of $70 million. The membership of the GPC and the sum it raises for Lincoln Center quadrupled between 2001 and 2014. The trustees in turn engage corporations and professional firms with which they are closely associated in the life of Lincoln Center. The institution benefits enormously from that collective, pro bono, intellectual firepower.

Lincoln Center has also benefited greatly from the tenth initiative undertaken, one that has the potential to transform Lincoln Center's operating budget and the way in which it conceives of its mission in the twenty-first century. It originated with a staff recommendation to establish an institutional consulting practice. Most trustees reacted favorably. They maintained that as the largest, best-known, and most consequential performing arts center in the world, Lincoln Center is frequently called upon to offer advice and guidance to its traditional and new counterparts around the world. Site visits; delegations; technical assistance; and one-on-one counseling of visiting staff, board members, and foundations from the four corners of the earth are virtually an everyday occurrence at Lincoln Center. Key trustees became convinced that the strength of Lincoln Center's brand and its accumulated knowledge could become an entrée to remunerative consulting.

If one of Lincoln Center's foremost assets is the combined talent of its incumbent staff, then why not exploit it to improve our institution's financial performance, to benefit our clients, and to enrich the experience of key employees, eager to tackle new and different assignments? This line of reasoning, in turn, caused us to reflect on whether and how Lincoln Center might help to improve the design and management of arts centers and promote international artistic exchange. For me, such activities fell right smack in the middle of Lincoln Center's mission. They are part of what it means to be the world's leading performing arts center in the twenty-first century.

It was this mix of considerations that prompted the board of directors to support my conviction that by entering consultant territory, we could at once further our mission, attract and retain world-class staff, substantially enhance our net revenue, and learn a great deal about ourselves in the bargain.

Lincoln Center Global (LCG) is the name of our consulting practice. A gifted staff member, formerly a Broadway producer and a Harvard Business School (HBS) graduate, Kara Medoff Barnett, led this unprecedented initiative. She performed with distinction. We decided to start small; our first client would be China. Soon afterward, the Harvard Business School, Harvard University, Mitsui & Co., Brown University, the New Orleans Musicians Village, and a performing arts and education center in the Phoenix metropolitan area called Consolari joined the city of Tianjin as LCG clients.

Overall, this major alteration of Lincoln Center's economic model took time to conceive and to implement, but the framework for its creation started on day one of year one. So did the notion of expanding the board of directors. I also set in motion task forces of trustees and executives from firms like McKinsey and UBS to help me think through how best to acquire federal and state funds to pay for redevelopment and how to maximize rental income from the venues that Lincoln Center owned and operated.

Even higher on my list of priorities was puzzling out what would be contained in the package of incentives that could move constituents from spectator seats to the playing field of redevelopment. What might convert them from opponents or passive bystanders to active participants?

That analytical challenge was sitting out there just waiting to be seized when reality intruded in June 2002. It came in the surprising form of a labor strike by the musicians of the Mostly Mozart Orchestra.

I WAS STARTLED by this sudden development. The Mostly Mozart Festival was a well-known Lincoln Center creation. Its featured ensemble in this widely emulated summer production has always been the Mostly Mozart Orchestra, which consisted of fine freelance musicians who were the best paid in the country. Their demand was not related to pay, or fringe benefits, or working conditions. Rather, they insisted on an outsized role in any decision about the possible dismissal of an existing player deemed by the music director to be performing below par and in the selection of new musicians to fill any vacancies. It appeared that the union players of the Mostly Mozart Orchestra intended to send management a message. But what was it?

Until recently, the Mostly Mozart Orchestra had been conducted by Gerard Schwarz, whose tenure lasted seventeen years. I knew Schwarz very well. In 1978, while I was executive director of the 92nd Street Y, Omus Hirshbein, the resident impresario and my close colleague, created and then nurtured the Y Chamber Symphony. We asked Schwarz to be its maestro. He performed very ably in that role, and as far as I could tell from a distance, he was also successful as the conductor of the Mostly Mozart Orchestra, particularly in his first decade on the job. However, by the time I arrived at Lincoln Center in 2002, Gerry's contract had not been renewed, and for the summer of 2001 the orchestra played with a series of guest conductors. The musicians anxiously awaited the decision of Jane Moss, Lincoln Center's vice president for programs, about who his successor would be.

Anxiety was mixed with trepidation. The critical reviews of the orchestra in Gerry's last years had not been favorable, and the orchestra's audience had begun to erode significantly. Early in its history, the festival ran for seven weeks. Reduced demand for tickets contracted its season to six, then five, and then four weeks. Concern was expressed about whether Moss intended not only to further shorten the already truncated season, but also to dilute the centrality of the orchestra in the festival's offerings. As an arts presenter, Moss was adept at bringing to Lincoln Center all kinds of excellent chamber ensembles, early music groups, chamber symphonies, vocal artists, and even modern dance troupes to enhance the festival. There were rumors, some of which reached the press, that the orchestra might simply disappear.

The message, then, seemed to be that the musicians of the orchestra wished to protect each other against dismissal and intended to exert control over the selection of future personnel. To me and to Moss, that meant any new conductor's authority would be diminished even before he or she could raise a baton. This demand seemed untenable. We both examined carefully the contracts of the Metropolitan Opera Orchestra, the New York Philharmonic, and other leading American ensembles with their musicians. In some, there was language about management's obligation to consult with musicians on vacancies or seek the advice of players in a given section of the orchestra. But none of the provisions came even close to the assertion of authority these freelance musicians were insisting upon for the Mostly Mozart Orchestra.

In June 2002 I had been exclusively on the payroll of Lincoln Center for a little more than one month. If the union members thought that a brand-new president might buckle under the pressure of a media frenzy, a disappointed audience, and the cost of a labor action that could not be offset by earned revenue, they had good reason. The chair of the Lincoln Center board, Beverly Sills, advised me to settle on the union's terms if necessary. Just conjure up some face-saving language for management, she advised. The issue at stake was obscure; no one really understood it, she opined. Why start off your tenure as president by alienating musicians, audiences, and union supporters, including most of the members of the New York City Council?

I held firm. The media pressure did not trouble me. Lincoln Center's board of directors, while not demonstrably supportive, seemed to be willing to cut the new guy some managerial slack. Whatever the resulting budget deficit, I was certain it could be closed by some more fund-raising hustle. Most important, Jane Moss needed and deserved my support. She was being unfairly scapegoated by elements of the press and reviled by the musicians. I was convinced that her strong track record and excellent intentions for the future of the Mostly Mozart Festival and for its orchestra fully merited my support. Moss needed the running room to rebuild and renew this festival. Being pushed around by musicians understandably concerned about their own future was no way to start that process.

We both wanted our soon-to-be-named music director to enjoy the full prerogatives of a maestro. The musicians of the Mostly Mozart Orchestra needed to be reshaped into a proud, energetic, fully engaged ensemble. That would take time and money. Scheduling extra rehearsals. Retaining world-renowned feature guest artists. Programming crowd pleasers and challenging repertoire. Encouraging the orchestra to learn from brilliant guest conductors. None of this could happen with a new maestro hobbled by a labor agreement that clouded the issue of who was in charge.

After several weeks of frenzied activity, including union demonstrations around Lincoln Center's campus, it became clear that neither the media nor the public were very sympathetic to the musicians' case. Two days after what was to have been the start of the season, the musicians in effect capitulated. They asked us to commence the Mostly Mozart Festival orchestral concerts about one week late. By then, opportunities for single ticket sales had diminished, and some important guest artists had changed their plans. By then, the opportunity for a buoyant opening had come and gone. We held fast to our position. The festival would carry on that summer, but without any Mostly Mozart Orchestra offerings. We were sure that the union musicians would be a lot more careful in the future about attempting to interfere with the prerogatives of management.

The rest is contemporary history. Jane Moss announced the appointment of the French maestro Louis Langrée. He is a conductor with a special flair for the music of Mozart. Engaging, energetic, and upbeat, he is a nonconfrontational leader possessed of a light personal touch, and he proved to be an inspired choice. As we had promised him and ourselves, Lincoln Center invested more time, energy, and resources in the festival than ever before.

Langrée developed a close working relationship with Moss. He was handpicked after Jane saw him perform in Europe. From the beginning, he was well received by the musicians. They rehearsed much more together. Langrée instilled in them a sense of pride and musicianship. He maintained very high standards. They responded by playing well, not only for him but *for* guest conductors who were going places: Yannick Nézet-Séguin (soon thereafter, selected to conduct the Metropolitan Opera Orchestra and to become the maestro of the Philadelphia Orchestra), Osmo Vanska (conductor of the Minnesota Orchestra), and Pablo Heras-Casado (also bound to conduct at the Met and to become the music director of the St. Luke's Orchestra). They played *with* special guest artists who were at the pinnacle of their careers: Stephanie Blythe, Susanna Phillips, Renee Fleming, Dmitri Hvorostovsky, Emanuel Ax, Leif Ove-Andsnes, Pierre Laurent-Aimard, Yo-Yo Ma, Alisa Weilerstein, and Martin Frost, among many others. And they performed not only the classical repertory, but also works *of* living composers, like Golijov, Adams, and Saariaho.

After some of the concerts in Avery Fisher Hall, a 2,700-seat venue, Moss would invite solo artists or trios and quartets to perform at 10:30 p.m. in the 240-seat, nightclub-like setting of the Kaplan Penthouse overlooking the Hudson River. In that candlelit, romantic venue, the age of the audience plummeted; hemlines rose; backpacks were unloaded; and music acquired spellbinding intimacy, proximity, and immediacy.

While the orchestra remained the centerpiece of the festival, it was surrounded by innovation. For the first time in its history, the Mostly Mozart Festival offered staged operas, among them *Don Giovanni* and *Le Nozze di Figaro*, both performed by the Budapest Festival Orchestra, conducted and directed by Ivan Fischer; *The Flowering Tree*, a new opera by John Adams, directed by Peter Sellars; Mozart's *Laide*, also directed by Sellars; *Il Re Pastore*, directed by Mark Lamos; and a revival of Jonathan Miller's *Cosi fan Tutte*.

Contemporaneous with such offerings were performances by William Christie and Les Arts Florissants, the Tallis Scholars, Gidon Kremer's Kremerara Baltica, the Leipzig String Quartet, the Emerson String Quartet, and the International Contemporary Ensemble.

A mainstay of the festival has been the Mark Morris Dance Company. It has performed *L'Allegro Il Penseroso ed il Moderato*, *Dido Aeneas*, and as a world premiere, *Mozart Dances*, among other pieces.

These are all expensive initiatives and actions. They required even more ambitious fund-raising. I enjoyed taking the lead in rallying the staff and board to acquire for Lincoln Center new and generous supporters.

What Jane Moss accomplished with the Mostly Mozart Festival was and remains astounding. She built on the basic idea of celebrating Mozart's brilliance, but construed that undertaking broadly and imaginatively. Who influenced Mozart, and which composers and musicians were most influenced by him? How is his work reflected in the music, the visual art, and the literature of his time? To what extent was Mozart the product of his own environment and extensive travel, and in what degree did he transcend them? How does Mozart's work influence today's musicians and composers? What mixture of nature and nurture accounts for his genius? These are some of the probing and fascinating questions that animated Moss's brilliant programming choices.

In working closely with Louis Langrée, classicism and innovation were viewed as entirely compatible. Mozart's music was enhanced and its essence revealed, not negated or superseded, by incorporating the music of other composers, dead and alive, into the festival. Adding different performing groups and programming elements into the festival also enlivened this summer tradition.

The ubiquity, consistency, and constancy of elaborate praise for the Mostly Mozart Festival was gratifying. While each critic was partial to his or her favorite features of this four-week cornucopia of events, what they seemed to share was respect. They held in high regard the fact that it was ideas that animated the festival, well-articulated points of view. One might take issue with some of them, but their worthiness as organizing principles was undeniable.

Peter Davies at *New York Magazine*, Justin Davidson at *Newsday*, Alex Ross at the *New Yorker*, and that *New York Times* cadre of critics—Anthony Tommasini, Allan Kozinn, James R. Oestreich, Alastair Macaulay, Steve Smith, and Zachary Wolfe, among others—wrote admiringly about what Langrée and Moss were accomplishing. Striking a theme that found echoes in all of their commentary, on August 5, 2004, the *New York Times* concert review read:

> What a difference a director makes.
>
> Youthful, limber, technically accomplished, full of ideas and seemingly tireless, Mr. Langrée has revitalized the Festival's orchestra . . . just two summers after the players went out on strike.

As a result of Lincoln Center's capital campaign, Jane received a special honor. The position she held became the Ehrenkranz Artistic Director of Lincoln Center. Louis Langrée was similarly recognized; he became the Renée and Robert Belfer Music Director of the Mostly Mozart Orchestra. These are the first positions ever to be endowed at Lincoln Center. In recognition of the publicly and critically acclaimed artistic reawakening of this beloved festival, these tributes were greeted with enthusiasm by colleagues, commentators, and audience members.

In the late summer of 2013 many of those musicians who had participated in that job action eleven years earlier asked to see me for lunch. They were joined by those who had accepted positions with the Mostly Mozart Orchestra after 2002. They offered me modest tokens of appreciation and genuine words of thanks. I told them how proud I was of what they had accomplished together. In return they recognized that without my energetic commitment, none of them could have enjoyed the artistic camaraderie and the critical praise that was now theirs to treasure.

In a whisper, I asked Jane whether she had a tissue handy.

THE SUSPENSION OF 2002 performances of the Mostly Mozart Orchestra was not the only instance of union friction at Lincoln Center with which I had to deal. Another occurred two years later.

I was told that James (Jimmy) Claffey, the notoriously brusque and tough-minded president of the New York Chapter of IATSE (the International Alliance of Theatrical Stage Employees), otherwise known as the stagehands' union, was intent on unilaterally asserting union jurisdiction for the first time over an event that Lincoln Center had mounted free to the public during each winter holiday season for years.

Lincoln Center organized a half hour of live outdoor entertainment that culminated in a holiday tree-lighting ceremony. It was held in December on Josie Robertson Plaza and on the surrounding balconies and porticos of the Metropolitan Opera, Avery Fisher Hall, and what was then known as the New York State Theater. Opera singers from the Met; dancers from the New York City Ballet; students from the School of American Ballet trained to perform in the *Nutcracker*; musicians from the New York Philharmonic and from Jazz at Lincoln Center; and jugglers, aerialists, and clowns from the Big Apple Circus all performed for no fee to an enchanted audience of children and their families that numbered as many as ten thousand. Organized by the Business Improvement District (BID), stores along Broadway, Columbus, and Amsterdam Avenues offered free refreshments and merchandise.

This event proved so enjoyable and visually arresting that the local ABC television station decided to broadcast it from 5:30 to 6:00 p.m. throughout New York, New Jersey, and Connecticut. It received very high viewership.

Sure enough, three hours before the television program was due to start, Claffey called to say, "We want that work on the plaza or we will picket and shut you down."

I reminded him that Lincoln Center's collectively bargained contract excluded IATSE jurisdiction over events offered free to the public in our outdoor spaces. I also mentioned that I would be present at this holiday event. At that time, I would be delighted to explain to the news media that the very best-paid union members in the world had taken it upon themselves to prevent a free event from being seen by tens of thousands live and on television as it had been for the last four years.

Lincoln Center simply could not afford to continue this joyful holiday celebration if union costs amounting to several hundreds of thousands of dollars were suddenly imposed, in violation of our existing contract.

This show would not be stopped by him, and I was not going to be threatened. There was heat under my collar.

Literally minutes after Claffey hung up, a member of the New York City Council, Christine Quinn, who was later elected speaker of that legislative body, called. She asked why the stagehands were being barred from Lincoln Center's campus. I patiently told her that there was no more unionized cultural complex in the world than Lincoln Center, but that the jurisdiction of the stagehands did not extend to Josie Robertson Plaza or our other public spaces for events that are free to the public. I asked her whether she had read or been briefed about Lincoln Center's contract with IATSE, or whether she was aware that the workers on whose behalf she was calling earned on average $250,000 annually. She dissembled.

Ignorant of these and other facts, Quinn was simply doing Claffey's bidding. She seemed flummoxed by my questions.

Politicians who are handmaidens of special interests—be they unions, real estate developers, retailers, or Wall Street lobbyists—do a disservice to the general public and to the office they hold.

I thanked her for calling.

The show went on as planned, without a hitch. Claffey's threat did not work. And Christine Quinn, hardly known as a supporter of the performing arts, was not heard from again.

CHAPTER 3

Curtain Up

Bit by bit, putting it together
Piece by piece, only way to make a work of art
Every moment makes a contribution
Every little detail plays a part
Having just a vision's no solution
Everything depends on execution
Putting it together, that's what counts!

—STEPHEN SONDHEIM, "Putting It Together,"
Sunday in the Park with George

The Mostly Mozart Festival is one of a number of productions and presentations Lincoln Center mounts every year, more than four hundred events in all. Preceding it is a beloved New York tradition, Midsummer Night Swing. Located in Damrosch Park, on the northwest side of Lincoln Center's campus, it runs for a period of two weeks every July. Between six and ten o'clock each evening, thousands of people arrive. They come to dance. Some arrive as couples. Most singles find it very easy to "couple up." The music breaks the ice. The rhythms introduce the shy to the outgoing.

Every age, size, shape, social class, color, and ethnicity is present. All are cordially invited. Dressed to the nines, or come as you are, be prepared to be surrounded by the sights and sounds of swing, reggae, the samba, the merengue, the cha-cha, the fox trot, the lindy hop, rock and roll, soul, Motown, salsa, the tango, the polka, funk, zydeco, country, disco, the jig, Afro-soul, Afro-Latin, and garage house. Hundreds spring for a $17 ticket, which admits them to an attractive, elevated dance floor and to a lesson. Thousands of others just show up. They dance free of charge in the park itself, around the stage on three sides. They also enjoy the carefully chosen musical ensembles, playing from a fully renovated and stunningly lit outdoor band shell. Four hours of sheer unadulterated, uninterrupted bliss transpire under an open sky.

And only yards away, at the Koch Theater, the Mark Morris Dance Company, the Bolshoi, the Paris Opera Ballet, or the San Francisco Ballet may be performing. Or equidistant, on the stage of the Metropolitan Opera, a celebration of the choreography of Frederick Ashton might be occurring, with the Royal Ballet of London and Birmingham sharing performance duties with the Joffrey Ballet of Chicago. Or, diagonally across the plaza in Avery Fisher Hall, audiences might be seeing a spectacular rendition of Sondheim's *Pacific Overtures* performed in Japanese, or Elvis Costello singing his catalog of hits, or Goren Bregovic crooning spirited and melancholy melodies from the Balkans.

In Damrosch Park, if you listen carefully, you will hear Albanian, Russian, Italian, Gaelic, Polish, French, Portuguese, Spanish, Japanese, Mandarin, and Cantonese, among other languages, being spoken. Be alert as you walk around not to trip over a stroller carrying a three-year-old, brought by her parents coming off the Number 1 subway line from the Bronx or the F train from Queens to enjoy a beautiful night under the stars at no charge. A fellow dancer offers to look after that little child, as her parents take a few minutes on their own to trip the light fantastic. The elderly prove that despite wheelchairs, walkers, and caretakers, they also can sway their hips, move their arms, shake a leg, and snap their fingers to the sounds of their adolescence. Mixed in with amateurs just having fun, aspiring professionals work on their routines for the competitions yet to come, surrounded by impromptu audiences of admirers, who applaud their virtuosity.

It is not for nothing that the *Wall Street Journal* called Midsummer Night Swing "democracy in action."[1] Nor is it a surprise that legendary *New York Times* photographer Bill Cunningham always elaborately displays decked out dancers in fine acrobatic form throughout his pages.

In this dense, crowded, and stressful city, on these July evenings, people seem free of worldly care.

That same feeling of joyful engagement suffuses Lincoln Center Out of Doors. It is a mélange of presentations that seems to pop up everywhere on and around (and sometimes underneath) Lincoln Center's public spaces. Music and dance of all kinds permeate Lincoln Center throughout August, every one of dozens of shows free of charge. The artists arrive at Lincoln Center from the far corners of our city and country and, occasionally, from abroad. Bill Bragin was the impresario of both Midsummer Night Swing and Lincoln Center Out of Doors. His encyclopedic knowledge of contemporary artists, whatever their genre, whatever their place of origin, made possible an exciting variety of performances.

You might even have been among the fifty thousand people lucky enough to see Dave Brubeck perform in one of his very last major concerts, or Chubby Checker twist again like he did last summer, or Roberta Flack, or Ruben Blades, one of salsa's most beloved icons, or the Silk Road Ensemble with Yo-Yo Ma or Eiko & Koma performing a site-specific water work in the Paul Milstein Pool and Terrace. They have all appeared on separate nights in seasons during the last decade of Out of Doors. As have the Asphalt Orchestra and *The Tangle*, The Polyglot Theatre's colorful and beautifully chaotic art installation that lovingly entangled kids throughout Josie Robertson Plaza.

Several years after the fresh breezes of reform swept over the Mostly Mozart Festival and after Bill Bragin began to reinvigorate Midsummer Night Swing and Lincoln Center Out of Doors, Jane Moss and I felt that something similar was needed for Lincoln Center's fall programming. She took a sabbatical. I encouraged her: "Take off four months or so. Read. Travel. Reflect. Come back with an organizing principle for a truly exciting festival. I can't wait to see what you develop."

Refreshed and reinvigorated, she reappeared with an artistic gift for Lincoln Center: the White Light Festival. The notion behind it came from two sources: the need to slow down and fend off the extraneous noise in our lives, on the one hand, and a yearning for a sense of spirituality, on the other. Are you too busy to think? Too preoccupied to relax? Too enslaved by the very appliances that are intended to liberate you? Then allow music to penetrate your consciousness.

Not everyone in a given audience or every critic agreed with Jane's premise, or even believed that it set forth a coherent theme on the basis of which a festival could be organized. But all seemed to acknowledge that the works selected to illustrate her point of view were of high quality. Many were arresting. And given the proclivity for programming in most places around the country to be ad hoc, a grab bag of unrelated performances, what everyone respected was the presence of a well-articulated theme.

Here is a sample of what audiences encountered in the first three White Light Festivals: the Manganiyar Seduction from India; the Whirling Dervishes from Turkey; the Schola Cantorum from Venezuela; the London Symphony Orchestra playing Beethoven's "Missa Solemnis"; Paul Lewis performing Schubert; the "Immortal Bach" rendered by Cameron Carpenter on Alice Tully Hall's refurbished Kuhn Organ; and the Philharmonia Orchestra conducted by Esa-Pekka Salonen, playing Mahler's Symphony no. 9. To these offerings add early music, Sephardic music, and Sufi mysticism.

The sources of humanity's spirituality and the art that moves us to transcendence are not confined by national boundaries or by centuries. Moss took audiences on her own carefully curated journey across the world and across time.

This high standard characterizes the excellent programs of Jane Moss and her team throughout the year. Orchestras have included the London Symphony, the Vienna Symphony, the Dresden Philharmonic, the Bamberg Symphony, the Academy of St. Martin in the Fields, the Kirov Orchestra of the Mariinsky Theater, and the Los Angeles Philharmonic. Recitalists have included Tetzlaff and Bell on the violin and Perahia, Aimard, and Ohlsson on the piano. The baritones Quasthoff and Keenlyside have appeared. Among the chamber orchestras that have performed are the Collegium Vocale Gent Choir and Orchestra, the Freiburg Baroque, and the Orchestra of the Age of Enlightenment.

The routine of many so-called curators and presenters in the performing arts is to dial up agents, choose artists, and negotiate a fee. What those musicians play or artists perform is usually their own decision. Rarely is there a meaningful exchange of ideas with the resident "impresario." There is little debate over whether each selection fits the context of a given season and does justice to the audience. No attention is paid to how much rehearsal time is really needed. "Roll them in and roll them out" is often the operating guideline. It's just a gig, after all. All around America, such "booking houses" order in touring productions and groups. Agents offer them up; you can take 'em or leave 'em.

At Lincoln Center and other excellent performing arts establishments around the world, such a method of operating would be considered a sacrilege. What and who appears on our stages is the product of collaboration and dialogue. The stakes are high, because the audiences are sophisticated and the critics demanding. We view what is mounted on our stages as a profound responsibility. It cannot be delegated or outsourced. And it certainly cannot be abdicated.

The artists who appear at Lincoln Center recognize that they are surrounded by talented administrators who understand what they are about and who are eager to create the best conditions for their performances. As a result, few do not long to return, early and often.

On Oscar, Tony, and Emmy evenings, when winners are announced, television audiences generally become impatient. From the podium, acceptance remarks almost always name names at great length, and quick shout-outs are offered to colleagues as time runs out. You may leave your living room when the litany of tributes begins. I sympathize with those winners. They are not holding their awards only because of their own natural talent or hard work. More often than not, that winner is part of a team. Jane Moss's staff are astonishingly bright and hardworking. They reflect well on her. For what you see at Lincoln Center, they fully share in the credit.[2]

IT ALL BEGINS and ends with a compelling piece of performing art. The director of the Lincoln Center Festival, Nigel Redden, is eager to bring to New York City something truly spectacular—as befits Lincoln Center. In this case, it was the only opera ever written by the German composer Bernd Alois Zimmermann, *Die Soldaten*. The subject matter is dark. It is about the traumatic damage inflicted on a young woman by World War II soldiers.

The twelve-tone score requires a huge orchestra of 110. At times the musicians, divided into three sections, are playing in completely different rhythms. They are joined by a 40-member cast of singers, dancers, and actors.

This daunting work requires that the audience be totally immersed in the theatrics of the opera. The director, David Pountney, conceives of a divided audience chamber that sits on top of tracks, allowing one thousand seats to move back and forth in the space, as if the audience were sitting in a trolley car while the scenes on the stage unfold.

But what space?

More often than not, the Lincoln Center Festival and all other Lincoln Center artistic presentations utilize the venues of constituents when they are available. This infusion of rental revenue from Lincoln Center helps our resident artistic organizations offset their overall fixed costs. To provide just one example, Lincoln Center regularly paid Jazz at Lincoln Center over $1 million each year for its use of the Allen (now Appel) Room and the Rose Theater.

In this case, Nigel Redden proposed that Lincoln Center use the mammoth fifty-five-thousand-square-foot Ward Thompson Drill Hall in the Park Avenue Armory. Opened in 1881 as a home for the military, the building had just been granted nonprofit status. Its fledgling board of directors, led by Elihu Rose, hired my close colleague Rebecca Robertson as its first president. She left being the first executive director of Lincoln Center Redevelopment to assume this new role. It played to her strengths. Restoring stunning but badly neglected rooms within the armory and activating this massive building was a natural for Rebecca. After all, for over a decade she led the transformation of 42nd Street between Broadway and Eighth Avenue.

The venue Redden proposed was arguably the only one in New York City that could house this awesome production. I was intrigued. If Lincoln Center demonstrated that the Park Avenue Armory was versatile enough to accommodate large-scale performing arts productions, then a magnificent new option could be exercised by presenters and producers the world over. We could help prove the value of this singular space for a certain scale of performing art.

The costs of presenting *Die Soldaten* in the summer of 2008 were formidable. And we were aware that an activist Park Avenue group wished to limit the number and kind of events presented at the armory and therefore the size of its audience. Petitions circulated anticipating excessive traffic and noise. Litigation was threatened. Still, none of these obstacles seemed impossible to overcome. The opportunity was enticing. I gave the production a green light, and it was deemed a success theatrically, critically, and civically.

What followed was a series of productions presented by the Lincoln Center Festival at the armory. First came the tender portraits of ordinary people that Ariane Mnouchkine and Le Theatre de Soleil called *Les Ephemeres*. Spread out over two evenings or in weekend marathons and performed during the summer of 2008, the stories were recalled by members of the company or improvised by them. Audiences were captivated. The following summer, in 2009, the festival also mounted in the Park Avenue Armory a very well-received *Boris Godunov* directed by Declan Donnellan.

Soon after, another production came to Redden's attention that only the armory could house. It is a haunting opera called *The Passenger*, composed by Mieczyslaw Weinberg (1919–1996). On the upper level of a formidable ship's deck, passengers without a care in the world are bound for Brazil. Down below is captured the living hell of the Holocaust. Beyond the height and width needed to accommodate the gigantic cruise ship, a separate expanse of space was set aside for a full orchestra. The sold-out performances were haunting and unforgettable. Only Lincoln Center could have brought the show to New York City.

By far the most ambitious Lincoln Center undertaking destined for the armory was the presentation of the Royal Shakespeare Company during the summer of 2011. It performed five plays in an auditorium literally shipped from Stratford-upon-Avon that was virtually identical to the one the RSC used in its own home. It took forty-six huge containers traveling by boat and truck over thirty-five hundred miles to transport this auditorium and everything else needed for the performances, from stage sets to costumes and props, from wigs to makeup. Only the Park Avenue Armory could hold 975 seats in a three-tiered auditorium that contains a thrust stage, so that actors and audience members are but an arm's length from one another.

Never before had the RSC's residency in New York City been as long (six weeks), and never before had its slate of shows numbered so many: *As You Like It*, *Julius Caesar*, *King Lear*, *Romeo and Juliet*, and *The Winter's Tale*. In effect, the armory invited the RSC to bring its own playhouse along for the ride to New York City and insert it into the cavernous building. Because the auditorium replicates the conditions with which the company is so familiar at home, lights, props, and sets did not have to be reconfigured, nor did the actors need to reblock the show.

We were most excited by the fact that the armory's column-free space would permit Lincoln Center to bring a true repertory company to a largely American audience. Watching the same actors perform in varied works with the same ensemble may be somewhat routine in Great Britain, but it is extremely rare in the United States. And it is thrilling. The RSC's residency, complete with its four-hundred-ton replica of an auditorium, was among the most expensive and the most gratifying artistic adventures in Lincoln Center's history.

As is often true in the arts, individual donors, in this case benefactors like Les Wexner and Suzi and Bruce Kovner, were the unsung heroes of the initiative. My colleagues and I roamed the earth, well, at least the borough of Manhattan, for prospects. We found them. Before too long, they became delighted philanthropic supporters. Before too long, I could give this massive artistic undertaking a thumbs-up.

This search for the best space available for the work of art being presented is characteristic of the festival. In 2012 and 2014, the Sydney Theater Company performed Chekhov's *Uncle Vanya* and Jean Genet's *The Maids* on the stage of New York City Center, to much acclaim. Both productions featured Oscar-winning actress Cate Blanchett. All agreed that the choice of venue worked well.

When the Druid Theater Company of Galway presented a cycle of three plays by the contemporary Irish playwright Tom Murphy, they were performed at the Gerald W. Lynch Theater, ensconced at, of all places, the John Jay College of Criminal Justice. Lovingly mounted in that same venue was the performance of "DruidSynge," a full cycle of J. M. Synge's six plays. The Druid Theater's Tony Award–winning director Garry Hynes no doubt regards the Gerald Lynch as her home away from home.

Returning to the festival for the third time, the Grand Kabuki Theater Company performed twice in Avery Fisher Hall and most recently in the Rose Theater at the Time Warner Center. The Rose Theater is also where the festival mounted the one-man *Macbeth*, starring Alan Cumming and directed by John Tiffany.

Nigel Redden and his colleagues are nothing if not adventurous. In July 2010 the Lincoln Center Festival presented a Russian play, *The Demons*, also known as *The Possessed*, based on Dostoyevsky's novel. It was staged in a spare theatrical space at Governors Island and was directed by the acclaimed Peter Stein. The running time for the play was roughly eleven hours. It was performed in Italian with English subtitles. Endurance was required, not only by the 26 European actors, but also by the 975 members of the audience in a fully sold-out, ten-day run. That day included two 45-minute breaks for meals, eaten communally and prepared by the staff of well-known chef Tom Colicchio. There were also four fifteen-minute intermissions. The audience was transported to a different time and place. And speaking of transportation, Lincoln Center provided a ferry, departing from lower Manhattan at 10 a.m. and leaving from the island for the return home at 11:30 p.m. It carried an audience that will fondly recall what transpired on the stage and how they enjoyed their theatrical marathon.

Perhaps the best illustration of real estate as theatrical destiny can be found in the Lincoln Center Festival production of Deborah Warner's *The Angel Project*. In the wake of 9/11, the destruction of the World Trade Center's Twin Towers, and the loss of some three thousand lives, Deborah Warner, the English director, created a site-specific set of installations spread out across a dozen locations in midtown Manhattan. In the summer of 2003, from Roosevelt Island to the top of the Chrysler Building, to an empty storefront on 42nd Street between Seventh and Eighth Avenues, she fitted out rooms filled with carefully selected and assembled objects intended to evoke feelings of remembrance, transcendence, and commemoration. The experience was meant to be solitary. At the Lincoln Center box office, participants were handed a map with *Angel Project* locations noted on it and given a Metro card to use on the subway or bus to get to some of them. Departures to the sites occurred at intervals of twenty minutes, three each hour, to minimize the chances of overlap between viewers.

To secure these spaces for an art project lasting three weeks was a major undertaking. It required the cooperation of property owners and real estate developers not necessarily sympathetic to the whole idea. We tried persuasion first, then groveling. And finally the intervention of third parties. The effort paid off handsomely. No one fortunate enough to have joined Deborah Warner on this journey will ever forget having done so.

Ben Brantley, the chief *New York Times* theater critic, wrote that this experience offered by the Lincoln Center Festival persuaded him, for the first time, to think of New York City as a "holy place." Until then, such a thought had no more occurred to him than it had to me, a born and bred New Yorker.

OF COURSE, WHILE it may be illuminating to view the Lincoln Center Festival through the lens of where productions are performed, location alone offers a limited perspective. Besides the suitability and availability of the proper venue, what determines the selection of performing art presented by the sixteen-year-old Lincoln Center Festival?

A group of Lincoln Center constituent companies is largely rooted in nineteenth-century western European art forms: opera, ballet, and symphonic music. The Lincoln Center Festival is intended not only to supplement this emphasis innovatively, but also to present classical forms from different countries and different centuries. An example of the festival's role in providing fascinating additions to standard constituent fare is its presentation of the Cleveland Orchestra under the baton of Franz Welser-Möst, performing all of Bruckner's symphonies, juxtaposed with those of composer John Adams. Examples of supplementing everyday Lincoln Center offerings are Kunqu Opera, Vietnamese water puppets, *The Secret History of the Mongols*, Robert Wilson's *Fables of La Fontaine* from the Comedie Francaise, and Middle Eastern religious epic theater from Iran—the Ta'ziyeh.

Complementary classicism is one continuing festival theme. Another is selecting work based on the sheer difficulty of presenting it or on whether it would otherwise be seen in New York City. But for Lincoln Center, *The Angel Project* would not have found its own angel, and Peter Greenaway's opera *Writing to Vermeer* would never have been presented in the cultural capital of the world. Bringing productions from Chile's Compania Teatro Cinema, Mexico's Teatro de Ciertos Habitantes, and Spain's Centro Dramatico Nacional offered New York audiences a sense of the inventiveness and exuberance of contemporary Latin American and Spanish theater. Only the Lincoln Center Festival would have made this happen.

The art of being a first-class festival presenter resides in posing and satisfactorily answering a series of questions, season after season. What combination of programs will attract an audience? Can they be packaged, priced, scheduled, and promoted in an attractive way? Are they planned far enough in advance to increase the probability that donations can be raised to defray costs for particular productions? Will the ideal venue be identified and available to mount the production? Is the content of this work, the way it is being mounted and performed, and by whom, worthy of Lincoln Center's imprimatur? Do the planned presentations complement and supplement the year-round artistic diet offered to Lincoln Center's far-flung audience? Have we adequately included performing art emanating from Russia, Eastern Europe, and the continents of Asia, Africa, and South America?

If there is an audience for these artists and their work, how fervently do we believe in both? If successful, can a given production burnish established careers or boost those of newcomers, moving them along the spectrum from "promising" to "proven"? Is it likely that once performed at Lincoln Center, the piece of work will have "legs"? How probable is it that audiences around the country and the world will have a chance to encounter it?

Finally, have we adequately prepared to greet and support our visiting artists in every conceivable way, from housing them, to feeding them, to transporting them, and to offering assistance of many other kinds?

The track record of Redden and his staff in responding to these formidable questions buoyantly and creatively has been superb.[3] Redden has held himself to a world-class standard of curatorial distinction for over three decades. His artistic taste and judgment are remarkable.

That Lincoln Center has been the beneficiary of Nigel's talent and of Jane Moss's expertise is really a tribute to my predecessor, once removed, Nat Leventhal. He selected them. He chose very well.

BUILT INTO THE DNA of Lincoln Center is visual art. The Alexander Calder and its stately presence at the entryway in Hearst Plaza to The New York Public Library for the Performing Arts. The Henry Moore Sculpture in the Paul Milstein Pool and Terrace. The Jasper Johns "Numbers" in the lobby of the David H. Koch Theater. David Smith's one-ton steel sculpture, entitled *Zig IV*, safely ensconced in Avery Fisher Hall. Louise Nevelson's *Nightsphere-Light* at The Juilliard School.

These are among the permanent pieces, many site specific, given as generous gifts to Lincoln Center in its early years.

Adding to this legacy is the Vera List Art Project, established by a gift from Albert and Vera List in 1962. Its goal is to have contemporary limited edition artworks commissioned and sold to the public to support Lincoln Center and its programs. The artists attracted to this project included, in its formative years, Roy Lichtenstein, Larry Rivers, Andy Warhol, and Helen Frankenthaler. In the last decade and a half, works have been commissioned from such artists as Jim Dine, William Kentridge, Karen Kilimnik, Guillermo Kutcha, Glenn Ligon, Richard Serra, and Terry Winters.

Looking forward, the question seemed to me not whether there was a place for visual art on our campus, but rather what form it would assume. What impact would the transformation of Lincoln Center's public spaces and performance facilities have on our thinking?

Lincoln Center is no longer interested in acquiring works of art as gifts. It is not a museum. It does not employ the expert staff needed to look after the physical condition of more than the couple of dozen pieces already in its possession. Instead, as the conclusion of the redevelopment project approached in 2010, we began to consider how best to deploy temporary exhibitions in our newly built indoor and outdoor spaces so that tens of thousands of visitors and ticketholders might view them. Could we commission new work, or mount existing work, in ways that would complement what was appearing on our stages, or in ways that would attract a new and different following? Could we call attention to artists of enormous talent who deserve the kind of exposure an association with Lincoln Center generates?

Our initial thought was to use visual art to animate Lincoln Center's huge public spaces, like Josie Robertson Plaza. We established a partnership with the Public Art Fund, a nonprofit organization dedicated to commissioning and presenting the work of important artists in outdoor spaces where they can be viewed free of charge. The partnership began with two major installations.

The first was the work of Franz West, the Viennese artist. In the summer of 2004, he installed seven huge aluminum sculptures in a rainbow of bright colors that sat across Josie Robertson Plaza, stretching from Avery Fisher Hall to the New York State Theater. They assumed compelling, whimsical shapes. Completely approachable, the bright yellow, blue, pink, and green figures all called out "Touch me," "Sit on me," "Lean on me," "Run around and through me." It was the human interaction with his art that West wished for most. To the delight of kids and families, his dreams were completely realized with this installation.

Also in cooperation with the Public Art Fund, the Malibu, California–based artist Nancy Rubins assembled her sculpture *Big Pleasure Point* on Josie Robertson Plaza. For two months in the summer of 2006, the sixty colorful vessels she accumulated and assembled included kayaks, canoes, rowboats, surfboards, sailboats, paddleboats, and windsurfing boats. They commanded attention. Forty feet tall, fifty-five feet wide, and weighing over six thousand pounds, the assemblage brought new shapes and new life to the space it occupied. All patrons and passersby, nautically minded or otherwise, paused to look and marvel.

These site-specific works made sense. Josie Robertson Plaza is a monumental, monochromatic space. Any installation prepared for it demands a keen sense of light and proportion. Figuring out the geography of the placement of objects and the color combination that would work best was a major part of any artistic assignment. Learning from these earliest, well-received trials, Lincoln Center next turned to Los Angeles–based artist Aaron Curry.

Taking the Revson Fountain as his central perspective, he created fifteen monumental aluminum sculptures shaped like anthropomorphic figures. Their bright colors and playful forms were impossible to ignore. As people walked by these human-like shapes, it was as if they were accompanying them to the theater, or they were waiting for the curtain to come down so the viewers could converse with them about how they had enjoyed the show. Kids and their families were drawn to them, and as with West's sculptures, thousands of photos were taken. These likeable and attractive figures captured the imagination. Families even gave them names and checked in on them, day after day. Fanciful conversations ensued. Aaron Curry received precisely the kind of public and media attention to which we aspired.

Other experiments on campus have enjoyed a closer affinity to the performing arts. In July 2007 forty-three dancers, among them Bill T.

Jones, Wendy Whelan, William Forsythe, and Judith Jamison, were projected on three huge screens suspended from the roof of the New York State Theater. What amazed and engrossed everyone was how slow moving the figures were and how sharp their renderings. The ripple of a muscle, the strand of a hair, the arc of a body in flight. To show dancers moving at less than one one-hundredth of their original speed was an amazing technical accomplishment, brought off by the gifted photographer David Michalek. To witness the progression of a gesture, the movement of a shoulder, the majesty of a jump, the delicacy of a turn, the subtlety of a foot landing was astonishing. The dancers moved side by side on the three screens. The overall effect was to be suffused in movement, form, and color. Tens of thousands of strolling pedestrians paused to look at the video presentation during the ten-week run of *Slow Dancing*, between the hours of 9:00 p.m. and 1:00 a.m. Others, like Mikhail Baryshnikov, brought their own beach chairs and bottles of wine and took their time to enjoy it all.

Slow Dancing traveled to several dozen cities around the world, and ultimately millions of people saw this remarkable piece. It was our privilege to have Josie Robertson Plaza be the site of its world premiere.

What David Michalek is to dance, Janet Cardiff is to music and Christian Marclay is to film, at least insofar as Lincoln Center's public art program is concerned. Cardiff's *Forty-Part Motet* is a sound installation artwork that was incorporated into the 2010 White Light Festival. The music is from a sixteenth-century motet by Thomas Tallis in which eight groups of five singers meet and diverge in sound. Cardiff recorded each singer separately, each projected by one or more speakers. As listeners step back from any single speaker, the ensemble coalesces. As they approach a single speaker, one of the parts emerges. The work is spellbinding and mesmerizing. Those who assembled in a rehearsal room and recording studio at Jazz at Lincoln Center to hear Cardiff's piece are unlikely to have forgotten their visit, as Justin Davidson explained in an article in the *New York Magazine* on November 1, 2010:

> Here . . . for eight hours each day, in a windowless sanctum, Cardiff offers a fourteen-minute bath of warm Renaissance counterpoint—a sauna for the mind. Physical and virtual space fuse. Normally, your

ears will tell you where you are in the world, but not here. Close your eyes and the room gets vaster, turning into a cathedral without walls, where exquisite music reverberates in the open air.

The Lincoln Center art installation that drew the most critical attention was Christian Marclay's *The Clock*, a twenty-four-hour collage of pieces of film that refer to time as depicted in objects of all kinds. Their appearance coincides with the very hour and minute when one is watching. For this enthralling masterpiece that wove together parts of over three thousand films, Lincoln Center built a theater in the David Rubenstein Atrium to Marclay's demanding specifications. He determined the weight, color, texture, and length of the drapes that surround the audience; the exact benches on which viewers would sit, and the space between them as they were positioned; and the quality of the speakers and their precise placement. Marclay insisted that each member of the audience should be able to remain in the theater for as long as he or she wished, free of charge. Hardly an empty seat could be found for any hour of any day during the three-week run in the summer of 2012.

The visual and sound editing are works of genius. They depict the role that time plays in film and how it is experienced differently around America and around the world, by the young and by the elderly, at work and at play, in the twenty-first century and earlier, by pedestrians and those in various modes of transport. It all adds up to a magnificent study. *The Clock* is a beautiful and evocative meditation on the meaning of time.

The reviews of Marclay's work were almost rapturous—apparently inspired by the quality of his work. Meghan O'Rourke, in the *New Yorker* on July 19, 2012, suggested that *The Clock* is nothing less than a definitive ode to film as an art form:

"The Clock" with its obsessive compiling, its miniature riffs, its capacious comic and dramatic turns, speaks to the completest lurking in all of present-day us. If montage is usually as cheaply sweet as Asti Spumante, "The Clock" is champagne: it's what the form was invented for, it turns out. Drink it in deeply and the days might just go on forever.

The curatorial parent of this new way to integrate visual art into Lincoln Center is trustee Peter Kraus, CEO of AllianceBernstein. He assembled some extraordinary curators and museum directors as informal advisors to suggest artists for commissioned work and to debate the pros and cons of how their visions and voices might be utilized in one or another of Lincoln Center's public spaces. The whole process is monitored by the trustees and volunteers on Lincoln Center's public art committee, chaired by Peter. Its meetings are fun; its exchange of views lively. Its results are embellishing the performing arts in a dramatic manner.

Public art has a bright future at Lincoln Center. Carefully thinking through the place of public art on the campus, the staff and trustees formulated a distinctive role, one that plays to the strengths of Lincoln Center's mission, generous outdoor space, and very large audience.

AT THE NUCLEUS of Lincoln Center's reason for being is the art mounted on its many indoor and outdoor stages. I cannot recall an important undertaking that either Nigel Redden or Jane Moss wished to see performed that was turned down because Tamar Podell, vice president for development, and I were unable to raise adequate funds. I am proud that their programs grew and flourished on my watch.

I was known as an easy touch for the programs generated by Moss and Redden. But saying yes required freeing up resources by keeping management expenses under tight control and keeping productivity high. Saying yes demanded relentless, round-the-clock fund-raising. Saying yes meant pursuing that new and altered economic model for Lincoln Center, finding alternative or enhanced sources of recurring net income. Saying yes meant lots of self-imposed pressure, on me and on the rest of the staff. Saying yes was a pleasure. Delivering on the "yes" was more than a full-time job.

But running Lincoln Center was only part of what I had been asked to do. Rejuvenating it conceptually, reconceiving it urbanistically, and rebuilding it physically were also in my job description. Achieving these objectives in the midst of continuing controversy would be a major endeavor.

CHAPTER 4

Transformation

The in-fighting at Lincoln Center resembles the kind
of insidious arguments that sometimes tear families
apart. Nearly every aspect of the redevelopment plan—
from basic questions of governance and veto power
to architectural details and artistic hegemony—seems
to be contested. The most powerful constituent of all,
the Metropolitan Opera, has taken what seems to be a
perpetually adversarial role, even threatening for a time
not to participate in the redevelopment. The air at Lincoln Center is as full of bewildering voices and implicit
threats as a production of "The Tempest." Only there is
no Prospero in sight.

. . . This kind of disagreement makes doing business
harder than it needs to be and makes Lincoln Center
look less like the commanding cultural institution it is
and more like a collection of petty fiefs.

—Editorial, *New York Times*, October 16, 2001

When you arrive at a place that has dug a hole as deep as the *New York Times* suggested, it does not take a mastermind to know that it is past time to stop the digging and start the building.

But how?

In the midst of constituents in disarray and what could fairly be called Lincoln Center's own midlife crisis, and in the face of strong internal resistance, inescapable major distractions, and forbidding economic conditions, how did we manage to secure forward movement?

The modernization of Lincoln Center's public spaces, artistic facilities, and infrastructure is a story worth recounting for what it explains about how leaders, trustees, and staff can advance from a situation rightly characterized as dire to one that today draws praise and instills pride.

Allow me to set the scene. The nerve-racking aftermath of 9/11 and the prolonged economic slowdown that followed. The very governance structure of Lincoln Center redevelopment, requiring unanimity, which seemed designed to prevent and delay forward movement rather than facilitate it. The cynicism of the media and other close observers, like foundations, trustees, and potential major donors, who had witnessed so many false starts and were not enamored of the divisiveness and turmoil on campus. The continued active resistance of key players, who sought to prevent what they couldn't entirely control.

With these and other challenges fully in mind, Bruce Crawford, my partner and Lincoln Center's chair from 2003 to 2005, joined me in recognizing a fundamental reality. Not every resident artistic organization was ready during the same period of time to plan in earnest for renovation. Many were not even prepared to offer informed opinions about the key steps to take in modernizing the public spaces near their own facilities. Determining which organizations were prepared to join forces and catalyze this stalled and stalemated project seemed like a good place to begin.

So we looked across the campus to find our coalition of the willing. The simplest way to proceed was by the process of elimination.

Beginning in 2003, the New York City Opera, one of two occupants of the New York State Theater, was intent on moving elsewhere. Its artistic director, Paul Kellogg, was convinced that the hall that had served New York City Opera's artists and audiences for forty years was now acoustically inferior, with too large a seating capacity. It would not work in the twenty-first century. He longed for an auditorium that wasn't built to Mr. Balanchine's specifications with only dance in mind, but to his own, with baroque opera and musical theater as its raison d'être. The founder of the New York City Ballet, and arguably the greatest choreographer of the twentieth century, George Balanchine, set the most important guidelines for how the auditorium in the New York State Theater was to be built. Kellogg chafed at the results. He couldn't bring himself to live with them comfortably.

Even those who agreed with Paul's goal, and I was not among them, were confused by his tactics and concerned about his seeming lack of realism. Why publicly tell your audience in 2001 and 2002 that the sound they hear emanating from the stage is inferior? At the very earliest, the New York City Opera could not move out of its New York State Theater quarters until 2008. It appeared to many that while Kellogg had intended to speak to potential donors and government officials about the hall's acoustic inferiority, his views were also reaching the City Opera's current audience. If so, wasn't he running the risk that, over time, many of its members would be persuaded that he was correct and quit paying for the privilege of attending? Beware of Sol Hurok's admonition: "If the public does not want to buy tickets, you can't stop them." Not surprisingly, dramatic declines in attendance followed.

It was no secret that Kellogg's restlessness was driven by the view that the 9/11 site offered the opportunity for the New York City Opera to develop its architectural plans with the federal and state governments picking up much of the tab for concept design and construction.

In its quest, the New York City Opera dream won the support of music critics like John Rockwell and Anthony Tommasini and curiously garnered a favorable *New York Times* editorial well before other artistic institutions had the chance to express interest.

John Whitehead, the president of the Lower Manhattan Development Corporation, was known to be partial to Kellogg and the New York City Opera. Even so, the outcome, not to mention its terms, was very much in doubt.

At community meetings, a strong predisposition was voiced in favor of film, visual arts, community center, and recreational activities to fill any available Ground Zero space. Opera did not rank high as a preferred art form for the new venue. Besides, it remained unclear whether the New York City Opera, if successful, would be granted its own facility or would share one, and if so, with what entity and with what sacrifice of Kellogg's artistic and acoustic objectives. What's more, audience surveys revealed that a substantial minority of the Opera's existing attendees would not follow it downtown. New ticket buyers from Brooklyn, New Jersey, and downtown would have to make up the difference.

On top of those obstacles, the New York City Opera board had a reputation for being weak in fund-raising, in both giving and getting. Of Lincoln Center's twelve constituents, the Opera ranked among the lowest in endowment size. In fact, the only known donor who publicly favored a move, Robert Wilson, was said to be offering as much as $50 million, but only if the New York City Opera found a location on the Upper West Side.

So in 2002 and 2003 the last thing in the world the New York City Opera thought about was redeveloping its portion of the Lincoln Center campus, the New York State Theater.

Subtract one from the desired coalition.

Until the Opera's future was crystallized, the New York City Ballet, with which it shared the theater, could not draw up its own capital plans. It was in a holding pattern. In any event, Howard Solomon, its chairman, expressed an active lack of interest in the whole redevelopment project, deeming it unrealistic and irrelevant to the future of the New York City Ballet. Period.

Down two.

For almost a year, it seemed as if the New York Philharmonic was serious about either building a new auditorium within the existing structure of Avery Fisher Hall or supporting substantial renovations to the front and back of the house, as well as in the auditorium, to be carried out in segments over time. All of the preliminary design work of Norman Foster and others, all of the travels to other halls around the world, all of the thought given to where the orchestra might play when Avery Fisher Hall was unavailable, were tossed to the winds on June 2, 2003, when the leadership of the New York Philharmonic announced an intention to migrate to Carnegie Hall.

Deduct three.

As for the Metropolitan Opera, it had moved into a new century seriously challenged, operationally and economically. Joe Volpe, its much-touted general manager, rode the previous decade of the 1990s with record-breaking box office revenue and satisfactory levels of contributed income. Emboldened by those results, he raised prices, often by double digits, year after year, for six years in a row.

In the wake of 9/11 came vastly reduced tourism in general and by Italians, Japanese, and Germans in particular, who during the good times had been responsible for purchasing a large share of single tickets bought by foreign tourists. Serious price resistance followed.

So the seasons 2001–2002 and 2002–2003 witnessed two successive operating deficits in excess of $10 million. In addition, Alberto Vilar, a flamboyant, publicity-seeking, and opera-loving donor, who had pledged well over $20 million to the Met, fell on hard times when the high-tech bubble burst. The Met was obliged to write down from its balance sheet some $16 million of his expected contribution.

As if that weren't bad enough, Chevron Texaco failed to renew its $7 million annual underwriting of the Met's radio program, placing in suspended animation the future of a show that had run for over four decades. Joe Volpe and Beverly Sills publicly acknowledged that they could not find a substitute corporate sponsor. Their annual plans to conduct an audience appeal over the radio and by direct mail seemed like a white flag being hoisted. Would the radio program go the way of Met television, which two years before had bitten the dust?

So the Metropolitan Opera had little appetite for facility or public space redevelopment. It had more than a few other problems to resolve. Mr. Volpe's difficulties were severe in number and kind. He probably viewed complaining about Lincoln Center and redevelopment as a pleasant break from having to grapple with them.

Minus four.

That completed the process of elimination. It might have been ideal if all resident artistic organizations were prepared for redevelopment simultaneously. But we would not let the best be the enemy of the good. Those that were ready comprised a highly motivated group of constituents occupying facilities on 65th Street.

The campus was naturally divided between those able and willing to plan for redevelopment and those not yet equipped or disposed to do so. We called those who were prepared the 65th Street Group. Their members were eager to raise the money necessary to realize strongly felt needs and aspirations.

As much by default as by design, then, Bruce Crawford and I gladly formalized and blessed the 65th Street Group. It was chaired by Bruce Kovner, a billionaire founder and CEO of the hedge fund Caxton, who also served as chair of the board of The Juilliard School and as a member of the boards of the New York Philharmonic and the Metropolitan Opera. He was a highly respected figure on Lincoln Center's campus. The professionals and trustees of The Juilliard School, Lincoln Center Theater, the Chamber Music Society of Lincoln Center, the Film Society of Lincoln Center, the School of American Ballet, The New York Public Library for the Performing Arts, and Lincoln Center itself rolled up their sleeves and worked diligently together.

The group was ably staffed by Rebecca Robertson, at that time the executive director of Lincoln Center Redevelopment. She had struggled since 1999 to achieve liftoff for the project, to little avail. Now, fresh reinforcements had arrived, determined to prevail.

Robertson was an able and resourceful partner. Indefatigable, extremely creative, and thoroughly familiar with the processes of architectural selection and concept design, her drive and energy were invaluable to the project. Kovner was methodical, disciplined, and extremely patient with his fellow trustees, many of whom had little background in design and construction. They were learning. Kovner rendered it easy for all to do their homework, with lots of staff support. Robertson and her small team supplied the teaching.

Together, we crafted a set of goals for the redevelopment of Lincoln Center:

1. To create a complex of the finest possible performance halls for the classical performing arts
2. To provide state-of-the-art performance support facilities that will create optimal conditions for the production and presentation of work in the twenty-first century
3. To create a heightened sense of welcome and occasion, much improved orientation, user-friendly accessibility for all visitors, and improved donor and patron amenities for Lincoln Center audiences

4. To project both an exciting and welcoming daytime and night-time image: at night as a place of luminous elegance and great performances, and during the day as a busy and active public and cultural campus where the performing arts are learned, rehearsed, and created

5. To develop the public space in a way that enlivens the image of Lincoln Center, encourages public use, and integrates the complex into its surroundings

6. To maximize efficiency and minimize costs for all constituents

My immediate preoccupation was less with the aesthetics and functionality of redevelopment than with creating an incentive structure that would activate the constituents. Sustained cooperation in this massive undertaking did not come naturally to the inexperienced, the ill-prepared, or the shortsighted. The focus of all on self-interest required Lincoln Center to create a set of attractive inducements for participation and engagement.

In formulating a workable scheme, I paid attention first and foremost to how our plans might appeal to private donors and to the state and federal governments. In the last days of the administration of Mayor Rudy Giuliani, the City of New York committed up to $240 million of capital funds to the physical redevelopment of Lincoln Center. It happened on Gordon Davis's watch. This was an important and often unacknowledged accomplishment.

It was surreal that some resident organizations like the New York City Opera and the New York City Ballet appeared to believe that these city funds were intended to be spent on virtually any capital request they articulated. The fact was that the city's capital appropriation had to be matched by noncity governmental and private dollars. Approved projects also had to satisfy specific and exacting eligibility criteria. These realities seemed to escape the attention of many of my colleagues and of the trustees to whom they reported.

With indispensable early funding from the city secured, it was imperative that funds be raised from individuals, foundations, and corporations and from the state and federal governments in unprecedented sums. Lincoln Center and its constituents needed contributed income in orders of magnitude higher than had ever been raised before.

Indeed, few at Lincoln Center had the slightest idea how the $1 billion or more needed to finance redevelopment expenses could possibly be found. Many believed it would never happen.

Of course, the post-9/11 economic recession was not the most favorable environment in which to begin. But was that temporary financial condition a reason to delay, or merely another pretext? After all, the endowments of the constituents hardly grew and balance sheets hardly strengthened during the decade of the 1990s, while the Dow Jones Industrial Average tripled.

Having recognized that not all resident artistic organizations were ready to tackle a redevelopment project at the same time, we formulated our plans accordingly and announced a collective goal in the $400 million range.

By 2004 Jazz at Lincoln Center had raised on its own some $140 million in pledges to move into its resplendent new Rafael Vinoly–designed venues: Dizzy's Club Coca-Cola, The Allen Room, and the Rose Theater, all on 59th Street and Columbus Circle, at the Time Warner Center, only four blocks away from Lincoln Center's traditional sixteen-acre campus. The location of Jazz was affectionately referred to as Lincoln Center South. This successful effort on the part of a fledgling organization in existence for less than two decades was nothing short of remarkable. A cadre of dedicated trustees, staff, and other true believers made it all happen. Their collective accomplishment provided some evidence that a much broader and more ambitious campaign could also succeed.

So WE BEGAN with those who were ready. As the campus landlord and the largest presenter of art in the world, Lincoln Center now also became the clear, bold, no-nonsense leader of public space modernization, infrastructure repair and replacement, and artistic facility renovation and creation. Except for The Juilliard School, this group— The New York Public Library for the Performing Arts, the Film Society of Lincoln Center, the School of American Ballet, the Chamber Music Society, Lincoln Center Theater, and Lincoln Center, the parent body—was regarded by the larger constituents as composed of organizational lightweights. We were called unrealistic and were thought to be unable to realize a capital campaign. The group was often referred to derisively as the "Northern Alliance."

The glue that held together these organizations was their eagerness for a street-level identity and ease of patron access on a campus and in facilities worthy of the artists, audiences, and students of the twenty-first century. That yearning was strong enough to overcome their stark artistic, managerial, educational, and economic differences.

This is the deal that Lincoln Center offered to these institutions.

First, we selected Diller + Scofidio (Renfro was added as a partner later) as our design architect. The choice of this firm, which at the time of Lincoln Center's decision had not yet been the lead architect on a single completed building, was a major surprise. Norman Foster, Richard Meier, or Cooper Robertson in collaboration with Frank Gehry—competitors all: any of these would have been a more logical and certainly safer choice.

We were betting on the creative, nonstop flow of ideas that emerged from the studio of Elizabeth Diller and Ricardo Scofidio. We appreciated very much Liz's explicit admiration of Lincoln Center and her desire to mix change with continuity. The firm respected what the founders had built, but Diller and Scofidio were convinced that Lincoln Center deserved to come off its pedestal, lower its barriers to entry, and embrace urban life in the form of an inviting pedestrian landscape. For Diller + Scofidio, Lincoln Center wasn't just a prestigious client; it was a place to inhabit, a series of intellectual and institutional challenges to be seized, and a set of players to be engaged in all of their variety, with all of their seemingly incongruous notions. Sooner than anyone thought possible, the selection of Diller + Scofidio became a unanimous choice. Even Volpe agreed.

Second, Lincoln Center committed to constituents that it would raise all the funds required for every improvement to public spaces: the removal of a huge plaza, the size of several football fields, suspended above much of 65th Street, allowing light to replace darkness at ground level; new outdoor green spaces and expansive seating in a totally Wi-Fi'd environment; ease of access for the physically handicapped; waterproofing and paving of badly deteriorated plaza stone; and a new information landscape consisting of twenty-first-century appli-ances that through beautifully designed video blades and three-shee cases would offer information about current and coming attractior Up-to-date news would also appear in scrolling and dissolving text o grand stairway facing the main campus, Josie Robertson Plaza, and an enlarged 65th Street stairway leading to that destination.

Travertine building facades would be replaced with glass. Transparency would allow for real institutional identity, which would be readily apparent to the passing pedestrian or to auto and taxi passengers. What had been a long stretch of garage entrances and exits, loading docks, and service corridors would become an inviting, foot-traffic-friendly street of the arts. And fully renovated, well-lit underground passageways would attract each day thousands of commuters and students walking to and from the subway and ticketholders bound for one or another venue.

Third, these public space improvements would also include state-of-the-art security measures to respond to post-9/11 concerns about terrorism and would embrace the construction of a new central mechanical plant to provide heat and air conditioning at a unit-cost reduction of 20 percent to virtually all of the theaters on the main campus. The charge for these changes and for much-improved access for the physically handicapped? None. Lincoln Center would raise every needed penny here, too.

Lincoln Center also agreed to pay for all insurance costs associated with construction. It offered to handle all federal and state regulatory requirements involved in shepherding this complex project through and around many administrative obstacles, including a major one called Urban Land Use Review Planning (ULURP). It required dozens upon ozens of meetings, with the community board, local politicians, pres-ation and environmental groups, the Business Improvement District), and the New York City Council itself.

ock for block, resident by resident, activist organization by advo-roup, pound for pound, the Upper West Side was well-known igorous exercise of the First Amendment, for its proclivity to nd for its constant courting of controversy. No resident orga-ompeted with Lincoln Center for the privilege of assuming ibility to cope with these often contentious forces.

s the matter of the expenses of the Lincoln Center Devel-t (LCDP): this staff group would oversee the work of io; convene the dozens of design review and organi-s required; master the intricacies of city rules; and set up competitions for the selection of theater designer, engineering firm, acoustician, and executive architect, among many other design and construction responsibilities. There was also the cost of research needed to mount a comprehensive, cohesive, capital campaign. Lincoln Center paid for it all.

If that were not enough, the deal closer was that for every approved artistic capital project, Lincoln Center volunteered to raise matching funds to those collected by the constituents, 20 percent of the first $25 million and 15 percent of everything above $25 million, up to a total of $120 million.

This unprecedented, concrete, dollars-and-cents offer came as a total surprise to the constituents of Lincoln Center. They had no reason to expect it. The proposal certainly caught their attention. It helped them to imagine what might be possible for their own facility wish lists.

For the School of American Ballet, the dream of Peter Martins was to double the capacity of its dance studios, and Diller's light-filled, arresting design delighted her client.

At Lincoln Center Theater, Andre Bishop advocated strongly for a third theater space, one dedicated to promising playwrights, directors, and actors introducing new work. In close proximity to the other performance and rehearsal spaces of the theater, this newcomer, designed by architect Hugh Hardy, was also to feature a rooftop outdoor space overlooking the Paul Milstein Pool and Terrace, the place in which the famous Henry Moore sculpture was situated. Bishop was passionate in his advocacy for a new venue, later named the Claire Tow Theater, that would allow promising artists using it to mix and mingle with the veterans staging productions at the much larger Mitzi Newhouse and Vivian Beaumont Theaters.

The Juilliard School aspired to a major 38,500 square feet of expansion and 58,000 square feet of renovation. It would accommodate practice rooms, rehearsal spaces, studios, study carrels, a library and archive, lounges, places to dine, and new and expanded performance venues. Once inward-looking, in the hands of Diller Scofidio + Renfro, students could peer out of the school and easily view the stages where they longed to perform professionally upon graduation.

What Juilliard, the Chamber Music Society, Lincoln Center itself, and the Film Society had in common was that all desired a modernized and much-improved Alice Tully Hall to call home. For Juilliard, Tully was the place where its orchestra and chamber music groups performed most. For the Chamber Music Society, Tully was literally created to be its home, financed by Alice Tully for that very purpose. For Lincoln Center, Tully was a venue receptive to diverse presentations of musicians and ensembles from around the world. There was chamber music. There were solo recitalists, vocalists, and instrumentalists, including organists utilizing the splendidly refurbished and renovated original Kuhn organ, soon to be reinstalled in the auditorium. There were chamber symphonies. Choral music. Jazz. Popular song. And even theater pieces and dance. For the Film Society, its two-week, world-famous New York Film Festival that opened the season was to return there.

The special accommodations shaped for these diverse needs by D S + R (design architect), Fisher Dachs Associates (theater designer), Jaffe Holden (acoustician), FXFOWLE (executive architect), and Arup (engineer) were nothing short of breathtaking. By installing sound-absorbing curtains lowered for film showings and moved out of sight for music, Alice Tully Hall would accommodate extremely well two art forms with opposing sound requirements. By allowing for stage extensions, the seating in Tully could be set up in three configurations, from 1,100 down to 850 seats. Smaller audiences could enjoy more experimental or contemporary work closer to the action, while dance and theater pieces could use the larger stage.

With the creation of an outdoor plaza accommodating 250 people and bleacher seating with equivalent capacity, a new performance venue had been born. It surprised and delighted residents and visitors exiting the busy subway station at 66th Street and Broadway. In addition, ticketholders could relax while waiting for their curtain time. And red carpets could be rolled out for stars to take their turns in front of the paparazzi.

The vaulting glass wall treated Broadway as a virtual stage set for those dining at Marcus Samuelsson's American Table in the lobby of Alice Tully Hall or imbibing a drink at its romantic, undulating bar looking east across that world-famous boulevard.

And above the Morgan Stanley lobby, one could find upstairs the Hauser lounge, graced by an outdoor terrace. Like the space below, it was frequently used for receptions and gala dinners, a crucial need never contemplated in the original design.

Add to all of this an expansive box office; special handicapped access; and a hall interior so comfortable, intimate, and stunning as to evoke amazement, most of all from those who knew the old Tully and had anticipated change with apprehension. They needn't have worried.

Working with the Film Society, the architect David Rockwell designed two new screening rooms, an amphitheater, and a canteen called Indie, to complement the Walter Reade movie house across the street. If there is a better, more inviting spot to view a movie than at the Elinor Bunin Film Center, anywhere, show me the way to it.

What the generous matching grant offer to constituents meant, as a practical matter, was that Lincoln Center, the organization I ran, became the single largest donor to all but one of every participating resident organization on the campus. And for what purpose? To help them realize their highest-priority artistic and educational ambitions.

Now what self-respecting trustee of any organization associated with Lincoln Center would fail to find this total incentive package less than attractive? All we asked for in return was a semblance of civility and a willingness to work long hours in good faith on problem solving and resolving conflict. Implicit in the individual bilateral legal arrangement Lincoln Center negotiated with each of its constituent organizations was an understanding that the project as a whole would be allowed to go forward. The formal veto power inherent in LCDP governing rules would be exercised, if at all, only when absolutely necessary.

In essence, Lincoln Center suggested that the constituents define carefully their vital interests. Informed views on these issues would be taken fully into account in an effort to satisfy and to avoid the casting of any veto. As to marginal interests, opinions really, on matters that were hardly central to an organization's operation or artistic future, it was informally understood that no veto would be exercised.

This was the formula that propelled us forward. This was the attractive and magnetic force that would eventually woo the "big guys": the New York Philharmonic, the Metropolitan Opera, and the soon-to-be-christened David H. Koch Theater and its occupants. In time they, too, could not resist cooperating.

And why not? Beyond the benefits enumerated here, there was even more to come.

THE DEAL LINCOLN CENTER offered to induce constituent cooperation was extraordinarily generous. It became even more so as detailed negotiations with each resident organization ensued. For the most part, we responded affirmatively to constituent requests supplemental to our already plentiful offer.

Call us magnanimous. Call us eager to please and indulgent. Or call us pushovers.

Our attitude was clear. We had overcome significant resistance and had built important forward momentum. No single supplemental request seemed so excessive as to warrant tediously long negotiations, let alone a project standstill. We did not wish to have our collective progress slowed down, with all of the attendant risks and costs. If pursuing this course of action meant raising even more money, so be it.

When, for example, The Juilliard School contended that its new facade, estimated to cost some $17 million, was really just another form of public space and should therefore be considered the financial responsibility of Lincoln Center, we gulped and then yielded in the interest of moving forward.

Building what is now known as the Claire Tow Theater, a third venue with an audience capacity of 112, to be added to the 1,089-seat Vivian Beaumont Theater and the 297-seat Mitzi Newhouse Theater, was estimated to cost $30 million. In view of Lincoln Center Theater's cooperation with such features of redevelopment as placing a garage entrance to its immediate east, we departed voluntarily from the 20 percent match formula and offered 50 percent, or $15 million.

The only constituent in favor of building a footbridge across 65th Street was the School of American Ballet (SAB). All others either opposed the idea or were indifferent to it. But the executive director of SAB, Marjorie Van derCook, longed to have an elevated crossing for students to safely cross the street on their way to and from the David H. Koch Theater. This wish was totally supported by her board of directors and by Peter Martins. The sculpturally expressive span that was ultimately put in place pleased everyone. It carried an $8 million price tag, picked up entirely by Lincoln Center.

Concessions were advanced to other constituents as well, above and beyond the standard package of rich incentives.

They all added up. In the end, of the $1.2 billion campuswide capital campaign a total of $790 million was Lincoln Center's share. Nearly $120 million of it was sent directly to constituents, either in the form of matching their own fund-raising or offsetting their costs directly. Nothing like a financial challenge of this size had ever before been undertaken. Raising this sum during the same eight years in which we required about $40 million in donations *annually* to balance Lincoln Center's own operating budget increased the total to $1.1 billion as our sole responsibility.

Lincoln Center is not a university with thousands of loyal alumni. Institutions like New York University and Columbia University are fund-raising machines. They no sooner complete one capital campaign than they launch another. They employ hundreds of fund-raisers. They organize by school and by graduating class. They exert all kinds of peer pressure.

Lincoln Center is not a hospital, blessed with grateful patients and their relatives, those who have left their lives in its care or hope for excellent service when they are in need.

In its first-ever massive renovation, everything depended on Lincoln Center meeting its unprecedented fund-raising commitments. Paying our bills on time. Setting an example for constituents who needed to satisfy their own ambitious funding goals. Avoiding reductions in scope or quality of work. Brooking no delays in construction.

Simultaneously, Lincoln Center continued to manage the campus and its annual support to constituents in financially beneficial ways. Each year I prepared an annual report card detailing all of the services provided by Lincoln Center to the constituents, as a group and individually. Leaving aside matching funds associated with redevelopment, in fiscal year 2012 these benefits totaled $12.9 million.[1]

WHY WAS I SO CONFIDENT that we could climb this fund-raising Mount Everest? Although the goal was daunting and unprecedented, Lincoln Center enjoyed some major advantages.

There was Lincoln Center's board. By 2008 it had almost doubled in size. It was possessed of considerable net wealth. Its members were deeply involved in the life of the institution. They were also extremely well connected to pools of capital controlled by corporations, foundations, privately held firms, and individuals of every kind and from every walk of life. Lincoln Center's board was highly ambitious and strongly motivated.

The trustees would take the lead in giving and getting.[2]

In its fifty-year history Lincoln Center had never engaged in a comprehensive, campuswide capital campaign. When we approached prospects, corporate and individual, who had never given a donation to Lincoln Center, none could claim that we had worn out our welcome.

Our case was compelling. The need for comprehensive renovation was almost self-evident. The architectural design was stunning. Lincoln Center's reputation was very strong. Prospects were impressed that in place of divisiveness and turmoil, cooperation and collaboration were now taking hold.

Lincoln Center enjoyed a valuable asset, hiding in plain sight: naming opportunities. We had an abundance of them in our outdoor spaces and our buildings. Unlike colleges and universities, which typically offered high-end donors the chance to have programs, departments, professorships, or even entire schools named after them, Lincoln Center had rarely done so.

Many companies liked the idea of having their multi-million-dollar gifts memorialized by a naming. The Morgan Stanley lobby. The Barclays Grove. The Hearst Plaza. Why not have customers, clients, partners, investors, and employees proudly take notice of company philanthropy? Why not burnish the corporate brand by associating with the visibility and the prestige that Lincoln Center enjoys?

For individuals, naming provided the chance to honor parents, a spouse, a friend, or a highly valued colleague. It is a nice feeling to have children or grandchildren admire your generosity to a place from which they now benefit.

For those not averse to public identification, the attractiveness of Lincoln Center's redeveloped spaces and our institutional reputation combined to render naming opportunities a valuable campaign offer.

Our appeal went well beyond the content of the performing arts. It highlighted Lincoln Center as an engine of economic development.

As an educator of kids and families. As a source of civic pride and of social cohesion. As a major tourist attraction. As another compelling reason why talented people would be drawn to New York City to live and to work.

The fund-raising pace was relentless. Rarely did a day pass without at least three face-to-face solicitations by members of the group. The chair, Frank Bennack, was fond of observing that any call from him was a collect call. David Rubenstein, the chair of the Capital Campaign, took on hedge funds, private equity, investment firms, and money-centered banks as his principal assignment.

Both men are extraordinary fund-raisers. They believe that a successful sales approach combines biography (their own and that of the prospect) and the cause. Properly briefed with up-to-date research on the potential donor, each was relaxed, focused, and unflappable at meetings. After exchanging pleasantries, inquiring about the state of the prospect's business, or the condition of the city, or the challenges before the nation, they would ask after members of the family or mutual friends. Bennack and Rubenstein would then state Lincoln Center's case, personally and compellingly.

Here is a version of Bennack's pitch:

After the attack on 9/11, I am, as the CEO of Hearst Corporation, exceptionally proud that my company became the very first to announce an intention to erect a new headquarters building here in New York City, one designed by Norman Foster.

We hoped this corporate affirmation about New York's bright future would be widely emulated. In parallel, as Hearst's President, I began to think of what I, born and raised in Texas, could personally do to express my thanks to this great town. Giving the matter lots of consideration and entertaining several possibilities, I concluded that being the Chairman of Lincoln Center at this exciting time in its history would be the most important role I could play.

As Lincoln Center approaches its 50th anniversary, the nation's oldest and the world's largest and most prominent performing arts center, has planned to reinvest in its physical plant. The design is comprehensive and elegant. It addresses all of the major public space, infrastructure and artistic needs of twelve world class constituents.

Collectively, all of Lincoln Center's resident organizations spend over $800 million annually. They attract over 5 million Americans and tourists to the campus each year. In addition, more than two thousand full-time students study at the much acclaimed School of American Ballet and The Juilliard School. Nothing of this size, diversity and quality in the performing arts exists in any one place anywhere else.

As a major source of civic pride, an engine of economic development and a center of artistic excellence, we need to raise a total of roughly one billion to get this job done.

New York City is on board with the commitment of $240 million. New York State and the federal government have each pledged $30 million. That leaves in excess of $700 million to be raised privately and we expect the board of directors of Lincoln Center to unanimously participate and to collectively donate the critical mass of that sum.

I am here this morning to ask you to please consider joining me and Hearst with a leadership gift of no less than $10 million.

You will not ever regret being a major part of this rejuvenation of a singular set of institutions. It is early in our campaign. But so far no one has turned us down. Please do not be the first to do so.[3]

Bennack's reputation and relationships with so many prospects were as solid as his rhetorical skills.

When Rubenstein approached prospects, all of them wondered why a guy who lives in Bethesda, Maryland; who cofounded the Carlyle Group, a major private equity firm headquartered in Washington, DC; and was a trustee of the Kennedy Center would be soliciting a mega-gift for Lincoln Center. They paid attention.

Katherine Farley, who took over major fund-raising responsibilities from both Bennack and Rubenstein, was more reluctant to invoke her own biography or to cite her own generosity, both very formidable. But her persuasiveness, charm, sense of humor, and seriousness of purpose yielded impressive results. In the three years that she was the chair of Lincoln Center and I was the president, twenty-five outstanding trustees were added to our board. Virtually all agreed to leadership gifts to the capital campaign ranging from at least $3 million to $5 million and to contribute $250,000 in annual support.

That kind of financial commitment to a single institution is extraordinary. It was clearly and explicitly requested as part of the invitation to join the board of directors, not just orally but in writing. The admired leadership of Farley resulted in a very high acceptance rate. She is as indefatigable and results-driven a leader as any I have ever met.

These top-drawer trustees would grace any nonprofit board. Wooing them to Lincoln Center was not only a boost to our campaign totals; it was also an enduring contribution to strengthening the institution's governance and influence. It was also very hard work. During Farley's tenure while I was her partner at Lincoln Center, every six and a half weeks a new trustee agreed to serve. Bennack, Rubenstein, and Farley were joined by about a dozen other active trustee solicitors for the campaign.

In its June 23/July 6, 2014 issue, *Crain's New York Business* featured the results of a study it had undertaken with Relationship Science to determine New York City's most prominent corporate and civic leaders. Lincoln Center and New York Presbyterian Hospital both ranked number 1 in terms of having more of the best-connected New Yorkers on their boards of directors than any other organization. Of the two hundred individuals named, seventy-eight are either current or former trustees of Lincoln Center or major donors to it, individually or through their place of employment.

Concurrently, the members of the 65th Street Group were also out on the hustings, raising funds. It is noteworthy that never before in their respective histories had the Film Society, the Chamber Music Society, Lincoln Center Theater, the School of American Ballet, and The Juilliard School appealed to more donors, for more gifts of higher size, more successfully. All were engaged, just like Lincoln Center itself, in soliciting for annual needs as well as for their capital projects. Each constituent CEO and his or her trustees stepped right up to that dual challenge with gusto.

For Lincoln Center, while the fund-raising was constant and I was in charge, there were many other demands to satisfy. Meetings with individual constituents to reach formal legal agreement and collective sessions called to arrive at design and construction decisions were booked back to back, day after day, and week after week. Diller + Scofidio described the process in their comprehensive account of redevelopment:

Working with the many [redevelopment] stakeholders was arduous
and sometimes contentious. After sitting through hundreds of meetings with still hundreds yet to go, what seemed like a disproportion-
ate ratio of creative work to political strategizing, ultimately led to
an important realization: building consensus among the many constituents and boards of trustees, working through the intricate city
processes, and satisfying all of the special interest groups—generally
enduring all it takes to realize a major project in New York City—
required every bit as much creativity as the design itself.[4]

From my vantage point, one could add to this intimidating agenda
many issues and obligations unrelated to our architects and their work.
Continuing to present the finest performing arts programs and services
in the world and drawing very large audiences to them, even as our
campus became a huge construction site. Interpreting our work to rav-
enous media, who were now eager to learn about the many pieces of redevelopment susceptible to attractive coverage. Raising the $40 million
needed each year to sustain Lincoln Center's programs and services at
normal levels. Implementing major changes to the outmoded economic
model in accordance with which performing arts centers, like Lincoln
Center, had operated ever since we were invented. Constantly building
trust between and among staff members and trustees.

I was not joined by many in paying careful attention to the operational costs and the financial consequences of design decisions. For
example, all of us grew to love replacing travertine with glass whenever
possible, leaving the campus far more inviting and transparent. Glass,
however, needs much more frequent cleaning than does travertine. At
one point, I observed that if there were any more such decisions, Lincoln
Center ran the risk of becoming a wholly owned subsidiary of Windex.

I was joined by a growing cadre of true believers, who functioned
without much sleep and without any vacations. The challenge before
us was complicated, and time was of the essence. So when Joe Volpe
fulminated, castigated, and interrogated, often without purpose, at our
meetings and often at a very high decibel level, it was tough to refrain
from responding in kind. Familiar with hammers—he was once a carpenter in the Met Opera workshop—Volpe apparently thought that
his constituent colleagues were nails. And he hammered away with

such ferocity as to suck oxygen from the conference room, leaving its occupants breathless.

Comic relief was in short supply. Soon the conversation focused on a subject that invited humor.

THE WORK ENVISIONED for 65th Street, most particularly new entrances and exits for Lincoln Center Theater, the Film Society of Lincoln Center, and the destination restaurant called Lincoln Ristorante, in addition to a new grand stairway leading up to Josie Robertson Plaza, necessitated the elimination of almost one hundred garage spaces. Notwithstanding the substantial loss of revenue that would result from this reduction, most of us who worked on that very busy block were delighted by the forthcoming change.

There were four vehicular entrances and exits on 65th Street, with many pedestrians walking in front of them all day. Thousands on their way to and from the subway came from the rental apartments and condominiums to the west, many of them built from 2002 to 2014. Thousands were Lincoln Center and constituent employees, students, and visitors. Over three thousand were students, faculty, and staff walking to and from LaGuardia High School and Martin Luther King School. And of course, tens of thousands of ticketholders rushing to one of many active stages used the street every month as well.

We were concerned for their safety, as cars moved very quickly into and out of the garages. Soon, since all of the pedestrian access would be brought down to grade level, the situation would move from bad to worse, unless we intervened. So we reduced the curb cut for parking entry and exit from ninety to eleven feet, eliminating three means of ingress and egress. Now just one entrance, on the southwest side of the street, was created. The result? The safety of all who traversed 65th Street was dramatically improved.

Of the ninety-six spaces being removed, sixty-eight were reserved for "executive parking," spots for designated administrators and VIPs. I could see my chairman Bruce Crawford's eyebrows raised at the very use of the term "executive parking."

The morning following the session at which these numbers were disclosed, Bruce and I were scheduled to meet. He began our conversation by indicating that out of sheer curiosity he had asked his driver to take him through the part of the garage designated for "executive parking."

"Some executives. Sixty-eight of them! Clearly that list is much too long. Reynold, one of those so-called executives owns a run-down maroon Mercury that should have been consigned to the junk heap years ago."

"Oh, Bruce, that's mine."

So much for my chairman's view of my mode of transportation. I was relieved that the next subject was not the inferior quality of my worn-out suit.

Just a few years later, Liz and I found ourselves at a fund-raising dinner held at Rockefeller Center. These can be very boring, tedious affairs, so we felt fortunate to be seated next to friends we hadn't seen for a while, Bill Aguado, the executive director of the Bronx Council on the Arts, and Kathy Pavlick, an executive at Chase Bank involved in corporate philanthropy. The conversation flowed freely. At the end of the evening, I offered to drive them home to their apartment house in Riverdale, not far from our own home.

Bill walked in laborious fashion to the garage, where my cherished Mercury was parked. As it pulled up toward us, this kid from one of the poorest sections of the Bronx, this proud, card-carrying member of the proletariat, saw my car and jokingly uttered these words: "No way. No way am I getting into that wreck. I have a reputation to uphold. I can't afford to have anyone see me in that thing. Besides, I doubt it can get us home without breaking down!"

In a course I once took on constitutional law at Columbia Law School, I became acquainted with this adage. When Felix Frankfurter, one of the Supreme Court's most conservative justices, and William Douglas, one of the Court's most liberal, both jointly dissent from the majority's opinion, well, the likelihood is that the Court has wrongly decided the case.

When the patrician, Bruce Crawford, and the working-class son of first-generation Puerto Rican and Italian parents both agree that the Mercury must go, do you think there is some merit to their opinion?

Nah. I did not give it up.

As the 65th Street Group's plans solidified, what had ranged from casual indifference to outright hostility to redevelopment on the part of the New York City Ballet, the New York Philharmonic, and the Metropolitan Opera began to morph into feelings of intense curiosity and latent envy. When the formal announcement of the planned transformation of the public spaces of 65th Street stretching from Broadway to Amsterdam Avenue and the artistic facilities that line it took place on June 12, 2006, hardened skeptics now began to wonder.

Might Lincoln Center and the feisty constituents with which it had joined forces, "the little engines that could," like the Chamber Music Society and the Film Society of Lincoln Center, and the School of American Ballet, together with The Juilliard School, Lincoln Center Theater, and Lincoln Center Inc., actually raise $400 million? This was the sum initially estimated as the total cost of the building and renovation projects along 65th Street. After all, Mayor Bloomberg, joined by a stalwart group of Lincoln Center trustees and other potential heavy-hitting financial supporters, had turned out for an impressive groundbreaking ceremony, at which the goal was announced.

Progress was reported positively and elaborately in the media. "Sure, sure," went the refrain of more than a few, "call me when the target is actually reached, when real money is raised." Once the notifications of solid commitments began to roll out from the City of New York; New York State; the federal government; leading foundations like Alice Tully, Ford, and Hearst; and important private benefactors such as Bruce Kovner, Ann Ziff, and David Rubenstein, that "show-me" attitude became a "what about us?" expression of concern.

The skeptics, cynics, and naysayers, along with the true believers, saw Anthony Tommasini in the *New York Times* call the transformation of Alice Tully Hall "remarkable" and "an indisputable achievement." The *Los Angeles Times* called it "swell," and the *Financial Times* "an extremely sophisticated and complex piece of urban surgery."[5]

The rave reviews for Tully and the rest of the 65th Street projects continued for months. Justin Davidson in *New York Magazine* and the *New Yorker*. Philip Kennicott in the *Washington Post*. Herbert Muschamp and Nicolai Ouroussoff in the *New York Times*, Paul Goldberger in the *New Yorker*, and many others joined in with words of praise.

But even before the completed Alice Tully Hall had been little more than a glimmer in my eye, almost all of those who had sat on the sidelines finally began to realize that the redevelopment train was leaving the station, and they were not on board. Well, not quite all.

If Mayor Bloomberg's analogy of Lincoln Center to the United Nations Security Council was accurate, then the Met Opera was playing the role of the obstructionist, veto-wielding Russia very well. On issue after issue, procedure after procedure, Volpe's fulminations amounted to "nyet."

The New York City Ballet, during the months when Howard Solomon was chair, seemed to be conducting itself like China. Howard's refrain was constant. What happens on the other side of the plaza "over there" on 65th Street has nothing to do with us, and we want nothing to do with it. It was as if the New York City Ballet had become a Pacific power, with a sphere of influence over Josie Robertson Plaza and 62nd Street, where the New York State Theater was situated. Those institutions located on the Atlantic side, as it were, could go their own way on 65th Street. Less an outright obstructionist than an isolationist, the Ballet could be counted on for resistance during Howard's tenure.

Howard's refusal to acknowledge the benefit to the New York City Ballet of the planned $45 million overhaul of the central mechanical plant at no cost to it or any other constituent was baffling. After all, it was the machinery that provided cool air and heat to the New York State Theater, in which the Ballet performed. It had been operating beyond its useful life and was in danger of breakdown. Howard's fellow trustees felt that his stance flew in the face of reality. Nor did they understand how Howard could deny that planned improvements to the concourses leading to and from the garage and New York City subways would benefit New York City Ballet patrons.

When the redevelopment work was complete, to his credit, Howard explicitly acknowledged what a positive difference it made to the quality of the patron and visitor experience everywhere on Lincoln Center's campus. "Count me an admirer," he declared. His Solomonic praise, slow to arrive, nonetheless meant much to me.

As for the New York Philharmonic, after its round-trip to and from Carnegie Hall, what Guenther and Mehta had to say was simply not taken seriously. Many at Lincoln Center and the constituents had become tired of their orchestral bravado. We all had enough of it. The New York Philharmonic needed to heal its self-inflicted wounds. It needed to find new board and staff leadership. It needed to figure out its direction. In 2014, twelve years after I arrived on campus, artists, audiences, and all occupants of Avery Fisher Hall, not least its owner and operator, Lincoln Center, were beginning to witness progress at "The Phil." But little of it seemed in evidence in the midst of redevelopment planning.

THE SELECTED EMISSARY for the New York City Ballet, the New York Philharmonic, and the Metropolitan Opera was Dan Brodsky, a real-estate developer and himself a Ballet trustee. Brodsky was well liked, a good man, a generous New Yorker. He was soon to become the chair of the board of the Metropolitan Museum of Art. His father had successfully built many apartment buildings on the Upper West Side of Manhattan. Brodsky inherited the business and expanded it in that geography and elsewhere in Manhattan.

Periodically, Brodsky would call and prod me to launch a Josie Robertson Plaza working group. He envisioned something not unlike the 65th Street working group that had been skillfully navigated by Bruce Kovner. I smiled. Not long ago Kovner's group was referred to by many of Brodsky's colleagues dismissively. Clearly things had changed. A number of former skeptics and cynics on the campus now believed that redevelopment was real. And by then Barry Friedberg, a former senior investment banker at Merrill Lynch, had been named Solomon's successor as the chair of the board of the New York City Ballet. Appointed in the middle of 2003, his tenure ran for a five-year period. Friedberg took a much more open and flexible view of redevelopment, understanding its many potential advantages. No doubt Brodsky was calling with Friedberg's encouragement.

At Lincoln Center, we were very busy. We had to fully realize a $400 million design. We needed to engage daily the city, state, and federal governments and comply with their rules and regulations in bidding and construction. We needed to manage engineering, acoustical, and construction firms and their suppliers. Most of all, we needed to be out and about, meeting prospects and raising money.

I told Brodsky of my concern about being distracted by constituents who had not thought through what they really wanted and who did not have a track record of playing well with others. I urged him to talk with his colleagues directly in an effort to assure me that all were now serious and prepared for reasoned discourse. I explained that I did not wish to be diverted from the huge undertaking of completing 65th Street successfully while engaged in some kind of fool's errand or major detour. Besides, I thought that playing just a little hard to get might provide Lincoln Center with some psychological leverage. Hopefully, Brodsky would prevail on his colleagues to cooperate.

By and large, he and they did so. With the concurrence of Frank Bennack, we asked Brodsky to chair the Josie Robertson Plaza group. The Lincoln Center board offered its blessing. To his enormous credit, Dan guided discussion with tact, patience, and finesse. We began in late 2006 and early 2007 by working through lots of options presented by Liz Diller to replace the fountain. After examining many ideas, we all concluded that our patrons, New Yorkers, and tourists generally liked the current placement of the fountain right smack in the middle of the plaza.

That is where Zero Mostel and Gene Wilder cavort in the film *The Producers*. It is where Cher in *Moonstruck* waits, decked out and gorgeous, looking for Nicolas Cage, the brother of her fiancé. Magic ensues. And it is where in *Ghostbusters* Bill Murray meets Sigourney Weaver after her cello rehearsal. Murray flatters her. "You were the best in your row," he fawns. With some trepidation, he asks her out on a date. When she accepts, Murray celebrates in a twirling dance. These are examples of how the Lincoln Center fountain is fondly remembered. As the site of love affairs, graduations, engagements, and marriages. Not one known divorce.

From our collective point of view, the frequently used phrase, "Meet me at the fountain," meant getting together at the existing location. So we asked D S + R to put aside their other imaginative but somewhat impractical and less popular designs. Instead, we suggested that the firm propose an intervention to replace the existing fifty-year-old structure with a modern revision. What they delivered astonished us.

A lighter, more transparent, more open fountain. Lit from underneath during the evening, it seemed to many like a flying saucer about to experience liftoff. Opened up, it allowed water to flow to the edges and invited visitors to move closer. Its disc shape welcomed those who wished to sit facing either the plaza or the fountain itself. What also drew attention was the collaboration of D S + R with Wet Design, the firm that specializes in the mechanics of water flow. Perhaps its best-known work is the Bellagio Fountain in Las Vegas.[6]

We made clear to Wet Design and to Liz that while we did not regard water displays as an art form, let alone a thirteenth constituent, a little fun in the form of fountain choreography would be welcome. The smiling faces of children and their parents as the fountain was put through its tricks, controlled by sophisticated software and intricate mechanics, testify to its success. As does the sheer number of photographers who show up at all hours to take photos, with or without human subjects in the foreground. Next to the Trevi in Rome, I do not know of a water fountain that attracts more donations of coins.

Having divined an elegant solution for the center of Josie Robertson Plaza, Liz Diller and her team now focused their attention on one of the knottiest and annoying design challenges before us.

At the very front of Lincoln Center was an inner roadway, a drop-off point for ticketholders arriving by limousine, black car, or taxi. These vehicles cut across pedestrians also making their way to Avery Fisher Hall, the New York State Theater, the Metropolitan Opera, Lincoln Center Theater, or Damrosch Park. I was fond of observing in speeches that if you successfully traversed nine lanes of traffic crossing Broadway and Columbus Avenue on your way to an event, Lincoln Center would reward you with one more opportunity to be hit by some kind of moving vehicle!

What D S + R conceived of was a subterranean drop-off location, one that would allow the main entrance to Lincoln Center to become a true pedestrian plaza. Diller and company seemed to stretch the plaza forward, creating a longer, more gracious entryway featuring elongated risers. As one ascended, the fountain and the classic monumental trio of venues suddenly came into view. They acquired a remarkable, welcoming quality. The arrival at Lincoln Center had become ceremonial, an early indicator that a very special and memorable experience was in store.

Across the back of each riser in the Grand Staircase is a self-contained mini-marquee with LED lighting that displays words of welcome, of coming attractions, and of special significance: the mention of a gala and its honoree, the greeting of a dignitary, the announcement of a birthday or an anniversary, and the like. This feature of the grand entryway caused much concern. Could it be maintained in New York City's notoriously cold and windy climate? Could the text of messages be seen on a hazy or foggy day? How would the software operate, and was this technology and its maintenance affordable? The creation of careful prototypes actually tested in all kinds of inclement weather and the explanations of geekish, high-tech experts convinced us to give this design feature the go-ahead.

The Grand Staircase scheme proved to be extremely popular. Everyone, it seems, loves to see their name up in lights.

To the left and right of the plaza, D S + R designed stunning glass canopies with entrances astride the stairs that are gentle and sloping. There are also easily accessible ramps complete with banisters to steady one's step, if needed. They allow theatergoers to arrive most of the time virtually unaffected by the elements.

And down below in the subterranean drop-off, escalators take patrons up to the plaza level and theater entrances totally protected from weather. This is part of a larger underground plan that allows for patron access to and from the subway, along passageways that are entirely refinished and pleasant to walk. So much so that all day long students, Upper West Side residents, and commuters who park their cars at Lincoln Center on the way to work or to shopping regularly use these concourses. They voted yes to this design—with their feet.

When Liz Diller first showed this proposed solution to the assembled constituents and Dan Brodsky asked for reactions, something unique happened in my experience at Lincoln Center. There was stunned silence, followed by acclamation. It was an aha! moment for everyone.

Praise then erupted from all parts of the room. Dan Brodsky noticed that Peter Martins was about to make his exit and that he had not yet spoken.

"Peter, before you leave, what's your opinion of all of this?"

"I am very impressed with all of these solutions to knotty problems. If we can realize this design, Lincoln Center will be much improved and we will take great pride in the result. *But who in heaven's name is going to raise the kind of money required for this elegant, but I am sure, very, very expensive plan?*"

All eyes turned to me.

CHAPTER 5

Rejuvenation

They all laughed at Christopher Columbus
When he said the world was round
They all laughed when Edison
Recorded sound
They all laughed at Wilbur and his brother
When they said a man could fly
They told Marconi
That wireless was a phony
It's the same old cry
They all laughed at Rockefeller Center
Now they're fighting to get in . . .
Who's got the last laugh now[?]
    —"They All Laughed," composed by George Gersh-
    win, with lyrics by Ira Gershwin

Before you do it, it's inconceivable.
After you do it, they wonder what all the fuss is about.
    —ANONYMOUS

In 2008 I completed and had published a book entitled *Yours for the Asking: An Indispensable Guide to Fundraising and Management.*[1] I wrote it to help others bridge the gap between the promise of the nonprofit organizations to which they were devoted and their performance.

Often the successful solicitation of funds made all the difference in realizing their goals.

To my surprise, the most quoted lines in the book, read to me word for word in astonishment by a moderator or a television or radio personality, are these: "Let me begin with a confession. I like raising money. I like everything about it."

Naturally, I took Peter Martins's exit line as a personal challenge. After all, no one else at Lincoln Center had pledged to take the lead in raising anything approaching $800 million, certainly not utilizing such funds to help realize the goals of their artistic neighbors or the needs of the general public. The other $400 million, more or less, is what the constituents set as their collective goal for new or renovated artistic facilities and for endowment.

Fund-raising took place virtually nonstop except for the interregnum after the Lehman Brothers collapse. It was both fun and exhausting. Figuring out what interested and motivated donors, who at Lincoln Center should best pop the question, and when and how much to request involved both solid research and well-organized consultations with experienced volunteer solicitors. While many donors shunned publicity, or even mention of themselves, there were some prospects for whom the size of their names etched on a building, or typed out in text, mattered a great deal. The larger, the better. Others truly cared about the amount of time their names appeared in a scrolling format on-screen. The longer, the better. In these minority of cases we found ourselves soliciting less and negotiating more.

We kept our spirits up, reminding ourselves how much rejection builds character. We could ask, short form or long. We became pretty adept at the elevator or bumper sticker pitch if that's all that time permitted. When prospects cared most about the company they would be keeping if they responded to our plea affirmatively, we focused not on the cause, or on naming opportunities, but on who had already given, names hopefully familiar to our target of opportunity. And we made ourselves available wherever and whenever an existing or future donor wished—evenings, weekends, early breakfasts, vacation homes. We aimed to please.

By the time I left Lincoln Center at the end of January 2014, more than one hundred sources—individuals, corporations, and foundations—had pledged $1 million or more, twenty-two had donated $3 million and above, twenty-one $5 million and above, twelve $10 million and above, and seven $20 million and above. Because this campaign was broad-based and not top-heavy, we had achieved one of our most important objectives. The idea was always for us to leave Lincoln Center, after completing a successful campaign, with a wider pool of donors, contributing more on an annual basis than had been the case when we began.

In fiscal year 2006, Lincoln Center raised $30.5 million to support its operating budget. By fiscal year 2014, it had raised $38.7 million for the same purpose. In other words, even while amassing close to $780 million to pay for construction and to supplement Lincoln Center's endowment, annual fund-raising grew simultaneously at 4 percent compounded for nine consecutive years.

Some first-time contributors to the capital campaign continued to donate to Lincoln Center for its annual needs when their pledge to the building and endowment initiative was fully paid. Moreover, when I arrived at Lincoln Center in 2002, its endowment stood at $133.7 million. At the end of my last fiscal year in office, it had grown to $236 million. Of this increase in the endowment, $43 million is attributable to funds raised during the campaign. Another $15 million more has also been pledged and is scheduled to be paid in the next few years. And Lincoln Center's pension needs have been fully funded.

Is it any wonder that by 2014 our solicitors were fatigued and that our donors could be officially declared generous, by any measure: number, amount, source, and purpose?

Peter Martins's question was, in the end, answered clearly and decisively.

THE TRANSFORMATION OF Lincoln Center took more than money. It took a new way of thinking and of operating.

An extraordinary dimension of Lincoln Center's physical modernization is how much of it was devoted to investing in public spaces. Close to two-thirds of every dollar Lincoln Center raised was allocated for this purpose. In addition to the comprehensive work on campus infrastructure, there were other, more accessible features of this work. For example, new places to sit were built along 65th Street at Barclays Grove, on the Tisch Illumination Lawn, atop the Lincoln Ristorante, in the Credit Suisse Bleacher, and on the steps of Tully Plaza. Also included in the public space portion of redevelopment were more green, more shade, and more trees.

Two public spaces deserve special mention because no one demanded their creation and now so many cannot imagine life at Lincoln Center without them. The first is located on the corner of 62nd Street and Columbus Avenue, where immediately outside the stage door entrance to the David H. Koch Theater was a completely barren space. Having worked at AT&T, I am familiar with the uniformly dreary switching centers it owned. The three sides of the Koch Theater not facing Josie Robertson Plaza resemble them. Dark. Windowless. Inert. Now, at least, one large corner of the building is miraculously softened by aspen trees and granite benches lit underneath when darkness falls. The Charles Benenson Grove is fully utilized. What was once an abandoned space is today animated and joyful. If you wish to converse with your favorite New York City Ballet dancer or request an autograph, hang out there during the daytime. You are bound to find your heartthrob on a coffee, yogurt, or cigarette break.

The second space in need of a metamorphosis was not controlled or operated by Lincoln Center. It was a privately owned public space (a POPS for those in the know), one of 530 such sites in the city of New York. Owned by the condominium board at 61 West 62nd Street and adopting the name of the condo itself, it was called the Harmony Atrium. The 7,000 square feet of space spanning from Broadway to Columbus Avenue, east to west, was to be set aside and maintained for public use in exchange for the city allowing the developer to build 25,314 square feet of extra floor area (roughly the equivalent of one hundred apartments).

My assessment of this deal from the point of view of the city of New York is simply stated. It turned out to be a hoax perpetrated on the public. The apartments were built and occupied, but the atrium space had been virtually abandoned. It became a temporary refuge for the homeless. It was dank, desolate, and not code compliant. Poorly lit; devoid of food service, proper seating, and functioning bathrooms; and neither well heated in the winter nor air-conditioned in the summer, it was a place to be avoided, a blight on the neighborhood.

Why the city of New York tolerated such conditions in this space and failed to enforce the public part of the bargain, I do not know. But I was utterly sure that the condition I found this space in was a complete embarrassment to the community and, given its proximity to Lincoln Center, to me. I was also certain that it represented a huge opportunity.

Located across the street from the most prominent performing arts center in the world, the atrium, I felt, could be converted into something very special. A light-filled space for public assembly or for those who wish to read, work, or meet. A pre- and post-theater hangout for ticket holders who wish to order a salad or a sandwich and a glass of wine at very affordable prices. If you desire an office away from home, or a place to meet friends, or an alternative site for staff meetings, a job interview, or a book club discussion, the atrium would be there for you—in all seasons and all times of the day.

So close to Lincoln Center, the atrium could be used for performances, free to the public and on weekends for shows appealing to young children and their families. The constituent companies of Lincoln Center could not only perform, but also hold lecture demonstrations on work that had been or was soon to be performed. At once a civic space and a Lincoln Center Commons, the atrium would be open 365 days a year from 8:00 a.m. to 10:00 p.m. It could serve both as an amenity for the Upper West Side and as an attraction for visitors from elsewhere in Manhattan and the other four boroughs of the city, or for American and foreign tourists.

The atrium could also be a civic space where nongovernmental organizations (NGOs) like the Community Board or Landmark West, or the BID or our elected officials, could convene meetings. Nestled inside the atrium could be a discount ticket operation that would allow for the purchase of off-price seats for constituent performances. In addition, I hoped that well-trained volunteer docents could respond to questions of newcomers about the basic content of performances and about more mundane matters, like how best to return to one's hotel by subway, or what restaurant would be most suitable for a family of five on a tight budget.

This inspiration of mine was not widely shared. Staff colleagues and trustees had a difficult time imagining precisely how the space would be used and occupied and why it was to Lincoln Center's advantage, or in Lincoln Center's interest, to invest so much time, effort, and funds in the atrium's conversion. I remain extremely grateful to the trustees of Lincoln Center for giving me the freedom to take the lead in realizing this vision. It was a splendid vote of confidence, especially when construction budgets were already very tight and fund-raising goals were already very ambitious.

After some deft negotiating and patient maneuvering over the course of more than a year, Lincoln Center legally arranged to assume responsibility for the space from the Harmony Condominium on a ninety-nine-year lease. Doing so required finding construction documents that hadn't been consulted since the creation of the space. It involved detailed negotiations with the city agency responsible for all POPS, the Department of City Planning, and with Harmony building board members.

We held an architectural competition and selected Tod Williams and Billie Tsien. Their charge was to totally overhaul the space into an indoor plaza that would serve as a lounge, a café, a meeting space, a discount ticket booth, a contemplative place to read and relax, and a performance venue, all at once. It was also to be the site where guided tours of Lincoln Center began. Over forty thousand visitors annually walked through our sixteen-acre campus and peeked into many of its theater spaces, accompanied by experts who could respond to all kinds of questions and satisfy all sorts of curiosity.

Williams and Tsien worked magic. They deployed huge plant walls, creating a delightful indoor urban garden. They made clever use of water elements. The purchase of movable seats and tables and the design of fixed marble benches worked well for the space. They wisely decided to commission enormous felt paintings that hung on the north and south walls, made possible by a gift from Betty and John Levin. These works gave this space a cozy, inviting character, one also conducive to good acoustics.

The Lizzie and Jon Tisch Media Wall was located on the north side of the room, providing up-to-date information on what was being performed throughout the Lincoln Center campus. It was part and parcel of an overall infoscape design driven by the same software that animated the infoblades on 65th Street, the scrolling text across the stairs, and what we called an infopeel, another information dissemination device in full video tucked behind the bleacher facing Alice Tully Hall and fully accessible to the thousands of passersby each day along Broadway. The media wall, one of the largest such installations in New York City, was also used regularly for film showings and for live television transmissions of events like the Oscars and the Tonys and, of course, fashion shows that were taking place twice a year only yards away in Damrosch Park. And the Barbara and Donald Zucker Box Office made it possible for thousands of people to attend performances of all kinds at heavily discounted prices.

The idea for what this space might become was informed by my service as the executive director of the 92nd Street Y. The atrium was a version of a community center. I was certain that if designed with maximum flexibility in mind, it would be heavily utilized, even in ways that we could not then fully contemplate. And that is exactly what Williams and Tsien delivered: a pliable space, capable of being a breakfast meeting location at 9:00 a.m., a civic organization's annual board meeting at noon, a reading room and study hall at 4:00 p.m., and a nightclub at 7:00 p.m.

By now, just five years after its opening, 1.75 million people have enjoyed the facility. I am confident that Lincoln Center can take credit for operating the single most popular and lively POPS in the city of New York. What pleases me immensely is that for so many working-class New Yorkers and schoolchildren, the atrium is their first encounter with Lincoln Center. It is their gateway and guide to what goes on throughout our bustling campus. Their exposure to Lincoln Center free of charge in such a delightful space is very gratifying.

To fully realize the design for the atrium and its enormous potential as a public space required raising from private sources over 90 percent of the capital cost of some $25 million. Lincoln Center also absorbed into its regular budget the $3 million annual operating expense of securing, cleaning, insuring, ventilating, programming, and staffing the facility. By city regulation, access to the space is completely free of charge, even for special events. There can be no earned income derived from the public utilizing this space. So offsetting the cost of the atrium year after year took marketing acumen (some very limited outside rental income was permitted), fund-raising hustle, and craftily resorting to the economics of scope and scale, since the atrium quickly became part and parcel of Lincoln Center's overall operation.

The facility is named after David Rubenstein in recognition of his extremely generous gift. He decided to associate his good name with what was then not so much an attractive space as an act of the imagination of a determined CEO. The David Rubenstein Atrium is a contemporary example of what sociologist William H. Whyte meant when he wrote these lines:

> I end then in praise of small spaces. The multiplier effect is tremendous. It is not just the number of people using them, but the number who pass by and enjoy them vicariously, or the even larger number who feel better about the city center for the knowledge of them. For a city, such places are priceless, whatever the cost. They are built of a set of basics and they are right in front of our noses. If we look.[2]

Consider this an invitation to follow your nose and happen on by.

IN ORDER FOR Lincoln Center's redevelopment to be formally approved, a vote of the New York City Council was required, following many meetings with our council member, Gail Brewer; borough president Scott Stringer; and Community Board 7. At each step in the process we also needed a green light from the office of the mayor and his key departments. No fewer than fifteen of them were involved.[3] Which had jurisdiction over what and when was a continuing source of either confusion or disagreement, even at the level of concurring on basic concept designs for redevelopment. When it came to drawings, bidding on contractors and subcontractors, and when construction would begin, no chain drugstore carried enough Extra-Strength Tylenol to see Lincoln Center staff through these tedious, excessive, and overlapping jurisdictions, all with their attendant delays.

To some extent, the price of building in New York City is making one's way through a regulatory gauntlet. Since for more than a few years Lincoln Center redevelopment was the largest construction project not only in our town, but in the country (when it wasn't second to the activity at the Ground Zero site), and since ours was so visible and newsworthy, normal oversight was ratcheted up, or so it seemed.

Beyond the formal players, there were those who influenced them. They enjoyed a voice—this being the Upper West Side, perhaps entitlement to a megaphone would be more accurate—but not a vote. They also could impede forward movement by appealing to state or federal departments or by reverting to litigation. Each in its own way—the Museum of Art and Design, the New York Public Library, New York University, the Museum of Modern Art, and Columbia University—would experience delays, constraints, and conditions in its own major building projects as a result of advocacy group activity.

In Lincoln Center's case, among the key nongovernmental players with which we regularly dealt were the BID, the Municipal Arts Society, Docomomo International, and Landmark West. The latter was by far the most knowledgeable, vocal, passionate, and determined. My approach to this and to any other interested party, like cooperative apartment boards, condominium associations, restaurateurs, and retailers in the neighborhood, was to keep an open door, to treat all views and concerns respectfully, and most of all, to listen. And by listen I mean with a readiness to change my mind or alter Lincoln Center's plans in response to solid studies, sound ideas, and well-articulated expressions of concern.

There were more than a few of those, and we adjusted our plans in response to them. There was also the usual mix of institutional self-interest, parochialism, showboating, and stridency on display. This is, after all, New York City.

We must have done something right. The ULURP process was completed without so much as a hiccup. No lawsuits were filed or even threatened. The accommodations that we made improved elements of the renovation. That so much time, energy, and money were devoted to public space improvement by Lincoln Center did not go unnoticed or unappreciated. And the fact that so many citizens deeply cared about its future was heartening. Their assembled data, perspectives, and points of view were worth taking fully into account—and we did. Repeatedly, D S + R and our staff were credited with being open to dialogue and faithful to a fair and thorough process. Our wide-open door won us much-needed goodwill.

And it established a precedent for the frequent communication required to prepare all Lincoln Center insiders and all of our neighbors for the noise, the dirt, the detours, the traffic snarls, and the inconveniences that would occur throughout the construction process. Here is how D S + R describe what Lincoln Center managed to accomplish:

> In a fashion akin to emergency medicine, Lincoln Center master-minded open heart surgery on a patient that was wide awake, as the work had to be carefully planned, translated and executed while [all] Lincoln Center's venues remained opened [except for Alice Tully Hall's eighteen-month closure].[4]

Amazingly, five million people were accommodated by Lincoln Center each year, even at the height of construction. Through meticulous planning, not a single curtain rose late, not a single student or faculty member at the SAB or The Juilliard School was displaced, and only a rare handful of complaints ever reached public officials or me in any given calendar quarter. I am certain that Lincoln Center's timely communication of construction plans helped keep our neighbors well informed and, by and large, content. But I am also convinced that E. B. White was on the money when he observed, "New Yorkers temperamentally do not crave comfort and convenience—if they did, they would live elsewhere."[5]

On time and under budget, the Lincoln Center development project team, led by Ron Austin, an experienced hand at building arts centers, performed masterfully. He was supported throughout by a superb chief financial officer, Dan Rubin.

We were also blessed with able and grateful subcontractor and construction employees. Most of them had been hired in the middle of America's deepest recession. Lincoln Center had created the equivalent of one thousand full-time jobs, paying a total of $70 million in wages. I felt terrific that so many working-class families could be sustained by the work Lincoln Center had undertaken.

A NEW WAY of thinking and operating was both cause and consequence of redevelopment. It did not only apply to lofty ideas like creating an alluring community gathering place where there had been a forlorn, desolate space. It was also relevant to mundane but important matters like getting to and from Lincoln Center in a car as conveniently and hassle-free as possible.

Ask anyone who was deeply involved in the redevelopment of Lincoln Center about Joe Volpe, and you are sure to hear a favorite story about our own homegrown enfant terrible. All will offer an example of obstinacy and obstruction on one issue or another—sometimes procedural, sometimes substantive, often just an effort to impede progress, seemingly just for the sake of doing so.

At critical moments, when Volpe's ultimatums reached their highest decibel level and crossed the boundary from being merely unreasonable to being simply outrageous, Bruce Crawford would see him and/or the Met Opera's chair, William Morris, behind closed doors. Generally, after these quiet conversations, somehow negotiations were put back on track.

Crawford is elegant, extremely well read, sophisticated in his tastes—in food and wine, in clothing, in furniture, in books, and, of course, in the performing arts, not least opera. Having left the business of advertising to run the Met as its general manager for two and a half years and to rescue it from a colossal deficit in the 1983–1984 season of some $8 million (inflation adjusted, that would be over $25 million today), he came to know Volpe well.

Crawford dined regularly at Grenouille. Volpe preferred red sauce Italian. Crawford's high-end shoes were never unshined. His clothing was impeccably chosen and worn. Joe's suits and shirts were not just off the rack and the shelf; they seemed to come entirely from someone else's closest, usually a size or two larger than he needed. Crawford is mild-mannered, rational, and even-tempered. Volpe is highly volatile. During his tenure at the Met, Bruce put the place back on a firm financial footing in a little less than three seasons. He then resumed his position as an important Met Opera board member and returned to corporate life as the president and CEO of Omnicom.

After a brief interval with a failed successor, Hugh Southern, Crawford neatly orchestrated Volpe's succession. They have been friends ever since, and Joe's treatment of Bruce in his own memoir—*The Toughest Show on Earth: My Rise and Reign at the Metropolitan Opera*[6]—is little short of laudatory.

Perhaps the most difficult issue to negotiate with Volpe and Morris was whether 65th Street would have any garage access at all and, if so, what kind. Some constituents wanted none. The Met wanted as much as possible. Volpe, supported by Morris, argued that the entrances on 62nd Street and Amsterdam Avenue were totally insufficient to satisfy Met patrons. Without a convenient way to enter and exit Lincoln Center's underground garage from the major west to east block, 65th Street, the Met feared that it would lose business. A lot of it.

Actually, it was impossible to know for certain. The Met felt strongly that those most concerned with the safety of pedestrians were exaggerating. After all, multiple points of ingress and egress all across 65th Street on its south side had been totally eliminated. Ninety-four feet of curb cut in all was to be reduced to eleven feet only, with one point of ingress being proposed on the southwest side of the street. Others felt equally strongly that the Met's representatives could hardly with a straight face claim that the future of its box office depended on the outcome of this one issue. The parties had squared off. Intransigence seemed to take over.

I offered Bruce several fresh options to consider negotiating as Lincoln Center's emissary. A compromise was struck. One point of entry. Ingress only. But not just pre-curtain for a couple of hours. Rather, the entrance would be open all day, with a guard posted at the curb at all times to check car trunks and to control traffic.

After a lot of hemming, hawing, harrumphing, and the generation of other sounds common to tough negotiations, the solution was accepted by all parties. It has been in effect ever since.

Not a single word ever reached me about either problems with pedestrian safety or any adverse effect of the arrangement on Met Opera patrons. Compromise worked well. Someone should tell the leadership of Republicans and Democrats in the House and Senate.

All praise goes to my friend, Lincoln Center chair and ambassador at large to the Met Opera, Bruce Crawford. His successor, Frank Bennack, also recognized the importance of maintaining personal relationships between and among trustees. Only by building trust could difficult agreements be reached. Toward that end, Frank twice invited all constituent chairs and their spouses or partners for weekend trips to his formidable ranch in Texas. There, in Kerrville, one hour northwest of San Antonio by car, bonds were formed amid the skeet shooting, the hikes, the stargazing, the horseback riding, and the picnic barbecues.

These forays, on which Frank and his wife Mary Lake played gracious hosts, were nowhere to be found in a chair's job description. But, wow, did they help to engender closer relationships and open up personal lines of communication.

Apart from reminding us how much relationships matter, Bruce's and Frank's success was attributable to their natural sense of pragmatism. They believed that at a high level of abstraction, differences are accentuated. But by moving to facts, to on-the-ground realities, they often can be bridged. The redevelopment of Lincoln Center is a series of such practical settlements. Moving trustees and staff from dogmatism to practical alternatives, trade-offs could be formulated that all parties found reasonable. Lincoln Center became a specialist in identifying that third way between contending groups.

Trustees enjoy accomplishing things, making a difference, contributing to a determination of Lincoln Center's direction, and helping it find the way across a finish line. They also enjoy being educated and having a little fun.

Katherine Farley regularly invited a single constituent to each meeting of the board of directors. The artistic or educational leaders of all resident organizations personally appeared before the board. They spoke about their accomplishments, their priorities, and their aspirations. Wynton Marsalis, Peter Martins, Peter Gelb, Joseph Polisi, Marjorie Van derCook, Andre Bishop, and Wu Han are among those who offered remarks and then engaged in a dialogue with trustees. These sessions built mutual understanding and a sense of community.

I endeavored not only to edify through extensive precirculated reading material and often through presentations by board committee chairs and senior staff, but also to lighten up the boardroom. Why just leave brochures on the seats of trustees, when staff costumed to impersonate a Shakespearean character, or Wolfgang Amadeus Mozart, or a jazz trombonist could hand the relevant literature to trustees as they came off the elevator?

Why just announce the renewal of the Big Apple Circus residency in Damrosch Park at Lincoln Center, when one could have the silent clown Grandma suddenly enter the boardroom, sit on the laps of selected trustees, engage in some hijinks, and unfurl a "Thank You Lincoln Center" banner?

Why not encourage a Lincoln Center staff a cappella group I named "The Donations" to thank Frank Bennack for his distinguished service as chair of the board for five years by singing, complete with bath towels at the ready, Rodgers and Hammerstein's "We're Going to Wash That Man Right Out of Our Hair and Send Him on His Way." That's a lot better than reading aloud a three-page resolution of gratitude, wouldn't you say?

Farley's regular meetings with all board chairs as a group, her special nights out together with a judicious mixture of Lincoln Center and constituent trustees, and her immediate response to the expressed needs of colleagues were all of a piece. These actions all aimed at building personal relationships and creating trust.

In her annual receptions at home for all Lincoln Center trustees, Katherine engaged in another form of personal diplomacy. Besides dinner parties, her calendar bulged with breakfast and lunch dates. Farley energetically reached out to secure the views of all trustees at Lincoln Center and among the constituents and to convey her own. These initiatives were respected. The investment of time and attention yielded dividends.

ANOTHER DIMENSION OF Lincoln Center's massive renovation is how well D S + R coordinated their work with other distinguished architects. David Rockwell was assigned by the Lincoln Center Film Society to design the Eleanor Bunin Film Center, Hugh Hardy was commissioned to create the rooftop Claire Tow Theater, and Todd Williams and Billie Tsien were asked by Lincoln Center to work miracles on the privately owned public space soon to become the David Rubenstein Atrium.

Each of these architects drew inspiration and guidance from the context that D S + R had created. All worked closely together whenever necessary. Mutual support and mutual respect seemed to prevail.

That is quite a contrast from what transpired when Lincoln Center was originally conceived and constructed. There is an iconic photograph taken by Arnold Newman in 1959 that captures nine men sitting and standing around oversized models of what were to be the New York State Theater, the Metropolitan Opera, and Avery Fisher Hall. Attired in suits and ties, the original architects of Lincoln Center and its patriarch, John D. Rockefeller III, do not look happy.[7]

In 1985, Philip Johnson reported that when that picture was taken hardly anyone was on speaking terms with anyone else. "Everybody pretty well hated everybody."[8]

A half century later, it was refreshing to witness a 180-degree change in the relationship of architects working for Lincoln Center and its constituents. Some important leaders even believed that vastly improved relationships extended well beyond the parties to redevelopment and the redevelopment process.

Truly present at the creation and a moving force behind Lincoln Center redevelopment, Bruce Kovner speaks with the authority of a major actor and with the detachment of an informed, insightful observer. What he has to say is very flattering and hopeful, particularly in view of the soon-to-be-described behavior of one constituent and the disappearance of another:

> The renewal of Lincoln Center was much more than a renewal of physical space. It was a process that connected constituents together in a way that they had never been connected. In the past, Lincoln Center was famously a place of silos, and I don't think it is anymore. Part of what happened during this whole process is we became much more of a community, a team trying to accomplish things that were important for all of us together. Speaking as a chairman of one of the constituent organizations [The Juilliard School], I can say there's been a tremendous, almost revolutionary change in the relationship of the constituent organizations. We do more together and we help each other. A lot of that was born in the process of coming together for the physical renovation. It made a big difference.[9]

Could it be that the very project that almost tore Lincoln Center asunder in 2001 and 2002 was a decade later partially responsible for an unprecedented level of cooperation, coordination, and cohesion?

LINCOLN CENTER MAKES eminent sense as an economic set of entities cooperating on revenue generation and expense controls. By taking advantage of the economies of scope and scale that exist among twelve different organizations, whenever possible, there are financial gains to be secured. The ability of this many performing and educational organizations to work together from an artistic perspective is also facilitated by their proximity. Redevelopment may well have solidified relationships all over Lincoln Center's campus. One of its consequences is that artistic cooperation seemed to increase appreciably.

It is no accident that Wynton Marsalis, the artistic director of Jazz at Lincoln Center, was selected to create and lead the first-ever matriculated major in jazz at The Juilliard School. Similarly, maestro Alan Gilbert, the music director of the New York Philharmonic, accepted a position as the head of The Juilliard School's Conducting Program. Whenever special guest artists are performing for constituents, Juilliard's president Polisi is attuned to how they might be invited to enrich the experience of students. Lectures, small-group discussions, and master classes abound.

Maestro Gilbert included a New York premiere of a Marsalis-composed jazz piece for the orchestra to open a New York Philharmonic season. Peter Martins commissioned Marsalis to compose a piece for the New York City Ballet. Lincoln Center retained Marsalis and the Jazz at Lincoln Center Orchestra to open its twenty-fifth anniversary Midsummer Night Swing outdoor dance series.

The Lincoln Center Festival has presented the New York Philharmonic playing the work of Varèse and jointly presented with the Metropolitan Opera the Kirov Opera Company and its orchestra performing a summer *Ring Cycle* conducted by Valery Gergiev. The festival also used the services of the New York City Opera Orchestra to accompany performances of the Ashton Festival at the Metropolitan Opera House in 2004, Julie Taymor's *Grendel* at the New York City State Theater in 2006, and the San Francisco Ballet at the same place in the same year. And it jointly presented with the Chamber Music Society a Prokofiev Marathon in July 2003.

Lincoln Center has recently reached an agreement with the New York Philharmonic to perform three pathbreaking staged operas. They will be cocurated by both institutions. The first, scheduled for August, 2015, is *Written on Skin* by the composer George Benjamin and the librettist Martin Crimp and directed by Katie Mitchell. The second, *The Importance of Being Earnest* by the composer Gerald Barry, will be mounted in 2016. A third opera, soon to be announced, is in the planning stages for 2017. To produce these rarely played works in America is expensive.

By joining forces, Lincoln Center and the New York Philharmonic will bring them to life in New York City. This major undertaking exemplifies artistic cooperation as between two constituents.

The Mostly Mozart Festival and the Great Performers series have frequently presented difficult-to-acquire films at the Walter Reade Theater with the cooperation of the Film Society.

When Lincoln Center reopened Alice Tully Hall and the New York City Ballet celebrated the one hundredth anniversary of the birth of George Balanchine, as many of the resident organizations as possible offered their artistry for these landmark occasions.

The Chamber Music Society frequently joined forces with Lincoln Center's programming department. In 2013, inspired by the codirector of CMS, David Finckel, a concert entitled The Cellists of Lincoln Center was arranged. Drawing from that instrument's repertoire, the first chair cello players of the Jazz at Lincoln Center Orchestra, the New York City Ballet Orchestra, the Metropolitan Opera Orchestra, the New York Philharmonic, and the Chamber Music Society all participated enthusiastically. It was difficult to discern whether the players—or the standing-room-only audiences—enjoyed themselves more.

The Metropolitan Opera, under Peter Gelb, has taken special initiatives with many of Lincoln Center's constituents. Perhaps the most notable has been joining forces with Andre Bishop at Lincoln Center Theater to develop new operas in workshop form. This process is guided by directors who frequently present plays at Lincoln Center Theater. Also notable is the Met Opera joining forces with The Juilliard School on the Lindemann Young Artist Development Program, launched in 2009, and in the New York Choreographic Institute beginning in 2002. In addition, Alan Gilbert has been invited to conduct the Metropolitan Opera Orchestra, as has Louis Langrée, the maestro of Lincoln Center's Mostly Mozart Orchestra.

The New York Public Library for the Performing Arts, the largest of its kind in the world, draws many of its special exhibits from the work and history of the constituents. To select just three, it mounted *Opera on the Air: The Metropolitan Opera Radio Broadcasts Turn 75* (December 2005–May 2006); *Historic Debuts at SAB's Workshop Performances* (April–July 2009); and *Lincoln Center: Celebrating 50 Years*, a fiftieth-anniversary exhibition (October 2009–January 2010).

And of course for forty years the nationally televised program *Live from Lincoln Center* has featured constituent performances for exposure around the country. These have included virtually every resident organization, many on multiple occasions.

These are only illustrations of the many and varied forms of artistic collaboration regularly occurring at Lincoln Center. So it is a source of annoyance to my colleagues and to me whenever some critics complain of insufficient cooperation between and among Lincoln Center and its constituents. There is a term of art for such carping: baloney.

LINCOLN CENTER AND its constituents are estimated to pump $3.4 billion of economic activity into the metropolitan-area economy. Data on employment, tourism, real estate development, retail business, restaurants, and New York City's sales and property tax revenue also support the revitalizing effect Lincoln Center has had on the Upper West Side.

But walking, over less than one square mile from the sixteen-acre campus, bordering from south to north, 57th Street to 79th Street, and from east to west, Central Park West to Twelfth Avenue, is just as telling. The changes are dramatic from the day I stepped foot on the campus on March 1, 2002, through almost thirteen years later. The streetscape, the skyline, and the rush of pedestrian and vehicular traffic, uptown, downtown, and crosstown, are not to be compared.

Not only has Lincoln Center been utterly transformed, but so have its surroundings. Just consider restaurants. On Lincoln Center's territory proper, in 2002 there were the Metropolitan Opera's dining establishment The Grand Tier and Arpeggio, a food service in Avery Fisher Hall. Eleven years later, they were joined by Tom Colicchio's "wichcraft" in the David Rubenstein Atrium, Marcus Samuelsson's American Table at Alice Tully Hall, a popular café called Indie tucked into the new Elinor Bunin Film Center, and of course, Jonathan Benno's Lincoln Ristorante.

These new venues range so widely in their cuisine, price points, ambience, comfort, and speed of dining that every pocketbook, taste, and schedule can be satisfied. They have become places where audiences, artists, employees, and administrators hang out. Lincoln Center has begun to have the feel of a campus, a name that its acreage has often been called.

The facts and figures are impressive. In 2013, over one hundred thousand people enjoyed a meal at Lincoln alone, roughly half pre- and post-theater patrons and half destination diners. All of the restaurants on the campus together grossed in the vicinity of $20 million. As striking, they served more than 425,000 diners. In 2013, compared to 2002, Lincoln Center's dining facilities were generating four times the dollar sum and serving five times the number of guests.

Beyond the statistics, they lured people to linger and enjoy themselves. Social encounter and cultural discourse became natural allies. Friends and companions found it easy to meet and anticipate the show to come or to share reactions soon after a curtain fell.

Artists and administrators, students and spectators, foreign tourists and domestic travelers, subway commuters, and drivers or taxi and black car customers all found common ground over a quick salad or sandwich or a repast that could run up an impressive bill and leave a wonderful memory of a terrific dining experience.

But as wide-ranging as are Lincoln Center's food service offerings, they almost pale by comparison to the abundance of choice now on the Upper West Side of Manhattan, an area regarded before 2002 as a culinary wasteland.

Sure, there were a few preexisting standbys when I arrived at Lincoln Center, like Café Fiorello, Café Luxembourg, Gabriel's, Picholine, and Shun Lee.

But now ticket holders and visitors can also dine at Asiate, The Atlantic Grill, A Voce, Bar Boulud, Bouchon Bakery, Boulud Sud, Ed's Chowder House, Jean-Georges, Nougatine, Landmarc, The Leopard at des Artistes, Le Pain Quotidien, Masa, Nick and Toni's Cafe, Per Se, PJ Clarke's, Porter House, The Smith, and Telepan, all within six blocks of Lincoln Center!

But for those who would venture just a little further, are prepared to dine earlier to make curtain or catch a meal after the show, or are willing to hail a cab rather than walk, the choices are also delectable.[10] Ask any of the chefs or investors in these establishments why they located on the Upper West Side of Manhattan, and one answer will inevitably pop up: Lincoln Center. Its year-round traffic is now estimated at 5.5 million people. They include 7,500 employees and 2,000 full-time students.

In a profession where few successful men or women are inclined to virtual anonymity, Lloyd Goldman is an exception: he's a low-key developer. He told me over lunch that one of the key criteria he uses to determine what residential properties to buy is the presence of a two-, three-, or four-star restaurant with a long-term lease and staying power on the same block. Its location is, in his mind, highly correlated to low crime levels, to the high net wealth of residents, to an attractive clientele, and to a terrific neighborhood amenity.

Goldman's observation underscores how development, once successfully started, can become a virtuous circle. The tremendous success of Steve Ross's Related Companies' Time Warner Center, which replaced the broken-down and forlorn New York Coliseum, helped to give those at the Hearst Corporation the confidence to build the first commercial skyscraper after 9/11, designed by Norman Foster.

Lenny Litwin built the Grand Tier Apartments in 2005 right across the street from Lincoln Center, charging rents two to three times the average of comparably located buildings. He is credited with proving that there existed a much more robust market for high-end rentals near Lincoln Center than was commonly believed.

Developers like Arthur Zeckendorf, Gary Barnett, Daniel Brodsky, John Avalon, Donald Trump, and Litwin himself all built major cooperative, condominium, or rental apartment houses near Lincoln Center during the period 2002–2014.[11]

And who, prior to 2002, would have ventured a guess that Apple, Barney's, Best Buy, Brooks Brothers, Century 21, Helmut Lang, Hugo Boss, J. Crew, Lululemon, MAC Cosmetics, Patagonia, Pottery Barn, Rag & Bone, Samsung, Theory, West Elm, Williams-Sonoma, and Zara would all have opened shops up and down Broadway, Columbus, and Amsterdam Avenue? Today, the costs of retail space, commercial space, and condominiums and co-ops per square foot on these streets are comparable to or in excess of their counterparts on Madison Avenue, or for that matter, on Park, or on Fifth Avenue, or in Tribeca or SoHo.

Hotels, some at the very high end, like The Mandarin or The Trump or The Phillips Club, and others, more affordable but less well known, like The Empire, The Hudson, and The Milburn, enjoy high occupancy levels year-round. Business is thriving. Lincoln Center's magnetic attraction to patrons and visitors contributes to that pleasant result.

Toward the end of my tenure, Glenn Dicterow, the first chair violinist of the New York Philharmonic, paid a visit to my office. Only twelve months before, after thirty-two years of service at "The Phil," he had announced that he would retire to a teaching post at the University of Southern California. I asked him what he was most looking forward to enjoying. "The beach," he said. He and his wife had bought a modest beachfront home where they could walk down a small flight of steps and be right on the sand to view the mighty Pacific Ocean.

In the early 1990s Glenn had purchased a condominium in the Harmony building. It was a very convenient place to live, located just steps away from Avery Fisher Hall. But the condo was poorly financed, poorly maintained, and adjacent to that much-neglected, non-code-compliant, seven-thousand-square-foot public space that had become a dismal hangout for the homeless: dark, dank, and poorly ventilated. Property values for Harmony residents plummeted accordingly. Now he revealed that following the completion of the David Rubenstein Atrium and more generally, Lincoln Center's stunning modernization, the value of his apartment had zoomed. The impact of Lincoln Center's renaissance enabled him to switch careers to teaching and occasional performing, while reserving plenty of time for glorious sunsets and glimmering seas.

"So, Reynold, I have come to thank you for making this future possible for me, my family, and countless others," he said.

This is what economic development looks like when personified.

When the Lincoln Center redevelopment project was stuck in the quicksand of controversy, extricating it required overcoming extensive negative print and broadcast coverage. Conversely, our success was aided and abetted by continued lavish public praise of each and every completed constituent project and of Lincoln Center's physical transformation as a whole. Donors like to associate themselves with a winner. The chattering classes were beginning to think that when it came to architecture, design, and construction, Lincoln Center could do little wrong.

What follows are the views of three important critics about what Lincoln Center was able to accomplish for artists, audiences, students, and tourists. Clearly, the close of the year 2010 found Goldberger,

Kennicott, and Tommasini reflecting on what Lincoln Center had wrought:

NEW YORK ARCHITECTURE: EVENTS OF THE YEAR

Their [D S + R] reconstruction of Josie Robertson Plaza, the central plaza of [Lincoln Center], brilliantly enhances the classical symmetry of this much admired but deeply flawed public space, yet at the same time, it sends clear signals that a new and different era arrived. Rarely has a change to a landmark been simultaneously so powerful and so subtle.

—Paul Goldberger, *New Yorker*, December 16, 2010

KENNEDY CENTER AND OTHERS SHOULD
TAKE NOTE OF LINCOLN CENTER REDESIGN

And even on a blustery winter day, the 16-acre arts center, which celebrated its 50th anniversary in 2009, is looking livelier, smarter, hipper and more inviting—it is a change that should be studied closely not just by the Kennedy Center and Washington's public art institutions, but by anyone who cares about the peculiar freedoms of urban life.

The architects have lightened and enlivened the space, opened it up to the city and added touches of humor and eccentricity that suggest both a subtle aesthetic and a playful one. [They understand that] the arts are about access, exposure, serendipity and comingling.

—Philip Kennicott, *Washington Post*, December 29, 2010

A CITADEL OF CULTURE SHOWS A FRIENDLIER FACE

Now the main stairs to the plaza slope gently down to the Columbus Avenue sidewalk, creating an entrance to the center that practically shouts, "Step right up."

. . . the radical transformation of [Alice Tully Hall's] lobby is a triumph. What used to look like a bunker hidden under a pointless pedestrian bridge has become an airy, spacious gathering space with tall windowed walls.

—Anthony Tommasini, *New York Times*, December 29, 2010

And this critical acclaim had its counterpart in professional awards and recognition of all kinds. A partial list appears in Appendix B.

WHEN LINCOLN CENTER hired Diller + Scofidio, the firm employed only about a dozen full-time employees and had yet to design a completed building. In fact, our engagement of their studio took place even before Renfro had become a partner. Although the Institute for Contemporary Art in Boston was a client Diller + Scofidio had acquired before we retained the firm, when Lincoln Center selected it a shovel had hardly hit the ground near Boston Harbor. And though Diller + Scofidio was enjoying a Whitney Museum twenty-year retrospective exhibit on its work, little seemed relevant to our massive project.

There were stage installations. There were set designs. There were conceptual sketches. There was the "Blur" building, a creation on the sea of nothing more than fog and a bar featuring more brands of the world's bottled water than had ever been gathered in one place. Stuff like that.

It is no wonder that architects and critics expressed surprise that Lincoln Center would hire Diller, rather than the much "safer" finalists like Foster and Partners, Richard Meier, and Frank Gehry. All of these competitors had substantial track records to their credit. Of real buildings, commercial and residential. Of prestigious awards, like the Pritzker. Of avid and well-known clients. Of sterling name recognition. What possessed the Lincoln Center selection committee to opt for the relatively unknown and unproven?

Well, as it happened, there is no single person during my tenure at Lincoln Center from whom I learned more than from Liz Diller: about different ways to see space; about the relationship between human beings and the built environment; and about breaking down barriers, real and perceived, between Lincoln Center and the city around it.

I have always been taken by Oscar Wilde's lament: "Nowadays people know the price of everything and the value of nothing." So Diller found in me a kindred soul when she wished to dip into Lincoln Center's pocketbook to achieve her vision. But that soul was lodged in an owner's representative. Me. And in that role I could not appreciate the value of everything at virtually any cost, often an architect's (or an artist's) propensity. I needed to avoid spending beyond the established budget.

So there was a natural tension between us. "Don't let the very best be the enemy of the very good, Liz," I would declaim, often in vain, at least initially. Eventually, Diller would find a way to achieve her aesthetic, functional, or design objective in rough proximity to what Lincoln Center could afford. Rarely were her ideas less than intriguing, imaginative, and thoughtful. She was a resourceful advocate for them, and as good as Lincoln Center's redevelopment turned out to be, dozens upon dozens of additional excellent design ideas were left on the cutting room floor.

On more than one occasion, Diller would utter words that strike fear into the heart of any client, like, "What I am about to propose has never been done before, so I cannot take you to see something similar. It simply does not exist." The curvature of the glass frontage in Alice Tully Hall had no precedent. Its "blushing" walls, which change color as the time for a performance approaches, did not exist elsewhere. The white text illuminating the grand stairs on the approach to Josie Robertson Plaza is unique to Lincoln Center, as is the scrolling text across the enlarged 65th Street entrance to the main campus. The dramatically contoured Tisch Illumination Lawn on the rooftop of Lincoln Ristorante has no equal.

These design ideas were greeted by some as impractical, too costly to build or maintain, or simply unnecessary. Diller persisted. She built exact prototypes to demonstrate beyond the shadow of a doubt that the stair text could be seen even in the haze of a 98-degree, steamy dog day in August, and that it could be maintained even when rain turned to ice. Or that the grass roof of Lincoln would not leak into the restaurant and was not dangerous to the urban climber in search of adventure, ascending or descending.

Beyond Diller's extraordinary strength as an architect, she had other very attractive qualities. She spoke compellingly and wrote persuasively. Her mind was restlessly creative. Her commitment to quality in design was ceaseless. She regularly crossed disciplinary, cultural, and geographic boundaries. Diller combines idealism with practicality. Something of a polymath, she holds a tenured post at Princeton University, and she and her husband, Ric Scofidio, were the first architects ever to win a MacArthur Foundation "Genius Prize."

It was these qualities of mind and creative spirit that we detected in Liz and her colleagues. They also exhibited energy, ambition, and the capacity to listen and to learn. Diller expressed a fervent desire to improve what was best about Lincoln Center, rather than replace it. She delivered fully on that expression of intent.

As Lincoln Center's redevelopment began to be realized, so did recognition of D S + R's work in the media and by prospective clients. Now, Diller Scofidio + Renfro are contracted to design or have already completed the Henry Kravis Business School at Columbia University; the Eli Broad Museum in Los Angeles; the High Line; the Granoff School of the Arts at Brown University; the new campus of the Columbia Medical School; the expansion of the Museum of Modern Art; and performing arts centers at both the University of California at Berkeley and Rice University.

But Lincoln Center really won an admirer in the person of Steve Ross, a highly valued Lincoln Center trustee and the chair of Related Companies. Steve hired D S +R to design their first-ever office building as part of his ambitious Hudson Yards Project. He also commissioned the firm to become the architect of record for the Culture Shed, a new indoor-outdoor entertainment and exhibition center, one on which the Bloomberg administration bestowed $75 million of New York City funds just before the mayor's term in office expired.

The very idea that Lincoln Center's nonprofit architectural and entrepreneurial forays were being validated by well-known and successful developer billionaires looking for solutions to their own personal, civic, and business undertakings was a special form of endorsement.

We could not be more pleased for Liz Diller, Ric Scofidio, Charles Renfro, and their talented colleagues at D S + R. They are helping to transform the look and the feel of some of New York's most important institutions, neighborhoods, and public spaces. They are also venturing far outside New York City, to California, Texas, Rhode Island, Rio de Janeiro, and China, among other places. It is nice to know that Lincoln Center was present at their validation and contributed to their studio's success.

To THE DEGREE that the total makeover of Lincoln Center has been viewed as a triumph, the victory is attributable to uncommon teamwork in staff and trustee ranks across many constituents. It required them to summon energy, persistence, and flexibility. It demanded of those of us at Lincoln Center even more.

During the course of design and construction and intensive fund-raising, we were preoccupied with refreshing and expanding Lincoln Center's far-flung arts presentation program. We were also intent on strengthening our staff and board of directors. We drew a bead on managing the campus in ways that would generate pride in its maintenance and applause for converting a drain on constituent resources into operating surpluses. We were bound and determined to revamp the economic model for our own operations. There was much else on our minds and agendas and no risk of being accused of indolence.

But concurrently, the New York Philharmonic and the New York City Opera were otherwise occupied. Working through the distractions and upheaval they caused while keeping an eye on the prize of campus transformation and solidarity tested our mettle and our patience.

The stories of how badly the New York Philharmonic strayed off course and how severe were the self-inflicted wounds of the New York City Opera have never been fully told. Occurring as they did on my watch, describing and analyzing both episodes is, I suppose, a point of personal privilege. More important, it is also an obligation.

The only saving grace of both adventures that occurs to me is the lessons that can be learned from them, providing a sobering contrast to the transformative work accomplished across the Lincoln Center campus.

CHAPTER 6

A Refugee Returns Home

Noah's principle says: No more credit for predicting rain; credit only for building arks.

—Anonymous

It was a Thursday afternoon—May 29, 2003, at 3:00 p.m., to be precise—when Paul Guenther, the chairman of the board of the New York Philharmonic, came to my office to meet with me and Bruce Crawford, Lincoln Center's chair. I had just completed my first full year of service as Lincoln Center's president.

His purpose was to report that, after studying all the alternatives, the New York Philharmonic did not wish to spend some $20–$40 million for mechanical, infrastructure, and cosmetic purposes on Avery Fisher Hall. Neither did it wish to demolish Avery Fisher Hall entirely and erect a new building and venue inside it. Nor did it wish to have designed and built a brand-new auditorium within the existing structure.

The first option, refurbishing, really amounted to addressing deferred maintenance on such items as the loading dock; elevators; heating, ventilation, and air conditioning; green rooms, changing rooms, and storage facilities; and seat and carpeting replacement as well as fresh coats of paint applied throughout the auditorium. The second, demolish and start fresh, would not only incur the opposition of the Fisher family, for whom the hall was named, but also mobilize the active resistance of preservationist groups and implicate a bundle of regulatory strictures and approval requirements. Moreover, a change in the structure of the building itself would upset the architectural symmetry of its relationship to the New York State Theater and to the Metropolitan Opera. Neither the Met nor the occupants of the New York State Theater, the New York City Ballet and the New York City Opera, were likely to allow this option to be exercised. They liked the fact that their dwellings were of equal height and aligned with a pleasing sense of proportion around the central fountain.

It was the golden mean, the third alternative, that all parties, including Guenther, had jointly agreed, just several weeks before, to bring to the executive committees of the New York Philharmonic and Lincoln Center, which would meet together for the first time. After months of work, the architectural firm of Pritzker Prize–winner Norman Foster, along with consulting acousticians and theater designers, had devised what appeared to be a very fine recommendation.

What they proposed was a brand-new auditorium within the existing structure. It would be moved south inside the building footprint, away from 65th Street, and toward Josie Robertson Plaza. In the auditorium, the seat count would be reduced from 2,738 to 2,400, and 250–300 seats would be placed behind the stage, facing the conductor. The stage itself would be thrust forward twelve to fourteen rows into the auditorium. The ceiling would be lifted to the bottom of the roof, the third balcony removed, and new floor and wall treatments applied everywhere.

By altering the cavernous and long shoe box design of the auditorium in Avery Fisher Hall to something resembling a vineyard-like configuration, the performers would enjoy a sense of intimacy and immediacy with the audience.[1]

The overall result would be improved aesthetics and acoustics. The "Foster plan" would also satisfy most of the program and functional needs set forth by the staffs of Lincoln Center and the New York Philharmonic. It could be accomplished in roughly half the time it would take to demolish the existing building and erect a new structure. It could be done for 75 percent of the cost (then estimated at $300 million versus $400 million). Because the building's dimensions and footprint wouldn't change, city and state regulation would be very lightly administered. And the Fisher family was amenable to our naming the new auditorium for a new donor as long as the building itself was called Avery Fisher Hall, as it had been since its opening in 1962.

The obstacles of too much time for the orchestra out of its home base, of having to raise too much money, of battling with the Fisher family over the naming of a new building, and of the heavy hand of government regulation, either were eliminated entirely or were significantly lowered by exercising this option. The prospects for major acoustic, programmatic, and aesthetic improvements all seemed to be substantially brightened by this approach, on which both institutions had worked together in good faith.

Or so we thought.

Foster's firm had become well known for reconfiguring the innards of famous buildings, while leaving their total original structure intact. The Reichstag. The British Museum. The Royal Academy of Arts and Sciences. And the then new, soon-to-be built corporate headquarters of the Hearst Corporation, only several blocks south of Lincoln Center. Foster's scheme for a brand-new auditorium in Avery Fisher Hall had generated much enthusiasm among all concerned.

Or so we thought.

At the request of the working group of trustees from both Lincoln Center and the New York Philharmonic, I had prepared a draft memorandum to the executive committees of both institutions formally presenting this option. It was framed as a united recommendation in advance of that joint meeting, scheduled for only a couple of weeks later. This unanimous agreement represented a major conceptual and procedural breakthrough, a source of hard-won consensus after months of intense work.

What Guenther told Bruce Crawford and me that Thursday at the end of May startled and shocked us. He said the New York Philharmonic intended to formally commence discussions with Sandy Weill, the chair of Carnegie Hall, to effectuate a merger of the two institutions. Nervously, Guenther cited two reasons for this decision. The cost of fixing up Carnegie Hall to house a full-time orchestra would be a relatively inexpensive $120 million, and the New York Philharmonic would be returning to an acoustically superior hall. He, and the few trustee colleagues who may have been consulted, viewed the Carnegie Hall option as no risk, low cost, and high return.

We asked whether the New York Philharmonic had considered the implications of a merger for its board, its staff, its artistic assets, its brand, and its donors. "Not yet" came the reply.

We reminded Guenther that Lincoln Center's constituency agreement with the New York Philharmonic as our anchor tenant and partner for the use of Avery Fisher Hall ran until 2012. It contained a list of obligations, and not the least of them was financial. These included payments for any dates between 2003 and 2012 that Lincoln Center could not fill in Avery Fisher Hall that would otherwise be occupied by the New York Philharmonic; payment of all legal costs; the loss of its share of the annual Lincoln Center Corporate Fund proceeds distributed to all constituents in good standing; and payment of discrete staff and consultant costs explicitly requested or caused by the New York Philharmonic.

We felt duty bound to see that these obligations were discharged with fidelity. "Understood" came the reply. We then noted that, with this news in mind, we had no alternative but to inform the members of the Lincoln Center executive committee of this completely surprising turn of events and, in so doing, cancel the scheduled June 16 meeting. "Fine with me," was Guenther's response.

The New York Philharmonic's bolt from the blue was presented by Guenther as firm, unwavering, and irreversible. We stressed that a leak of this sudden change of position could easily become front-page news.[2] We urged Guenther to treat the matter with the utmost discretion, so that we could arrange for a dignified joint announcement the following week, on Tuesday or Wednesday. "Of course" he said.

The story was leaked less than thirty-six hours later. It came as little surprise to Bruce Crawford or me.[3] President John Kennedy once noted, in referring to the source of leaks, that "the ship of state is the only ship that leaks from the top." Well, Lincoln Center had been a notorious source of leaks for years, and many believed that Paul Guenther could rightly claim a share of them.

We knew that the New York Philharmonic had retained Skidmore, Owings & Merrill to explore the technical issue of whether the orchestra could logistically fit into Carnegie Hall. But we were told that this inquiry was low key, that it was conducted at the behest of a very few vocal members of the board, and that it would go nowhere.

In March, Guenther had told me in a telephone conversation that he was going to walk into the office of Zarin Mehta, the New York Philharmonic's executive director, and tell him to "knock off this Carnegie Hall inquiry." In April, Bruce Crawford told me Guenther had assured him that the notion of the New York Philharmonic going to Carnegie Hall was so unlikely that Guenther would resign as chair if it ever came up for serious consideration. Crawford also reported that in another conversation, Guenther had pledged that the New York Philharmonic would relocate to Carnegie Hall only over its chairman's dead body.

Either the Paul Guenther we saw that May 29 afternoon never had that promised showdown with Mehta, or it yielded an entirely unsatisfactory result. He didn't resign as chair of the New York Philharmonic. In possession of all his vital signs, he failed to redeem his pledge.

Bruce Crawford and I resolved not to become entangled in any personality issues. The most that Crawford would allow himself to say for public consumption was that he and Lincoln Center had been treated in less than collegial fashion by his counterpart at the New York Philharmonic. Crawford's low-key and cool reaction set the tone for Lincoln Center's modus operandi in the months ahead. From our perspective, Lincoln Center's mandate was to serve the public. We turned our attention almost immediately to how best to physically transform Avery Fisher Hall's venue, its programming, and its identity in the wake of the New York Philharmonic's anticipated departure. At our request, Lincoln Center's vice president for programs, Jane Moss, crafted a white paper outlining many exciting artistic initiatives that could take place in Avery Fisher Hall on dates now available for the first time. Its alternative futures were extremely promising. We were enthusiastic about them.

While we were determined to avoid the ad hominem and to attend to wounded feelings, not least our own, we were also confounded by the lack of any logical explanation for what had just happened.

One school of thought had it that Guenther's leadership style was so disorganized and mercurial that to assume negative motives would be to pay him a compliment. Robin Pogrebin, the indefatigable *New York Times* reporter who rightly regarded the redevelopment of Lincoln Center as her exclusive beat, quoted a Philharmonic board member as characterizing the chairman's decision-making process as nothing other than "ready, fire, aim."[4]

Evidence for this opinion included what were widely regarded as two bungled searches for music director. According to multiple news accounts, neither Kurt Mazur nor Lorin Maazel was the New York Philharmonic's preferred choice. The sense was widespread that in Mazur and Maazel the involved trustees had settled rather than selected. Both were septuagenarians, retained at the tail end of their careers. Neither would introduce new repertoire, new energy, or new direction to an orchestra many felt to be in need of them. Neither could connect to New York City in any meaningful way.[5]

Mazur brought discipline and Maazel superb baton technique and rehearsal efficiency to the musicians, but little to excite audiences and impress critics. Indeed, virtually no young conductors—Robert Spano, David Robertson, James Conlon, and Michael Tilson Thomas among them—were given serious consideration in either search. The hiring process in both searches was criticized even by prominent members of the New York Philharmonic board for being uninspired and tactically clumsy.

This same lack of clarity and purposefulness of the orchestra was fully reflected in its confusion throughout the process of thinking through a new hall. First, Guenther and Mehta argued that nothing less than tearing down the existing structure and starting afresh would suffice. Then they contended that following that approach would be too costly and too huge a fund-raising task and would keep the Philharmonic homeless for too long. Then their view shifted to preferring a new auditorium in the existing structure. But soon Mehta, Guenther, and a few other trustees complained that without a new footprint the Philharmonic's needs couldn't be satisfied, that the new auditorium couldn't guarantee world-class acoustics, and that even it would cost too much money.

In 1962, a new baseball team was formed in the National League. Its name was the New York Mets. The near-term prospects for the franchise did not look good. The idea occurred to management that perhaps hiring out of retirement Casey Stengel, the legendary New York Yankees manager, to nurture the motley collection of young players and to guide the "over the hill" types who constituted the Mets' first team would make good sense. Stengel accepted in the hope of creating a decent franchise.

After the first two months of the season, it became abundantly clear that Stengel's hopes would be dashed. The Mets were the laughingstock of the National League, consigned to its basement, last place. At the end of the year, their record stood at 42 wins and 120 losses. And nothing that Stengel could do helped matters much.

Jimmy Breslin reported that Stengel at one point during the season looked forlornly down the Mets bench, shook his head, and plaintively asked, "Doesn't anyone here know how to play this game?"

In October 2003, when the New York Philharmonic announced that it hadn't meant what it said five months before and was "returning," having never really left Lincoln Center, I was quoted as saying, "Welcome home. All's forgiven. We have a lot to discuss."[6]

That remark was not off-the-cuff. It expressed my careful, if seemingly lighthearted, attempt to build a bridge back to a battered and chastened refugee orchestra. After leading the IRC for six years, during which time it had resettled a total of about seventy thousand refugees in America, I could credibly claim to know something about the process. To return home, the refugee needs to advance the case convincingly that he or she is fleeing from danger or is reuniting with family. By my lights, the New York Philharmonic, an institutional refugee, had met the latter test and was therefore entitled to come home. That explains those three pithy sentences. They came by way of an embrace.

Had I been less responsible, or more accurate, or had I simply given vent to my true feelings about the performance of the New York Philharmonic's leadership, I might just as well have quoted Stengel.

THE FLIGHT OF the New York Philharmonic to Carnegie Hall was purportedly designed to achieve freedom from the strictures of the Lincoln Center relationship. But its position as an anchor tenant at Avery Fisher Hall and a partner of Lincoln Center in financing its operations offered the orchestra what Carnegie Hall could not or would not. A wide, almost unlimited choice of performance and rehearsal dates in season. Complete freedom as to what would be performed in the symphonic literature and by whom. The choice of music director and all other staff, artistic and managerial. Control over the New York Philharmonic name and how it is depicted, the sources from which it chooses to raise funds, and the number and kind of trustees that would populate its board of directors as an independent 501(c)(3) nonprofit organization.

Apparently, soon after the triumphant expression of an intention to merge operations was announced with great fanfare, it became abundantly clear that all of these freedoms enjoyed by the New York Philharmonic at Lincoln Center might well be relinquished if it returned to Carnegie Hall.

For decades, orchestras from domestic and foreign cities like Vienna, Berlin, Boston, Chicago, Cleveland, and Philadelphia performed at Carnegie Hall on certain agreed-upon dates. These rarely varied. The New York–based donors and the expatriate supporters of these ensembles attended with enthusiasm. Fund-raisers were held. Some orchestral players brought family members to New York City on holiday. In the media capital of the world, feature stories and critical reviews were much sought after.

Neither Carnegie Hall nor these world-class ensembles were prepared to yield their prime dates to the New York Philharmonic.

As a practical matter, and not even counting the number of needed rehearsals, the 120–130 desirable performance dates of the New York Philharmonic soon began to shrink as the utterly predictable laws of physics were thrown into sharp relief. Two orchestras cannot rehearse or perform on the same stage at the same time. Something had to give. And what ultimately yielded was the New York Philharmonic's wishful, even magical thinking.

How could Carnegie Hall guarantee that one of its world-class visiting orchestras would not play the same music the New York Philharmonic planned to perform in the same season?

How could Carnegie Hall ensure that there wasn't competition for special guest artists between the New York Philharmonic and these visiting orchestras?

How could Carnegie Hall allow free rein to the New York Philharmonic's fund-raising, given the substantial overlap in appeal of both organizations to existing and potential donors?

Lorin Maazel was scheduled to be replaced with a new conductor. As the "owner" of the New York Philharmonic, why wouldn't Carnegie Hall select his successor?

And in the mix was another septuagenarian, Zarin Mehta, the executive director. He must have assumed that a major role would be reserved for him in the new arrangement. The much-respected head of Carnegie Hall, Robert Harth, about three decades Zarin's junior, but with plenty of experience, was extremely well-liked and respected in the field. Anyone who knew Harth understood that he had not joined the venerable organization of Carnegie Hall to be deposed or undermined. Naturally, Carnegie Hall wished to determine who would run the outfit. Rumors spread that if this merger were executed, in a matter of months Mehta would be shown the door.

Shrouded in mystery was whether the New York Philharmonic would actually give up its independent charitable status and dissolve into Carnegie Hall, becoming, in effect, a "line of business." If so, what number of New York Philharmonic trustees would be added to the Carnegie Hall board, and who would they be?

What looked so tempting in theory to the New York Philharmonic faded in the face of these thorny questions. They amounted to one, really: Who would be in charge?

As for Carnegie Hall, what did it find when it belatedly examined with care the books of the New York Philharmonic? Years of consecutive operating deficits and a large unfunded pension liability in excess of $10 million. Harth and Weill also learned to their dismay that the New York Philharmonic's announcement and potential departure from Lincoln Center might well carry heavy legal liabilities. They could cost well over $20 million. Lincoln Center meant business. It intended to pursue its legal remedies.

We patiently explained to Guenther that from Lincoln Center's point of view its constituency agreement with the New York Philharmonic had been breached. As a result, we contended that the New York Philharmonic would be responsible for payment of damages, and its privileges as a resident artistic organization of Lincoln Center were subject to nullification.

One might consider the New York Philharmonic's plans from either the perspective of pursuing freedom *from* a constrained and constricted relationship at Lincoln Center or gaining freedom *to* a promised better deal at Carnegie Hall. What became clear was that the situation at

Lincoln Center was not so bad after all, and the one at Carnegie Hall was more complex and vexing than either side had imagined.

If there were an Olympic gold medal for a sport called backpedaling, the New York Philharmonic would have won hands down. The public reversal of its plans less than six months after a grand public announcement of them was a colossal humiliation.

So much of the difference between the two sides could have been determined by just a little staff homework and by careful consideration of the likely legitimate interests of each party. Apparently, neither happened. I was put in mind of Napoleon's epigram: "Never ascribe to malice that which is adequately explained by incompetence."

Beyond Napoleon's explanation, could there be another? My view is that the New York Philharmonic simply did not wish to raise its share of the cost of a brand-new auditorium in Avery Fisher Hall, $100–$125 million. Even though Lincoln Center had generously offered to pay as much as 75 percent of the $400 to $500 million total price tag, the prospect of a major capital campaign gave many trustees at the Philharmonic the shivers. In its storied history, nothing approaching that sum had ever been raised, and the orchestra's chief professional, Mehta, had not the experience, the willingness, or the ability to take the lead in directing such a campaign. Nor did its board chair, Guenther.

To this day, I do not understand why the nation's oldest orchestra, located in what is by far its largest and wealthiest city, does not perform much better in raising funds. For the fiscal year ending August 31, 2013, the New York Philharmonic's endowment totaled $187.4 million, with an operating budget of $74.2 million. In other words, its endowment stands roughly at 2.5 times its annual spending needs.

Why is it that the Chicago Symphony, by comparison, ended its 2012–2013 fiscal year with an endowment of $257 million on an operating budget of $73 million, or 3.5 times its annual operating budget?

And why did the Boston Symphony's endowment total $421.7 million on an operating budget of $83.5 million, five times its annual spending requirements?

The New York Philharmonic seemed to view its lackluster endowment and its consistent annual operating deficits as reasons to shortchange itself. There is, of course, another option. More generous trustees.

More energetic and compelling fund-raising, by the board and the staff. More galvanizing ideas that spur contributed income.

In most of my experience with the New York Philharmonic, tepidness and an absence of zeal have carried the day. Instead of seeing a new auditorium as an exciting investment opportunity that could catalyze superior fund-raising for both capital and endowment needs, it viewed a major fund-raising campaign as out of reach and unrealistic.

Not so in Dallas, where Meyerson Hall was built for the Dallas Symphony in 1989. Not so in Philadelphia, where the Kimmel Center was erected for the Philadelphia Orchestra in 2001. Not so in Los Angeles, where Disney Hall was christened as the dazzling home of the Los Angeles Philharmonic in 2003.

For the New York Philharmonic, the dominant challenge seemed to be how to find a new home without having to raise substantial funds to pay for it. How sad.

Rumors had it that Sandy Weill, Carnegie Hall's chair, might have offered some kind of substantial commitment to the New York Philharmonic. It was suspected that what Mr. Weill had up his sleeve was an intention to give or raise most, if not all, of the funds needed for the orchestra's relocation to Carnegie Hall. Given his extraordinary generosity to Carnegie Hall for so many of its major initiatives, financial support directed to helping make possible the New York Philharmonic's return there would hardly be out of character.

Besides any financial incentive, moving to Carnegie Hall made it unnecessary for the orchestra to perform for a couple of seasons outside its home while construction occurred. Like the renter who keeps his original apartment until he moves into a new one gradually and conveniently, the Philharmonic envisioned staying at Lincoln Center until Carnegie Hall was ready for it to relocate.

If there were an explicit or implicit offer of financial support to the New York Philharmonic, from a sheer real estate perspective one might call this anticipated arrangement a free ride. But from an institutional, managerial, artistic, and operational vantage point it was nothing short of a disaster in the making. All of this could have been fully predicted by looking at the calendar. Just ask the question why no great orchestra has merged with another institution. Ever. Anywhere. Just consider the issue of who would be in charge managerially and artistically. And what about governance?

Why didn't the Philharmonic staff obtain a current Carnegie Hall calendar and project onto it all needed New York Philharmonic performance and rehearsal dates? Doing so would have immediately clarified how much displacement of Carnegie's regular schedule was needed to accommodate the New York Philharmonic's expectations.

Why didn't the New York Philharmonic board debate the consequences of a merger for the identity of the orchestra, for its artistic integrity, for its management, and for its governance?

Why wasn't basic homework done regarding the impact of a merger on fund-raising, on trustee composition, and on the balance sheet of the merged entity? And why didn't Carnegie Hall's staff and board undertake similar due diligence from its point of view?

The aftershocks of this orchestral round-trip to and from Carnegie Hall permeated the media. No one followed this story more closely than Robin Pogrebin, who originally broke it for the *New York Times*. No one had more or better sources. Writing on October 14, 2003, she summarized the whole affair this way:

> [T]he Philharmonic board itself may ask him [Paul Guenther] to step down [as chair]. Several trustees, who would not comment for the record, said Mr. Guenther mishandled the Philharmonic's planned departure in a way that cost him the confidence of his board.
>
> Several Philharmonic trustees said that Mr. Guenther decided on the merger without consulting the full board, and that he agreed to a merger before having even begun to consider—or had the board consider—the logistical and programming ramifications. They said he assumed the Philharmonic would have primacy at Carnegie Hall without ascertaining whether Carnegie would agree.

I am aware that grade inflation is quite common in colleges and universities, but as an erstwhile professor myself, I'd conclude that there is no way the New York Philharmonic could have received anything other than a failing grade in Management 101 and Governance 101.

THE ULTIMATE IRONY is that not only did both organizations fail to look forward to the first-order consequences of their future relationship, but also neither appeared to look back to their own history together.

Famously, Santayana once observed: "Those who cannot remember the past are condemned to repeat it." I am more partial to Mark Twain's view: "History doesn't repeat itself, but it does rhyme."

A visit to the New York Philharmonic archives reveals that when the orchestra performed at Carnegie Hall, well before it ever moved to Lincoln Center, the relationship between these two artistic institutions was fraught and embattled. From the New York Philharmonic's perspective, the records are replete with complaints, from very serious issues to minor irritants. The lateness of Carnegie Hall in scheduling performances and rehearsals. The terms and conditions of the use of the venue. The sloppy deployment by Carnegie Hall of the New York Philharmonic's chairs and music stands. The feeling was that when given a choice, Carnegie offered foreign orchestras favored dates, to the detriment of its resident orchestra, the New York Philharmonic.

> We ask why the Carnegie Hall administration always favors a foreign orchestra which takes a few dates over and above New York's own orchestra which leases more than one hundred dates. Our objections are both important and numerous and I wish to set them forth so that you will see our position more clearly.

So wrote Arthur Judson, the Executive Secretary of the Philharmonic Society, to Wilton M. Bergerman, acting president of Carnegie Hall, on December 15, 1942.

On January 28, 1944, Bergerman returned the favor in a written volley to Judson, complaining about the Philharmonic's failure to offer a reasonable sum to rent Carnegie Hall's quarters for future seasons:

> Except for the conditional offer of $250,000 contained in Mr. Field's letter, of September 1st, 1943, I have received no direct word from the Philharmonic on their position. I have informed Mr. Field and told you on a number of occasions that an offer of this amount was unsatisfactory and contained no possibility of an ultimate agreement.

> I, too, regret that it has required so much time for the [Philhar-
> monic] Society to formulate an offer of a character warranting seri-
> ous consideration by us.

By the end of the very same year, on December 20, 1944, the matter
still had not been resolved. Bergerman claimed in writing that he was
being treated rudely. The Philharmonic, in the person of associate manager Bruno Zirato, denied that such was the case. He expressed his own
frustration that settlement discussions were at a standstill.

The correspondence is replete with complaints about major matters and small details. It seethes with animosity. The Philharmonic protested other events booked by Carnegie Hall on inconvenient dates. It
importuned management to install water coolers in the corridors and
to repair fans causing a draft on the stage. It beseeched the administration of Carnegie Hall to provide clean meeting rooms free of refuse;
supply toilet paper, paper tissue, and soap in bathrooms; and ensure
that rental tenants began and ended their occupancy on time. There
were arguments about access to the green room, about the cleanliness
of the hall itself, and about the comportment of the ushers.

And all of these matters were aired *following* an ultimatum that was
issued by the Philharmonic in a letter to Robert Simon, the president of
Carnegie Hall, dated three years before, on January 13, 1941:

> If Carnegie Hall is not seriously concerned about the artistic success
> of the Philharmonic, we are seriously considering curtailing again
> our dates at Carnegie Hall and resuming our concerts in Brooklyn
> and the Metropolitan, giving in this way an opportunity of playing
> concerts in a larger auditorium in the case of the Metropolitan, or
> of bringing the music to another borough as in the case of Brooklyn.

Does this sound like a happy tenant? Do these exchanges depict a
benevolent landlord?

COULD THE NEW YORK PHILHARMONIC possibly believe that the
reception accorded it at Carnegie Hall seventy years later would be
much different? Commitments to other ensembles are now far more
numerous, as is the number of Carnegie Hall's own presentations, as

is the number of its rental agreements. For all of these reasons, satisfying the Philharmonic on performance and rehearsal dates would be much more difficult today, not less. To compound these difficulties, the orchestra's expectations of how it would be treated at Carnegie Hall had risen, not fallen.

Even worse is the distinct possibility that the staff and trustees at the Philharmonic and at Carnegie Hall never consulted their own history. If they failed to do so, they willfully ignored their past, Santayana and Twain notwithstanding. If they did pay any attention to yesteryear, then both parties ignored the explicit warnings contained in their history. Either way, shame on them.

Sure enough, over the summer months of 2003, representatives of Carnegie Hall and the New York Philharmonic found that they could agree on very little.

The New York Philharmonic, in the person of Zarin Mehta, expected Carnegie Hall to accommodate all of its needs and to acquiesce in its plans virtually unchanged—on scheduling, on artistic and managerial leadership, and on program content. In a stunning display of naiveté, Mehta wondered why Carnegie Hall would want to merge with the world's third-oldest orchestra only to change it.

For Carnegie, the New York Philharmonic would become only one orchestra among many it would present in the Isaac Stern Auditorium. Although it may have historically played 120–130 dates in Avery Fisher Hall, Carnegie could offer it only about 80 desirable dates in its home. No more. And accommodating the orchestra's request for rehearsal time on the stage of the Isaac Stern Auditorium before every performance was deemed to be simply out of the question.

There was nothing to be gained by pretending. The effort to avoid fund-raising for capital purposes thrust the New York Philharmonic into a subsidiary role at Carnegie Hall, the true cost of which grew clearer and larger by the day.

For all of the bombast that the merger would be a "win-win" arrangement for both parties and a "perfect deal," the incompatibilities between these two important organizations were too basic to overcome. The New York Philharmonic Board was left gasping for breath, wondering about the fecklessness of its leaders, who could allow such a breathtakingly public spectacle to occur on their watch.

The announced merger was star-crossed from its inception, and both parties abandoned it. What we witnessed was a travesty, an escape from responsible governance.

Putting our private, personal feelings aside, the Carnegie Hall caper inevitably set back the New York Philharmonic's relations with Lincoln Center. In attempting to refute members of his own board who had revealed to the press that they were uninformed about the move to Carnegie, Guenther told the media that the matter had been discussed openly at meetings for at least a year.[7] He never revealed to Lincoln Center officials that a New York Philharmonic move to Carnegie Hall was being seriously considered. We had participated instead in what we thought were good-faith discussions about the future of a fully renovated auditorium in Avery Fisher Hall.

In the weeks following the initial announcement of a merger, Guenther, Mehta, and Glenn Dicterow, the concertmaster of the orchestra, disparaged Avery Fisher Hall's acoustics, the very place where the New York Philharmonic had played for four decades.[8] At one point, Guenther was quoted by Deborah Solomon of the *New York Times* as saying that the acoustics in Central Park were preferable to those in Avery Fisher Hall.[9] All of this hall bashing was not only unnecessary, it was unseemly.

Naturally, the trustees and staff of Lincoln Center and many of the constituents were furious. The gratuitous bad-mouthing of Avery Fisher Hall's ambience and acoustics amounted to rhetorically kicking their forty-year host on the way out. It was the height of irresponsibility. We were all angry about the wasted time that had been invested in exploring options that the Philharmonic may have never intended to exercise. And we were upset with the negative fallout of the trashing of the reputation of the hall. After all, Avery Fisher Hall was also the home to Lincoln Center's own successful and critically acclaimed presentations as well as to dozens of highly valued ensembles that rented the space.

Avery Fisher Hall and Lincoln Center deserved better, much better.

Nonetheless, Bruce Crawford and I extended ourselves to Guenther, Mehta, and their colleagues. We swallowed hard and tried to look past the incivility and half-truths to which we had been subjected. We saw our role, publicly and privately, as soothing the ruffled feathers of trustees and employees and rising above the fray. Perhaps the most significant of many steps taken toward these ends was dropping the threat of litigation and of demands for damages, claims we were very confident we could have won had we pursued them.

By our taking the high road, we hoped the New York Philharmonic would learn its own lesson as a barrage of criticism and ridicule swept over the institution and its leaders. We refused to participate in what must have been a humiliating aftermath. We very much hoped that the passage of time would heal wounds.

IT DID.

Belatedly, Guenther resigned. In September 2009 he was succeeded by Gary Parr, a leading investment banker at Lazard Frères. Lorin Maazel was succeeded by the son of two New York Philharmonic musicians, a hometown boy made good, Alan Gilbert. And Mehta was followed by Matthew VanBesien, an experienced executive director of the Houston Symphony and the Melbourne Symphony Orchestra.

We could feel the fresh air. Parr moved to supplement the trustee cohort of the New York Philharmonic with new members. Vital matters were now discussed openly at executive committee and board meetings. The relationship of Parr with Lincoln Center board chairs Bennack and Farley was excellent. Both worked in every way possible to support him in rebuilding trust between our two institutions, as did all of Lincoln Center's employees, with my explicit instruction and encouragement.

Alan Gilbert exhibited poise, intelligence, and reliable leadership from the podium and otherwise. His programming and conducting were extremely well received by the critical press and Philharmonic audiences. He became the head of Juilliard's conducting program. He was a staunch advocate for maintaining and even expanding free concerts in New York City's parks. He championed the music of living composers, not only in a major new Biennale, but in the core subscription program of the orchestra. He participated willingly in the resumption of serious and sustained discussions about the future of Avery Fisher Hall. He understood what it takes to be a cultural leader.

To the delight of all concerned, Gilbert's contract with the orchestra was renewed and now runs through 2017.

On the subject of Avery Fisher Hall, Gilbert's view was far from cramped. It was ambitious. As he energetically communicated to me and others: if we are going to modernize this auditorium, then let's do it thoroughly and imaginatively. Let's get it right. Avery Fisher Hall is now surrounded by a magnificently renovated and rejuvenated campus. We need to catch up in terms of the quality of our facility and the level of energy and imagination we bring to it.

No furrowed brow. No defensive crouch.

He even saw a positive side to being unable to play in Avery Fisher Hall for a couple of seasons while construction was under way. Traveling to different venues around New York City would be healthy for the orchestra. It would enlarge audiences, reach out to new donors, and secure additional loyalists. It would put "New York" back in the name of this venerable organization.

And VanBesien? He was a hardworking, experienced, and competent partner to Parr and Gilbert.

During my last few years at Lincoln Center, cooperation and goodwill dominated the relationship with the New York Philharmonic: in clearing dates for the use of Avery Fisher Hall, in artistic consultations, in refreshing a constituency agreement that required a significant overhaul, and in thinking through what kind of auditorium in Avery Fisher Hall would work best for artists and audiences of the twenty-first century.

Even so, the New York Philharmonic remained beset by challenges. That nagging operating deficit just wouldn't go away. The 2013–2014 operating deficit was $2.1 million, and it was $6.1 million in the prior season. Tellingly, for that just completed fiscal year, the board of directors approved using 6.75 percent of its endowment to support current operations, up from the traditional 5 percent. Had it not instituted this change, the 2013–2014 deficit would have been closer to $5 million.

So, it is clear that the orchestra simply must learn how to live within its means. It also needs to address long-standing structural issues like the continuing lack of a summer home, an asset of so many of the New York Philharmonic's counterparts: Chicago at Ravinia, Boston at Tanglewood, Cleveland at the Blossom Festival, Los Angeles at the Hollywood Bowl. The absence of this source of earned income and an associated, enhanced donor base was difficult to compensate for in other ways.

Retaining a consultant to advise it on setting a course for enhanced fund-raising, the New York Philharmonic became acutely aware of how much, offstage, it had fallen behind some of its admired counterparts around the nation. Too little had been asked of trustees. With a new energetic and cooperative leadership team in place and with the future of the orchestra consensus-blessed, now seemed to be the time for raising expectations of giving and getting. Besides, with the stock and real estate markets at record highs in 2014, there could hardly be a more receptive environment.

It was very refreshing for me to witness the frankness with which the Parr, Gilbert, and VanBesien trio acknowledged these challenges and endeavored to deal with them. Positive changes were frequently announced. They established a partnership with the Shanghai Philharmonic Orchestra and created an annual fund-raiser on the Chinese New Year. They built on a successful summer residency in Vail, Colorado, by arranging for another with the Music Academy of the West in Santa Barbara, California. They began an effort to enhance their endowment and to set aside funds for the future modernization of the auditorium in Avery Fisher Hall. How serious, sustained, and successful the New York Philharmonic's capital campaign will be is an open question.

Together, we hoped to prove that, by looking forward and by moving to higher ground, a most unfortunate episode in the life of our organizations could be overcome. Nations do it all the time. So do corporations. How could two sister performing arts organizations with so much in common conduct themselves any differently?

CHAPTER 7

A Death Foretold and a Turnaround Unheralded

AUTOPSY REPORT ON THE DEATH OF THE NEW YORK CITY OPERA

Office of the Medical Examiner

Symptomatology and Clinical History:	attention deficit disorder; severe hearing and listening deficiencies; sudden wanderlust bordering on edifice complex; low self-esteem; steady audience decline; poor relations with closest neighbor; many months of program suspension and shrinkage; patient given to flights of fancy and magical thinking
Causes of Death:	succession of self-inflicted wounds; severe case of governance failure; poor succession planning, resulting in flawed decisions on CEO selection; trustees too few and too disengaged; charitable contributions wanting; budgets out of balance; endowment shrinking; patient living beyond means; displacement and uprootedness
Contributing Factors:	owner of the David H. Koch Theater aka the City of New York; music critics as cheerleaders and enablers

Institutions are rarely murdered; they meet their end by suicide. They are not strangled by their natural environment while vigorous; they die because they have outlived their usefulness, or fail to do the work that the world wants done.

—DR. A. LAWRENCE LOWELL, President, Harvard University, Inaugural Address, October 6, 1909

The New York City Opera vanished. On October 1, 2013, it declared bankruptcy. A victim of governance failure and management ineptitude, its death was completely avoidable. The cultural capital of the world can easily accommodate two full-time and full-fledged opera companies. Metropolitan-area audiences are substantial enough. Donors are ample and generous enough. Tourism is plentiful. And yet the New York City Opera is no more.

The early signs of serious problems can be found not so much in its programming and even less in its home at Lincoln Center, the New York State Theater. Yet critics prattled endlessly about Paul Kellogg's, then Gerard Mortier's, and finally George Steel's choice of repertoire, as if some perfect formula could be devised that would, once and for all, satisfy their aesthetic preferences and draw ample audiences. Attractive, compelling productions are utterly necessary, but hardly sufficient, to maintain and sustain a healthy opera company. For the enterprise that Mayor La Guardia was reputed to have called "The People's Opera," much more was needed.

Meanwhile, beginning in 2002 Paul Kellogg complained publicly and repeatedly that the house acoustics were not fit for opera. The New York State Theater was built to choreographer and founder of the New York City Ballet George Balanchine's specifications. They required that the footsteps of dancers hardly be heard, a muffled condition supposedly incompatible with a hall acoustically fit for the human voice.

This point of view drove Beverly Sills to utter distraction. Sills had been one of the New York City Opera's biggest stars throughout the 1960s and 1970s. After retiring in 1979 from a singing career that brought her global recognition, she took over as the company's general manager, a post she held for a decade. Kellogg was her successor once removed, and his comments set off a flourish of rhetorical questions she regularly posed to me in confidence.

How could it be, she asked, that an opera company performing in the very space with supposedly poor acoustics could also be closely associated with the rise to worldwide prominence, not just of herself, but also of Placido Domingo, Norman Treigle, Phyllis Curton, Beverly Wolff, Samuel Ramey, and Catherine Malfitano, among many others? What did Kellogg know about acoustical deficiencies that such stars and musical directors, maestros like Julius Rudel and George Manahan, did not? This company was born in 1943, and it had sustained itself at Lincoln Center for almost four decades. And why did Kellogg assume that existing deficiencies, such as they may be (no hall is perfect), could not be addressed by remedial measures to improve the acoustics?

Besides, didn't Kellogg appreciate that the baroque and chamber operas he regularly transferred from Glimmerglass (a summer opera company he also directed, located in Cooperstown, New York) took productions from a nine-hundred-seat hall to the twenty-seven-hundred-seat New York State Theater? Naturally, these programs were likely to be inappropriate for that much larger space, acoustically and otherwise.

Sills's unvarnished view was regularly communicated to me, but in far less temperate language.

While there was much controversy about Kellogg's contention, there was little debate about its consequences.

Audiences listened—to him. If the New York State Theater was not good enough for the New York City Opera to perform in, why should opera-going audience members part with good money and time to buy tickets and see performances, or at least as many as in prior seasons? Persistent declines in attendance started in 2002. No other resident artistic organization at Lincoln Center experienced such severe and sustained reductions at the box office.

Although a dubious proposition at best, if the house that Balanchine built was truly an ill fit for the New York City Opera, then it followed that the search for a new space should be pursued with vigor and as a high priority. With all of the energy the staff and board of the New York City Opera could muster, months were spent investigating the

World Trade Center site in the hope, no doubt, of securing a new hall with substantial federal, state, and local subsidies.

That offer was never tendered, as the city struggled, without success, to have instead the Drawing Center, the Signature Theater, and the Joyce Theater occupy a Frank Gehry–designed, multifunctional space. Twelve years later and counting, the question of whether there will be any resident companies in a Ground Zero arts facility and what may be presented there artistically remains unresolved. Why the City of New York encouraged the Opera to spend so much effort investigating and then applying to occupy this downtown site remains a complete mystery.

The New York City Opera, disappointed that the local community near Ground Zero found its offerings less to its liking than other arts fare, then turned its attention to a private developer, who had purchased what came to be called the American Red Cross parcel, on 67th Street and Amsterdam Avenue. Its footprint was large enough to house not only an upscale all-glass rental apartment complex, but also a modern opera house. Its proximity to Lincoln Center's sixteen-acre campus meant that, at least in theory, the New York City Opera could remain a constituent, with all the associated benefits.

Actually, the Opera requested of Lincoln Center some estimate of how often it might rent the new facilities for its own presentations, just as it was doing in Jazz at Lincoln Center venues at Columbus Circle and just as it continued to do when the New York State Theater was available for events offered by the Lincoln Center Festival and the Mostly Mozart Festival.

The time and resources expended by architects; theater designers; city and state officials, appointed and elected; private developers; engineers; community boards; and trustees to engage in sufficient due diligence on both the Ground Zero and American Red Cross sites was considerable. The regular operations of the New York City Opera suffered as a result of this huge distraction.

Audiences diminished. Operating deficits grew. Staff morale suffered. Uncertainty about the company's future hung in the air like a brooding presence.

Where would it be located? Who would lead it? What was to be its raison d'être?

On April 27, 2006, the *New York Times* reported:

The New York City Opera is close to a deal to build a concert hall in the base of a new apartment building planned for the former American Red Cross site near Lincoln Center.

"They're very close to making a deal; it all looks very good," said Martin J. Oppenheimer, a Vice Chairman of New York City Opera. "The City is very supportive. Lincoln Center was very supportive."

I was astonished. The City of New York had not advanced a financial commitment to the project. No private parties had stepped forward with pledges of monetary support. How could the New York City Opera possibly afford a $300 million capital construction bill? How could it possibly manage to pay for the substantially higher operating cost it would incur post-construction, when operations would begin? After all, this very company had recorded an operating deficit of $3.3 million in 2002, $6.3 million in 2003, $3.9 million in 2004, $5.6 million in 2005, and nearly $3 million in 2006.

Looking for a new home? How, pray tell, board of directors, could the New York City Opera possibly afford one? When asked this question, individual trustees responded with blank faces or assumed that Susan Baker, as board chair, or others close to her knew the answer.

Two months later, on July 4, 2006, this headline appeared in the *New York Times*: "High Hopes Frustrated, City Opera Stays Put—Is the Long Quest for a New Theater Scaring Away Customers?" The "very close to a deal" with the developer A & R. Kalimian Realty had fallen through.

Publicly, the firm stated that incorporating an opera house into the condominium project would be too complex and potentially would be delayed for years, given a likely extensive public approval process. Privately, the Kalimian family expressed little confidence that the New York City Opera could raise the needed funds and become a financially sound, reliable anchor tenant.

At the same time it was generally known that Paul Kellogg, the general and artistic director of the New York City Opera, would retire in June 2007, the decision having been publicly disclosed on September 15, 2005.

Kellogg's announcement gave the board members of the New York City Opera almost two years to find a successor. They inexplicably selected Gerard Mortier, a Belgian impresario. He was unfamiliar with three key elements of running the New York City Opera: earned income (marketing and selling largely unsubsidized tickets), contributed income (raising funds from corporations, foundations, and individuals), and reporting to a board of directors that would determine policy. All of his professional life, Mortier had operated in the European way. National and municipal governments supported opera, with very generous sums. He had hardly ever raised funds in the private sector or fretted about the state of the box office. If he worried at all, it was about maintaining good relations with public benefactors—the ministers of culture.

How could the New York City Opera Board of Directors assume that at the age of sixty-five, Mortier would suddenly develop these new skills? Why did the search committee have confidence that his well-known flamboyant temperament would be transformed so that he could manage compatible relationships with the board *and* successfully solicit private funds *and* offer affordable programs that would attract paying audiences? What could the search committee members have been thinking? There was simply no evidence in Mortier's considerable work history that suggested he could meet these challenges.

Perhaps the search committee hoped that the selection of Mortier would generate excitement and signal the arrival of cutting-edge, avant-garde, artistic adventurism. If so, it seemed to others, to revert to a sports metaphor, that Mortier's selection was a fourth-quarter artistic Hail Mary pass.

As Justin Davidson put it in *New York Magazine* on November 24, 2008, after Mortier was selected,

> some opera watchers warned that he would blaze through a couple of groundbreaking but financially disastrous seasons, then retire back to Europe, leaving the company covered in ash. They were too optimistic.
>
> Mortier made his exit even before his entrance; when the budget he wanted failed to materialize, he walked away, leaving the New

York City Opera with a stack of visionary plans and the specter of a Lehman Brothers–like future.

Mortier contended that he had been promised an annual budget of $60 million, a number he claimed was explicitly specified in his written contract. But the board was prepared to provide "only" $36 million, not nearly enough for the innovative productions he wished to finance. Indeed, Mortier noted that the smallest opera company in France enjoyed an operating budget in excess of what he was being offered. The Paris Opera alone, which he had been running, was blessed with a budget of $300 million, half of which came straight from national coffers.

How could the New York City Opera, after pursuing two different sites to build a new opera house without securing substantial pledges for either of them, then promise to increase its budget by some $24 million, only to renege?

The conclusion of this sorry episode was neatly captured by Heidi Waleson in the *Wall Street Journal* on November 11, 2008. She minced no words:

> In the end, the whole affair was a remarkable act of hubris. To summarily jettison an opera company's history, completely alter its artistic and audience profile, and redesign its funding structure without having identified sources of capital beforehand seems like an exercise in wishful thinking and a highly irresponsible act.
>
> City Opera is an essential public institution with a valuable history. Boards are supposed to take that trust seriously, but this one was blinded by a shiny new toy. Like financial engineers with an outsized appetite for risk, but little understanding of it, they are now left with the shell of a company. It's time for a change in governance, a bailout, and a restructuring. Rescue is needed. City Opera is too valuable to lose.

It cannot be said that the trustees of the New York City Opera failed to be openly taken to task and warned. The press was hardly alone in its assessment of the abject performance of the board of directors. Its many acts of omission and commission were cause for anger and dismay all over Lincoln Center's campus.

THERE IS MORE to this grim epitaph. On August 13, 2008, George Steel was appointed the general director of the Dallas Opera after serving for eleven years as the executive director of the Miller Theater at Columbia University. The choice of Mr. Steel was somewhat of a surprise, as he had no experience running an opera house, and as the Dallas Opera's budget, at $12 million, was four times that of the Miller Theater. Yet only five months later, the New York City Opera, by now in a state of utter turmoil, announced that George Steel would come back from Dallas, where he had just moved, to become its general manager and artistic director.

The Miller Theater housed 688 seats. Its audience consisted largely of students. The price of admission was not much more than the cost of a movie ticket. It was heavily subsidized by its owner, Columbia University. It encompassed no separate governance structure, such as a board of directors. It demanded very little private sector fund-raising.

Steel was credited with imaginative contemporary and early music programming, but the New York City Opera's challenge was several orders of magnitude larger and more formidable than running the Miller Theater. The David H. Koch Theater contained twenty-seven hundred seats, four times more than the Miller Theater. The Opera's budget was a minimum of ten times larger than that of the Miller Theater. I was reminded of Karl Marx's observation that a difference of degree, if large enough, becomes a difference in kind. In moving Steel from either the Miller Theater or the Dallas Opera, it is an understatement to suggest that the search committee of the New York City Opera had chosen someone about to encounter a difference in kind. The selection was nothing short of stupefying.

Satisfying the formidable private funding requirements of the Opera was an utter necessity of the post. Steel had never before confronted anything like it. The New York City Opera also came with a board of directors, and its general director would need to engage it in the context of the whole environment of Lincoln Center, a complex entity. And not least, the New York City Ballet shared the David H. Koch Theater as its home.

If it is true that good fences make for good neighbors, it is also the case that no fences are to be found in this building for which Phillip Johnson was the architect. The Opera and the Ballet quarreled incessantly over matters like scheduling, cleaning, insurance, security, catering, cost sharing, and much, much more. For example, live music played well is integral to beautiful dance making. Kellogg's complaint about acoustics at the New York State Theater could adversely affect not only the New York City Opera, but potentially the New York City Ballet as well. Peter Martins, the ballet master in chief, was said to be livid. He felt strongly that Kellogg was speaking out of turn.

Around Lincoln Center, my colleagues were deeply disturbed by the embarrassing and very public amateurishness of the New York City Opera board and its leaderless and beleaguered staff.

We wondered why the search committee had not opted for a seasoned expert to replace Mortier, one fully acquainted not only with the art form, but also with the basics of leading and managing a formidable nonprofit enterprise. Just to name two possibilities, there was Francesca Zambello, then the director of the Glimmerglass Opera, who had expressed keen interest. Turned aside, she later added director of the Washington National Opera to her responsibilities. Another highly regarded professional, David Gockley, had been the general director of the Houston Grand Opera from 1972 to 2005 and then assumed a comparable post at the San Francisco Opera.

There were others inside Lincoln Center who could also have been excellent candidates. Two hardened, well-regarded veterans reported to me. One was Nigel Redden, the director of the Lincoln Center Festival and the Spoleto Festival in Charleston, South Carolina, who at one point in his career served as the director of the Santa Fe Opera. He is a superb professional. Jane Moss, Lincoln Center's vice president for programs, was the other. She had built an excellent curatorial track record and had won the respect of artists, critics, audiences, and professional peers. Apparently, neither was seriously considered.

The interregna tolerated by the City Opera board between CEOs was also mystifying. The vacuum left after Paul Kellogg's announced resignation and Mortier's on-again, off-again arrival, and the second vacuum as the Opera considered who would step into the stubbornly vacant post, were both extremely damaging.

Each resident artistic organization at Lincoln Center takes pride in its autonomy. Lincoln Center is careful to offer advice and support only when a member of its artistic family asks or when irreversible damage threatens.

After consulting with the chair of Lincoln Center's board, Frank Bennack, I decided to act. I asked Joseph Polisi, the president of The Juilliard School, and Adrian Ellis, the executive director of Jazz at Lincoln Center, to join me in meeting with George Steel as soon as possible after his appointment.

Our purpose was to ask leading questions and to help Steel think about how best to address his major challenges. Polisi had been the president of Juilliard for over two decades, and Ellis, prior to assuming his post at Jazz at Lincoln Center, had founded a successful strategic consulting firm focused on arts organizations. They were highly qualified to join me in offering good counsel.

We met with Steel for some two hours of intense conversation, after which I offered to draft a paper for him and his chair, Susan Baker. If the New York City Opera was going to disappear while I was Lincoln Center's president, it would not be because I had failed to offer my best, uninhibited, and frank advice.

The paper was entitled "The New York City Opera: A Road to Recovery." It pulled no punches. It characterized the Opera's situation as a crisis and called for a revitalized and expanded board of directors, beginning with the resignation and replacement of Susan Baker. It made the strong case to reduce, contain, and control costs immediately. It called for the development of a serious three-year operating plan and business model. It suggested ways and means to raise substantial funds and to begin to repair the damage to relationships with key opera stakeholders.

The report also contained a serious and generous offer of Lincoln Center support.[1]

I had sent along an advance copy to my colleagues for comment and then to George Steel in case he thought some changes were in order before he showed it to Susan Baker. It was important that she have the chance to examine the white paper and think about it as soon as possible. We then arranged to meet with Baker and Frank Bennack for a thorough review of the document.

All of us gathered in my office some weeks later. There, it quickly became clear that Steel had not shared the paper with Susan at all. It even seemed that Steel himself had never read it!

No wonder I had not heard back from him about the paper before our meeting.

Accordingly, it fell to me that afternoon to talk both the beleaguered board chair and the CEO of the New York City Opera through the document. While I spoke, Susan Baker was seething, realizing that her very competence was being called into question. Steel's face was completely blank, as if he now recognized that not giving the paper so much as a cursory look was a colossal error of judgment.

At the end of a very difficult hour and a half, I could tell that Baker was livid.

As she and Steel departed, my mind wandered to the subject of how this disaster in the making could have been avoided. In the life of many professions and institutions, there are solemn moments of declared intent and resolve. For physicians, the Hippocratic oath. For lawyers, fealty to statutes and to judicial rulings. For public officeholders, an inviolable promise to uphold the Constitution.

In nonprofit institutions, such a dignified rite of passage occurs when one is formally elected to the board of directors. And yet seldom is such an occasion accompanied by an articulated pledge of any kind.

Just imagine if Susan Baker and her fellow New York City Opera trustees were expected to affirm their institutional commitment upon election before all of their assembled peers with something like the following oath:

> As a trustee, I pledge to participate actively in the governance of the New York City Opera. As such, I will take care to look closely after the selection of a Chief Executive Officer, to regularly monitor the CEO's performance in office, and to carefully review both the organization's financial affairs and the discharge of its artistic mission.
>
> I recognize that the Opera requires financially supportive trustees, and I will offer generous contributions, consistent with my means. I shall also encourage friends, colleagues, and associates to donate funds.

In executing my responsibilities, I will first and foremost consider the best interests of the institution in its service to audiences and artists. I will not hesitate to voice my view if either my fellow trustees or senior management appear to be straying from the path of fiscal and programmatic solvency in pursuit of the New York City Opera's clearly stated mission.

Would an oath of this kind help to set a peer-driven expectation of responsible governance? Surely it would allow a well-disciplined nominating and governance committee to review the conduct of every trustee and judge the adequacy of his or her financial and service contributions. Come to think of it, this idea of a statement of initiation that all newly inducted trustees would be required to avow might well work for any or all nonprofit institutions.

My reverie about what might have been did not last for long. Soon after our meeting, Susan Baker called Frank Bennack and gave him a piece of her mind about my effrontery. But our conversation had not been about me or her. It was about the future of a precious forty-seven-year-old opera company that she and her board colleagues held in trust for artists and audiences. It was about an imperiled institution well on its way to collapse unless drastic action was taken quickly, as in there was not a moment to lose.

As painful as it may have been for Baker to hear from me behind closed doors about the condition of the Opera and the need for her to part company with it, how much more painful must it have been to read the headline and opening paragraphs in a Pogrebin article in the *New York Times* on June 18, 2009, shortly after our tense session:

> If nonprofit cultural organizations were run like corporations—in which chief executives are at least, in principle, held accountable for financial performance—then the Chairwoman of New York City Opera, Susan L. Baker, might well be out of a job.
>
> During Ms. Baker's tenure, City Opera has raided its endowment—which now stands at $16 million, down from $57 million when she was appointed in December, 2003—to pay off debts and cover operating expenses. The practice, known as endowment invasion, requires approval from the State Attorney General's Office

and the State Court of Appeals and is widely considered a last resort for any arts institution.

. . . During the fiscal year ending June 30, 2008, the company's revenue from ticket sales, donations, and investments fell 23% to $30.9 million, while expenses increased 11% to $44.2 million, amounting to a loss of $11.3 million.

This was the state of affairs that George Steel inherited. Even so, he could have worked much more quickly and effectively to expand the board of directors and to build on the New York City Opera's good name and goodwill. New Yorkers love an underdog. Donors and ticket buyers would need to be convinced that the New York City Opera now knew what it was about, financially and artistically; that it possessed the energy, the will, and the stamina to recover; and that it would reach out to its friends and allies in doing so. Nothing emerged from months of Mr. Steel's tenure to instill confidence in the organization's future. Indeed, in his first full year as director, Mr. Steel presided over a $5.9 million deficit, hardly a source of encouragement.

As I watched in sadness Steel's flailing performance, I was certain of two things: Lincoln Center had not been called upon for help until it was too late to matter, and for the New York City Opera, it was all over. An accumulation of poor decisions had taken their full toll. The die had been cast.

FROM APRIL 20, 2008, until November 5, 2009, for almost eighteen months, no New York City Opera performances were held while the David H. Koch Theater was being renovated. The new hall was hailed, most of all by Steel himself, not just because the space was more comfortable to be in, center aisles having been created in its orchestra, but because the removal of carpeting, the replacement of seat covers, the creation of a stage lift for the orchestra, and the various uses of acoustic shells, among other measures, appeared to have improved its sound. Critics, musicians, and audiences all said so.

Then Steel, having elaborately praised the renovation of his organization's newly modernized artistic home, suddenly announced on May 20, 2011 that the New York City Opera would leave Lincoln Center forever and perform at various places around New York City: City

Center, the Brooklyn Academy of Music, and El Museo Del Barrio, for starters. It would, in itinerant fashion, "go to where the people were." Well, five million of those people who love the performing arts were at Lincoln Center every year, the very place City Opera was leaving. By Steel's calculation, the costs of operating at Lincoln Center were higher than the brand equity of staying in place. The likelihood that Lincoln Center's cachet and prominence would have less appeal to donors than a "now you see me, now you don't" vagabond company was apparently his best guess.

No one followed the New York City Opera's fortunes more closely than Anthony Tommasini, the chief classical music critic of the *New York Times*. He writes with nuance and texture. His prolific reviews have taught me much. Attentive New Yorkers pay heed to the paper of record, and his voice is an influential one.

How disappointing then, that his running critique was so inconsistent, so incomplete, and ultimately unhelpful, even whimsical. Tommasini contributed to the magical thinking that seemed to permeate the New York City Opera's decision making. He supported the City Opera's quest for a new home seemingly without considering its financial consequences or its adverse impact on the company's artistic productions. He was in a very small minority that welcomed the Mortier appointment. He offered an almost Panglossian view of George Steel's selection and of the Opera's future with Steel at the helm.

On November 30, 2009, in "Better Acoustics in Koch Theater Give City Opera a Much Needed Boost," he argued that the "acoustical improvements to the Koch Theater are real and encouraging, and nothing will help City Opera more."

Tommasini was right about the sound, but dead wrong in his conclusion. What would have helped the New York City Opera more were generous benefactors, an enlarged and committed board, and a company truly dedicated to living within its means. These are all matters to which Tommasini paid little heed.

When the New York City Opera surprisingly announced that it was moving out of Lincoln Center, Tommasini declared, "I am all for the City Opera's leaving Lincoln Center." This he wrote less than four months after calling the Koch Theater's acoustics significantly improved and observing that "nothing will help City Opera more." No diligent reader could reconcile these strongly held but diametrically opposite points of view.

In supporting the New York City Opera's decision to leave Lincoln Center, Tommasini found himself in sharp disagreement with no fewer than 120 of opera's most important figures. They had crafted a letter beseeching the New York City Opera to reconsider. Placido Domingo, José Carreras, Sherrill Milnes, Samuel Ramey, Hal Prince, and Frederica Von Stada all were among those who signed their names to that missive. It declared that "to lose City Opera as a vital part of the Lincoln Center family would be felt as a personal loss to each and every one of us, as well as to this great city, and we find it unnecessary and unacceptable."[2]

That letter accused management of "dismembering the City Opera, piece by piece, person by person." It was filled with anger, even fury.

The authors knew what Tommasini did not. A nomadic opera troupe would lose its identity and in fact would quickly become a company in name only, utilizing freelance orchestras, choruses, and soloists in multiple locations for extremely short runs all over the five boroughs.

For years, Tommasini paid little attention to what it took to run a serious performing arts institution. Earned income, contributed income, cost controls, and responsible budgeting appeared to be of little interest to him. He seemed consumed by the artistic properties he wished to see performed in New York, whatever the costs, whatever the risks. His cheerleading for the New York City Opera to take on more elaborate and expensive programming in the face of its financial meltdown was quixotic.

At almost every point of critical decision for the Opera, Tommasini's advice was well intentioned but misguided, his track record unerringly wrong. In a February 9, 2009, *New York Times* online interview, "Talk to the Newsroom: Chief Classical Music Critic," he had admitted: "I can't balance a check book or even organize my desk, let alone run anything." Such self-awareness is laudable, but it did not deter Tommasini from offering many opinions early and often on the City Opera's future as an artistic organization.

With America and Wall Street reeling from the 2008 banking meltdown and with the deepest recession since the Great Depression looming, Tommasini seemed to be living in a world of his own. He was preoccupied with preparing a personal bucket list of artistic preferences, cast in the guise of offering helpful advice to a tottering New York City Opera. Here is what Tommasini wrote on July 4, 2009, offering his recipe for the New York City Opera's success:

> Yet now more than ever, [the New York City Opera] should be bold. Maybe the new Director will adopt some of Mr. Mortier's more intriguing ideas, like importing the haunting English National Opera productions of Britten's "Death in Venice," which starred Ian Bostridge as Aschenbach, one of the hottest tickets in London in 2007. And how about the new staging of Philip Glass' "Einstein on the Beach," with which Mr. Mortier wanted to inaugurate the renovated Koch Theater. And please, New York must finally have a production of Messiaen's visionary "St. Francois D'Assise," another Mortier promise. The Met is not about to take on this five hour spiritual epic. Go to it, people's opera.

The New York City Opera had determined that it couldn't afford Mortier's extravagant opera adventures. They were simply too expensive. So Tommasini had an idea. Why not mount them without Mr. Mortier?

The Met Opera finds it imprudent to produce *St. Francois D'Assise*, so why not prevail upon a financially hemorrhaging New York City Opera instead?

Tommasini was perhaps the most prolific and unrealistic commentator to offer his views regularly on the affairs of the New York City Opera right up to and even following its disappearance. Alas, he was not alone among respected critics in offering unhelpful advice that seemed almost "drive by" in character. Alex Ross, the Pulitzer Prize–winning critic at the *New Yorker*, was also capable of volunteering guidance that at times bordered on the tangential, even the frivolous.[3]

Ignoring the fast-approaching day of reckoning, some still hoped for the best. As late as July 16, 2011, the *New York Times* editorial board continued to harbor and perpetuate the illusion that the revival of the New York City Opera was possible.

> The New York City Opera can no longer afford to be what it once was, and the overwhelming reason was bad management. In the past five years . . . the Opera has overspent its budget and reached into its endowment while underselling its tickets.
>
> . . . Now what is left under George Steel—a roving troupe with a sharply reduced schedule—is a ghost of the Opera's former creative self.
>
> . . . We hope Mr. Steel can begin to rebuild what has been lost.

The best one can observe about such an opinion is that it embodied the triumph of sentiment over reality.

Writing a moving and foreboding plea for the *New York Times* Op-Ed page of June 7, 2011, Julius Rudel, the general director and principal conductor of the New York City Opera from 1957 to 1979, had refused to don rose-colored glasses. After first acknowledging Lincoln Center as the place that solidified the New York City Opera as the town's other opera company, he then offered a fervent request and a forlorn prediction:

> Once before, in 1956, City Opera faced the threat of bankruptcy, but instead of retrenching and cutting, the Board boldly moved forward, securing the financing we needed to stabilize the company and then grow. The current board must reconsider its decision and demonstrate the commitment and vision its predecessors had.
>
> If the board and management of City Opera cannot finance, produce, and support all seasons of new works and standard operas in interesting productions with first rate casts, as we once did, they should be replaced.

Less than six months later, the New York City Opera declared bankruptcy. It performed *Anna Nicole* at the Brooklyn Academy of Music, while publicly announcing that it could not go on as an operating entity without the emergency infusion of $7 million, or two-thirds of its $10.5 million operating budget, by the end of September 2012. No one stepped forward with that kind of financial rescue.

Only twenty months earlier, Chuck Wall, a retired general counsel of Phillip Morris, who had been a member of the board of directors of the New York City Opera since 2001, had taken over as chair, on January 1, 2011. As with much about the New York City Opera, his election was too little and too late. Even the generosity of Mr. Wall, who had donated almost $3 million over two seasons, reportedly more than the rest of the entire board of directors, did not matter in the end. It was all for naught. Leaving Lincoln Center to become an itinerant company was the final act of desperation.

Lest there be any doubt that the captain of the sinking ship had truly lost touch with reality, George Steel gave the New York City Opera's final epitaph during a *New York Magazine* interview, published on October 2, 2013. It was headlined "George Steel on Trying to Save City Opera: 'It Almost Worked.'"

It almost worked? Steel somehow reminded me of Soviet president Mikhail Gorbachev. When he was asked to describe the economic condition of the Soviet Union, he replied: "If you allow me one word, I'd say 'good.' If you allow me three words, I'd say 'not so good.'"

"It almost worked." That's three words.

The fantasies of an inexperienced chief executive in over his head remained intact until the very end. So did the embittered realism of maestro Rudel. At the age of ninety-two, he was very upset and disconcerted. He allowed himself these moving few words on a "real operatic tragedy": "I would not have thought in my wildest dreams that I would outlive the opera company."[4]

May the New York City Opera rest in peace. And may those who lost their jobs and their dreams forgive others who held the company in trust for service to artists and audiences. We all deserve to be very upset with the powers that were. Sacred fiduciary duties were not honored. Accountability for the disappearance of a cultural jewel in New York City's crown was nowhere to be found.

Had the search for a new space outside Lincoln Center, driven by supposed severe acoustical deficiencies, been largely unnecessary? Was Mortier's conviction that there was nothing fatal to the future of the New York City Opera in its staying put at the David H. Koch Theater correct? It surely seemed so.

In any event, the New York City Opera's leaderless condition, combined with a prolonged period of being unable to perform, accelerated its loss of audience and deepened its sense of drift and crisis.

Pulitzer Prize winner Manuela Hoelterhoff, the executive director of arts and culture for Bloomberg News, published a number of reflections on the damage done to the careers of artists and technical staff and to their financial condition. For them, the consequences of poor governance and mismanagement could not have been more tangible:

> Raiding the endowment was a suicidal thing to do. The Board made reckless decisions without thinking of the lives of artists they were ruining. [The Opera's musicians, singers, and stagehands] don't have trust funds. Most don't have pensions. They have nothing but their memories. It makes me angry that there's no accountability.[5]

I stand second to none in my distress about the saga of the New York City Opera's downfall. Its fate was not determined by market forces, or by its location at Lincoln Center, or by proximity to the Metropolitan Opera. These are excuses and scapegoats, not causes of the New York City Opera's demise.

Its misfortune was largely self-inflicted. A suicide, not a homicide. A reckless disregard of Governance and Management 101.

The coroner's report told the tale accurately.

THE ECONOMIST JOSEPH SCHUMPETER developed the idea of "creative destruction." He argued that in a free market, there will always be enterprises that weaken and fail while others grow and thrive. The disappearance of a useful, and even noble, entity is never a pretty sight, but what replaces it can be a surprising delight. We mourn the self-destruction of a beloved organization like the New York City Opera. We could not so easily have anticipated what was about to emerge in its stead, with remarkable speed.

WHILE THE NEW YORK City Opera was disappearing, expressions of concern mounted about the economic viability of the David H. Koch Theater. It had lost not only an anchor rent-paying tenant, but also a cost-sharing partner to the New York City Ballet in paying the over-head expenses of maintaining and operating this mammoth hall.

I was not at all concerned. Here is what I told journalists on background.

> Now that the New York City Opera has left the David H. Koch Theater, it can become the leading dance house in the world. The void left will be filled with this nation's and the world's greatest dance companies delighted by the opportunity to perform much more regularly in New York City and at Lincoln Center.
>
> Expect this new opportunity to be seized by the Paris Opera Ballet, the Royal Ballet of London, the Bolshoi, the Mariinsky and the San Francisco Ballet, among many others. Americans will no longer need to leave their hometown to see a favorite world-class dance ensemble.

Concern about the impact of the Opera's dissolution on the New York City Ballet was not unwarranted. In the program and fiscal year 2009/2010, the Ballet experienced one of its worst box offices in over two decades, and its operating deficit ballooned to $8.5 million on a roughly $60 million budget.

The board of directors was alarmed. John Vogelstein, a founding partner of the firm Warburg Pincus, was about to pass the baton as chair to Jay Fishman, the CEO of Travelers Life Insurance. But before doing so, Vogelstein was bound and determined to fill the vacancy in the post of executive director with a highly qualified professional. Indeed, the leading candidate would be offered the opportunity to join ballet master in chief Peter Martins in reporting directly to the board of directors.

Such a decision, a first in the history of the New York City Ballet, signaled the board's deep concern about the management of operations, from marketing and sales of tickets to customer service, from hall maintenance to auditorium and adjacent space rental, from properly scaling the house to freshening the New York City Ballet's image, and from foundation and corporate fund-raising to major gifts and special events. For an executive director to be accountable directly to the board of directors, along with Peter Martins, was a radical change.

Peter Martins, in his twenty-fifth year as the ballet master in chief and in his forty-seventh year with the company overall, was stretched thin. He needed a collaborator, one in whom he could confide and whom he could totally trust. No one for a moment misunderstood that if Martins was unhappy with the executive director selection, this scheme of dual reports to the board would not work. But all agreed that a shake-up was in order, especially in the aftermath of New York City Opera's departure from Lincoln Center. Concern about an already poor operating performance, which could worsen in light of that recent development, was prevalent.

Vogelstein called during the search process and asked me to be candid about a leading candidate for the job. Her name was Kathy Brown. To my mind, Brown was close to a perfect choice. She loved dance as an art form. She adored the New York City Ballet as an institution. She had been, for a seven-year period, its major gifts fund-raiser, and as such knew her way around the board, the important individual benefactors, the repertoire, and the institution's leading figures, not least Peter Martins. She had held a similar post at the New York Public Library and had enjoyed a successful run there. During that stint, I tried hard to recruit her to become the development director of the IRC while I was the president, a change of field that did not engage Brown's interest.

Instead, she joined Jazz at Lincoln Center's staff, moving from being its superb head of development at a critical early stage in the life of this fledgling institution to become its executive director. From that post, she was wooed to be the chief operating officer of WNYC, the largest and most successful radio station in the National Public Radio network.

Quite unlike Mortier or Steel, here was a professional with truly relevant experience, and then some. Familiarity with trustees and a temperament to relate well to them. Experience in all dimensions of fund-raising. A close student of the New York City Ballet—its programs, its dancers, its rhythms, and its routines. Someone who knew her way around the operations of a complex house, including some difficult unions that had been the beneficiaries of years of sweetheart deals. Most of all, Kathy Brown admired Peter Martins and genuinely empathized with his huge job. It included not only artistic direction of

America's largest ballet company, but also oversight of a closely related nonprofit, the School of American Ballet, directed with skill and finesse by Marjorie Van derCook. SAB is also a substantial operation, with its own operating budget nearing $12 million. Kathy understood Martins. His workload, operating style, personality, and pace of decision making.

She was appointed executive director of the New York City Ballet in mid-December 2009. Positive change was not long in coming. Much of what should go up, rose: trustee contributions, foundation and corporate support, ticket income in a completely rescaled house, rental revenue, morale, and favorable press coverage.

Most of what should go down, declined: head count, marketing expenses as a percentage of earned income, and complaints from patrons and licensees.

Sooner than even I had thought possible, dance companies flocked to perform in the David H. Koch Theater, either as renters or enjoying the good fortune of being presented. The Nederland Dance Theatre. The Paris Opera Ballet. The Alvin Ailey Dance Company. The San Francisco Ballet. The American Ballet Theatre for its fall season (the late spring to early summer run would remain at the Metropolitan Opera House). The Mark Morris Dance Company. The Paul Taylor Dance Company. The Bolshoi Ballet.

As predicted, dance enthusiasts within hailing distance of the David H. Koch Theater were deliriously happy. Only the airlines and City Center were disappointed. The former is now less used by dance mavens traveling around the world. The latter had previously housed Alvin Ailey, Paul Taylor, and ABT and had to bid them good-bye.

By the time I departed Lincoln Center and less than four years after Brown arrived, the New York City Ballet's budget had improved from that significant $8.5 million deficit to a modest surplus. A fund-raising campaign to strengthen the company's balance sheet and to finance additional capital improvements was well along in the planning stages. Touring of the company as a whole and in a nimble, lower cost version had been reinvigorated. And experiments in digital media, including putting some ballet performances in movie theaters, were in advanced stages of planning.

In reflecting on the speed of this remarkable turnaround, I was reminded of a remark of Lenin's that I had first come across many years ago while in graduate school: "Sometimes decades pass and nothing happens; and then sometimes weeks pass and decades happen."

Kathy Brown would be the first to acknowledge that what was accomplished so rapidly resulted from team effort. But high-performing teams need skilled leaders. In Brown, the board of the New York City Ballet found a smart, savvy, hardworking, and utterly likable chief executive.

THE OPERA AND THE BALLET, occupants of the same home, dealt with their challenges very differently. The Opera engaged in escapism and avoidance of its central challenges. The basic blocking and tackling of a successful organization was ignored, as a search for a new home diverted energy and attention from hard and unyielding realities.

The board of directors of the Opera did not insist on a budget in which expenses and revenues were in balance, nor engage in a vigorous debate about the identity of future executive leadership. Its members contributed financially far less than most were capable of offering and far less than what the Opera needed.

At the Ballet, the lesson to be learned is that the quality of trustees and management matter. If they are clear about their respective roles and responsibilities, and if all agree on the challenges to be seized, an organization can turn around and recover quickly. From 2008 to 2010, the Ballet was in an institutional funk, its finances in the red, its audiences eroding.

What changed? Not the market for classical dance, not Mr. Balanchine's and Mr. Robbins's choreography, not even the principal dancers, very much. What changed was the energy, determination, and persistence of sound and purposefully led management and trustees, working together, asking one another for improved performance. What changed was the establishment of a new fall season and improved marketing, as reflected in better box office results. What changed was disciplined trustee monitoring of operations, the establishment of clear benchmarks to be met, and the increasing generosity of the board, with many providing annual contributions of $100,000 or more.

The contrast in board and management comportment was stark. The Ballet now thrives. The Opera died. Why?

Yes, Mr. Martins's choice of the repertoire to be performed, the selection of commissioned work, and the artistry of the New York City

Ballet dancers all matter a great deal to the success of the enterprise. Reasonable fans of ballet naturally differ from season to season and decade to decade in their assessment of the company's performance on the artistic side. But the solidity of the stage on which dance (or music, or theater) is performed depends as much or more on the excellence of management, the effectiveness of trustee oversight, and the size of their benefactions. The New York City Ballet now enjoys first-rate performance in management and governance. It will require continued persistence to maintain that track record.

It is as if all concerned parties had decided to sacrifice on the altar of a cause larger than themselves. At the New York City Ballet, the board and staff might just as well have taken that solemn oath of the kind I had imagined. Its key commitments were being honored rather than ignored or violated. The trustees of the New York City Ballet held themselves accountable for the fiscal and artistic health of the organization.

CHAPTER 8

The Fashionable Landlord

It is not the strongest of the species that survives,
nor the most intelligent but the one most responsive
to change.
   —CHARLES DARWIN

Nothing will ever be attempted if all possible
objections must be first overcome.
   —SAMUEL JOHNSON

For a number of years before my arrival at Lincoln Center, it failed, and by a wide margin, to cover the true cost of maintaining its plant, even accounting for handsome parking revenue and modest public space rental income. One major reason for the deteriorated state of Lincoln Center's buildings and infrastructure was the unwillingness or inability of all involved parties to collectively cover those deficits and to maintain adequate cash reserves to pay for very much-needed remedial work. The well-known developer Marshall Rose told me before I officially assumed my post at Lincoln Center that its budget and those of the resident artistic organizations were in substantial part balanced on the back of deferred maintenance. A decade later, little had changed in the resistance of constituents to joining Lincoln Center in setting aside ample funds for plant upkeep.

With the redevelopment of Lincoln Center concluded, collectively offsetting any public space deficit that might arise or contributing to an adequate reserve fund to pay for future plant repairs should have been acceptable to everyone. After all, the new campus was splendid, modern, and up to date. Its infrastructure was in excellent shape. But in view of the financial condition of most Lincoln Center constituents, varying, in many cases, from problematic to dire, such an expense was one many thought they could ill afford. Instead, they preferred to minimize the assessments needed to keep the physical plant sound. Some simply wished they would disappear entirely. They wanted a free ride. A few constituents even held to the view that if they did not offer financial support, eventually Lincoln Center, "the landlord," would be compelled to absorb the entire bill, just as had been the case in redeveloping all of the public spaces on campus.

Under these circumstances, Lincoln Center sought to limit increases in the expenses of security, engineering, and maintenance staffs to no greater than the rate of inflation. We worked to ensure that all suppliers were subjected to rigorous and frequent competitive bidding. And we looked to generate additional earned revenue in new, entrepreneurial ways.

In 2011 IBM mounted its THINK exhibit on the future of world cities in the underpass to the garage drop-off in front of Lincoln Center as part of its one hundredth birthday celebration in Alice Tully Hall and adjacent spaces. Film premieres and television episodes of all kinds were viewed in Avery Fisher Hall or Alice Tully Hall or shot in Josie Robertson Plaza or Hearst Plaza. Photography shoots also frequently occurred out of doors.

Among the popular premieres featured in the new Alice Tully Hall and in Avery Fisher Hall were *Harry Potter and The Deathly Hallows Part I* and *Part II*, *The Great Gatsby*, *War Horse*, *Lincoln*, *Sherlock Holmes*, *Waiting for "Superman,"* *Les Miserables*, *Mandela: Long Walk to Freedom*, *The Grand Budapest Hotel*, and *Superman: Man of Steel*. The public spaces of Lincoln Center attracted *Gossip Girl*, *Black Swan*, *Sesame Street*, *The Celebrity Apprentice*, *Glee*, and *House of Cards*.

As a result, the redeveloped Lincoln Center now draws into its network newcomers and veterans who regularly rent facilities, such as Warner Brothers, Paramount, Walt Disney Studios, DreamWorks, HBO,

ABC, Universal, Netflix, AOL, PBS, Discovery, Fox Searchlight, and The Weinstein Company.

There were annual investor conclaves. Birthday, graduation, engagement, and wedding celebrations. Product introductions of cars, consumer goods, and clothing. Ceremonies and parties preceding or following film premieres.

Memorial services for famous New Yorkers like Beverly Sills; Robert Tisch; Estée Lauder and her daughter-in-law, Evelyn Lauder; former chair of Lincoln Center Martin E. Segal; Nora Ephron; Lou Reed; and Edgar Bronfman were also held at Lincoln Center. That these families wished to honor the memories of their loved ones on our campus spoke to the centrality and symbolic importance of Lincoln Center.

All of these uses to which our campus was put helped to generate income and to have Lincoln Center be viewed as serving the public, broadly construed. These steps not only assisted Lincoln Center and its resident organizations financially, but it drew to it new fans and loyalists. Over 286 outside, nonconstituent rentals of Alice Tully Hall, Avery Fisher Hall, the Kaplan Penthouse, and the David Rubenstein Atrium generated approximately $6.3 million of net income, and more than thirty-five rentals of all public spaces generated about $4 million of revenue in the last fully recorded fiscal year, 2013–2014.

BY FAR THE BOLDEST achievement was responding favorably to New York City's request that Lincoln Center accommodate a move of Mercedes-Benz Fashion Week from Bryant Park near the New York Public Library to Damrosch Park on the Lincoln Center campus.

After they had spent seventeen years at Bryant Park, even taking into account growing complaints about that venue, it was still necessary to overcome a naturally strong desire on the part of some fashion designers to stay put. Many recognized that needed runways and adjacent spaces were much larger than Bryant Park could accommodate. Others were aware that tempers often flared between the "landlord," in the person of Dan Biederman, the president of the Bryant Park Restoration Corporation, and the firm IMG, which ran Mercedes-Benz Fashion Week. Nonetheless, moving "uptown" and west seemed disorienting to many.

For others, though, the physically transformed Lincoln Center was more than one step up in glamour and comfort. The many venues and restaurant options in close proximity to the fashion tents were a designer's and party planner's dream.

Lincoln Center could offer a 25 percent larger footprint than Bryant Park for both runway and support services and an elegant entryway through one of New York City's most iconic and beloved public spaces, Josie Robertson Plaza, adorned by a brand-new Charles Revson Fountain. We provided plenty of space for generous signage, fixed and dynamic. Within the tent structure, there could be commodious areas for meetings and presentations. No area of the city of New York is better served by mass transportation, subways, buses, and taxicabs. And no public space anywhere is more secure in an already extraordinarily safe city.

Within easy walking distance of Lincoln Center, dozens of restaurants offering all kinds of cuisine at every conceivable price point are available. On the Lincoln Center campus itself, there are no fewer than five dining establishments. Plenty of green spaces have been created for relaxation outdoors, and many indoor spaces as well now have comfortable seating for individuals and groups to relax before and after fashion shows—all in a totally Wi-Fi'd environment.

Even more, Lincoln Center offered many ancillary spaces—for fashion presentations, for press conferences, for social gatherings—in venues like Alice Tully Hall, Avery Fisher Hall, the David H. Koch Theater, the Stanley Kaplan Penthouse, the Metropolitan Opera House, the David Rubenstein Atrium, and the Library for the Performing Arts.

Lincoln Center thought of design and fashion as a key element on the creative spectrum of which the performing arts is an integral part. Lincoln Center, as a prominent civic institution, wished to come to the aid of what was once a thriving garment industry in New York City. The rag trade had seen better days. Even so, according to the New York City Economic Development Corporation, it accounted for a total of 165,000 jobs, generating about $2 billion in tax revenue and $9 billion in annual wages.

Perhaps by elevating the visibility and prestige of its centerpiece show twice a year, in February and September, Lincoln Center could help grow these numbers and strengthen the place of design and fashion in New York City's economy. Besides, the rental fee for a five-year relationship with IMG, beginning in September 2010 and running through September

The most prominent performing arts campus in the world: Lincoln Center.
Photo by John Meloy

The reinvented Alice Tully Hall, inside and out. *Photos by Iwan Baan*

The liberation of Josie Robertson Plaza saw the removal of the mandated concrete blocks and the vivid introduction of sculpture.
Photos by James Ewing/Otto (top) and Tom Powel (bottom)

The author in a rare moment of serenity. © *Joshua Bright*

Lincoln Center welcomes all to its public spaces, free of charge.
Photos by Kevin Yatarola (top) and Mark Bussell (bottom)

A performance of Eiko + Koma in the Paul Millstein Pool and Terrace, adjacent to the Henry Moore Sculpture. © *Kevin Yatarola*

The huge facade of the David Koch Theater was used by David Michalek in his video presentation titled "Portraits in Dramatic Time." © *Nan Melville*

"Meet me at the fountain" acquires a new luster. © *Nan Melville*

The President's Bridge. © *Joshua Bright*

2015, not just for the use of public spaces, but also for designer use of many Lincoln Center indoor venues, was substantial, approaching and perhaps exceeding $20 million. That sum would help to defray the annual operating and capital costs of securing, cleaning, and lighting Damrosch Park as well as maintaining its trees, plants, shrubbery, and adjacent spaces at far less constituent expense than would otherwise be the case.

So, what was there not to like?

Just ask the Peters. Levy and Gelb.

Peter Levy was the relentless and shortsighted manager of Fashion Week for IMG, a high-powered firm representing important clients in sports, fashion, and media. Straight out of the Pulitzer Prize–winning David Mamet play *Glengarry Glen Ross*, Levy didn't bargain or negotiate. He haggled over everything, even after a clear and quite detailed contract was signed, sealed, and fully acceptable to both parties.

Listening to his Cassandra-like cries, you would think the fashion business was disappearing at any moment, and with it, Mercedes-Benz Fashion Week as an enterprise. Listening to him, you'd think that Lincoln Center had not negotiated a rental agreement with IMG at all, but rather that we were some kind of foundation, with IMG its largest grantee!

One of the most energetic and forceful advocates of Lincoln Center as a new home for Fashion Week was the first deputy mayor of the Bloomberg administration, Patti Harris. Apparently the city, together with IMG, had scoured Manhattan for alternative sites to Bryant Park, and Lincoln Center was deemed to be the best.

But in our meetings, I could sense tension and unhappiness everywhere. Between the Parks Department and IMG. Between the Council of Fashion Designers of America (CFDA), chaired by Diane von Furstenberg, the outfit that represented the interests of designers, and IMG.

To develop a better sense of what designers really felt about the impending move to Lincoln Center, I met individually with Tommy Hilfiger, Calvin Klein, Leonard Lauder, and Jason Wu, among others. In marked contrast to the dour Peter Levy, each evinced excitement and enthusiasm for the change in locale, the manifest advantages it brought, and the power of the Lincoln Center brand, one fully compatible with fashion.

If fashion has a reigning priestess, surely it is Anna Wintour. I was somewhat uneasy about meeting her, but David Remnick, the editor of the *New Yorker* and a fellow Condé Nast employee, encouraged me to do so. "Fundamentally, Reynold, Anna is smart, she knows everyone in fashion. Don't confuse her shyness with unapproachability. If you are genuine in seeking advice, you cannot repair to a better source."

We met for breakfast in a private space in Condé Nast's dining room on a hot August morning. Naturally, I paid more than the usual attention to what I was wearing. A neatly pressed and well-fitting, though quite inexpensive, cotton Haspel navy suit, a powder blue shirt, and a very light green silk tie with speckled yellow on it. Anna's first words were memorable, and I have quoted them ever since. "Good morning, Reynold. It's a pleasure to meet you. By the way, that color combination is not half bad."

Now, that's a compliment to take home. Anna Wintour liked what I was wearing!

Wintour provided a tutorial on the history of Fashion Week in New York City. What she liked was that it provided a center of energy, a fixed point around which many other shows of all kinds and all sizes inappropriate for the IMG tents could be spread throughout New York City. In European capitals, there was no such center of gravity. Fashion shows are highly decentralized. Publishers, bloggers, and buyers had to hustle from place to place all around a given city. Just getting to them through the traffic-clogged streets of London, Paris, and Milan was exhausting. Being so spread out is hardly conducive to community or to relaxed conversation between shows.

She also held forth on Bryant Park's severe limitations as a site. No stately entrance. No easy place for black car pickup and drop-off. No orderly lines for entry and exit before and after shows. No place for attendees to conveniently dine or hang out while they waited for their first, second, or third show of the day. An inadequate number of poorly maintained bathroom facilities. Too small a footprint to accommodate designer needs, spanning from the world renowned to the new and the promising.

Lincoln Center would represent an improvement in every one of these dimensions. It also held out hope to accomplish something entirely new—namely, to capture the excitement and allure of these shows for the trade by finding ways to invite the public to participate as well.

The deficiencies of the current arrangement were not simply physical. The former executive director of CFDA and the creative director of Fashion Week for IMG, Fern Mallis, was soon to depart the firm. That left Peter Levy, who was widely viewed as a guy too focused on costs and lacking an appreciation for value to be the key figure to relate to designers. Many of them were eager to collaborate with someone from IMG or elsewhere in crafting their shows. Levy could not be that someone.

He employed a technically proficient staff for building sets and for scheduling cheek by jowl eleven- to fifteen-minute shows with amazingly short load-in and load-out intervals. They also handled the some one hundred thousand people who attend one or another event in a compressed eight consecutive days with relative ease. By nature, Levy himself seemed quite shy and more than a little intimidated by the creative side of the fashion business. His BlackBerry was his escape mechanism. He stared at it or placed phone calls while the VIPs of the industry walked right by him.

So Anna asked me directly: Who will be Lincoln Center's ambassador to the design community? Who will listen to the needs of insecure new designers and ambitious designers of prominence and help them organize their shows, presentations, and parties at Lincoln Center? And who might help Wintour herself plan a huge fashion show right on Josie Robertson Plaza that would be nationally broadcast and would help launch what would become a countrywide post–Labor Day shopping experience called Fashion's Night Out?

I was having a lot of fun regaling female trustees like Ann Ziff, Anna Nikolayevsky, and Katherine Farley of Lincoln Center with lines like, "Did you know that Dennis Basso was no longer working so much with fur?" "Have you caught up with Francisco Costa's new line (it is fabulous)?" "Do you plan on seeing Jason Wu's show at the St. Regis (the buzz is that it will be sensational)?" "Aren't Oscar De La Renta and Carolina Herrera unbelievably inventive? What a track record of consistently beautiful and alluring clothing." "If you check out the latest from Rag and Bone, Theory, Rick Owens, and Prabal Gurung, you won't be sorry."

But truth to tell, my knowledge of fashion ran, as Dorothy Parker would have put it, from A to B. And besides, I had no time to be that fashion ambassador. Done properly, it was more than a full-time post.

By now, Anna Wintour's reputation was as outsized as the September issue of *Vogue*, so laden with advertisements that the Equinox Sports Club could package two or three issues, tie them together, and use them for weight training. The documentary *The September Issue* had just been released to movie theaters, to excellent notices. And only two years before, Meryl Streep had played an Anna-like character with style and aplomb in *The Devil Wears Prada*. Anne Hathaway portrayed her harried, omnicompetent assistant, and Hathaway's career had flourished ever since.

Wintour's recommendation to assume that role of ambassador was a case of life imitating art. Her name was Stephanie Winston Wolkoff, and she was as close as one can come to the Hathaway character in real life. Having worked for Wintour for the better part of a decade, the strikingly beautiful, six foot one, former Fordham University basketball standout was credited with executing the annual event dreamed up by Wintour: the Metropolitan Museum of Art Costume Institute gala.

The highlight of the New York social season, no event matches it for glamour, glitterati, and paparazzi. Many a marquee movie and television star and others from the worlds of journalism, sports, theater, opera, and of course fashion, gather together to enjoy each other's company. It sets the standard for fund-raising in high fashion, not only in New York City but around the world.

Apparently Wolkoff also handled many other special events for Anna and did so with poise, polish, and painstaking attention to detail. After a couple of meetings between us, she was retained as Lincoln Center's director of fashion, and she took our place by storm. Suddenly, spaces that had never before been utilized for fashion shows, or presentations, or parties were transformed into perfect venues. Such results required verbal dexterity, problem solving, creativity, inexhaustible energy, and not a little forceful charm. When one of our senior staff members was caught having committed some seating errors at an event Wolkoff was planning, she became so angry that he expressed concern about the possibility of being subjected to "death by stiletto."

Tommy Hilfiger held his twenty-fifth anniversary celebration at the Metropolitan Opera House. Avery Fisher Hall and the David H. Koch

Theater became venues for Lagerfeld and Valentino as successive award winners of the Fashion Institute of Technology's annual prize for career achievement. Fashion shows sprang up outdoors in Hearst Plaza and around the Paul Milstein Pool and Terrace; in the new restaurant, Lincoln; at a white box space in the Library for the Performing Arts; in various locales of Alice Tully Hall; and in the Kaplan Penthouse. The CFDA Fashion Awards; photo shoots by *GQ* and Michael Kors; presentations by *Harper's Bazaar*, Rachel Roy, and Derek Lam; a book party for Eleanor Lambert; a blogger conference by Decoded Fashion; and a Barbie's Dream Closet installation in the David Rubenstein Atrium numbered among dozens more such attractions.

Serving as the intermediary between high-strung, ego-laden designers unaccustomed to new spaces and uptight facility managers at Lincoln Center, who were far more comfortable with concert artists than with famous models (and their handlers), wasn't easy. When Wintour chose the word *ambassador*, I soon learned that she meant that the height of diplomacy would be required. In recommending Wolkoff, she knew who would best fit that bill.

Wolkoff was part of the Harry Winston jeweler family, a mother of three, and married to a very accomplished and successful real estate developer. In terms of status and net wealth, she was more like a trustee than a staffer. Her employees took their vacations at home. She took hers at exotic destinations. But for her own impeccable sense of style in clothing and accoutrements (over some two years, I do not recall ever seeing her wear the same item of clothing more than once), you would never know her economic status. She was as hardworking and unspoiled as anyone employed by Lincoln Center.

Eventually, the incessant feuding with IMG and the reality of Lincoln Center as first and foremost a performing arts institution wore her down. I could intervene on her behalf and ask staff to bend and flex to accommodate the whims of fashion designers not known for advance planning, by which I mean next week or even day after next. But I could not insist that staff treat fashion designer needs as the be-all and end-all of their working days while neglecting other key responsibilities. After a couple of years, Stephanie took her leave of Lincoln Center, but not before she had successfully identified the world's strongest brand in the performing arts with fashion. No small accomplishment.

When Lincoln Center took the high road and engaged designers in genuine dialogue, it was they who demanded to use our ancillary spaces. No corporate suit from IMG could cite any obscure provision in a legal agreement to get in the way. Peter Levy attempted to use an embargo clause in our contract, which would have prohibited any fashion event in Lincoln Center public spaces or private facilities ninety days before a February or September Mercedes-Benz Fashion Week. It was effectively neutralized. Ultimately, the success of IMG ownership of Fashion Week depends on the cooperation of talented designers, famous models, and influential publishers. By cultivating them directly, Lincoln Center largely checkmated Peter Levy.

When Lincoln Center joined forces with Ralph Lauren to hold a fund-raiser that also featured Oprah Winfrey, to benefit both the Ralph Lauren Cancer Center and Lincoln Center, IMG had no choice but to acquiesce. In fact, the firm contributed handsomely to a $7.5 million gate by purchasing a table.

SOON AFTER IT WAS announced that Lincoln Center would become the home of Mercedes-Benz Fashion Week, the fashion designer Ruben Toledo grabbed collaborator/wife Isabel and cornered me at an El Museo del Barrio gala. He wanted to know whether I really had any idea of what I was doing. "We are all crazy, Reynold, really crazy. We are totally self-referential."

When I pointed out that world-famous sopranos were not exactly selfless creatures, he shrugged his shoulders as if to say "you ain't seen nothing yet." Isabel nodded in assent.

Well, they were both right, but not about the identity of the source that would give me the most headaches.

Yes, the other Peter. Gelb.

From the moment the very idea of Mercedes-Benz Fashion Week moving to Lincoln Center was mentioned, Gelb vigorously opposed it, and very publicly. He claimed that the name Mercedes-Benz emblazoned on signage would commercialize Lincoln Center (as if we didn't already enjoy dozens upon dozens of corporate sponsors who were not shy about being visible on our campus). He professed grave concern that the bass level of the sound track that accompanied models as they strode down the runways in the tents would "bleed into" the opera house and interfere with rehearsals and performances. (At Lincoln Center's expense, extra sound absorption baffling was installed in the tent adjacent to the Met, and the doors leading to the opera house were treated with special insulation so no noise could possibly penetrate.) He worried that crowds entering the tents would be noisy, maybe even rowdy, and would interfere with the "peaceful enjoyment" of Josie Robertson Plaza. (Who in their right mind would gather in the below-freezing plaza in February waiting to attend either a fashion show or a Met performance, and how could any such assembly in September interfere with Met audiences when the Metropolitan Opera doesn't even open until after Fashion Week concludes?)

These baseless contentions—*rowdy* crowds?—were easily addressed. Infuriatingly, Peter willfully ignored all of the advantages—financial, reputational, artistic, and civic—Fashion Week and Lincoln Center brought to all concerned parties.

What's more, Gelb insisted on seeing a copy of the contract that Lincoln Center had negotiated with IMG. Indeed, he actually wished it to be reopened so that the Metropolitan Opera could be made a party to it!

At this point, my even-tempered chairman of the board, Frank Bennack, fully aware that Peter's legitimate concerns were being satisfied and knowing well, as the chair of the Metropolitan Opera's audit committee, how much the Met could use its share of funds derived from Fashion Week, told his mildly protesting Met board chair counterpart, Bill Morris, that Peter should back off. Frank did so in a most soft and gentle manner by offering to summarize the contract orally for Mr. Morris, if he wished. To my knowledge, that offer was never accepted, and the issue was not raised again.

As I write in 2014, it is no small irony that the person most concerned about how long Fashion Week would remain at Lincoln Center and about whether Lincoln Center's contract with IMG for Fashion Week can be extended is none other than Peter Gelb. He acknowledged no contradiction or irony in the 180-degree turnaround. But every time I saw him, he asked how my efforts to elongate Fashion Week's length of stay were proceeding. All concerns, real or feigned, about commercialism, acoustical bleed, and noisy, loitering campus visitors seemed suddenly to have completely disappeared. Amazing.

I RECALL AS a child growing up in Brooklyn turning the pages of my mother's copies of *Women's Wear Daily* at nine years of age. In part, I was motivated to do so by sheer curiosity. Why was Mom devouring this newspaper, which arrived daily in our mailbox? But I was also curious because my dad earned a living for years as a presser in the garment industry. Up at 5:00 a.m., he worked from 6:30 a.m. to 2:30 p.m. every weekday and then boarded the D Train in Manhattan, traveling halfway home, to complete his bachelor's degree at Brooklyn College.

Weekends were largely devoted to Dad studying. But there were also long walks on the boardwalk, playtime at the beach, and meals out together as a family. We watched the fireworks from the rooftop of our apartment building every Tuesday night, brought to us by Schaefer Beer. We sometimes spent a summer night sleeping across the street in Seaside Park to escape from the stifling heat of an un-air-conditioned apartment with no cross-ventilation, facing only an inner courtyard.

Not infrequently, Dad talked to Mom about the latest style of pea coat, the hottest colors for the coming fall, the pros and cons of the one- or two-piece bathing suit, and the proper length of a hemline.

In our family, window-shopping, as distinct from buying, was a frequent activity. At an early age, I knew that a man's shirt sleeves should protrude about one and a quarter inches from the suit jacket and that cuffed pant legs should drop ever so gently over the back heel of a shoe. By the time I was twelve, I could recognize the names Hart Schaffner Marx and Hickey Freeman, well before I ever became familiar with Beethoven, or Bach, or Brahms.

In a real sense, then, I grew up in the rag trade. Dad left it for the mutual fund and insurance business, but a sense of fashion and style never left him or Mom.

That Lincoln Center in some modest way helped a struggling garment industry to revive in New York City would have given them an enormous sense of pride. That Diane von Furstenberg, a Hungarian Jewish refugee of wrap dress fame, would know me by my first name could only have been a source of utter astonishment to my parents.

LEST IT SEEM that this initiative was totally successful, be assured that there were problems, particularly from the perspective of some of Lincoln Center's neighbors. These quality-of-life concerns are worth highlighting. You will find them at the intersection of almost all major public events and occasions. While citywide in their importance, they impose collateral costs on the local community.

How do East Siders feel about the bumper-to-bumper traffic up and down First, Second, and Third Avenues for days on end when the United Nations is in session, particularly during its opening weeks in September, as heads of state from every continent make their way around that small and dense island called Manhattan?

What is the reaction of most New Yorkers to crowded midtown streets cluttered by tourists, whose annual numbers almost doubled during Mayor Bloomberg's tenure?

The new, very tall residential skyscrapers on 57th and 59th Streets that cast shadows on Central Park from apartments often uninhabited by foreign investors drew loud protests from park advocates and preservationists.

This conflict between the interests of the commonweal and the adverse impact on a given local community was at play on the Upper West Side.

In preparation for the arrival of each Fashion Week, which runs about thirty-five days, including load-in and load-out, Lincoln Center urged the City of New York to insist that IMG conduct its business with careful attention to minimizing community disruption. After all, Lincoln Center's immediate neighbors had just endured more than a billion dollars of redevelopment construction activity. During that six-year period, our staff was exceedingly careful about formulating and communicating plans in ways that took fully into account the concerns of the BID, the Community Board, elected officials, and key co-op and condominium owners. All of these stakeholders had also experienced the construction of an unprecedented number of high-rise residential skyscrapers with attendant escalating motor vehicle traffic and demands on public services—fire, police, sanitation, and schools among them. Just south of 62nd Street, the site of Fashion Week, Fordham University was in the midst of constructing a new law school and dormitories. And developer Lenny Litwin was building a new rental apartment house immediately to the west, on the corner of Amsterdam Avenue.

We warned the city that completely closing off 62nd Street to automobile passage would result in a traffic stranglehold on Amsterdam

Avenue and across 65th Street to the East Side of Manhattan. We implored the city to have IMG erect well-marked and well-lit pedestrian walkways for Lincoln Center patrons, for the students and faculty of Fordham, as well as for tenants to the south and west. We urged that attention be paid to the noise emanating from generators temporarily installed to provide electricity to the tents or emitted by unloading dumpsters after 10:00 p.m. and before 6:00 a.m., or by trucks backing up during the same hours. We outlined the ways and means Fashion Week could manage its operations with far less disruption to the lives of Lincoln Center's patrons, employees, and neighbors.

City Hall simply would not listen. The prevailing attitude seemed to be that Fashion Week was good for New York City and that it brought considerable business and employment to the neighborhood. According to IMG, each fashion season attracted a total audience of one hundred thousand and generated about $800 million of favorable economic impact. In every community, there are complainers and cranks. So be it. We at Lincoln Center were far more sympathetic. We "lived" on the campus and understood that some of these grievances were legitimate and could be readily and easily addressed.

Not until a lawsuit was threatened and then filed were many of the action recommendations we advanced taken seriously. Mufflers were installed on those generators. Pedestrian walkways suddenly appeared. Vehicular traffic was permitted on a reduced schedule. Crews took care to engage in garbage disposal only during work hours, as did most trucks when in reverse gear. Fashion Week and neighborhood serenity became more compatible when representatives of the city were ordered by their superiors to listen more attentively and to act accordingly.

Maintaining New York City as an economically vibrant world capital and keeping Manhattan a relatively pleasant place to live and work are sometimes conflicting objectives. Most often, reasonable compromises can be reached and accommodations struck. Ultimately, such was the case with Fashion Week. The generation of $800 million of economic impact and the maintenance of a semblance of serenity for its neighbors were both possible. But only if citywide economic imperatives were reconciled with legitimate community concerns.

CHAPTER 9

A Year of Reckoning at the Met

> A convalescing patient who does not finish their course
> of treatment takes a grave risk.
>
> —LAWRENCE SUMMERS

The figures are staggering.

In a single year, more people come to see a performance at the Metropolitan Opera House than reside in all but nine of America's cities. The Met stages twenty-three operas annually. To view as many pieces of repertoire in a single season elsewhere would require you to attend the entire seasons of at least four, sometimes five, other leading opera companies around the nation.

The Met's 2013 annual operating budget stood at about $330 million. No performing or visual arts organization of any kind approaches that figure in America, except for the comparably sized Metropolitan Museum of Art. The Met Opera's operating budget is actually larger than the next eight largest opera companies in America combined. Number two is the San Francisco Opera, and its annual expenditures are only 20 percent of those of the Metropolitan Opera, or $68 million.

The Met's payroll embraces 3,400 full-time, part-time, and seasonal employees. They include 140 musicians, 80 full-time chorus members, and employees represented by no fewer than sixteen trade unions. To appreciate the complexity of just the unionized workforce, consider its composition by functional category. Orchestra musicians and librarians.

The chorus, principal singers, directors, and stage managers. Ushers and ticket takers. Cleaning staff. Porters, security guards, and office service workers. Call center employees. Building engineers. Box office treasurers. Costume and wardrobe. Camera operators. Wigs, hair, and make up. Scenic artists and designers. Parks crew. Bill poster. Painter.

Both in the sheer number of employees, union and management, and in the intricacy of its organization, the Met Opera's workforce dwarfs any other performing arts entity in this country.

The Met Opera's artistic productivity also knows no equal. In Peter Gelb's first decade at the helm, the Met will have presented sixty-two new productions and introduced seventeen new works to its repertory. The comparable number in Joe Volpe's last decade as general manager was forty-five new productions and twelve Met premieres.

To be in charge of an operation of this astonishing size, scope, and elaborateness is a formidable management assignment. For someone who works in this or a related field, the likes of Joe Volpe or Peter Gelb, the two Met Opera general managers who presided during my tenure as Lincoln Center's president, must evoke empathy. Theirs is a tough job. It is not easy to balance divas and dollars, season after season. Satisfying demanding audiences and critics, particularly in the media capital of the world, is a constant battle. And endeavoring to contain expenses and expand earned and contributed revenue every single year cannot be easy.

When it was announced in October 2004 that Gelb was to succeed Volpe, effective in August 2006, the Met Opera's board of directors wisely put him on the payroll immediately. Volpe remained in charge of the place, fully accountable for its operations. Everyone recognized that there can be only one general manager at a time. But for about eighteen months, Gelb was free to study the inner workings of the Met, to become acquainted with its personnel, to meet board members and important donors, to travel extensively, and to begin to sketch out his plans. Allowing for this kind of prolonged transition is a smart move, one that other complex nonprofit institutions would do well to consider, particularly when the incumbent being replaced has enjoyed a long tenure.

As a result, Gelb's first years in office were well planned. With relentless energy and a single-minded ferocity, he implemented a broad and sweeping action agenda. Mount more fresh productions of standard repertoire and more commissions of new operas. Engage theater directors to shape creative approaches to the stage, coaching the world's greatest singers in dramatic settings that do them justice. Open one of the oldest art forms to new and wider audiences. Subsidize low-priced, day-of-performance tickets. Offer free-of-charge broadcasts on Josie Robertson Plaza, allowing some four thousand attendees for ten successive evenings to enjoy shows in the open air. And, most significant, simulcast operas, eventually to several thousand movie theaters around the world.

Superbly telecast and featuring inventive interval content, this initiative now reaches three to four times the some eight hundred thousand operagoers who make their way each year to the Met itself. At about $22 a ticket, this come as you are, bring your children and grandchildren, munch on popcorn, relaxed approach to opera attendance has spread rapidly. It has been emulated by many other opera companies and in theater and dance as well. Arguably, these cinema transmissions, an initiative justifiably credited to Gelb, may have in a single stroke accomplished as much for the exposure of opera as an art form to an enlarged audience as did simultaneous language translation projected onto screens or seat backs. Truly, movie simulcasting is a transformational development for opera as an art form.

Of course, not all of Peter's new productions have been well received. His selection of directors has resulted in a mixed record. Perhaps his most criticized step was to commission a new *Ring Cycle* from the director Robert Lepage. It was an unmitigated disaster. Critics abhorred it. Audiences stayed away. The computer-driven pyrotechnics often did not work. Writing in the *New Yorker*'s March 12, 2012, issue, Alex Ross described Lepage's *Ring* as "pound for pound, ton for ton . . . the most witless and wasteful production in modern operatic history. Many millions of dollars have been spent to create a gargantuan scenic machine of creakily moving planks, which have overshadowed the singers, even cowed them, without yielding especially impressive images." Another poorly rated production was Luc Bondy's *Tosca*. From dreary lighting and vacuous sets to simulated onstage sex, this was not the Met at its best. In these cases, Gelb's risk-taking did not pay off.

Other shows—like *The Nose*, directed by William Kentridge; *Madama Butterfly*, directed by Anthony Minghella; *Le Compte Ory*, directed by Bartlett Sher; *Maria Stuarda*, directed by David McVicar; *Don Carlo*, directed by Nicholas Hytner; Verdi's *Falstaff*, directed by Robert Causen; *Prince Igor*, directed by Dimitri Tcherniakov; and *Parsifal*, directed by Francois Girard—were among many much-applauded productions.

The curatorial staff at Lincoln Center admire Gelb's boldness, even though they may not agree with all of his artistic choices. His drive to marry theatrical flair and superb staging to singing and music of the highest quality merits respect and enthusiasm. There will be ups and downs in any given season. So what? No one can point me to an artistic season that has been uniformly and universally praised, let alone in the world's busiest opera house.

What has been everywhere admired is the consistently high quality of the Metropolitan Opera Orchestra. With the fragility of music director James Levine's health and his on-again, off-again ability to conduct, Peter has secured guest maestros of enormous stature and promise. Daniel Barenboim. Esa-Pekka Salonen. Yannick Nézet-Séguin. Riccardo Muti. William Christie. Valery Gergiev. And of course, Fabio Luisi, who stepped in on very short notice in 2011 to become the principal conductor of the Metropolitan Opera Orchestra when Levine could not perform. Levine's baton has been in very good hands awaiting his return to a consistent workload. Gelb could not have handled this delicate situation more elegantly.

IT REMAINS UNCLEAR whether free performances, low-cost tickets, and cinemacasts have improved full-priced attendance at the Met or actually reduced it. The stakes are high. In recent seasons, according to the Met, the percentage of the house sold has been around 79 percent. What share of those sales were at full price and what proportion discounted is not readily knowable. But each percentage point, up or down, is worth roughly $1.5 million to the Met's coffers, if the tickets are sold at "rack rate."

Even as Gelb expanded discount prices at the lower end, he has experimented with hiking them elsewhere in the Met's more desirable seating areas, earned income being critical to the struggle to balance the budget. During his seven-year tenure the Met's annual expenditures catapulted from $210 million to $330 million. To pay for this stunning budget escalation requires major growth in earned income from ticket sales and close to double-digit percentage increases in donations year over year. Projecting that both would mushroom simultaneously has proven to be a very high-risk bet.

On the earned income side, some of the Met's price increases have met with resistance and had to be rolled back. As to contributed income, annual fund-raising totals, impressive though they may be, still fall far short of what the Met Opera requires to truly balance its budget and to build a healthy balance sheet.

Some close observers of the Met, most particularly its loyalists, have been heard to complain that expense growth during Peter's tenure has not only outpaced inflation many times over, but has also been too dramatic to be covered by either the aggressive marketing of tickets or the multiplication of fund-raising events and solicitations.

This bridge too far has caused the erosion of the endowment. In some years, for the Met to "balance its budget" more than 8 percent of the endowment was tapped. Few nonprofits permit greater than 5 percent of endowment spending as a matter of prudent and strict policy.

The Met's more relaxed and flexible approach has caused its endowment to be reduced to some $267 million, roughly $50 million less than its fiscal 2013 operating budget. In 2006 that endowment number stood at $305.8 million. Its $40 million decline since then is especially noteworthy, as the stock market from 2009 forward has experienced record gains, from which the Met hardly benefited because funding its operations required annual reductions in endowment principal.

Even that pattern and practice proved insufficient. As a consequence, the Met found itself needing to borrow $100 million in 2012 to access cash for its operations. It was the Met's first bond sale in its 129-year history, but without it, there would be far more bills than available funds to pay them.

The Met has also carried a large and growing unfunded liability for its union pension funds. And the necessary expenses of maintenance, repair, and the purchase of new equipment, for the most heavily used opera house in the world, have been frequently deferred.

The tough and bitter negotiations with all of the Met's unions were a response to these realities. When it is compelled to place the world-famous Chagall tapestries that grace the front of the Metropolitan

Opera House as collateral on a loan, then it must be concluded that the Met's financial situation is grave.

BY THE SPRING of 2014, it had become abundantly clear that the course Peter Gelb had set for the future of the Metropolitan Opera was not working. Anticipating tough collective bargaining to come, Gelb told the *Guardian* that the Met now faced a serious crisis. On June 6, 2014, the *Guardian* carried this startling direct quote from Gelb: "This battle is an existential one that has to be won. If we're not able to create a more sustainable business model now, we know we will face a bankruptcy sometime in the next two or three years." In other words, if collective bargaining did not result in major union concessions, then the Met would confront economic insolvency. The *Guardian* quoted Gelb as saying that the Met was at "the edge of the precipice."

This was a remarkable admission in both its suddenness and its gravity. By the summer of 2014, I'd been gone from my post at Lincoln Center for only six months. Yet the starkness and the specificity of Peter's foreboding alarmed even me. Of course, it was intended to let the unions know that the Met was serious and that its financial condition required of them unprecedented concessions. But it also sent a message to donors, current and potential, that the economic model in accordance with which the Metropolitan Opera had been operating was fatally flawed. And it did nothing to lift the morale of Met Opera employees increasingly concerned about their own professional security.

Indeed, the faithful reader of the *New York Times* might remember Daniel Wakin's reporting on July 27, 2011, fully three years earlier. In an unusually precise story about the state of the finances of the Met, he summarized them in one paragraph. It crisply foretold what would soon come to pass:

> The Metropolitan Opera under Peter Gelb has an accumulated deficit of $51 million and pension funds are $78 million underfunded. The endowment stands at $243 million, off more than $100 million at its pre-recession peak.

Even sixteen months earlier, Nina Munk, in a very long story written for *Vanity Fair*'s March 30, 2010 issue, "The Met's Grand Gamble," commented on the unusual difficulty in acquiring accurate information about the Met's financial condition. She then summarized what she had learned:

> In the past three fiscal years, since Gelb became general manager, annual expenses have soared by 27% to a frightening $252 million in fiscal 2009—almost four times what it costs to run the San Francisco Opera, the second biggest opera company in North America. This, while revenues from box office, movie tickets and other media (television, radio, video) were a mere $110 million last year.
>
> More worrisome data emerged: the Met's endowment, never impressive to begin with, had collapsed from a high of $336 million in fiscal year 2007 to $247 million in fiscal year 2009. The stock market is down, of course, but that's not the only reason the endowment has shrunk: badly in need of cash for its operations, the Met has quietly (and in retrospect) imprudently drawn down its endowment by a total of $61.5 million in the past three years. At the same time, the so-called draw down rate jumped to 8.3% of the endowment last year, well above the 5% rate considered appropriate for nonprofits. How long can that aggressive draw down rate possibly last?
>
> All of which is to suggest, Gelb does not have much time.

Munk's prediction proved accurate. By 2014, time had run out. The economic situation had grown much worse. The Met's budget had continued to escalate, from $252 million in fiscal 2009 to around $330 million in fiscal 2013. The drawdown figure may well have increased even beyond the 8.3 percent cited by Munk.

Belatedly, Gelb was now being quoted around Lincoln Center as enunciating a new refrain for the Met: "Spend less. Earn more." This bumper-sticker message fell somewhat short of a strategic plan, but at least it was more than a prayer. The question remains why that simple directive could not have been fully internalized and then widely communicated much earlier during Gelb's tenure. When decisions are reached, year after year, to decant the endowment in excess of the income it generates, then its erosion, and an accompanying financial crisis, is inevitable.

The reasons given by Gelb for the plight of the Met began to proliferate as union negotiations approached:

1. The Met's audience was aging.
2. Opera was not taught in elementary and secondary schools.
3. What was happening to the Met was also occurring elsewhere around the world at leading opera companies.
4. Superstorm Sandy cut into attendance.
5. Raising funds was highly competitive.

On item 1, 'twas ever thus. To attend opera regularly requires substantial discretionary time and income. Older people have both. From 1960 to 2010, according to the U.S. Census Bureau, those over sixty-five years of age as a percentage of the US population doubled. More and more baby boomers are becoming senior citizens, and those over sixty-five will soon grow to 20 percent of the population. In New York City, the figures are just as dramatic. Its Department for the Aging reports that the number of those over sixty years of age increased 12.4 percent between 2000 and 2010. The population of those over age sixty is projected to increase by 35.3 percent by 2030, to a total of over 1.85 million people. This trend should have been viewed by the Met as an extremely lucrative opportunity to exploit, rather than one to bemoan.

Regarding item 2, when was opera ever taught in elementary and secondary schools? Even in the days before the performing arts were virtually eliminated from the primary and secondary school curriculum in New York City, opera was rarely if ever embraced as a subject.

On item 3, spokesmen for the English National Opera, The Royal Opera, and the Opera Bastille all denied that their companies had been adversely affected by the same trends afflicting the Metropolitan Opera. On the contrary, the leadership of these European companies asserted that recent seasons had been good to excellent from an attendance and earned income perspective. Quite unusually, they publicly parted company with Gelb. They left little doubt of their view that he was incorrect in lumping the financial condition of their institutions with his own.

As for item 4, Superstorm Sandy was a temporary phenomenon at worst and did not seem to have badly damaged other Lincoln Center constituents or Broadway in any kind of serious way. There seemed to be a touch of futility in citing it as an important cause of a full year of disappointing results at the box office.

On item 5, the Dow Jones Industrial Average, the S&P, and the Nasdaq were all hitting record highs. The real estate market in New York City was booming. The bull market in stocks and in commercial and residential real estate offered huge opportunities to recruit new, wealthy trustees and to solicit major gifts from existing supporters and prospects. As a veteran fund-raiser, I find it difficult to imagine a more receptive and upbeat environment in which to tap the generosity of the affluent.

What's more, tourism remained at record highs, and the hotel business was booming. Were vacationers and expatriates attending the Met Opera in ample, or even anticipated, numbers? Was the Met Opera winning its fair share of their time and resources?

What troubled Met Opera loyalists, myself included, was that the faultfinding all seemed to be "out there," in the economy, in the school system, in demographic trends, in competition for contributed income, even in extreme weather, rather than "in here," in the Met Opera's own economic model, its soundness in formulation and execution.

To fail to acknowledge Gelb's energy, drive, innovativeness, and entrepreneurial flair would be churlish. But all who care about the future of the Metropolitan Opera are entitled to ask how this desperate financial condition arose, and whether the steps taken to date are nearly enough to address it successfully.

ONE ENGAGED AND interested party that shared this concern was the Met's unionized workforce.

The Met's proclivity until the run-up to the negotiations in the summer of 2014 was to act as if economic matters were well in hand or at least under control. Downplaying or sugarcoating realities was now at an end. It was past time to blow the whistle. And ironically, it was Gelb who became the whistle-blower in chief, issuing dire warnings about the Met's financial future.

Savvy union members were not buying these sudden Cassandra-like cries of a change in fortune. Tino Gagaliordi, the president of Local 802 of the American Federation of Musicians, asked why such significant costs needed to be cut by the Met from union wages, benefits, and work rules to manage what until recently Gelb had contended was a minor deficit in the last fiscal year:

> It is our hope that the mediated negotiations will finally yield transparency on the part of Met management, requiring it to prove why it needs upwards of $30 million in cuts to address a deficit of $2.8 million.[1]

The reason was simple. As Wakin and Munk had reported years before, the Met treated its endowment quite casually, moving funds from the balance sheet to the operating statement so as to pay bills and to claim that budgets were balanced or very close to it. By 2012, realizing that this practice was no longer practical, the Met was compelled to issue $100 million of bonds to help satisfy pressing cash needs.

Now, it was claimed, the day of reckoning had come. The endowment had reached the point where it was less than half a year's expenses, leaving aside entirely the need to pay back borrowed cash, or to address the alarming unfunded liability of pension funds, or to satisfy deferred maintenance and equipment needs. Gelb turned to the unions as a critical source of assistance.

They weren't flattered by the attention. What they wanted instead were clear answers to these questions:

1. Why had the Met's budget ballooned in the Gelb years, from $220 million to close to $330 million?
2. Isn't it true that the HD movie opera initiative, however it may have worked elsewhere in America and around the world, actually reduced attendance in the opera house from those residing in New York, New Jersey, and Connecticut? If so, might a blackout of some highly popular operas in the tristate region encourage live attendance?
3. Why didn't Gelb better control overtime costs?
4. Wasn't Gelb's scheduling of rehearsals excessive and largely controllable by him?
5. Where is it written that the Met Opera must put on twenty-three different shows each season? Why not twenty-one or

twenty or nineteen? And why not slightly fewer new productions or new operas? And isn't there room for more coproductions, in which two or more companies split the cost of new operas?

These questions must have rankled Peter. They suggested that treating the unions as a scapegoat for the Met's travails was unfair. Surely, the unions claimed, management changes were also in order if the Met's financial condition were to improve and stabilize. These questions indicated a few significant pathways to cost cutting. I'll add one in the form of revenue enhancement.

If, over time, the Met can organize its productions so as to free up a consistent week to ten days in its venue, then one or another televised award show is likely to commit to a very lucrative multiyear arrangement. Whether it be the Tony Awards or the MTV Awards, the Oscars or the Emmys or the CMT Awards, the Met is a highly desirable place for such televised productions. Its sponsors all have deep pockets. Just one or two such extremely lucrative rentals every year could help contribute to the Met's annual revenue needs and reach a national audience in the bargain.

I am confident that this opportunity is real. For several years running, I received phone calls from City Hall asking me to determine which of our venues could be made available consistently for several mega-televised events. Because its seating capacity nears four thousand and because of its front- and back-of-house versatility, the preference of interested parties was to use the Met Opera House. But it was always unavailable.

On July 25, 2014, the musicians of the Metropolitan Opera, Local 802, handed a very detailed, sixty-page document to Gelb that was highly critical of his management of the Met and of his artistic choices. Gelb could have thanked the union, his highly praised musical colleagues, and treated with respect their constructive effort to identify cost savings. He could have promised to review these detailed proposals and to consider them on the merits. Instead, within twenty-four hours the Met responded in a point, counterpoint style, conceding nothing and rejecting every union argument and proposal.[2]

It was as if for Gelb there was only one way to run the Metropolitan Opera. His way. Message sent. Message received. Message rejected.

Being at the helm of a complex institution is not just a matter of juggling facts and figures and reaching sound decisions. It is more than finishing tasks and completing transactions. It is certainly more than always trying to win arguments and prove that you are correct. It is about building relationships and creating trust.

IN THE CASE of Volpe and Gelb, appearances are deceiving. They seem to be an unmatched pair. But in my capacity as the president of Lincoln Center, I found it was their similarities and not their differences that struck home.

True, Gelb is to cultural royalty born. His father, Arthur, served as the cultural editor of the *New York Times* when that position was truly powerful. His mother, Barbara, was the stepdaughter of the playwright S. N. Berhman and the niece of violinist Jascha Heifetz. The Gelbs wrote two definitive and much-praised biographies of the playwright Eugene O'Neill. Their son, Peter, worked for Sol Hurok, the legendary impresario. He also served as Vladimir Horowitz's manager, as the public relations director of the Boston Symphony, and as the president of Sony Classical. By contrast, Volpe began his career as a carpenter at the Met and rose up through the ranks.

For me, the major differences end there. Neither Volpe nor Gelb attended college (nor, for that matter, did Rudolf Bing, their famous predecessor). Each is, by his own admission, a control freak. In reading about and personally observing their respective tenures (Volpe characterizes his as a reign), there is seldom a favorable reference to the colleagues with whom they worked closely at the Met or elsewhere around the world. They both behave as if they are one-man shows. In discussing the Met, they do not just personify the institution; they personalize it. They seem to conflate themselves and their views with its interests. In hundreds of news and feature stories about Volpe and Gelb, it is difficult to find nouns like *team, colleague, partner, collaborator,* or *coworker.*

In my judgment, each has attempted personally to resolve too many issues and hammer out too many decisions. For management gurus like Peter Drucker, such overreaching unilaterally displaces experts in an organization who are likely to be closer to the issues and the problems at hand than is the CEO. Delegating smartly not only resolves matters nearer to their source, but leaves the CEO with fewer decisions, those for which he or she is most needed and most knowledgeable. It preserves valuable time for that which only the CEO can accomplish, like high-end fund-raising and important donor cultivation:

> The least effective decision makers are the ones who confidently make too many decisions. The effective ones make very few. They concentrate on the important decisions. And even people who work hard on making decisions often misapply their time. They slight important decisions and spend excessive time making easy—irrelevant—decisions.[3]

For all of their apparent differences, neither Volpe nor Gelb seemed to enjoy company in reaching decisions or in executing them. If either played a musical instrument for a living, I am confident that each would prefer to be a solo artist. Chamber ensembles are not for them.

LABOR NEGOTIATIONS REQUIRE, by definition, sitting down with one's counterparts and bargaining. Gelb deserves credit for calling into question union costs that have grown increasingly unaffordable and work rules that have become both rigid and expensive. Yes, his hand was forced by the Met's dreadful economic condition. Even so, acknowledging that under his watch the greatest opera house in the world had allowed itself to arrive only two to three years away from going out of business could not have been easy. Nor could being subject to merciless criticism of his management by his own workforce.

The unions merit some praise as well. By pointing to ways and means under Gelb's control to reduce and contain costs, they refused to allow themselves to be perceived as the only or even the principal cause of the Met's financial woes. They attempted to be constructive.

Ultimately, both parties seem to have offered important concessions, and what would have been a disastrous lockout or strike was avoided.

On the union side, singers and orchestra members agreed to take a 3.5 percent cut in pay immediately and an equivalent cut six months later. There would be no pay increase until the second half of the last year of a four-year contract. That upward adjustment in 2018 will be 3 percent. The Met claims that all of its other unions agreed to a roughly comparable wage savings package. Technically, that may be true. But the stagehands, while taking an immediate cut of 3.75 percent, then receive raises of 2.5, 3, and 3 percent in the fourth, fifth, and sixth years of their new contract.

These are significant, historic concessions. While nowhere near the 17 percent Gelb claimed the Met Opera required, they are the first pay cuts experienced by the Met unionized workforce in decades, and they will result in millions of dollars of savings.

What all of the unions refused to yield on is also very significant. No changes to health-care benefits. No changes to pension benefits. No changes to work rules. Each of these categories of cost offers plenty of room for give and take that could have saved meaningful sums overall. Their complete rejection by the unions must have come as a bitter pill to Met management. And so did this most unusual provision: apparently the Met agreed that any return on its endowment above 8 percent will be equally shared with union employees, 50:50.

The plot further thickens as one reviews the rest of the Met's part of this bargain. It agreed to cut $11.25 million in expenses each year in addition to the savings yielded from the cuts to union wages. The Met also agreed to retain Eugene Keilin, an independent financial analyst who had been hired originally to analyze the Met's books and to assist the federal mediator in negotiations. Now he will stay on, reporting to both labor and management and paid by both of them equally.

These Met concessions beg two important questions.

First, the Met claims that roughly 60 percent of its $327 million budget is paid to its unionized workforce, or $196 million. That leaves $131 million. Of that amount, the Met has now agreed to cut $11.25 million in expenses, or 8.5 percent of the balance. If the Met can accomplish this significant a cost reduction in a single twelve-month period, why did it not do so in the first seven years of Gelb's tenure? Instead, expenses went only one way. Up. Way up. Couldn't the organization have avoided bringing itself, by its own admission, to the razor's edge of bankruptcy? And where were the checks and balances that are supposed to be provided by the scrutiny and oversight of the board of directors during these years of cost escalation?

Second, precisely what role is Keilin to play? The Met Opera has as part of its board structure a finance committee, an executive committee, and an audit committee. Its books are audited annually by the accounting firm KPMG. Both S&P and Moody's closely monitor the Met's finances as part of their oversight of its $100 million bond issue.

Apparently these multiple sources of review are insufficient for the unions. Their level of trust in management has sunk so low that they feel a truly independent watchdog is needed. An inkling of what has motivated the unions was disclosed to the *New York Times* on August 19, 2014, by Jessica Phillips Rieske, a member of the orchestra committee. Rieske told journalist Michael Cooper that she found it gratifying that federal mediators and Keilin had

> agreed with our assessment that in addition to our agreeing to wage reductions, Met management needed to look at its own budget, introduce important efficiencies and curtail unlimited spending.
>
> Now, in the contract itself, there are mechanisms in place to address management's cost inefficiencies and provide greater financial oversight as we all move forward.

Such an arrangement is highly unusual. It is difficult to find a management-labor agreement in the nonprofit sector that is conditioned on the presence of a third-party monitor. Keilin's role is to validate and authenticate management's collectively bargained commitments. For the unions to have spent finite collective bargaining capital on this kind of management concession must mean that there really is no love lost and little trust remaining between the union and Met management, together with its board of directors.

Such acrimony is not a pretty sight. But Keilin is a top-flight professional who will conduct himself fairly, competently, and by the book.

What a paradox. The unions, whose members are accused of excessive and unaffordable pay, fringe benefits, and work rules, publicly argue that it is management that needs economic discipline. If there is to be a sound Met economic future, employee "give backs" must be matched by the Met's own self-control and self-restraint in spending.

Could it be that with Keilin's help the unions studied the Met's finances more carefully than ever, and what they saw was a future that resembled nothing more than that of the New York City Opera?

Is it possible that this agreement and Keilin's continued presence will bring to the Met's financial management a large dose of the discipline that Peter Gelb and the board of directors had not demonstrated on their own?

This much seems clear. If Gelb had hoped that the union settlement would go a long way toward easing the Met's financial woes, he must have been keenly disappointed with the outcome. In an operation of the Met's size and complexity, there is no single answer to the economic challenges before it. The end result of the negotiations was a step in the right direction. Many other measures and acts of self-restraint will be necessary for this artistic patient to fully recover.

Let us assume that Gelb builds on the unionized labor concessions and pares expenses under his own control, as he is now contractually bound to do. Let us assume that in all other respects he manages the opera's operations much more tightly. Let us also assume that major stumbling blocks like the financial and artistic setback of the commissioned *Ring Cycle* do not recur. If administrative expenses are streamlined, if the number of new operas and newly commissioned productions is even modestly reduced, and if coproductions are just slightly increased, so much the better.

Were all of this to come about, it is claimed that the Met Opera would save $90 million in expenses over the four-year contract. Impressive. But consider that the $90 million is only roughly 7.5 percent of the $1.3 billion the Met is expected to spend at an annual rate of $320 million per year over the next four years. As a result, the Met Opera will need many more generous trustees and benefactors. It requires a much larger endowment, ideally three to four times the size of its operating budget.

The stated willingness of the board of directors to endeavor to double the size of the Met Opera's endowment over the next four to five years is important and helpful, but it is just a beginning. When the endowment reaches that $520 million total, a 5 percent drawdown from it will yield $25 million, or about 7 percent of its current $330 million operating budget. Reaching a $520 million endowment is a good beginning. But that's all.

The Met also needs to buttress the value of its pension funds. And it must set aside resources for its maintenance and repair needs. They cannot be deferred much longer. Only surplus capital generated by a multiyear, extremely ambitious, and successful fund-raising drive will allow for significant progress toward each of these ends.

Writing in the *Wall Street Journal* of August 29, 2014, Terry Teachout surmised that either Gelb exaggerated the Met Opera's financial plight, or the union "ate his lunch." These alternatives are not mutually exclusive, of course. More telling is Teachout's warning, proclaimed with the New York City Opera's recent demise fresh in mind: "Given sufficiently bad management, no arts organization is too big, too old or too famous to fail. Not even the Metropolitan Opera." Teachout's article is titled "Apocalypse Later." The two-word sentence does not end with a question mark.

Sure enough, on November 20, 2014, the Met Opera revealed that its operating deficit for the completed 2013–2014 season came in at an astounding $22 million. As a percentage of its budget, nothing of this magnitude had been experienced for three decades, going back to 1984. In absolute terms, this loss was among the largest ever experienced by the Met Opera. Even more dangerous, that $22 million deficit in one stroke reduced by 8 percent its $265 million endowment as it was valued at the end of July 2014.

It is no wonder that Gelb had spoken about the Met Opera's finances in such grave terms as collective bargaining approached. In FY 2013–2014, charitable contributions had fallen. Earned income in the form of ticket revenue was well short of expectations. Expenses, though modestly lower than in the prior year, were still in an elevated state of $316 million. Overall, during Gelb's tenure the Met's endowment has badly eroded.

For the Met Opera, the growing gap between its annual costs and revenues had reached crisis proportions, as had the Met's net asset position.

Clearly 2014 was the Metropolitan Opera's year of reckoning, its moment of truth. It will take at least a decade of extremely hard work to deal with its problematic financial condition and bring it to a reasonably healthy state. And it will take mature leadership to act on the realities revealed by this dramatic and important episode in the life of the Met. Little would please me more than to conclude that Teachout's foreboding proved to be a useful expression of alarm, rather than an accurate prophecy.

IN VIRTUALLY EVERY country in the world where they exist, the performing arts, including opera, receive large government subsidies. Considered national treasures, support comes to them regularly and more or less reliably. Not so in America. If we wish to keep government small(er) and taxes low(er), then especially those who benefit most from such policies should offer generous philanthropic support.

Whether contributed income can be maintained and increased at needed levels is an open and critical question. At least some of the answer resides in how energetic, compelling, and persuasive are those who solicit on behalf of noble organizations and causes. The difference between a successful "call to alms" and a "farewell to alms" is often in the artistic and financial performance of the organization asking and in the sense of urgency with which it does so. It would help the Met a great deal if mutual trust between management and its employees were to be restored over time and if this period of bad feeling were to subside.

I hope that as long as Peter Gelb continues to play his extraordinarily important role as the general manager of the Metropolitan Opera, he will arrogate to himself fewer important decisions and delegate more to others. This recommendation comes out of respect for the extraordinary demands placed on him. It recognizes that no single human being can assume and discharge as much responsibility as he has done. The Metropolitan Opera requires a strong team of executive leaders working in tandem if it is to see its way through what will be an extremely challenging decade. Building that team could well be one of Gelb's most important accomplishments.

An identical challenge faces the Met Opera's board of directors. Is it properly sized and composed for the tough years ahead? Doesn't it need many more fresh, enthusiastic, well-heeled, and generous recruits? I suspect that the Met board's leadership also has their work cut out for them.

The Metropolitan Opera is a marvelous and indispensable organization, possessed of a very distinguished history. It now raises the remarkable sum of $160 million annually. Until and unless the Met's economic model radically changes, its board and staff will need to do even better, as it first restores and then expands the value of its endowment. Doing so will require broadening its appeal and increasing the number of its most munificent benefactors.

For the sake of preserving grand opera as an art form in our country, I earnestly hope those blessed with an abundance of wealth, not least the members of the board of the Met, will answer the call. They are out there, waiting to be asked. New York is the wealthiest city in the richest country in the world. If orders of magnitude of more funds for opera can be found anywhere, it is here, in the Met's hometown and among lovers of the art form throughout the nation and even beyond it.

I am rooting for Gelb and his trustee colleagues to successfully lead the way.

CHAPTER 10

Close Encounters

> Whether a man is burdened by power or enjoys power;
> whether he is trapped by responsibility or made free
> by it; whether he is moved by other people and outer
> forces or moves them—this is the essence of leadership.
>
> —THEODORE H. WHITE, *The Making of the President*, 1960

The talent, character, and drive of those holding high office matter a great deal. The health of an enterprise depends in no small measure on the qualities of mind and the management acumen of its leadership.

Where does that leadership come from?

For me, a vital source of inspiration and emulation has been observing carefully the lives of others, whether by reading about exceptional people or seeing them depicted across the footlights of a stage or on a screen at home or in a darkened movie theater.

I have also been fortunate in coming to know personally some leaders whose influence on me has been profound. It is my privilege to introduce you to a few of them. Some of my depictions portray public figures, revealing features of character or accomplishment that are either not well known or are underappreciated. Others delineate personalities who are hardly household names.

These individuals share three traits. They work very hard to achieve uncommon results. They wish to make of this world a better place. They offer time, treasure, and talent to advance the public good.

By examining their lives closely, I have grown personally and at the workplace. How others assess situations, unearth opportunities, respond to threats, and conduct themselves more generally has always been an essential wellspring of learning for me. My career has been immensely enriched by dozens of such associations, models to closely watch, lively examples of how to inhabit a life of consequence.

BEVERLY SILLS WAS SINGULAR. A global superstar on the world's opera stages, she retired at fifty years of age, never to sing again. Not even in the shower, she claimed.

In our family, my mother revered two Jewish women. One was Bess Myerson, who in 1945 became the first Jewish Miss America. There has not been another since. That Myerson went on to also become the first commissioner of the Department of Consumer Affairs in the city of New York and a favorite of Mayor Ed Koch was another point of pride for Barbara Levy.

Her second heroine, Beverly Sills, was regarded as virtually a neighbor. If you take a two-and-a-half-mile stroll on the boardwalk going west, starting off across the street from my apartment house on Bay Seven in Brighton Beach, to its very end, passing by all of Coney Island, you reach Sea Gate. That is where Sills was raised. The very idea that a child brought up in a Jewish home in such a place could rise to global prominence was amazing to my mother.

Is there an opera star you know of who could hold her own on *The Johnny Carson Show*, or with Carol Burnett on a one-hour television special in prime time? How many divas can you name who served on four corporate boards of directors, including American Express and Macy's? Sills could count as close friends not just CEOs and fellow household-name artists, but also mayors, governors, and US senators.

There are only a handful of artists who could move deftly from a career in singing to running an artistic institution like the New York City Opera, which Sills did as its general director from 1979 to 1989.

Sills once told me, tongue in cheek, that she learned all one needed to know about finance from the developer Peter Jay Sharp, the owner of the Carlyle Hotel. Apparently he told her that two things were not good to find when examining an operating statement: any number in parentheses and any number colored red!

Sills's effervescence was everywhere apparent. She was always upbeat, always smiling. In the business of the arts there are setbacks, of course. But Sills really believed that for every door that closes, a window opens.

Her positive spirit at work and in public was remarkable given the private setbacks she and her husband Peter Greenough endured. Their daughter Muffy was diagnosed as deaf before she was two years old, and their son Peter Jr., "Bucky," was very severely disabled at birth. That Bev could manage to deal with these setbacks and not let them dilute her indomitable spirit was remarkable. It is not for nothing that she decided to title her book-length self-portrait *Bubbles*.

When it came to attending opera performances, Beverly was the least stuffy person I ever encountered at Lincoln Center. Just enjoy it, she would advise. Don't treat attending this grand art form as some kind of stress test. Lead with your senses. Study up on the opera later, after you have seen a show, rather than before. If you are too tired to enjoy the performance after the second act concludes at 10:20 p.m. and all you can think about is your 7:00 a.m. breakfast the next morning, then just take your leave. Act 3 will be ready for you when you are better prepared for it. Sills often followed her own advice, stealing away from performances as inconspicuously as possible.

For all of Lincoln Center's disorganization and for all of the problems that afflicted it, being around Beverly always made me feel relaxed and comfortable. I count myself fortunate for having had the couple of years our lives touched. Barbara Levy would have thought that there was no greater success than to proclaim that one knows, let alone works with, Beverly Sills.

In July 2012 the staff at Lincoln Center decided to hold a party to bid Sills good-bye and to thank her for the service she had rendered as chair for more than seven years. She insisted on planning the luncheon menu: fried chicken, French fries, three quarter sour pickles, and for dessert, s'mores, cotton candy, ice cream, and the ingredients to make your own sundae: wet walnuts, maple and chocolate syrup, whipped cream, and cherries. And for those who preferred them, root beer floats. Of course there were also egg creams.

Alice Waters, forget it. The choices of our honoree came right out of her Sea Gate origins. There was not a vegetable to be found. There were words of praise and tears of remembrance from all of those gathered in the grand lobby of Avery Fisher Hall. We expressed our appreciation and, in honor of Beverly, we gained some weight. For all of the glamour and glitter, the ball gowns and the white-tie occasions, for all of the globetrotting and the hotel suites in world capitals, and for all of the admiration in which she was held, at bottom, when given her choice, the sights, smells, and sounds of her youth prevailed.

Egg creams in hand, we offered our final toast to a star more indelibly identified with Lincoln Center than any other.[1]

I FIRST MET David Koch months after setting in motion his dramatic entrance onto the public stage of Lincoln Center. It happened this way. The New York State Theater, which was owned, notwithstanding its name, by the city of New York, had virtually always housed the New York City Ballet and the New York City Opera. In a fit of pique, Governor Nelson Rockefeller, who did not like fellow Republican, Mayor John V. Lindsay, decided to name the space, designed by Philip Johnson, after New York State.

In anticipation of the desirability of the entire building carrying the name of a private donor as part of a campuswide, comprehensive capital campaign, Lincoln Center took the initiative. On behalf of the New York City Opera and the New York City Ballet, we proposed to Assembly Speaker Shelly Silver, Senate Majority Leader Joe Bruno, and Governor Eliot Spitzer that a bill be passed permitting the New York State Theater to be renamed for an as yet unknown private party, hopefully a very generous donor.

The statute embodying this purpose was passed by unanimous consent and signed into law on April 23, 2008. That act paved the way for the solicitation of David Koch, who readily pledged $100 million, to be paid out over ten years, for the renovation of what for ballet fans was a hallowed space. The gift was publicly announced on July 10, 2008.

In one decisive move, Koch elevated the way in which donors viewed cultural institutions, and places of public accommodation more generally. Before Koch's donation, only hospitals and universities were receiving gifts of such size. Now places like Lincoln Center were transformed in the minds of wealthy philanthropists into fully worthy recipients of mega-gifts.

Earlier, the largest-known gifts received by Lincoln Center or any of its resident artistic organizations had been $25 million from financier and Lincoln Center trustee Julian Robertson; $25 million and $30 million from Mercedes Bass and Ann Ziff, respectively, to the Metropolitan Opera; and separate donations, each of comparable size, to The Juilliard School from its board chair, Bruce Kovner.

As if to prove a point, several months later Stephen Schwarzman, the cofounder of the Blackstone Group, donated $100 million to the New York Public Library. The headquarters and main branch, located on 42nd Street and Fifth Avenue, now carries his name.

Several years later John Paulson, a leading hedge fund manager, donated $100 million to the Central Park Conservancy.

David Koch's gift not only set an extraordinary precedent, but as a practical matter it enabled the frequently quarreling New York City Opera and the New York City Ballet to cooperate on a marvelous modernization. The gift made possible the removal of carpeting and layers of material from the floor and walls of the theater, significantly improving its acoustics. It allowed for the creation of an orchestra lift that would elevate the musicians from the pit to become level with the stage if the repertoire so demanded. It created a media room that could potentially broadcast and narrowcast what was appearing on the stage outdoors on Lincoln Center's Josie Robertson Plaza and to movie theaters, television sets, and mobile devices. It enlarged and improved bathroom facilities. It created aisles for easier access to seating in the orchestra, originally built to the specifications of George Balanchine as the home of the New York City Ballet, the place with which his name will forever be indelibly associated.

Koch, of his own volition, took another very unusual step. Typically, buildings and parts of them are named in perpetuity by way of acknowledgment for appropriately sized gifts. David Koch voluntarily offered to have his name on the building for a fixed period of fifty years and not a day longer, thereby enabling that funding opportunity to be "resold," charitably speaking. His generosity on this score is rare and much to be admired. He had created nothing less than a timeshare opportunity that could be renewed and renamed for another family. Alas, no such provision exists for the likes of Alice Tully Hall, or Avery Fisher Hall, or Frederick P. Rose Hall, or the Vivian Beaumont Theater, or any other space, indoors or out, that carries a benefactor's name on Lincoln Center's sixteen-acre campus.[2]

Koch and I met on February 22, 2009, at the first concert in the completely new and refurbished Alice Tully Hall. He could not have been more engaged or curious. He marveled at the idea that the wood paneling of the entire auditorium came from one African moabi tree, cut into the thinnest slices in Japan and shipped to New York City. He was very impressed with the geometric contours of the space, likening it to a cruise line or a spaceship. He couldn't quite believe the dramatic effect that light-emitting diodes carefully placed behind the thin wood veneer had on the room, "blushing walls," in a hall where the interior was fitted out as if it were a "bespoke suit." And Koch, who holds an engineering degree from MIT, put many questions to me about why musicians, audiences, and critics were so captivated by the acoustics, referring to them as heavenly, among other words of praise. What is it about the shape of the hall and/or the three stage configurations and/or the volume of the space that allowed for just the right reverberation time, leading to splendid sound?

I found Koch genuinely enthusiastic about what Lincoln Center had accomplished and eager to learn more about its whys and wherefores. His excitement extended to other elements of Lincoln Center's physical transformation, not least the new fountain. Its engineering enabled hundreds of spigots to create a kind of water choreography that enchanted David as it did thousands of visitors each week. All eagerly witnessed the various configurations of water that staff fondly called by names like "The Wedding Cake" and "The Swan Song."

Koch showed up at the fountain's inauguration and was mesmerized by all the tricks it could play. He asked to be taken to the mechanical room underneath the plaza at Lincoln Center that ran the fountain and to be tutored in the software that drove it. He even wanted to see the manual that explained to staff how it worked.

Apart from his natural curiosity, he had a specific purpose in mind as he put these questions to me. Serving on the Board of Trustees of the Metropolitan Museum of Art, he found its Fifth Avenue frontage in general, and its ill-kept and unkempt fountains in particular, forlorn and depressing. Its renovation was very much on his mind.

Working together with developer Dan Brodsky, who in a volunteer capacity had guided the Josie Robertson Plaza renovation, Koch ultimately donated $65 million to the Metropolitan Museum to modernize its Fifth Avenue frontage. It turned out that Brodsky was also the chair of the Met's real estate committee, and as such had oversight over this modernization as well. Soon thereafter Dan, a good friend, was appointed chair of the board of the Metropolitan Museum.

A couple of years later, Koch was invited to serve on Lincoln Center's board of directors. That invitation was not without controversy. He and his brother Charles were among the principal benefactors of the right wing of the Republican Party. They lavished tens of millions of dollars on their own super PAC, Americans for Prosperity, on the election campaign of Mitt Romney, and on Karl Rove's super PAC, American Crossroads. These investments had paid virtually no dividends. President Obama was reelected with plenty of room to spare. The Democrats gained two seats in the US Senate and eight more in the House of Representatives.

Nonetheless, as word spread about how tens of millions of dollars had been pumped into 2012 election campaigns and separate committee advertising campaigns by the Koch brothers, among others, strong supporters of the Democratic Party were not pleased by the New York State Theater's new name, nor with David's presence on our board. Displeasure was expressed at a few poorly attended demonstrations and in a steady flow of protest letters, many originating from bastions of liberal Democratic strongholds, like the Upper East Side and West Side of Manhattan, gentrified Brooklyn, and even Greenwich, Connecticut, the world's hedge fund capital.

How could Lincoln Center accept "guilt money" and lend legitimacy to a family notorious for taking so much advantage of the Supreme Court's decision in the *Citizens United* case? That ruling treated money as speech and determined that it would be unconstitutional to place any limits whatsoever on how much cash could be given to support candidates without violating the First Amendment rights of citizens. Moreover, the Supreme Court had also determined that corporations are people, and therefore Koch Industries, as a company, enjoyed similar campaign contribution prerogatives.

How could we, a performing arts center that cooperated fully with dozens of unions, countenance a huge gift from David Koch, who was bound and determined to weaken, if not destroy, them?

Dismantling the New Deal, shrinking the federal government, and favoring policies that strengthened still further the wealthy at the expense of the poor and working class were policy stances attributed to the Kochs and widely opposed. By accepting his outsized donation and asking David to be on the boards of the New York City Ballet and Lincoln Center, we were accused in some quarters of virtually endorsing them. In the view of what appeared to be a small but strident minority, we were thought to be guilty by association.

There are more than a few trustees at Lincoln Center, and for all I know, at the New York City Ballet, who do not share David Koch's values or agree with his politics. So what? In the toxic partisan environment that characterizes our divided nation, what purpose is served by infusing such differences into the nonprofit boardroom? The Lincoln Center Board of Directors, in deciding to elect David to its ranks, affirmed the principle that the institution's mission did not admit of a political litmus test for service on its governing body. David Koch was no less welcome on Lincoln Center's board than would be George Soros, whose politics were the mirror opposite.

Of course citizens are free to object to the politics of the Koch brothers and to the way Koch Industries is run. Similar objections were directed in their time at the "robber barons," including Andrew Carnegie and John Rockefeller. But who among us would deny the benefits countless Americans have enjoyed from their benefactions? To cite just two examples from Mr. Carnegie, how about the public libraries and Carnegie Hall? To mention just two illustrations from John D. Rockefeller, how about the University of Chicago and the Population Council?

Try to explain to the first-generation American student studying for a college degree in a well-lit and well-ventilated branch library reading room in the south Bronx, or to a student on full tuition scholarship at one of the world's great universities, that he or she is enjoying the tainted philanthropic fruit of the poisonous capitalist tree.

Many institutions and those they serve have received gifts from $20 million to $200 million from David Koch, and I would be very surprised if their beneficiaries would quarrel very much with Koch's legal (but objectionable to some) activities and with his political proclivities and financial support of them. The roster of grantees is astounding: MIT, the University of Texas M.D. Cancer Center, New York-Presbyterian Hospital, Memorial Sloan Kettering Hospital, Johns Hopkins University, the American Museum of Natural History, the Metropolitan Museum of Art, the New York City Ballet, and Lincoln Center.

I like David Koch. He and his wife are friendly people, good conversationalists, patriots, eager to use some of their wealth to help others. I also vehemently disagree with many of his political views.

It has been said that differences of opinion among elected officials should stop at the water's edge. Likewise, one's political views should not be allowed to intrude on decisions about who serves on nonprofit boards of directors. Such a course of action is a slippery slope.

From my vantage point, on the battleground of politics, the Kochs and their allies deserve a good drubbing. And if David Koch or his firm violates the law, the remedies of our justice system should be invoked. But his willingness to devote so much of his time, talent, and treasure to cancer research and treatment, to higher education, and to strengthening our nation's museums and performing art institutions is entirely meritorious.

When it comes to David Koch's philanthropy, I have four words for him: *THANK YOU VERY MUCH.*

IT WAS A good old-fashioned cold call. Everyone on Lincoln Center's nominating and governance committee knew of David Rubenstein, but no one knew him personally. And all thought that recruiting David to be on the board of Lincoln Center was a terrific idea, even though the chances of succeeding were slim.

After all, he lived in Bethesda, Maryland, regarded himself as a Washingtonian, and appeared to be waiting in the wings to succeed Steve Schwarzman, the cofounder of Blackstone, as the chair of the Kennedy Center for the Performing Arts.

I dialed the phone. He picked up. I told him we had a lot in common. We both were fascinated by the performing arts. His business took him to my hometown, New York City, with some frequency. In fact, over 125 employees of Carlyle worked in Manhattan, its second largest location.

I wondered aloud. Is that enough for the two of us to become acquainted in my office over a sandwich lunch? Sure, he replied.

We met, and the conversation flowed easily. David said yes on the spot when I suggested that he join the board of Lincoln Center.

Rubenstein is not just a piece of work; he is all work. He is simply indefatigable. No one logs as many hours on behalf of Carlyle, the company he cofounded and dearly loves. In a quarter century he and his colleagues have built a firm that now has over $200 billion under management and is widely admired around the world. It is a world that Rubenstein has gotten to know, as he spends, by his own count, 190 days in the air every year on his private jet, prowling the planet for sovereign wealth funds and other pools of capital that could do far worse than invest in Carlyle.

In the last decade or so, Rubenstein has matched his propensity for business with a passionate commitment to philanthropy and non-profit institutions. By last count, he serves on the boards of directors of over a dozen nonprofit organizations, including the Kennedy Center for the Performing Arts and Duke University (he is the chairman of both), Johns Hopkins University, the University of Chicago, the Brookings Institution, the Council on Foreign Relations, and the Smithsonian Institution.

He is no letterhead trustee. He works hard to advance the mission of every one of these institutions. I know. Lincoln Center is among them. David served with determination and distinction as the chair of Lincoln Center's unprecedented capital campaign for the physical redevelopment of the campus.

Even after associating with David for almost nine years and spending lots of time with him, it is still tough to know what makes him tick. He is highly competitive, for sure. He keeps close track of how Carlyle is faring relative to plan and to competitors. No one is a more successful private equity fund-raiser, and no one has logged more miles, delivered more speeches, and pitched more business to more people.

Rubenstein also loves American history and politics. He has purchased original documents like the Emancipation Proclamation and the Declaration of Independence, both on loan to the National Archives. And his knowledge of US presidents before and after the one he served, Jimmy Carter, is breathtaking. But no one I know who is acquainted with David has been able to locate his "off switch." He seems "on," always.

For Rubenstein, food is merely fuel to keep him working. I have never seen this teetotaler and vegetarian truly enjoy a meal or spend more than fifteen minutes consuming one. Clothing is just garb, necessary coveralls. David seems to own about a half dozen of the same navy blue pinstripe suits, and he wears them with Hermes ties and white shirts. He treats his clothing as if he were donning a uniform.

For him, sleep is highly overrated, and if you are longing for a very brief conversation, ask him when he last enjoyed a break from work that lasted more than a few days.

I was a weekend guest in Nantucket at the home of Rubenstein and his wife, Alice. It sits on one of the largest and highest pieces of property on the island. Its promontory offers stunning views of the Atlantic below.

As we were treated to a personal tour by David, my wife, Elizabeth, seeing the dock on the property, asked whether David sailed.

"Elizabeth, Jews don't sail. The instructions are too complicated, it is too much work, and it takes too much time. Besides, I can't swim very well, and in the highly likely event that I crash into something or capsize the boat, I'll be in deep water and in deep trouble."

Ten minutes later, we were shown a gym on the lower level of the main house. My wife asked whether David used the facility, one that any Four Seasons Hotel would be proud to offer its guests.

"Elizabeth, just look at me. Do I look like a guy who does much more than drop in on this place occasionally to see which equipment my kids and their friends enjoy the most?"

"Well," Liz wished to know, "how about skiing? Your parents tell us you have a place in Beaver Creek, Colorado. Surely you ski?"

"Elizabeth, I wasn't meant to put those strange contraptions on my feet."

When approaching David's home in Nantucket, there is a huge round stone propped up against a majestic tree that guests circle around in order to arrive at his front door. On the stone is handwritten in paint these words:

"Honest, I'd rather be working."
—David

One would be hard-pressed to find a human being who is more austere and self-disciplined or less interested in material comforts. Plain and simple, Rubenstein is an ascetic billionaire, at least six times over. He is also as humble and self-effacing a successful businessman as one is likely to find.

After he joined Lincoln Center's board, Elizabeth and I offered to accompany him on a couple of evenings out at Lincoln Center. Many of his fellow stars in America's financial firmament came to Lincoln Center frequently. David, of course, knew of them. And leading executives of Carlyle often worked with their counterparts in the firms they founded, owned, or helped manage, but David and they had never met. It was fun for me to introduce him around to other financial and real estate titans.

David was in typical humble form one evening when I arranged for him to have dinner with Gail and Carl Icahn in the Grand Tier of the Metropolitan Opera prior to seeing a performance at Lincoln Center Theater. Icahn, for all of his notoriety in the press, is really a loner, even in the field of activist investing. Being reasonably sure he had never met Rubenstein and that he might need a reminder about his background, I composed a succinct e-mail on the subject and sent it to him before the event.

Over dinner, Icahn regaled us with his then view of Time Warner. He had bought a substantial position in the company. He was no fan of its stodgy management or of its CEO, Richard Parsons.

I asked a few questions about Icahn's life and learned that his father was a cantor who didn't much understand or appreciate what Carl was about professionally. Carl's father would have preferred that he become a physician, or a musician. Striking to all of us was Icahn's response to my question about what continued to motivate him to work so hard at the age of seventy-four.

"I'll stop only when I think my dad would have respected me."

After Icahn's extended monologue, his wife Gail suggested that Rubenstein might have a point of view about Time Warner. Carl paused over his second martini to ask, "David, remind me of your background and tell me what you do now." Clearly, my e-mail had gone unread.

Unfazed and unflustered, Rubenstein summarized his professional life this way: "Well, Carl, I began my career as a lawyer at Paul, Weiss, Rifkind. But after a couple of years, I really wasn't enjoying it, and when I told the hiring partner that I was thinking of leaving, I noticed that neither he, nor anyone else in the firm, nor my clients, protested very much. On the advice of Ted Sorensen, I then relocated to Atlanta to work on the Carter campaign for president, and after his election found myself with a White House job. That experience didn't work so well either, as I helped bring the United States an inflation rate of 19 percent, an Iranian hostage crisis, prolonged oil shortages, and infuriatingly long lines at America's gasoline stations. Ever since, I have been trying to build a business."

"What kind of business?"

"Well, my colleagues and I search for undervalued firms. We buy them at attractive prices, endeavor to fix them, and find a purchaser prepared to offer a premium or arrange for them to become public companies."

"And what is the name of that business?"

"The Carlyle Group."

"Oh. Now I know who you are."

One tycoon met another that night. David, self-deprecating as always, would probably contend that he is not in Icahn's league, financially or otherwise. But perhaps David would allow himself to be called a mogulette, or at least a low-single-digit billionaire with aspirations to make something of himself.

I HAD MET Mayor Bloomberg only once before becoming the CEO of Lincoln Center. He was being honored by the International Rescue Committee when I served as its president. Bloomberg's interest in Lincoln Center began before he became mayor. He was wooed onto the board of directors by Beverly Sills, an extremely close friend. During his service as a trustee, he came to respect Nat Leventhal. He asked Nat to lead in the transition planning as he was assuming office and to help him select key personnel for his cabinet. More than a few other Lincoln Center trustees felt entitled to call the mayor Mike.

As I could add little value to such relationships, I kept my respectful distance from the mayor. That ended in a memorable and disquieting conversation one Wednesday morning about a year and a half after I arrived at Lincoln Center. Michael Bloomberg was on the line.

"Good morning, Mr. Mayor."

"Good morning. Okay, Reynold, who leaked the specifics of my gift?"

His tone was angry, his manner rough.

"I don't know, Mr. Mayor."

"Oh, come on. I am furious. I asked for that gift to remain anonymous, and I am holding you responsible for the public disclosure."

Days earlier, Robin Pogrebin, the *New York Times* reporter, had revealed that before he became mayor, Bloomberg had pledged $15 million for the planning and early "soft" costs of Lincoln Center's physical redevelopment.

"Mr. Mayor," I said. "Last week, the New York City Police Department, during a search for illegal drugs, broke down the wrong door in an apartment house in Harlem. A fifty-nine-year-old African American mother and grandmother, shocked by the suddenness of the forced entry, died of a heart attack, on the spot. Immediately you, who knew nothing of the whys and wherefores of the police action, apologized to that woman's family on behalf of the entire city of New York.

"Well, I feel similarly. You pledged the gift in question to Beverly Sills over two years ago. I have no idea to whom she may have spoken, or who inside Lincoln Center knew the details. But I wish to sincerely apologize to you. And, of course, as the president of Lincoln Center, I assume full responsibility for what could have been an unauthorized disclosure from someone working or volunteering here."

Understandably, the mayor wished to prevent letting trustees of other arts and culture institutions in town with which he was also associated know the details of his generosity to Lincoln Center. Why have his friends and colleagues who served on the boards of other institutions "complain" that they were less favored by his benefactions? For that reason, and others, I am sure, he wished to maintain some semblance of privacy.

Much to my relief, I think the mayor was surprised by the firmness of my reply, disarmed by the analogous reference to his own recent praiseworthy act, and pleased that I took full responsibility for the disclosure.

Evasions, circumlocutions, and running away from rather toward problems are not part of Bloomberg's character. He certainly does not admire these traits in others. The conversation then shifted. He recalled his own service as a trustee of Lincoln Center and how frequently matters discussed in the boardroom somehow became public knowledge, rather quickly.

"The place has always leaked like a sieve," he acknowledged.

The conversation ended far less coldly than it began, but fell considerably short of the mayor warmly accepting my apology.

In general, Bloomberg's relationship to Lincoln Center was extremely positive. Beverly Sills was his very close friend, one of only a handful of people annually invited to his small private birthday parties. The physical redevelopment of Lincoln Center was to be a massive undertaking and would not have happened without Bloomberg's $15 million pledge.

In fact, Bloomberg, not given to off-the-cuff humor, regularly used these lines on the campaign trail while running for election to his first term in office:

> Some people think that my spending $75 million is a lot of money to run for mayor.
>
> But what they do not know, is that I served on the board of Lincoln Center and might have succeeded Beverly Sills as its chair.
>
> And if that had happened, it would have cost me a hell of a lot more than $75 million.

As well as leading by his own example, Bloomberg stuck to an agreement reached by Lincoln Center and his predecessor at the very end of Mayor Giuliani's second term in office. In rough outline, it committed $240 million of city capital funds to a Lincoln Center campuswide physical redevelopment campaign.

It was the first campuswide capital investment since Lincoln Center had been created forty-five years before. Mayor Bloomberg was an indispensable partner in seeing this complex set of projects through from inception to completion. While success may have a thousand parents, the private party who was present at the creation with a generous gift and the public sector angel throughout was without doubt Michael Bloomberg.

Greatly influenced by a trusted colleague who was soon to become first deputy mayor, Patti Harris, Bloomberg was conspicuous for his supportive presence at cultural venues in every borough—established and fledgling, general and audience specific—and in all genres: theater, ballet, modern dance, opera, jazz, vocal music, chamber music, orchestral work, and visual art.

Bloomberg viewed arts and culture as good business, part and parcel of his notable success in increasing tourism from twenty-nine million visitors annually in 2001 to fifty-three million by 2013, the last year of his third term.

His enthusiasm for the arts as an engine of economic development and as a magnet that drew creative talent to the city of New York, combined with his personal generosity and his commitment of city capital funds, was responsible for nothing less than a renaissance of unprecedented building projects: the Whitney Museum and the Museum of Modern Art, the Metropolitan Museum, the New Museum, El Museo Del Barrio, Theatre for a New Audience, the Queens and the Bronx Museums, the Brooklyn Academy of Music, City Center, the Museum of the City of New York, the Manhattan Theatre Club, the Roundabout, the Second Stage, and the Public Theater all experienced major renovation, expansion, or both, backed by the City of New York. As, of course, did Lincoln Center and all of its resident artistic organizations.

Yes, the mayor's bureaucracy could be confounding. The multiple and staggered city agency reviews of the work of redevelopment at every single stage was costly and time-consuming. I learned that taking on a huge building project in New York City was not an assignment for the impatient or for those with a low tolerance for frustration. And the decline in annual operating support from city tax levy dollars to cultural institutions was worrisome.

But these are quibbles. Bloomberg and his colleagues got the big picture right. Art works on many levels. And nowhere more so than in New York City, the cultural capital of the world. His administration supported arts and culture like no other, as did he.

The city began to attract first-rate architects—Renzo Piano, Norman Foster, Elizabeth Diller and Ric Scofidio, Herzog and de Meuron,

Christian de Portzamparc, Jean Nouvel, Frank Gehry, Tod Williams and Billie Tsien, and David Rockwell—to design new and expanded artistic spaces. Stimulated by public support, foundations, corporations, and individuals donated unprecedented sums to complement the commitment of government.

I can think of a few but not many very successful, creative businessmen who have become billionaires many times over within a period of three decades. I can list a handful or two of creative, seminal, philanthropic leaders whose gifts have made a real difference in this world. And I can enumerate some outstanding public officials and mayors. But I cannot identify any figure in the twentieth or twenty-first century who has played all three roles with the determination, drive, and brilliance of New York City's 108th mayor.

His track record of fidelity to the arts and to Lincoln Center was almost enough for me to accept blame for a disclosure to the press I knew nothing of and had nothing whatever to do with.

A HUNGARIAN REFUGEE, resettled as a teenager by the IRC, Andy Grove took one glance at America and fell in love. He had found freedom. Fate had bestowed on him the IRC. It resettled Andy in a foreign country, the United States of America. It outfitted him with a hearing aid, offered counseling and financial support of all kinds, and advised him that he could enroll as a matriculated student at no cost in The City College of New York.

When I arrived at the IRC, Grove was a world-renowned figure and a modest (very modest, relative to his means) donor. No one from the IRC had endeavored to contact him personally, until I did.

We met in an unpretentious suite in a midtown hotel. He was with his wife, Eva. Andy came across as a no-nonsense, all-business interrogator. America was then in the midst of the Kosovo crisis. Grove asked to be briefed.

"The IRC is one of only four NGOs present in Kosovo when the NATO bombing began," I started.

During the half hour that followed, Andy asked many probing questions. I had but one request of him. Would he join the IRC's board of directors?

I was elated when he said yes.

Several years later came another question from me. Would Andy agree to be honored at a gala held in the heart of Silicon Valley?

As the president of the IRC, I was struck by how distant the world of high-tech was from humanitarian refugee causes, even though hundreds of senior executives up to and including CEOs were themselves first- or second-generation immigrants or refugees. Grove provided the chance to break through into this wealthy, scientifically sophisticated, and very influential community.

We were told that Silicon Valley types did not show up at fund-raising events. We were informed that those relatively few who live in San Francisco would not trek up to Burlingame, where the event was to be held at a hotel close to the airport and convenient for the landing of corporate jets. We were informed that those who worked in the valley wished to go home at the end of the day and would not assemble in a hotel room for dinner and speeches, even to honor one of their own. To do so was, well, "so New York."

The naysayers underestimated our bicoastal determination, and they certainly didn't account for how beloved was Andy Grove, as a founding father not only of Intel but more generally of the high-technology community.

Tom Labrecque, then CEO of Chase Bank and an IRC board member, readily agreed to emcee the event. Bill Gates, then a very active CEO of Microsoft, served as its chair. Secretary of Defense Bill Cohen, at the request of another IRC board member, Henry Kissinger, agreed to be the featured speaker.

But the centerpiece was Grove, who spoke of the kindness of strangers. About how the IRC helped situate him in a new country with counseling, financial support, and that new, relatively inconspicuous hearing aid. He held it up for all to see, together with his identity card, which he had saved all these years, a precious piece of paper prepared by the IRC that permitted him to be admitted to the country.

Grove offered his heartfelt thanks not only to the organization that had rescued him from his native Hungary during the 1956 revolution through its office in Vienna, but also to his immediate personal family and to his extended professional family, present in that packed ballroom.

The message was simple and powerful. Today's Andy Grove is not Hungarian. He or she is Cambodian, Vietnamese, Sudanese, Burmese,

Bangladeshi, Russian, or Indian. It matters not. America has been blessed by newcomers, brave and ambitious people who flee persecution in their own countries and envision a future for themselves and their children here. Not so long ago, he had been one of those "tired and poor," a member of the "huddled masses yearning to breathe free." He told those gathered in the ballroom that it was up to them to guarantee that the words etched on the pedestal of the Statue of Liberty are given new life, generation after generation, not just for the benefit of refugees and immigrants, but for the future vitality and creativity of our country, to which they have contributed disproportionately.

The IRC won many friends that night, and Grove rekindled his own interest in the refugee cause by becoming a major and important contributor of time and treasure.

PERHAPS THE LAST of the generation to legitimately claim to be a founding father of Lincoln Center was Martin E. Segal. I had been proud to call him a friend ever since I had first met him and his wife Edith when I was executive director of the 92nd Street Y. Marty was a confidant, an informal advisor, an indispensable part of Lincoln Center's intelligent memory.

Born in Russia on July 4, 1916, Segal was a life force. He once told me that his very first involvement in the arts occurred when he was about six years old. He played the role of Spinach in a first-grade play. Rumor has it that he insisted on top billing. His wife of seventy-three years, Edith, the love of his life, overheard him telling this story. She whispered that Spinach was Marty's first and last nonspeaking role.

Segal progressed from a vegetable that's good for you to becoming the founding president of the Film Society of Lincoln Center. During his tenure, Marty arranged for Charlie Chaplin's very controversial return to America to become the first Film Society honoree. The second was Fred Astaire. There were few things that Segal didn't much like, but going to the racetrack was one, cigars another. To woo Fred, who loved both, Marty smoked from the stands at the Kentucky Derby with Astaire, his host.

With Nat Leventhal as Lincoln Center's president at his side, Marty chaired its board of directors with consummate skill, finesse, and prodigious fund-raising from 1981 to 1986. After concluding his term as chair, for the next twenty-five years Segal faithfully attended Lincoln Center board meetings and participated fully in the active board emeriti group, serving with distinction and characteristic flair as its cochair.

He could be a stickler for detail. Few acts of omission were as inexcusable to him as failing to show up, as promised, on a gala occasion or at a Green Room Dinner, without at least calling in advance. Whenever that happened, Segal is reputed to have asked his secretary and assistant, Bonnie Zitofsky, who worked closely with him for almost half a century, to follow up with a telephone conversation of her own, which went something like this.

Bonnie: "Hello, is this Mr. Adler's secretary?"

"Yes."

"Well, I'm calling for Mr. Martin Segal, and he asked me to express his grave concern about Mr. Adler's health and to inquire as to what hospital flowers should be sent, or whether Mr. Adler is convalescing at home."

"Well, Mr. Adler is perfectly fine, and he is in the office."

"Oh, I see, I'll report that to Mr. Segal. I am sure that he will be relieved to learn of Mr. Adler's good health. And I am also very certain that Mr. Adler will be hearing directly from Mr. Segal very soon."

Marty Segal loved the arts, and he adored artists. He found it simply magical that a violinist or pianist could walk into a grand space, like Alice Tully Hall, and fill it with beautiful sound. Or that an actor could transport one into another time and place, inhabiting a character as one might wear a custom-made suit or a made-to-order dress. For Segal, there was nothing like a night at the movies or opera, preceded or followed by animated conversation between and among friends about art, politics, current events, and what could be done to help repair our broken world.

Each year, Marty presented to two promising artists the distinguished Martin E. Segal Award, which helped launch or sustain their careers. It was another example of his desire not simply to enjoy established artists, but to nurture the new and the promising.

In addition, Segal knew that world-class art attracted commerce; created jobs; lured tourists; swelled the coffers of restaurants, retail establishments, and hotels; and fed the property tax rolls. Lincoln Center as an engine of economic development, as another reason that talented people are attracted to New York City, as a source of civic pride.

Segal, who was the guy behind the very idea of creating the Cultural Affairs Department in the City of New York, was accustomed to explaining why by asking this rhetorical question: "Do you know anyone who comes to Manhattan to ski?"

Segal was an immigrant who never graduated from high school yet was as well-read as any PhD, and he became the chairman of the board of perhaps the most prestigious intellectual retreat in the world, the Institute for Advanced Study at Princeton University.

This self-educated entrepreneur and shrewd businessman could write a letter as charming and as persuasive as any I have ever received. The sheer elegance and expressiveness of these missives rendered them keepsakes. I treasure the several hundred he sent me.

In the very week of his death, Marty was at our Mostly Mozart Festival Gala celebrating the tenth anniversary of Louis Langrée as its music director. That same week, we met in my office. Ostensibly, I was seeking advice. Really, I just wanted an excuse to see him. He arrived at 10:00 a.m., dressed to the nines, a trademark fresh red boutonniere in his lapel, walking with a cane and seeing through only one eye.

Marty sat down and sipped his coffee. He spoke of a trip he planned to take to London and Paris. He remarked on how amazing Alan Cumming's one-man *Macbeth* had been, how splendid it was for Lincoln Center to present the Paris Opera Ballet, and how much he had enjoyed seeing Christian Marclay's *The Clock*. He asked me what I was looking forward to most in the fall season to come.

Segal's secret for life was, in the words of a James Taylor song, "enjoying the passage of time." He looked ahead with the energy, the optimism, the prodigious work habits of an immigrant who loved America.

This is what Marty believed. That seemingly insoluble problems are really only tantalizing challenges in disguise. That working together, smart people of goodwill can build durable institutions of the highest quality, causes and organizations that matter. That the key to longevity is engaging fully in the life of our great city and country. That private joys and public achievements are meant to be seized.

DANNY MENDEZ AND Chris Ullman mean as much to me as the more celebrated mentors in this chapter. Mendez and Ullman embody the talent and drive of artists. Someone like them is working just around the block from where you live. Such is the ubiquity of performing art.

As the president of Lincoln Center, I enjoyed the authority to present performing arts ensembles in our halls. During the course of my tenure, I rarely offered concrete suggestions to either Jane Moss or Nigel Redden. To my relief, whenever I did, each readily accepted them. Perhaps my ideas had merit, or perhaps I was being rewarded for self-restraint.

Producing and presenting events on a regular basis was not part of my job description. Moss and Redden are world-class professionals. What these veterans needed from me was support, financial and otherwise. What they didn't need was second-guessing.

While I was having an MRI scan on August 20, 2007, about six weeks after I had an operation on my right wrist at the Hospital for Special Surgery in New York City, I found the lab technician in charge knew not only my name, but what I did for a living.

He explained that the MRI would take almost forty-five minutes and handed me a looseleaf notebook in which a single page was devoted to a selection of music in different genres—pop, rock, indie, folk, world music, and the like. He explained that the MRI made something of a racket and that music muted its clatter.

He also suggested that if I didn't particularly care for any of the choices in front of me, there just happened to be another option.

Danny Mendez, the technician, had formed a rock band in the Throgs Neck section of the Bronx, and it had produced a CD. I could always listen to "Danny Mendez and His Latin Project."

Why not?

The next thing I knew, a conveyer belt was moving me into the MRI contraption accompanied by the beats of that rock band organized by Mendez. Naturally, he seemed as eager to learn my reaction to the music as he was to determine whether my wrist was healing properly.

When the examination was concluded, he asked what I thought of the CD, and I told him the truth—actually, I rather liked it.

He was ready for me. Another copy had been giftwrapped in anticipation of my positive reaction, together with a handwritten letter addressed to Wynton Marsalis. Danny requested that I be the courier of this important missive and the accompanying package!

Any doubt that artists are natural entrepreneurs was dispelled during a meeting I had with the Carlyle Group, one of the largest and most influential private equity organizations in the world.

As I was being introduced to executives, one of them in charge of public relations mentioned in passing that he was also a musician.

"What do you play?"

"I whistle."

"What do you whistle, and where?"

"Almost anything. Almost anywhere."

"Would you whistle something for me now?"

"Of course. What would you like to hear?"

"How about Duke Ellington's 'Take the A Train'?"

To my astonishment, Chris Ullman whistled a perfectly modulated and spirited version of Ellington's classic piece. The sounds wafted through the corridors of offices in which, no doubt, at that very moment mega-deals were being discussed and plans to raise the next new fund were being concocted.

I then learned that Chris had performed with the National Symphony at the Kennedy Center and at the National Mall during a July 4 celebration, and I was handed his own vintage CD, *The Symphonic Whistler*.

It was made clear to me that should Lincoln Center ever have an opening in its concert schedule, I could always reach a talented whistler in Washington, D.C., who would be pleased to drop everything and in a New York minute, take himself to one of Lincoln Center's famous venues.

Each of the characters profiled here, though situated in different settings and confronting starkly different challenges, showed me how to change the world for the better, in large chunks and small.

All of them taught me lessons about applied energy, selflessness, and ambition. All helped to repair a world in need of mending. None indulged in acquisitive behavior, whether in search of power or material goods.

To remind myself that such role models are all around us, all I have to do is whistle.

CHAPTER 11

Civic Leaders Come and Go: In Search of Accountability

Many forms of conduct permissible in a workaday world for those acting at arm's length, are forbidden by those bound by fiduciary ties. A Trustee is held to something stricter than the morals of the marketplace. Not honesty alone, but the punctilio of an honor the most sensitive, is then the standard of behavior. As to this, there has developed a tradition that is unbending and inveterate.

—BENJAMIN CARDOZO

It is fascinating to observe how corporate, institutional, and political leaders decide when to stay and when to go.

Supreme Court Justice David Souter and Pope Benedict, though enjoying lifetime appointments, resigned from their posts: the first because he wished to return to a scholarly, monastic life in a Vermont cabin, the second because of illness and an inability to perform acceptably while in office.

At IBM, the CEO is out at sixty years of age, no questions asked, no protest to be lodged. Lou Gerstner and Sam Palmisano, arguably in their prime, stepped down in deference to that rule. It is designed to encourage internal aspirants to the top spot to stay and not leave IBM for other available senior executive positions. Whether and which internal contenders for CEO are successful is determined well in advance of the time needed to look for outside candidates. A fixed, relatively early retirement age is viewed at IBM as a key to senior executive retention.

When Hosni Mubarak was finally toppled as the president of Egypt after a twenty-nine-year dictatorship, albeit one that featured regularly staged rigged elections, a joke circulated throughout the country explaining that his departure was no loss.

It is said that on the day he first took office, Mubarak's limousine driver was taking him through downtown Cairo when they reached an intersection requiring one to turn either left or right.

"Mr. President, which direction would you prefer that I turn?"

"Well, what would Nasser have done?"

"Oh, sir, he would have taken a sharp right."

"And what direction would Sadat have taken?"

"He definitely would have had me turn left."

"I see. Well, then, why don't we just stay put."

Staying put is the best that can be claimed for Egypt's society, economy, and polity during all of the Mubarak years.

That prolonged stall also characterized the New York Philharmonic during Paul Guenther's thirteen-year tenure as its board chair (1996–2009). He stayed on too long.

He failed to lead, and he failed to leave.

In the immediate wake of the excruciatingly embarrassing round-trip of the New York Philharmonic to and from Carnegie Hall, it was widely thought that Paul Guenther and Zarin Mehta would surely find a speedy and dignified way to resign, or failing that, the trustees would insist on both taking their leave. Neither happened. At galas, Paul would introduce himself this way: "I am Paul Guenther, and yes, I am *still* the chairman of the New York Philharmonic."

Resigning from office is straightforward. Announce a date. Appoint a search committee of the board to look for your successor or refer the matter to a well-functioning nominating and governance committee, if there is one. In other words, leave a time-certain vacuum and allow your trustee colleagues the freedom to fill it.

Instead, Guenther took it upon himself to find his own successor. Could there be a less persuasive recruiter? At least a few individuals were offered the post. All declined. Months passed. Then years. Finally, in desperation and perhaps for the first and only time at Lincoln Center, a search firm was consulted to help find a board chair, one who did not come from the trustee ranks, numbering some sixty strong. So much for succession planning.

Matters were hardly better at the New York City Opera. Its weakened condition, particularly after Paul Kellogg's resignation; the on-again, off-again, shaky agreement that Gerard Mortier would serve as Paul's successor; and the designation of the ill-prepared George Steel all suggested strongly the desirability of Susan Baker resigning as the chair of the board. Her leadership was identified with unconsummated institutional wanderlust, with the severe erosion of the New York City Opera's endowment, with confused and shrinking audiences, and with persistent operating deficits. One sign that her credibility and judgment were in doubt was the disappointing charitable contributions of most trustees. Another indicator was her unwillingness or inability to expand that group and to raise its performance in giving and garnering donations.

As with the last-gasp selection of Steel, only when it was too late to matter did Baker relinquish her post, to Charles Wall. It fell to Wall to close up shop, once and for all, and he did so with as much class, dignity, and generosity as could possibly be imagined.

The moral of these stories is surely that the choice of when a CEO or a board chair comes and goes should not be left entirely to the incumbent. An orderly and regular review process is required. In government, we call that process free and fair elections. In free enterprise, we refer to it as sound corporate governance. In nonprofits, the terms of the chair and the CEO are the province of the board of directors. Sound succession planning is imperative if highly valued institutions are to remain healthy.

My own decisions about when to leave various positions were largely determined by what had been accomplished during my tenure. Had important milestones been reached, rendering it less productive, less necessary, and less satisfying for me to stay in place? Was the institution ready for another leader? Was I physically and psychically ready to move on?

IN DECIDING WHETHER and when to step down, a CEO faces a serious danger. Will his or her tenure in office be so long as to conflate the interests of the incumbent with the needs of the institution? Is the very personal identity of the officeholder so intertwined with his or her institutional role that voluntary separation becomes too threatening to contemplate? It is always a bad sign when the board member or the CEO appears to need to occupy the position more than the institution needs that individual to serve. Trustees and CEOs hold institutions in trust for service to others, not the other way around. Often, when lengths of stay are prolonged, a key attribute of good governance—healthy turnover—is ignored. There is then a major risk that talented potential successors inside the organization will leave in search of challenging service opportunities elsewhere.

At Lincoln Center we enjoyed a rigorous nominating and governance committee process that annually assessed trustee performance. Not infrequently, improvement was called for and, on rare occasions, a request for the resignation of a negligent or disappointing trustee was in order. We also benefited from an annual executive committee review of CEO performance. Both processes created regular opportunities to discuss succession and its timing.

In my case, the board twice requested that I extend my stay. First from seven years to nine, and then from nine to twelve. These discussions about transition also led to the selection of Katherine Farley as the chair designate, a post she held for a full year before she formally succeeded Frank Bennack. Part of our thinking was to ensure that Farley remained as chair when I left the CEO post. The next president would then have at least a couple of years to serve with an experienced board leader at the helm.

There is wisdom in knowing not only when to leave your post, but also when to really "let go." In his definitive work on the subject of corporate CEO retirement, Jeffrey Sonnenfeld reaches this conclusion: "Corporate leaders who leave office positively and enthusiastically may meet both their personal needs for renewal and the needs of their firm and society."[1]

For an excellent example of proceeding just this way, I think of the conduct of Harvey Golub, the CEO of American Express. When retiring, he decided not to be the chair of the board when his successor, Ken Chenault, became the CEO or even to remain on the board as a plain director. Interviewed in *Business Week*, Golub, who became and remained during much of my tenure a trustee of Lincoln Center, acknowledged how much he had enjoyed his days in the driver's seat. He was available for advice if and when Ken needed it. "If Ken wants my input, he knows where to find me."[2] For Golub, retiring meant truly departing from American Express, not casting a shadow on his replacement.

It is said that Episcopalians always leave the scene without saying good-bye, whereas Jews always say good-bye and never leave. Harvey said good-bye *and* left, clearly an ecumenical approach. And a model worthy of emulation.

YOU CAN LEARN a lot about any destination—a hotel, a gym, a hospital, a college, or an employer—by how each greets you and how each bids you good-bye.

Are you welcomed by name? Is the place prepared for your arrival? Are you thanked for completing your term of service? Are you asked genuinely about what might be improved, and is there intelligent feedback to your suggestions? Well-functioning organizations should always conduct exit interviews, particularly of their most valuable personnel.

And what about your length of stay? Have you ever felt that the vacation you planned was longer or shorter than the destination warranted? Or that the third year of law school was one too many? Or that you were discharged prematurely from a hospital stay?

These sorts of issues are different in degree, but not in kind, from those that involve you and your employer. Throughout our tenure, from entry to exit and at all points in between, how we treat one another matters. And when it comes to the CEO, the impact is far-ranging and often enduring.

When Leonard Lauder, the then CEO of Estee Lauder, decided in his capacity as the chair of the 92nd Street Y's search committee to offer me the post of executive director, little did I know how consequential this decision would be. At the time, I was just thirty-one years old. Henry Kohn, the president of the board of directors, called me with the good news. But he didn't mention that my predecessor, once removed, would remain something of a fixture at the place. His name was Carl Urbont, and he and his predecessor, Jack Nadel, had together served more than sixty years as CEO of the Y. When Urbont resigned, Jack Boeko was appointed executive director, but he departed some eighteen months later.

Throughout the search for Boeko's successor and during his brief term of service, Carl Urbont held the post of executive vice president, supposedly in charge of fund-raising. Actually, Urbont acknowledged that he was unfamiliar with raising funds and had engaged in very little of it during his long tenure. It struck me as awkward in the extreme to have my predecessor working every day only yards away from my office at a salary higher than my own, and with a full-time assistant at his disposal, assigned to a task he was admittedly incapable of completing successfully.

As it happened, I was too self-confident and too challenged by the state of drift and underutilization in which the Y found itself in the summer of 1977 to be very much bothered by his presence. He could have been an irritant. A constant second guesser of my every move. He could have been an in-house critic with the trustees, whom he knew very well, and with staff, many of whom he had hired or who had previously reported to him. That the board of directors did not recognize the potential for mischief in Urbont's continued presence, holding a job for which he was clearly unqualified and with which he was very uncomfortable, well after retirement age, seemed amateurish.

Almost twenty years later, as I became the president of the International Rescue Committee, all was not well with the organization. My predecessor, Bob De Vecchi, and the leader he followed, Carel Sternberg, were the only CEOs the IRC had known in its storied fifty-plus-year history. Strapped for resources, having great difficulty finding enough cash to meet payroll, and organizationally challenged, the institution, I learned after the fact, needed rescue almost as much as the refugees it served. Rather than bid De Vecchi a fond farewell with warm thanks for his extraordinary service, which had been heroic in many ways, the IRC's board of directors saw fit to elect him to be one of its own.

Playing that role was an invitation to Monday morning quarter-backing. Perhaps I should not have been surprised, because the IRC was institutionally immature, and nowhere more so than at the board level. Some key players, like John Whitehead, Winston Lord, and Dr. James Strickler, were outstanding leaders and recognized the need for change in board composition and expectation. And De Vecchi never once interfered with my chief executive role. Nonetheless, on the board there was a trustee married to a senior staff member who reported to me. On the board were also both a father and his son and a husband and his wife, serving simultaneously. As was the case at the Y, there was no common understanding about the financial obligations or the service requirements expected of trustees. It is hardly surprising that their charitable contributions and commitment of expertise and service were highly uneven. Taken together, they left a great deal to be desired.

Neither the Y nor the IRC could find a red carpet to roll out for their new CEO. Each was thoroughly unprepared to greet me and had given virtually no thought to an appropriate orientation or introduction to the institution, its key actors, and its formidable challenges.

Later, after I had announced my plans to step down as the CEO of the IRC, I interviewed with the search committee of Lincoln Center, chaired by the president and CEO of the Hearst Corporation, Frank Bennack. It was the IRC and the 92nd Street Y all over again. Strange governance practices seem to follow my career path. Serving on the search committee was my friend and former CEO Nat Leventhal. Leventhal, who had been president of Lincoln Center for some seventeen years, was an extremely close friend of his successor, Gordon Davis. They had practiced law together. They had both served in the administrations of Mayor Lindsay and Mayor Koch. Davis was also a trustee of Lincoln Center for part of the time that Leventhal served as president. Leventhal must have been pleased that Davis was selected to take his place, and he must have been saddened that Davis's tenure as president lasted only nine months. Not only was Leventhal then given the opportunity to help select a second successor by serving on the search committee after Gordon's resignation, but he had earlier been elected to Lincoln Center's board as a full-fledged voting member.

Such a state of affairs is an invitation to difficulty and discomfort.

To put a new CEO in the position of being judged by a predecessor who held the post for almost two decades was problematic. Leventhal now served alongside trustees whom he knew quite well and staff with whom he had worked closely, if not actually hired. The temptation to ask him how I was performing and vice versa must have been irresistible. It is a credit to Leventhal that I cannot recall a single problem. He addressed all of his questions and observations to me only, personally and confidentially. I felt completely free to ask for his advice. Not everyone would have been as circumspect and thoughtful.

There was no organized preparation for my arrival. No formal briefings. No systematic way to meet key trustees, donors, and constituents. No budget for the following year. Few fund-raising plans were in place. I felt very much on my own.

Surprised by these experiences, I drew lessons from them. When I took my leave of the Y, the IRC, and Lincoln Center, I refused to become a trustee, to serve in any way (unless explicitly asked to do so by my professional successor), or even to be a member of an emeriti group. Nor would I play any formal role in the selection process for my successor.

Having served for eight, six, and twelve years, respectively, at the Y, the IRC, and Lincoln Center, there had been ample opportunity to influence the culture, the staffing, and trustee expectations at each organization. That was enough, indeed more than enough. There is a time to pass the torch. The responsibility for the future of an institution resides in the staff and the board being left behind.

In politics, from my viewpoint, nothing brought more honor to George W. Bush than his conduct after leaving office. Unlike his hand-picked vice president, Dick Cheney, who was an incessant source of consistent and shrill criticism of President Barack Obama, Mr. Bush simply refused to publicly comment on the performance of his successor. The same can hardly be said of Jimmy Carter, with his running commentary on many of the policies of his successors, which accounts for his relative unpopularity with all of them.

A departing CEO should do everything possible to ensure a solid first year of institutional performance after his or her departure. Mobilize staff to present thorough and thoughtful transition briefings. Offer the successor an opportunity to meet and greet key figures in an efficient, congenial way. Kick no cans down the road. And then leave the premises. Lock, stock, and barrel. But be available to provide advice whenever it is requested.

It has been rumored that some outside candidates to succeed the handpicked successor of Bill Gates, Steve Ballmer, as the CEO of Microsoft, were put off by the presence of both men on the board of directors and decided not to compete for the job.

Can you blame them? Those privileged to be in charge in government, in corporations, or in nonprofit institutions should first and foremost ask what is best for citizens, shareholders, customers, patrons, and clients. Rare are the occasions when retired CEOs hanging around the institutional water cooler can be helpful to such key stakeholders. Resist the temptation to continue to feel needed. Do not stay beyond what the organization realistically requires.

When in doubt, leave.

Consider the words attributed to Oliver Cromwell, speaking to the Rump Parliament in 1653: "You have sat too long here for any good you have been doing. Depart, I say, and let us have done with you. In the name of God, go!"

WHY DO OTHERWISE intelligent and sophisticated board chairs and those closest to them fail to speak frankly with each other and with their CEOs about individual and collective performance?

Why is it so difficult to point to areas in need of leadership improvement and to insist on the development of a plan to remedy a state of affairs requiring high-level attention? For that matter, why do so many trustees of an institution fail to call themselves and their CEO to account for serious performance shortfalls?

Gary Parr once commented at a meeting that the New York Philharmonic had experienced fourteen successive years of operating deficits. *Fourteen.* It carried out two conductor searches, one resulting in the retention of Kurt Masur, the other, Loren Maazel. Both were widely regarded as botched in process and disappointing in outcome. The board also took the orchestra on the round-trip to and from Carnegie Hall that squandered credibility and goodwill. This is not a record of performance to boast about.

Would all of this not be reason enough to expect the resignations of Paul Guenther and Zarin Mehta?

In the face of a declining audience and a deteriorating balance sheet, the Metropolitan Opera remains a troubled institution. Evidence abounds that Peter Gelb's management and artistic responsibilities are simply too much for any one executive to shoulder, no matter how creative and hardworking.

Why didn't the Met's board of trustees demand early on the development of an economic model that held promise of a viable financial future?

In meeting privately with Gelb, I was struck by his response when I asked what would happen if his effort to hike ticket prices and raise unprecedented amounts of funding for ambitious programs, infrastructure improvements, and working capital were not successful. What if seeking surpluses from operas in movie theaters did not work according to plan? What if price increases met with significant resistance?

Peter's response was surprising.

"It has to work. There is no Plan B."

I know of no successful CEO without a backup plan in the event of failures or shortfalls. Gelb's insistence that he had charted a course and was going to pursue it no matter what obstacles he faced, foreseen or otherwise, struck me as bordering on dangerous. The Met's board of directors should have seen to it that considered alternatives were seriously entertained.

If the New York Philharmonic faced chronic operating deficits, and the Metropolitan Opera's economic model seemed seriously flawed, the New York City Opera's devolution also occurred not suddenly, but over at least a decade.

Ten years or more of spending well in excess of annual income and of drawing down on an endowment until there was hardly any left would surely weaken any artistic organization. What Paul Kellogg, Gerard Mortier, and George Steel had in common as successive CEOs was a board of directors and a chair who simply refused to call a halt to irresponsible management. One wonders whether they even recognized the harsh realities. Sometimes in human affairs, the capacity for self-delusion knows no limits.

Even worse, recall that board members indulged Paul Kellogg by traipsing around the island of Manhattan, looking to build a new opera house with no prospect whatsoever of being able to raise the funds to build or sustain it.

The famous sociologist Albert Hirschman wrote a treatise on what to do when you disagree in principle with an institution's policy. He referred to the choice as voice or exit.[3] Either protest the organization's direction inside its corridors with a view toward change, or leave it entirely, in the hope that others will follow or that leadership, stunned by defection(s), will change course or resign.

Clearly, every difference of opinion is not a difference of principle. One should not take lightly offering a strong dissenting view or a resignation in protest.

In my general experience at Lincoln Center, very few trustees or staff exercised either option: voice or exit. Those who choose either course of action deserve a special place on any trustee honor roll.

The failure to engage in "voice or exit" is hardly confined to Lincoln Center's constituent artistic organizations or to nonprofit institutions more generally. Consider contemporary American foreign and domestic policy.

The Iraq conflict led by President Bush has been called a war of choice.[4] That choice and the way the war was conducted became publicly controversial. But who raised a contrary voice in the Bush administration during the course of a conflict that was costly in lives and treasure and was unjustified by the rationale of weapons of mass destruction readily available for use by Saddam Hussein? As to exit, one can search in vain for any high-ranking official who even threatened to resign on principle.

Instead, it seems to be a rule of human behavior that to get along, you must go along. One can count on fewer than two hands those in significant positions who expressed strong dissenting views inside almost any post–World War II administration or those who resigned on principle over policy differences.

Secretary of State Cyrus Vance in the Carter administration did so over the Iranian hostage crisis policy. Attorney General Elliot Richardson did so rather than carry out President Richard Nixon's orders during the notorious Watergate affair. FBI Director Robert Mueller and Deputy Attorney General James Comey threatened to resign if President Bush compelled Attorney General John Ashcroft to authorize the illegal surveillance of American citizens. Before his untimely and premature death, Ambassador Richard Holbrooke spoke forcefully about President Obama's "mistaken" policy toward Afghanistan and Pakistan. Christina Romer, President Obama's chair of economic advisors, argued that the economic stimulus package of the administration was too small to promote a rebound sufficient to overcome the most drastic downturn in America's financial history since the Great Depression. These are notable exceptions to the general rule of passivity in the face of important policies or practices with which one strongly disagrees.

Notwithstanding his reputed differences with President Bush, Secretary of State Colin Powell never gave voice loudly or clearly enough to be heard inside or outside the administration. The director of the Central Intelligence Agency, George Tenet, who called finding weapons of mass destruction and victory in Iraq a "slam dunk," and General Tommy Franks, largely responsible for a failed occupation policy, were not held accountable for deficient performance. Instead, each was granted the highest award our nation can bestow, the Presidential Medal of Freedom.

What is it about speaking truth to power, or about holding authorities accountable for their acts, that is so difficult?

As I write, no one, not a single senior executive of Bear Stearns, Countrywide, Lehman Brothers, Merrill Lynch, Goldman Sachs, Fannie Mae, Freddie Mac, the Bank of America, or Credit Suisse, has been found guilty of a felony. Indeed, no official from these firms has even been indicted for gross failures of omission and commission that brought our country to the "brink of economic Armageddon" in 2008 and 2009. That is the phrase used by none other than the former chairman of the Federal Reserve Bank, Ben Bernanke.

This pronounced tendency to avoid both conflict and the risk of alienating friends and colleagues runs rampant in all sectors of our society. It is no small part of the reason that our major institutions are far less trusted by citizens than they were decades ago.

The failure to exercise the option of voice or exit can badly maim an organization, even bring it to the brink of dissolution. Acknowledging grave mistakes and resigning, or being asked to take one's leave, may be difficult, uncomfortable, and painful for those directly involved. But it is sometimes the only honorable course of action and best for the institution or country.

DURING THE LAST two years of my tenure as the president of Lincoln Center, Katherine Farley, my chair, whom I had known for two decades, did not hesitate to give strong voice to her opinion if she felt that management, sometimes a euphemism for me, needed clear criticism.

For example, Farley argued for reducing the cost base of Lincoln Center's artistic programs. She felt that too many were too expensive and were attracting too small an audience. She examined the deficit of various program series—expenses minus ticket income—and expressed concern that the gap to be bridged by contributed funds was growing too large.

She credited management with first-rate cost controls, particularly over administrative expenses. They rose on average only 3 percent per year, including escalating health-care costs and collectively bargained salary and fringe benefit increases. She also acknowledged that on more than one occasion, program expenses had already been reduced to lower levels.

Still, since program cost commitments often extended several years ahead of the next budget cycle, Katherine felt that "out year" expenses needed to be reduced and contained even further.

We joined issue.

I argued that Lincoln Center was operating within the context of more than a decade of balanced and surplus budgets during my tenure. I advanced the view that daring, unusual, and challenging programs are precisely the kind that attract donors and that bring needed subsidies. The Andrew W. Mellon Foundation was not about to offer a major grant to support the presentation of mere entertainment. Besides, surely the only measure of Lincoln Center's artistic success could not be the size of a paid audience attracted to a given set of programs.

What about our obligation to commission new work, world and American premieres? What about our dedication to promoting new and exciting artists, ensembles, choreographers, and composers? What about the important positive recognition accorded our senior artistic curators, Nigel Redden and Jane Moss, by audiences and critics for their adventurous programming? What about the fact that very often what is produced and presented first at Lincoln Center is then performed elsewhere, nationwide and worldwide?

Didn't such considerations deserve a place in Lincoln Center's performance box score? Weren't these salutary consequences of our programming central to Lincoln Center's mission? Not everything that counts can be measured. Not everything that can be measured counts. We should not run the risk of weighing the costs but ignoring value that doesn't fit so neatly on a spreadsheet. Like the power of Lincoln Center's brand and the trust it enjoyed among artists, patrons, and critics for high quality. Like the audience its programs attracted outside of our campus venues, through tours, run-out performances, and digital media.

Farley pushed back. She acknowledged these other Lincoln Center roles and recognized that management enjoyed a praiseworthy track record of balanced and surplus budgets.

But Lincoln Center should climb a wall of worry when it comes to its financial condition. Economic times change. The fund-raising climate can become more forbidding. Box office business can disappoint. And my successor should be given an easier budget to balance, the best possible flight path to a smooth landing.

To pull Katherine's leg at one finance committee meeting, I played a song from Steven Sondheim's musical *Merrily We Roll Along*, falsely suggesting that my chair preferred the easy and the popular over the challenging and the worthy.

Farley grimaced at the mere suggestion that she failed to appreciate Lincoln Center as the progenitor of high art. And she was right to do so. I had overstepped my bounds.

It was tough for me to debate a friend whom I respected enormously. But our differences were about matters of degree, and the contention between us was creative and constructive. Fortunately, good humor prevailed, compromise was struck, the cost basis of programming was reduced (yet) again, and budget guidelines for the "out years" were established. But the board allowed for exceptions if artistic opportunities warranted and if financial planning for larger budgets proved sound.

Good for Farley. She is a rare board chair, and I tip my hat to her. Hold management accountable even if it comes at the cost of more than a little discomfort. After all, one definition of leadership is speaking uncomfortable truths. Lincoln Center is too important a place to smother genuine differences rather than to air them. Our friendship was too precious to be based on false pretenses. In the end, I learned a few lessons. I may have disagreed with the board's judgment, but ultimately, I served at the pleasure of its members, not the other way around. Given Farley's responsibilities, her cautiousness was entirely merited. Holding management accountable for sound performance is precisely what an excellent chair should be about.

Would that all of my CEO colleagues experienced similar debates and were compelled to respond to trustee pressure to perform better or differently. Lincoln Center would be far stronger if the options of voice or exit were exercised more frequently. As would our country's corporations, not least its financial institutions. And so, for that matter, would the management of our nation, the United States of America.

What is needed to close the deficit of trust that Americans harbor toward virtually all institutions is responsible, accountable leadership. And one of the most important responsibilities is knowing when to walk away. Nothing less will do.

CHAPTER 12

Hale and Farewell

One must wait until the evening to see how splendid
the day has been.
—SOPHOCLES

The voluntary routine of rising every morning at 4:45, no matter what time I fell asleep and without the benefit of any alarm clock, and arriving at the office no later than 6:15 a.m., was beginning to take its toll.

I enjoyed the solitude of that early hour. Uninterrupted time to read and write and to respond to incessant e-mails. The space to think about how best to manage the day, the week, and the month ahead most effectively. You can accomplish a lot between 6:15 and 9:00 a.m., not least reaching important people who are also at their desks before their assistants arrive.

If that was the start of most days, at least four nights a week, often five, there were fund-raising prospects and visiting dignitaries to be hosted by me at dinner and then a show. Most often I chose what to see, and with the help of staff members I'd select a dozen or so couples to invite. Generally, three to four were available, making for a party of eight to ten.

Spending all of an evening in such company was a terrific way to come to know donors and donor prospects and what they are about. The aim was to puzzle out how Lincoln Center might entice each to contribute a significant first gift or renew and enhance a previous commitment. Part of what made the job at Lincoln Center so much fun was meeting new and intriguing people. Their professional and personal lives, their interests, opinions, and convictions, were almost always engaging. And one thing I learned for sure. People generally love, and those who do not love do not mind, talking about themselves.

Done well, the beginning and the end of every day, not to mention what happened in between, demanded my full and undivided attention. In between deskwork at dawn and social duties in the evening, I found myself motivating, energizing, supporting, and directing staff colleagues, on whom many psychic calories were spent. Embracing trustees and volunteers loaded with ideas and eager to make their mark, to leave an impression on Lincoln Center, also fell largely to me.

The job description did not end there.

Cultivating corporate and foundation donors, coping with the seemingly endless expressed needs of Lincoln Center's constituents, who treated the "mother ship" as an endless supply of resources with demands that ranged from the serious to the petty. Dealing with appointed and elected officials at all levels of government from around the city, state, country, and world. Responding to requests from outside Lincoln Center for meetings, speeches, and counseling sessions. Launching a start-up consulting practice for Lincoln Center. Helping staff and trustees in need of a reference, a recommendation, a nominating letter, a good word to an admissions officer, a co-op board, or a hospital trustee.

Managing expenses down and revenue up. Recruiting and retaining best-in-class staff and trustees. Keeping one eye on the operating budget and the other on Lincoln Center's balance sheet. And communicating, consistently, about Lincoln Center's priorities, goals, and mission.

After some eight nonstop years of all this and more, I longed for a respite. A truly huge undertaking, the campus renovation, was almost all done, with just a couple of elements left to complete. It was 2010, and I had overdelivered on my promise to the Lincoln Center search committee to serve at least five to seven years in office.

That new theater for which Andre Bishop longed, the Claire Tow Theater, was to be opened soon. And a sculpturally expressive pedestrian bridge across 65th Street was also on the drawing board. The bridge was perhaps the most challenging piece of the entire redevelopment project, as Liz Diller and her team had to satisfy the very different requirements of her Lincoln Center clients and the Department of Transportation, the Department of Buildings, the City Planning Commission, and the Design Commission, among others. All but $75 million of the $1.2 billion needed to pay for the massive renovation and supplemental endowment funds had been raised.

Programs were flourishing. Staff and board ranks had been replenished, both the beneficiaries of energetic, persuasive recruitment.

I felt like it was time to step down and bid Lincoln Center good-bye. But the advice I received from friends and colleagues was almost uniformly to stay for another two or three years. They advised me to try to enjoy the ride and revel in the ribbon cuttings. Why not spend some time actually enjoying all that I had helped make possible?

That turned out to be sound counsel. Not the part about easing the pace. Having Lincoln Center move from strength to strength after my departure was very important to me. That meant the smoothest possible handoff to my successor. Transitions are delicate. Getting it right takes time. I fully intended to race against the clock, not run it out.

I could not have anticipated how pleasant bidding Lincoln Center farewell would be. Its gracious and generous chair, Katherine Farley, her Lincoln Center trustee associates, my professional colleagues, and friends from all walks of life gathered in various configurations and settings on separate occasions to offer fond good-byes. Their odes and gifts were very touching.

At the Lincoln Center Gala held in my honor on May 9, 2013, Bryan Lourd, the managing director and cochair of Creative Artists Agency, brought with him as guests Anne Hathaway and Jimmy Fallon. Anne had recently seen in Alice Tully Hall the American premiere of the film *Les Misérables*, for which she won the Oscar for Best Supporting Actress in 2013. She marveled at how fine were the sightlines, the visual acuity of the film images, and most of all, the sound.

Alice Tully Hall was best known for projecting unamplified sound: the human voice, solo instrumentalists, choruses, and chamber ensembles. Projecting classical music requires a reverberant hall, one that invites clarity and timbre. Film needs the exact opposite: sound that is dampened. It is no accident that Alice Tully Hall serves both ends and does so very well. Only weeks before Jeff Katzenberg, the CEO of DreamWorks, had told me that he knew of no other concert hall in the world as good for watching a movie.

Lourd, well aware that it had been my life's ambition to become a stand-up comic, introduced me to Jimmy Fallon. He too commented on the excellent reports he had heard about Lincoln Center's physical redevelopment in general, and particularly about Alice Tully Hall. He asked me whether I would be good enough to spend some time on the phone advising him about the acoustics of the new Rockefeller Center studio being built for him. In less than a year, by February 2014, he was scheduled to succeed Jay Leno and bring the *Tonight Show* back to New York City, forty years after Johnny Carson had left town for Los Angeles.

Did I have time for JIMMY FALLON? Oh, my.

So we arranged a call. It went something like this:

Reynold: "Jimmy, rest assured, Lincoln Center can recommend an excellent acoustician to help the NBC in-house team. The challenge, though, often has to do with the client, namely, you."

Jimmy: "What do you mean?"

Reynold: "Well. When you sit down to dinner at a first-rate restaurant and tell the waiter or sommelier that you would like a good red wine, he is likely to ask you questions about what you mean by good. Fruity? Aromatic? Smooth? Complex? Questions like that. We should talk about what you want in studio sound. That process can take some time."

Jimmy: "Reynold, I beg to differ. The answer is simple. I know exactly what I want."

Reynold: "Oh you do? Tell me."

Jimmy: "Well, there are 350 seats in the studio. I will tell a joke. 35 members of the audience will laugh. I WANT IT TO SOUND LIKE 350. Just deliver to me an acoustician who can make that happen."

After promising to do so, I reminded Jimmy of my own aspirations and asked whether he would indulge me by listening to just two jokes and assessing my potential for comedic stardom. He readily agreed.

And I reported for weeks to everyone I knew that Jimmy Fallon loved my jokes and that he thought I had a future in stand-up comedy.

Memorable, no? This whole incident was scrapbook worthy. A keeper. One of the many farewell scenes I cherish.

AT THE INTERNATIONAL RESCUE COMMITTEE, I learned anew why it is that I am so enamored of so many donors. There are many reasons to fall madly in love with them. Some are obvious. Others less so. In the surprise category is the fact that most benefactors think about the institution or cause you represent in a simpler and more penetrating way than many who work full-time in the organization.

One winter afternoon in the middle of my six years of tenure at the IRC, I accompanied my chairman, John Whitehead, the former cochair of Goldman Sachs and deputy secretary of state in the Reagan administration, on a solicitation call to Arthur Ross.

We met over lunch at the highly exclusive Links Club right off Madison Avenue on 62nd Street. It is not identifiable, except for the address, and its membership is confined to the wealthy.

In my experience, most clubs in New York City offer pretty mediocre food, and the service leaves a lot to be desired. The Links is an exception.

John and Arthur didn't agree with this observation entirely. In fact, lunch began with both bemoaning the limited selection of white wine, as neither cared for chardonnay and the sauvignon blancs available by the glass apparently left a lot to be desired.

Arthur and John were good friends, so John asked about Arthur's place in Jamaica, how his golf game was faring, and what his prognosis was for the stock market in the next quarter. As members of the Board of Directors of the United Nations Association, they bemoaned the UN's slow and steady deterioration.

With the entrée consumed and coffee on the way, Arthur turned to me and said, "Reynold, I strongly suspect that John has brought you here for a reason, so tell me a little bit about the International Rescue Committee."

I mentioned that refugee organizations were generally divided into two types. There were hundreds in our country that provided relief services to refugees outside of the United States. And there were about a dozen and a half that helped to resettle refugees from around the world in America. The IRC was the only NGO that performed both functions.

"So, Arthur, which of the two areas would you like most to be briefed on?"

He chose resettlement.

Trying to be as concise as possible, I told Arthur that there were essentially two legal justifications for refugees coming to the United States. They needed to prove that they were either fleeing from persecution in their home country or were reuniting with family members in the country of resettlement. The IRC helps refugees advance their case for entry into the United States on either or both of these grounds with the Immigration and Naturalization Service (INS). Once the IRC succeeds, the refugees are then flown to the United States, where they are met by IRC staff and volunteers, who arrange for housing, for US financial and social service support, and for cultural orientation services.

"Arthur, the results are amazing. Within ninety days, 90 percent of the heads of refugee households are fully employed, many even before they have learned to speak much English."

"Let me see if I have got this right, Reynold. I think I can describe what you have said in one sentence. The IRC takes refugees from the INS to the IRS in less than three months!"

There you have it. Arthur compressed pages of the IRC's description of resettlement into fifteen words. I have been plagiarizing them shamelessly ever since.

It is a mark of donor influence that I can't recall precisely how much Arthur pledged to support the IRC's resettlement work that afternoon. Memory may not serve. But I am reasonably certain it was no less than $100,000. What I am crystal clear about, however, is how Arthur so quickly penetrated to the essence of what the IRC's domestic mission is all about.

Donors have that uncanny ability to get to the heart of the matter.

To MY DELIGHT, the board of directors voted to name that footbridge after me. In a ceremony with Katherine Farley presiding, Mayor Bloomberg crossed that span with me behind him, each of us hand-in-hand with a School of American Ballet student. It was a splendid, well-planned event, and when a banner was removed from each side of the bridge revealing these words, "The President's Bridge: In honor of Reynold Levy, October 1, 2012," I was truly moved.

There I was, up there in the ranks of Brooklyn, Manhattan, Williamsburg, George Washington, and 59th Street. A New York City bridge, named after me!

To reconcile the differing views of so many city agencies and her client, Diller had prepared dozens upon dozens of conceptual designs for the bridge, which I was given as a keepsake of the final product that carried my name. Appropriately, it is entitled *The Book of Bridges*, and it has found a proud place in my home library. By the way, there are over one hundred concept designs of bridges contained in it. I kid you not.

Before our maiden bridge crossing, in my own remarks recognizing the accomplishments of the staff, donors, and government officials assembled to celebrate the conclusion of this huge and unprecedented capital campaign, I asked all present to think about the tribute to the great English architect, Christopher Wren, who is buried in St. Paul's Cathedral. Near his tomb, there is a plaque that reads:

> Here in its foundations lies the architect of this church and city, Christopher Wren, who lived beyond 90 years, not for his own profit, but for the public good. Reader, if you seek his monument, all you need do is look around you. February 25, 1723.

Then I asked everyone present to look around them at the new Lincoln Center. It was, I argued, the product of their benefaction, their dedication, and their civic mindedness. It was, I contended, their monument.

IN THE FOLLOWING YEAR, at the gala held in my honor on May 9, 2013, the very event at which I was introduced to Jimmy Fallon, a record $9.4 million was raised, and one of my very favorite artists offered a concert at Avery Fisher Hall that was aired on public television.

Audra McDonald is in many ways the epitome of what Lincoln Center is about. She is a graduate of The Juilliard School. She has performed on virtually every stage in every venue of our campus. She has won a record six Tony Awards. She is now the host of *Live from*

Lincoln Center, the longest-running program of the performing arts on television. It is produced by Lincoln Center and features presentations staged by the resident artistic organizations on our campus. And she is the first and only artist ever to have been elected to serve on Lincoln Center's board of directors.[1]

To have her perform on a night in my honor was very special. Surrounded by friends, supporters, and well-wishers, I indulged myself in reflecting on an accomplishment or two.

The remarks that evening were delivered to some thirteen hundred guests by Bruce Crawford, Frank Bennack, Katherine Farley, and David Rubenstein. Outrageously, Rubenstein compared the physical redevelopment of Lincoln Center to God's creation of the earth, except that while the Lord rested for one day out of seven, I rarely, if ever, had been able to take time off, for any reason. Rubenstein also reflected wryly that God never had to raise money; attend committee, subcommittee, or task force meetings; select architects or contractors; or deal with multiple layers of government.

Rubenstein proposed that I next take on such challenges as Middle East peace or balancing the federal budget. He even suggested that after leaving Lincoln Center I could successfully move on to the highest calling humankind had to offer: private equity.

I was amused, bemused, flattered, and embarrassed all at once.

My remarks focused on two groups: professional and trustee colleagues and generous attendees who had resources to spare.

For the Lincoln Center family of organizations, I distilled down to its essence all that we did together, always aspiring to the highest professional standards. We produced art. We presented it. We studied it. We commissioned it. We toured it. We televised it and digitally transmitted it. We taught it. We offered it more affordably and free of charge more often than ever before in our storied history.

For the benefactors, I reminded them how important they were and how much Lincoln Center depended on their generosity, since they had built and sustained the most prominent and consequential set of performing arts organizations to be found anywhere. I implored them to nurture, preserve, and protect what they had created and never to take that unique achievement for granted.

I closed with Sophocles's observation that "one must wait until the evening to see how splendid the day has been." Well, my evening had arrived, and I could say that I had enjoyed many truly splendid days at Lincoln Center.

ON THE *CHARLIE ROSE SHOW*, I was asked whether at the end of a very successful tenure at Lincoln Center I would have done anything differently. At that time I essentially demurred. I won't now.

I do not have many reservations, and I will not run the risk of burying the lead. Lincoln Center enjoyed a pretty darn good run during my tenure, just shy of thirteen years.

But regrets, I guess I have a few.

I left Lincoln Center with the uneasy feeling that in our zeal to create an encouraging environment for constituent artistic organizations to cooperate on their physical redevelopment and on other business and artistic arrangements, such as celebrating our fiftieth anniversary, we may well have sent an unintended message. Lincoln Center was very generous in the interpretation of what constitutes public space, and therefore, of how much money it would raise. Lincoln Center also absorbed costs for redevelopment services for a period of time well beyond what was originally anticipated. It erred on the side of design excellence, and the cost of materials and quality construction rose accordingly. Lincoln Center also liberally interpreted the purposes for which constituent fund-raising was matchable. The consequence of these expressions of leadership generosity is that Lincoln Center may unintentionally have encouraged an unrealistic and excessive dependence on the parent body.

By indulging the unanimity principle and working around it rather than facing it head-on, we may have reinforced the view that in matters small and large, consequential and otherwise, everyone's assent was required. The law of unintended consequences was at work.

My wife Elizabeth's analysis seemed exactly right. In her view, Lincoln Center was hardly a landlord in the classic sense.

First of all, none of our constituents paid rent, except $1 a year.

Second, the conditions of tenancy were determined not by Lincoln Center but jointly between the so-called landlord and the so-called lessee.

As a result, Liz concluded that I wasn't the president of a real estate concern, but rather the chairman of a co-op board. Lincoln Center was governed like other prestigious cooperative apartments on the Upper West Side, like the San Remo, the Dakota, and the Beresford.

We all had strict criteria for the admission of new members.

We all set high standards for capital improvements.

But when they would be done, how they would be done, who would finance them, and under what terms and conditions resulted in a pile of multilateral and bilateral written agreements. They were extraordinary in their complexity and in the tediousness with which they had to be negotiated and recorded.

Liz concluded her analysis by saying that with the possible exception of the mayor of the city of New York, there was no assignment more dreaded, or tedious, or demanding than being the chair of a co-op board.

In the interest of overcoming passive and active resistance on the part of more than a few constituents to the physical redevelopment of Lincoln Center, had the so-called landlord yielded too much, too often?

AFTER THE FALL of Lehman Brothers in 2008, the setback to the American economy was enormous. It was experiencing the most severe downturn since the Great Depression. Few at Lincoln Center, least of all my chair Frank Bennack, were in any mood to solicit gifts for our capital campaign. He and his colleagues thought that doing so was a fool's errand. I was less certain.

As is always the case, some saw opportunity in crisis and created or embellished a fortune. Others were not adversely affected, and even for those who were struggling, keeping in touch was important, because when their businesses bounced back, Lincoln Center did not wish to be forgotten or placed on some backburner. I know that I annoyed Bennack and some others by continuing to press for meetings and failing to take no for an answer. In retrospect, perhaps I should have "harassed" my superiors somewhat more frequently, or at least more persuasively. As was the case with almost all nonprofits, our capital campaign was at a virtual standstill for almost eighteen months. And in any such effort, the passage of time is almost always an enemy, never an ally.

IN AN OTHERWISE highly laudatory and extensive *New York Times* piece on July 14, 2006, about my performance as Lincoln Center's president, Robin Pogrebin opened her story this way:

> Understandably, perhaps, some concert goers were not pleased by the sight of a man floating in a glass tank, smack dab in the heart of Lincoln Center Plaza, as crowds and television cameras looked on for a full week in May.

By 2012, I was prepared to admit that I agreed with her. So eager had I been to demonstrate Lincoln Center's accessibility to a wider public, to turn it inside out, and especially to invite in those who normally would not consider themselves welcome, that I had succumbed to the blandishments of David Blaine, who offered to set a record for living in an aquarium, underwater, at Lincoln Center.

The spectacle drew a television audience of millions, on ABC, nationwide, in prime time. My chair, Frank Bennack, had approved. Nonetheless, if I had to do it over again, I would decline. As my close colleague Bernard Gersten, the executive producer of Lincoln Center Theater, observed, Blaine's presence created a carnival-like atmosphere. His tricks are not to be confused with the values that an institution like Lincoln Center should symbolize and project. Lesson learned. If New Yorkers want water, they can go to the beach.

AND THEN THERE was the one that got away.

During my term in office, Lincoln Center completed one of the most admired physical transformations in New York City. The success of this bold renovation—architecturally, civically, acoustically—is demonstrable. A once-imposing design now encourages exploration and engagement; a once-failing infrastructure is now robust; formerly inhospitable public spaces are now inviting, lively, and green; dated venues and facilities now welcome the most established and avant-garde artists with ease; serpentine and forbidding passages are now bright and easily navigable; and a shunned and walled-off cityscape is wholly embraced.

Public space expansion and modernization, like the creation of the David Rubenstein Atrium, have been accompanied by the development of new artistic facilities, all extremely well received.

As a result, Lincoln Center can be found where cultural experience meets social discourse, where artistic programming meets dining and relaxation, where event-driven attendance meets a destination in and of itself.

In short, the new Lincoln Center is one of New York City's best calling cards. Ask anyone.

The singular exception is Avery Fisher Hall. Ask anyone.

Avery Fisher Hall was the first venue to open its doors at Lincoln Center; home to the acclaimed New York Philharmonic, Leonard Bernstein, and Gustav Mahler; home to countless world-class musicians, composers, and conductors; home to classical music lovers from around the corner and across the globe; and home to Beverly Sills, whose first Lincoln Center performance was on its stage.

The history of Avery Fisher Hall and the memories it holds for generations of audiences are to be admired. But physically, Avery Fisher Hall's best days are long gone. The artist and patron experience is woeful. The stage is inflexible. The seating plan is archaic. The acoustics can be improved. Physical access is forbidding. The backstage facilities offer "amenities" basically unchanged since the 1960s.

The building is simply worn down, well past its useful life. While this reality was widely known, we could not bring the renovation of the auditorium in Avery Fisher Hall to a successful conclusion.

On reflection, the failed attempt to get this done was the single most frustrating and baffling exercise of my tenure.

Lincoln Center tried everything.

We offered an extremely generous fund-raising division of labor to the New York Philharmonic. In essence, Lincoln Center expressed a willingness to raise no less than 75 percent of the total bill for a new auditorium. To clear away a potential obstacle, we also reached an understanding with the Fisher family that the existing building would continue to be named Avery Fisher Hall. However, Lincoln Center is free to acknowledge a major capital pledge by naming the auditorium inside the building for someone else, not unlike the Isaac Stern Auditorium in Carnegie Hall. Such a lead mega-gift could help launch a fund-raising campaign in fine fashion.

We worked at length, together with the New York Philharmonic, on reaching a common understanding of the objectives for a brand-new, twenty-first-century venue in the existing structure. We shaped consensus on the major changes in the auditorium configuration required to realize them.

Lincoln Center commissioned a new stage installation for use by the Mostly Mozart Festival Orchestra. It incorporated some of the design intent of the planned eventual overhaul of that 2,750-seat space. It worked. Well regarded for intimacy, immediacy, and sound quality, the portable stage, its location, and its lighting were applauded by musicians and audiences. Critics wondered why the New York Philharmonic would not wish to adapt something resembling it as part of an enduring, year-round solution.

We supported in every way we knew how the successors to Paul Guenther as board chair and Zarin Metha as executive director, Gary Parr and Matthew Van Biesen, respectively. We encouraged everyone at Lincoln Center to treat the New York Philharmonic's round-trip to and from Carnegie Hall as a caper. It was time to let bygones be bygones.

The relationship between Lincoln Center and its constituents is governed by a negotiated agreement. The existing document had not much changed since it was originally drafted in 1966. It had expired many times. At the Philharmonic's request, we granted many extensions. These delays troubled us. In order to jointly occupy a new venue, complicated issues like pricing, scheduling, the process for reserving dates, and many other details of a hall's operation needed regulation. A new century and a new auditorium necessitated a new agreement.

The best that we could do was sign a carefully negotiated document that took both parties up to but not including operations for when the replacement venue actually reopened. That task was set aside for another day.

At Lincoln Center, to accomplish some goals, one needs a willing and able partner. For more than half of my tenure, when the matter at hand involved committing to the transformation of the auditorium in Avery Fisher Hall, I could be excused for doubting that the New York Philharmonic was either willing or in the least prepared to be that partner.

For roughly the last third of my tenure, the orchestra appeared to be more than willing. Their key leaders actually seemed to be preparing for a major venue overhaul and all that it would entail. How would the

New York Philharmonic's share of the capital funds be raised? How would it reduce or eliminate its persistent operating deficits, enhance its endowment, and fix its pension fund liability? Where would it perform for the two years that the auditorium in Avery Fisher Hall would be closed? Could it proceed in a way that would protect its subscriber and single ticket holder base during that period? It took time for the New York Philharmonic to grapple with these questions. For those of us engaged in planning for the future of the auditorium with the New York Philharmonic since 2002, it was exasperating to watch the slow-motion progress. When it came to redevelopment, the orchestra seemed to play only in adagio.

And yet I left the premises with some reason to be hopeful. An active committee of the New York Philharmonic and Lincoln Center trustees, staff, and musicians, chaired by the developer Philip Milstein, had been working constructively for the last year and a half of my tenure. Certainly Katherine Farley regarded this huge project as a very high priority. A theater designer and an acoustician had been selected by unanimous agreement after the conclusion of a competitive process, and all looked forward to the selection of a design architect and to detailed campaign planning as the next steps.

I had hoped for more. But the proverbial shovel remained in storage. And it was premature for me to solicit that mega-gift. Time ran out on me.

On Friday, November 14, 2014, Lincoln Center publicly announced that it had successfully negotiated an agreement with the Fisher family. In exchange for a payment of $15 million and a promise of featuring tributes to Avery Fisher in the new lobby of a modernized concert hall, the family agreed to have its name removed from the building.

Now Lincoln Center is free to seek a new, generous benefactor, not only for the overall hall, but also for the transformed auditorium inside of it. Other pertinent facts were disclosed. This comprehensive design and construction project was expected to cost in the vicinity of $500 million. Akustiks had been chosen as the acoustics firm and Fisher-Dachs Associates as the theater designer, with the design architect to be selected in the following months. Both the New York Philharmonic and Lincoln Center agreed that the reconstruction would begin in 2019.

Lincoln Center was well on its way to answering the six key questions any potential mega-donor might ask: Who? What? Why? When? How? At what cost? Lincoln Center was now in a position not only to reply, but to ask prospects a question of its own: Will you join us by offering a nine-figure gift in exchange for a singular, signature naming opportunity?

Speaking for the family, Nancy Fisher was quoted in the *New York Times* on this auspicious day about the family's motivation: "I watched as the campus started to change. It invited the public in, it didn't look so forbidding and formal anymore. [By contrast, Avery Fisher] Hall was like an old slipper. How could you avoid sensing that?"

If there was any lingering doubt about Lincoln Center's resolve, the concrete action steps and timetable that had been announced conveyed Katherine Farley's and the Lincoln Center board's clear intent.

Only one month later, the New York Philharmonic announced that Oscar Schafer, the chairman of Rivulet Capital, a private investment firm, would succeed Gary Parr as the chair of the board of directors. *New York Times* reporter Michael Cooper described Schafer as being enthusiastic about realizing a new home for the resident orchestra of what was once called Avery Fisher Hall.

Then, on February 6, 2015, in a startling development, Alan Gilbert announced that he will step down as the music director of the New York Philharmonic when his contract expires in 2017. Suddenly, the "who" became an open question.

Who shall lead an august orchestra is always a weighty and consequential decision. In this case, the identity of Gilbert's successor will be portentous. Will the board's search committee recommend a civic leader who appreciates New York City and who understands the urgent desirability of replacing Avery Fisher Hall, after so much delay and so many false starts? Will it choose a musical leader with a flair for performing superbly not just the warhorses of the repertory, but the work of living composers as well? Will it choose an energetic and ambitious leader who recognizes the opportunity to shape the future of one of the world's leading orchestras? Key decisions beckon.

How quickly can the new conductor take hold? Less than two years after Gilbert's replacement is identified and on board, the orchestra is scheduled to vacate its home to allow for demolition and construction.

Under the best of circumstances, leaving its historic venue for two seasons and keeping an audience with you is a daunting challenge. The new music director will need to accomplish that feat, assist in closing the orchestra's persistent operating deficits and help raise charitable contributions in unprecedented sums. A very tall order.

The gift of a world-class venue will be worth all of the work and sacrifice required to design, construct, and pay for it. Having demonstrated that Lincoln Center and seven other constituents could raise $1.2 billion in a collective capital campaign, above and beyond the formidable donated sums needed for annual operations, the positive mood of trustee leaders would be fully justified. And not just by a successful Lincoln Center comprehensive capital campaign track record, but also by the economic climate, especially for fund-raising.

When President Bill Clinton was inaugurated in 1993, the Dow Jones Industrial Average stood at 3200. When President Barack Obama was sworn into office for his first term in 2009, that figure had risen to 7200. In the third year of Obama's second term it exceeded 18,000.

Fortunate New Yorkers have increased their net wealth inordinately. Investors, financial intermediaries like hedge funds, private equity funds, and investment advisory firms are faring well. Commercial and residential real estate developers are in the money. Property values are at record highs. So is the mood of many wealthy people. And why not? For a wide swath of our town, the joint is jumping financially. The so-called 1 percent has never had it so good in New York City and around the nation.

Fund-raising conditions will not always be so favorable. Seize the day. For bold ideas, breathtaking designs, demonstrations of solidarity between Lincoln Center and the New York Philharmonic, the funds are there. For the asking.

Should the key players from both organizations hear sounds in the distance, it's just me, cheering them on.

I FOUND IT DIFFICULT to believe that I had served as the president of Lincoln Center for 22 percent of its entire life as an organization.

The Mercury, clocking in at 185,000 miles of travel, had certainly been driven beyond its useful life. I was stubborn about keeping it. Liz was genuinely concerned. She didn't think it was safe to drive any longer. But like that old favorite sweatshirt and that now thirty-three-year-old raincoat I had purchased in an outdoor flea market in Florence on our honeymoon, I just could not bring myself to give it up.

I had come to believe that my tap-dancing dad was with me whenever I got behind the wheel. I missed him very much. A beat-up old car was a poor substitute for his palpable presence. But better than nothing.

Yet even I eventually came around to admitting that its time had come. In Riverdale, it was not uncommon for homeowners to keep old oil storage tanks buried in their yards. New York City regulation required that they be filled with sand or removed entirely. Liz had long wanted ours hauled away in anticipation of an eventual sale of our home.

Well, as luck would have it, the tank and the car were roughly the same size. Why not, I proposed, bury the car under the front lawn where the tank had been as a lasting tribute to Dad? The look I received from my dear wife was indescribable. I tried a compromise: "Okay, okay. Then why don't we just cremate it? I can leave an urn of some kind in my study as a reminder of the decade-plus experience with Dad's car and as a remembrance of him."

The verdict? Macabre.

Instead, I settled for writing a note to the next owner, imploring him or her to take care of this relic, as if it were a pet collie being left to a new home. Bidding the Mercury good-bye on a trade-in was not easy. I had not been inside a dealer's showroom for at least a dozen years. I was very rusty. So I turned to the latest special *Consumer Reports* issue on cars. Following its advice, I bought the highly recommended family car, a 2012 Honda.

On Friday, January 31, 2014, I drove the by now two-year-old Honda out of the Lincoln Center garage onto Amsterdam Avenue. There was no longer a vehicular egress onto 65th Street, much to the relief of pedestrians.

I drove north, hanging a left at 71st Street, to West End Avenue. Traffic on the West Side Highway looked smooth. I then turned left onto 72nd Street and, driving past several dozen formidable condominium, co-op, and rental apartments to the south that did not exist in 2002 when I started at Lincoln Center, made my way home in less than fifteen minutes.

Almost thirteen years had passed. It is estimated that during that short span of time, as many as ten thousand additional residents had found a new home within walking distance of Lincoln Center. America's first and oldest performing arts center had been transformed. So had I.

Chief executive officers are often judged by what transpired during their tenure. That's fine as far as it goes. But they should also be evaluated by institutional accomplishment after their departure. Did they build enduring value? Did they leave behind a foundation for sustained success?

In my case, the 92nd Street Y never returned to its forlorn status as a rather underutilized, undercapitalized, neighborhood community center, largely confined in influence to its Upper East Side location. Its reputation and its services continued to grow.

The International Rescue Committee was no longer hemorrhaging cash and in danger of breakdown and dissolution. After almost six years of nonstop professional management and leadership, I left a solid track record on which my successor, George Rupp, the former president of Columbia University, could build. That he did. Today the IRC is larger—in size, in impact, in influence, and in stature—than ever before in its storied history. The excellent staff and trustees recruited during my tenure and the unprecedented private and public financial support that was raised were assets that George could and did enjoy and significantly enlarge.

To witness institutions and causes flourishing after you have left them is like observing a child moving from a state of dependence to one of liberation. Little is more pleasurable.

Driving home, I imagine that Mercury completely overhauled and refinished, its now proud owner offering it a new life.

My reverie also envisages Lincoln Center thriving long after I have left the stage.

CHAPTER 13

Futures: The Third Sector's and My Own

They say eyes clear with age,
As dew clarifies air
To sharpen evenings,
As if time put an edge
Round the last shape of things
To show them there;
The many-levelled trees,
The long soft tides of grass
Wrinkling away the gold
Wind-ridden waves—all these,
They say, come back to focus
As we grow old.

—PHILIP LARKIN, *Long Sight in Age*, 1955

After I left Lincoln Center, Liz and I deferred taking a vacation in the interest of enjoying our first grandchild, who had just been born, and of giving whatever help we could to the new parents, Emily Feinstein, our daughter, and Eric Olney, our son-in-law. They named their child Colette Elyse Olney. Given Colette's initials, CEO, I'm quite sure that Sheryl Sandberg, the COO of Facebook and the author of the best-selling manifesto for female aspiration and achievement, *Leaning In*, would have no cause for complaint.

When answering the question most friends and colleagues asked me—What next?—I surprised them. Certain of what I did not want—another demanding, full-time spot running an organization, or a life quite as much in the public eye—my thoughts about the future had me traveling back to where I had begun: to solitude, reflection, ideas, and a return to teaching at Columbia University, my alma mater. Taking on occasional consulting assignments for foundation and nonprofit clients. Continuing to serve on the Board of Directors of First Republic Bank and as chairman of the board of the Charles H. Revson Foundation. Becoming a special advisor to the private equity firm General Atlantic. Enjoying my three-year term of service as a recently appointed member of the nominating committee of the Tony Awards.

But before I could embrace my new life, I needed to reduce to its essentials the leadership lessons of my professional journey. What were the keys to any success that I may have enjoyed, the "how-tos" and the "takeaways" from which others might benefit? How to get things done inside complicated organizations is a constant puzzle and a perennial challenge. Whether you work in government, business, or a nonprofit institution, I hope you will find as you read this book's next, final chapter that Larkin is correct. Perhaps my eyes have cleared and come into focus with age and experience.

Building and sustaining vibrant institutions is a continuous process, something of a relay race. I carried my baton proudly and ran as fast and as far as I could. I know that I left the place much stronger than I found it.

My unwillingness to serve as a trustee of Lincoln Center after retiring as president is symbolic of my strong belief that institutions are far more important than those who serve in them. From this conviction it follows that my successor, Jed Bernstein, should not in any way feel crowded by the presence of a predecessor. My deliberate choice is also an expression of faith in the community of volunteers and employees who propel Lincoln Center forward.

I am confident that one could search in vain for a more talented staff and a more gifted, generous board of directors. With its sights raised, its aspirations amply realized, and its momentum very strong, Lincoln

Center's prospects look promising. And with Katherine Farley at the helm as board chair, I am sure that Lincoln Center will not shy away from carrying out a broad definition of its mission as a performing arts presenter and educator, as a campus leader and a prominent civic actor.

New York City deserves as much, as do the artists and audiences Lincoln Center serves.

The world looks to Lincoln Center as a seminal source of creativity and artistic inspiration. That leadership role will assume many new forms in the twenty-first century. It should never be relinquished.

At Lincoln Center and thousands of other nonprofit institutions across America, the challenge of properly discharging trustee and executive accountability looms large. At stake is the proper governance and the quality of performance of the third sector.

It is not an accident that America's nonprofits are sometimes referred to as the "voluntary sector." In virtually all cases, trustees serve entirely without financial compensation. The role they are asked to play is nothing less than to hold the institution they help govern in trust for service to others. That means fully exercising their prerogatives in monitoring CEO performance, adhering to the organization's mission, keeping the nonprofit financially sound, and controlling risks to the enterprise: economic, programmatic, and reputational.

When trustees and those who report to them perform poorly, troubles abound.

The New York City Opera vanishes.

Yeshiva University so mishandles its investment portfolio as to bring this 128-year-old academic institution, including the Einstein School of Medicine and the Cardozo School of Law, to the brink of bankruptcy.

The University of Virginia fires its president, Margaret Sullivan, arbitrarily and capriciously, and then quickly reverses course in the face of unprecedented, highly visible student, faculty, and alumni protests.

Such failures of governance are more prevalent than is commonly appreciated.

The Los Angeles Museum of Contemporary Art slides into desperate financial straits. Its board acquiesces in the appointment of New York City gallery owner Jeffrey Deitch as CEO. That news, and his decision to fire a highly regarded senior curator, results in the resignation of four trustees, the only visual artists on the board. Staff tumult and negative publicity ensue. Deitch resigns less than thirty months after his appointment, leaving the museum in disarray.

The American Academy of Arts and Sciences Board of Directors publicly acknowledges that its CEO of seventeen years, Leslie Cohen Berlowitz, had misrepresented her academic record and was overpaid. The trustees did not discharge their duty to set and monitor compensation by ensuring fairness and a measure of comparability. They failed to perform as a responsible fiduciary.

The Corcoran Gallery of Art in Washington, D.C., agrees to a controversial takeover by George Washington University in a deal signed on May 15, 2014. Many charge that the museum has relinquished its mission in the transaction due to trustee unwillingness to preserve its independence by raising adequate funds.

The premature and failed attempt in 1988 to merge Mount Sinai Hospital and Medical Center with its counterparts at New York University inflicted significant financial and reputational damage. In the case of Mount Sinai, this mistaken course of action took more than a few years to repair.

From such illustrations there are many lessons to learn. Mercifully, there are also some safeguards, checks and balances to prevent such conduct or to expose and remedy it. Audiences, students, patients, and donors can vote with their dollars and their feet when universities, museums, or hospitals lose their way. Attendance falls, applications for admissions drop, and donations plummet. Journalists report on the travails of what are, after all, public institutions. Accreditation commissions and peer review procedures are healthy forms of institutional discipline and reform. Those with standing can resort to the judicial system for relief.

Contrast these forces at work monitoring nonprofits with their absence in the domain of private foundations. Of all the parts of the third sector, foundations stand apart for the pervasive weakness of their accountability. They have no real customers. Few if any grantees or aspirants to that status would dare to criticize foundation officials. Dwight MacDonald once observed in describing one philanthropic fund: "The Ford Foundation . . . is a large body of money completely surrounded by people who want some."

Want some? Then never run the risk of biting the philanthropic hand that can support you. On any given day, there is very little media coverage of foundation activity save in the trade press. Self-regulation by the Council of Foundations is weak and ineffectual. Public regulation by state attorneys general or the Internal Revenue Service is episodic at best.

Yet these entities constitute 15 percent of the $335 billion estimated by Giving USA to have been donated to charities in 2013, or $43.25 billion. And every penny of these benefactions is subsidized by the tax-paying public with generous incentives that have no equal in any other country in the world.

What prevents these relatively insulated private foundations from engaging in illegal, unethical, or unprofessional conduct? Who ultimately is accountable for the efficiency, effectiveness, and comportment of grant making? The trustee. In the definitive work on this field, Joel Fleishman identifies arrogance, discourtesy, inaccessibility, arbitrariness, the failure to communicate, and constant change in priorities as the besetting sins of a private foundation.[1] These important entities in American life need reform and oversight.

My experience as chair of the Nathan Cummings Foundation and the Charles H. Revson Foundation suggests that their success relied heavily on the discipline and judgment of my fellow trustees. Such was the case as well when I served as the architect and CEO of what was then one of America's largest asset-based corporate foundations, AT&T. Although AT&T answered to constituencies rarely encountered by private foundations—shareholders, customers, communities, tax authorities, journalists—the policies, operations, and procedures of corporate philanthropy remained largely the province of senior employees playing the roles of trustees and fiduciaries.

By asking the right questions; setting the appropriate measures; and insisting on responsiveness, openness, modesty, and professionalism, trustees can exercise a positive influence on both nonprofit performance and foundation conduct. Little else can.

And when trustees and those who report to them perform superbly, institutions take flight. Those who work inside them soar as proud professionals. Those who receive their services are changed for the better.

In my lifetime, institutions like New York University, Duke, Johns Hopkins, Stanford, the University of Michigan, the University of Texas, and the City University of New York have catapulted to levels of accomplishment that once seemed highly improbable. Small liberal arts colleges like Amherst, Haverford, Pomona, Reed, Middlebury, and Vassar have distinguished themselves. And what about the Mayo and Cleveland Clinics? New York Presbyterian and Emory University Hospitals? The Los Angeles County Museum of Art and the Metropolitan? The Steppenwolf Theater Company and Lincoln Center Theater?

My list is partial and arbitrary. Yours will be as good or better, no doubt. Why? Because attracted to so many nonprofit institutions of higher education, health care, and the arts and to so many other fields of endeavor are professionals of uncommon talent. They are committed to their work. They aspire to excellence. When supported by trustees who take their measure, mind their missions, and invest in their future, hundreds, if not thousands, of these nonprofits flourish.

At their best, trustees and senior management struggle to strengthen the nonprofit institutions they are privileged to lead. America's third sector is distinctive. It is large, sprawling, and influential, and its very pluralism strengthens the commonweal. Mediating between the powerful state and individual citizens, nonprofit organizations protect us from tyranny and help to support participatory democracy. And the high-quality services delivered by many draw patients, students, and tourists to our shores from around the world.

My journey through some of this territory may be useful to others. If the lessons I have learned prove worthy of emulation, I will be pleased. If those who occupy privileged positions as executives and trustees hold themselves more accountable to those they serve, I will be delighted. And if nonprofits take the lead in restoring the trust of Americans in institutions and their leadership, that is all to the good.

Consider the hospital president. What share of America's approximately one hundred thousand deaths estimated by The Institute of Medicine to occur annually due to medical error happen on his watch?[2] What about the spread of avoidable infections among inpatients? Hospital employees who don't regularly wash their hands? The mistaken prescriptions or not administering them in proper doses? The breakdown of triage systems that occurs in overly crowded emergency rooms with unconscionable waiting times? The sleep-deprived residents and overworked, harried nurses whose impaired judgment adversely affects patient care?

Surely if senior executives and hospital trustees owe an obligation to the public, it is first and foremost to remedy these and other sources of medical harm. Carefully monitoring patient lengths of stay. Avoiding unnecessary readmissions. Assuring that the medically indigent are served with the same care and dignity as third-party reimbursable or self-pay patients.

Is measurable progress occurring in each and every one of these problem areas?

Consider the issues facing the private college or university president. How to keep the costs of room, board, and tuition affordable enough to lower the barriers to entry for youngsters from poor and working-class families. How to relieve a collective student debt of well over a trillion dollars, more than Americans collectively owe on their credit cards. How to resist pressures from parents, students, government, and prospective employers to transform colleges and universities from educational to vocational institutions. How to keep schools safe places for young men and women, where sexual harassment is shunned, emotional distress is detected and addressed, and attention and learning disorders receive ample attention. How to effectively use twenty-first-century technology without undermining the value of human interaction, professor to student, in the classroom.

Are these challenges being addressed frontally, and are trustees holding management accountable for demonstrable progress?

Consider the performing arts administrator. As the costs of labor gallop ahead of inflation and as ticket prices begin to approach premium levels, what can be done to protect access to the performing arts for the poor and the working class? How can the proper place of the arts in elementary and secondary schools be secured? Can performing arts centers resist succumbing to the coarseness of popular culture? Can they present the classics and promising new work of high quality rather than shallow entertainment? Can they identify and adopt new economic models to sustain themselves?

These threats and opportunities are not for the faint of heart or the unambitious. They are as complex and taxing as those any politician or corporate executive might confront. What's needed are accomplished, skilled, and resourceful people to lead nonprofit institutions and occupy seats in their boardrooms. People who yearn to serve beyond self, who wish to convert private resources to the public good.

Maybe these issues are best addressed through imaginative use of technology or the analysis of big data. Maybe the keys to unlocking new value in organizations are fresh sources of revenue and novel productivity measures. Maybe gain-sharing breakthroughs in collective bargaining can offer a contribution to needed solutions. Or new ways to devise incentives that lead to breakthrough big ideas.

I do not know. What I am sure of is that brilliant young people can be found in more than Silicon Valley garages, investment firms, and consulting practices. Attracting bright minds to third-sector habitats and to the formidable problems found there, charging them to help devise solutions, offering needed resources and the freedom to wander intellectually, and then listening to what they formulate cannot help but create a new order of things. Blending the benefits of experienced hands with the unconventional approaches of the relatively uninitiated can lead to answering questions like those I have posed.

And I am certain of something else.

Unconstrained by petty partisan politics and the necessity for reelection every two, four, or six years, and uninhibited by the pressure to report quarterly financial results, this American third sector is free to invent, to create, and to innovate. Blessed by diversity in its institutional ranks, the sector offers plenty of room for experimentation, for thousands of flowers blooming, and for tackling some of this nation's and the world's most pressing challenges.

That is why the health of this realm of American life remains so important. It is why I took those jobs. It is why I wish for others the excitement, the pleasure, and the gratification of this form of professional or voluntary public service.

I always offered all benefactors, trustees, and volunteers four ironclad commitments in return for donations of consequence to Lincoln Center: give generously of your time, talent, and treasure, and you will be rewarded with a better night's sleep, a longer life, an unobstructed pathway to heaven, and aisle seats when you get there.

Lincoln Center is hardly alone as a noble cause or worthy institution in being bold enough to offer such "guarantees." My life in public service provided me with the chance to help others. To save lives.

Relieve pain. Educate. Elevate. Realize dreams. Help repair a broken world. Even transcend it through the medium of art.

No material reward, no worldly possession could possibly offer as much pleasure or satisfaction.

You can do far worse than to seek the job that some tell you not to take.

CHAPTER 14

The Leadership Lessons
That Matter Most

Between the conception and the execution
Lies the shadow.

—T. S. ELIOT

Being the CEO, or for that matter any kind of leader, entails placing a high priority on the identification and allocation of resources. The most precious of these is human talent. It follows that I have always conceived of my role as creating and sustaining an environment in which gifted employees can do their best work.

The Art of Employee Recruitment and Retention

Leaders must place a high value on attracting and keeping first-rate staff. I am always on the prowl, seeking energetic, intelligent, curious, and ambitious new employees who wish to achieve extraordinary results. I look for both solo actors and team players, recruits brimming with the confidence to go it alone if necessary and able to work with others productively, whenever desirable.

David Rubenstein observes that he has never encountered an outstanding performer in his professional life who worked from nine to five. Nor have I. The colleagues I value most are those who challenge themselves. They seek constant improvement. They yearn to bridge the gap between Lincoln Center's enormous promise and its current performance. When they leave the office, their work accompanies them, because little is more thrilling or gratifying than what they are up to professionally.

I have found that human resource departments and executive search firms can be helpful. They can prepare position descriptions, delineate roles and responsibilities, and usefully brief candidates. What they often do not handle well is drilling down on the content of the prior work of applicants and determining how, in fact, they really performed. What is the precise relevance of their experience to the situational setting and the culture of the hiring organization?

When filling important posts, do not completely delegate to others contacting key references. You know best the right questions to ask. You can pick up many clues and cues by attentive listening. Because the costs of a mistaken hire are so high and the benefits of a correct choice so valuable, your personal attention is imperative.

Be careful. Be methodical. Be deliberate. Sleep on your decision. It is no accident that the business sage Peter Drucker urged management to take time to reach key personnel decisions. Drucker rarely counseled delay. But on recruiting talent, he urged that one should not rush.

Just as it is far easier to retain a good existing customer than to acquire a new one, so it is far harder to recruit a star employee than to retain those already in your employ. Do not neglect them. Their morale, their sense of importance and self-worth, and their belief in having contributed to the success of the enterprise matter a great deal to whether they stay or take flight.

Pay close attention to the very valuable human assets in your midst. Your colleagues yearn for self-realization. They aspire to fully tap their potential. If training is needed, provide it. If mentoring is called for, supply it. Acknowledge good work, early and often, privately and publicly.

Identify high-potential employees in the organization who over time can succeed existing senior staff. Offer them custom-tailored advancement programs to supplement their existing skill set and to expose them to leadership challenges. Spend time with them. They will be flattered by the CEO's attention, and you will learn much about the organization you lead from paying heed to the perspectives of middle management.

Besides, you will experience joy in witnessing those with whom you work blossom professionally. Fortifying staff and fostering their growth is a legacy that will endure. You deserve to take pride in it.

Accountable for Results and Open to Improvement

With the possible exception of nature, nothing abhors a vacuum more than a nonprofit board of trustees. Unless trustees are deeply and properly engaged in the life of the organization, they are likely to act inappropriately and to undermine the effectiveness of the CEO. What do I mean by properly? The board of directors of established nonprofit institutions has several very important, indisputable roles to play.

It hires, determines the terms and benefits of compensation, and assesses the performance of the CEO. It judges whether or not proposed activities fall within the mission of the organization. It reviews and passes, with or without significant modification, an annual budget proposed by the staff. And it assesses risk to the institution: budgetary, managerial, and reputational.

In a well-functioning organization, the board pays attention to policy, not operations, to ensuring that the institution does the right things, while avoiding the temptation to tell staff how to do things right. At Lincoln Center, I drew up a set of objectives for the new fiscal year and sent them to my chairman for review and discussion. Our exchanges of views were substantive and serious, and once agreement was reached, a plan was presented to the executive committee of the board of directors for the considered reaction of its members.

This annual undertaking was designed to compel Lincoln Center's key players to focus on what we wished to accomplish in the year ahead, and how I, as the president and CEO, would be held accountable for delivering the results projected in our annual forecast.

At the end of the fiscal year, the chairman then met with the executive committee in executive session, at which my performance was formally reviewed—no holds barred—without any staff present. Bruce Crawford, Frank Bennack, and Katherine Farley, my respective chairs, would listen carefully to the views of trustees and then offer their own assessment. Recommended compensation treatment would be aligned to the consensus appraisal.

After each such evaluation, the chairman would meet with me to report on feedback. I was always eager to learn of any performance or stylistic shortfalls, with a view toward improvement. Lincoln Center's board of more than ninety members, including emeriti, is large and sprawling. Its agenda is ambitious and far-ranging. Its trustees are smart and experienced, and its stakeholders are many and varied, as are the constituents to be served. I looked forward to a frank evaluation, and if it wasn't fully forthcoming, I was ready with questions like these:

- Were there any trustees feeling marginal or relatively uninvolved whom we could activate to Lincoln Center's advantage?
- Were committee and board meetings properly balanced among staff reports, information dissemination, and policy discussion?
- Did any ideas emerge for improving my relationship with Lincoln Center staff or with the resident artistic organizations or external constituencies like government officials, advocacy groups, and the media?
- And what about us, chair and president? Are we communicating sufficiently? Should we adjust the number of face-to-face meetings, phone calls, or e-mails? Are we focused in our conversations on the right things, the subjects that only a chair and a CEO can address? Are we resisting the temptation to spend our time on tactics and implementation details better left to others?

My sincere openness to frank appraisals, not just once a year, but all of the time, helped to create an atmosphere of honesty and a free-flowing exchange of thoughts.

These executive committee sessions that reviewed my performance as a proxy for how well Lincoln Center was functioning were extremely well attended and animated. Central to them was a sound and healthy, mutually respectful relationship between the CEO and the chair of the board of directors. Fortunately my chairs understood the zone of trustee prerogatives and welcomed an energetic and capacious role for paid staff, first and foremost the CEO.

Stay Focused, Avoid Distractions

Intense focus leads to outstanding performance. Superior programming. Balanced and surplus budgets. Audience enthusiasm. And a positive reception among trustees, donors, and critics.

Undiluted concentration on work can go to extremes, I'll confess.

Early in our marriage, my wife Elizabeth appeared one weekday evening at around midnight in my study, where I was toiling away on some important memoranda and correspondence for AT&T.

"Ren, excuse me for interrupting, but I have been working on next year's calendar and need to enter some important dates."

"Liz, do we have to do this now?"

"Oh, it will only take a moment. When is your mother's birthday?"

"I don't know."

"Reynold Levy. You are forty years old. Surely you can tell me what month your mother was born in."

"Liz, honestly, I don't know."

(Long pause.)

"To tell you the complete truth, Liz, Mom's birthday is three weeks after [my sister] Joyce calls to say that it is coming and to discuss what we are going to do to celebrate."

In other words, why clutter my mind (and lose focus) with what someone else will remind me of in a timely fashion anyway?

Here is another example. Remember that beat-up old Mercury I held on to until its last gasp? I was able to keep it limping along well past its natural life because of two car mechanics, brothers, Mark and Bruce. They owned and operated Riverdale Auto. These guys are the local version of the Tappet Brothers, who have been featured for decades on National Public Radio's exceedingly popular program *Car Talk*.

Mark and Bruce love cars. They seemingly know everything about them. They also like most of their customers. And they are very curious about them. They fix whatever new car or jalopy you bring in, and charge you next to nothing for the privilege. So after about a year and a half of owning a four-door Honda, I brought it in for an oil change, a check on all of its fluids, and to have air put in its tires.

Bruce greeted me warmly and asked, "So I know you must miss the Mercury, but how are you liking the Honda?"

"Well, it runs smoothly, I suppose."

"You sound disappointed."

"I am."

"In what?"

"The gas mileage. In the Mercury, I could travel about 247 miles on a full tank of gas. Now, with the Honda, supposedly a fuel efficient car, I only get about 360 miles. Not much more."

"You bozo. Don't you realize that the Mercury Marquis has a gas tank large enough to fuel half of the vehicles in the Bronx!? It holds twenty-seven gallons of gas, whereas your Honda holds seventeen. You are getting more than double the miles per gallon with your new car."

"Oh."

"So, here's what I want to know. What idiot gave you the title President . . . of anything?"

Okay, there are some costs to focus and concentration, I suppose. And taking lip from Bruce is one of them.

But not being aware of all kinds of practical stuff, like the date of Mom's birthday or the capacity of the gas tank of my car, leaves me the space to keep on top of what I need to know at work, as undistracted as possible.

Winning Friends and Influencing People

For over a decade, Norman Vincent Peale's book of this title topped all best-seller lists.

What alliances are to nations and partnerships to companies, donors, investors, and cooperative parties are to nonprofits. By definition, an eleemosynary institution must win friends and influence people in order to thrive. Places like Lincoln Center are in the business of asking: for time, talent, treasure, and the sweat equity of employees, trustees, volunteers, donors, and sister institutions.

One terrific metric to gauge whether Lincoln Center is winning friends pivots around donors. How are acquisition and retention rates of donors at various levels of generosity faring? Are they increasing in number, holding steady, or decreasing? Do these results compare favorably with other admired institutions? The same question should be asked about trustees, and more broadly, about ticket buyers.

The ability to lead an organization effectively often depends on the relationships you have cultivated during your career. Calling in favors or just requesting fair play from existing and potential donors, or media outlets, or politicians, or foundation and corporate officials, or members of your board of trustees is possible only if you have spent time with them and invested in creating an enduring connection.

In the ATM machine of leadership, asking for withdrawals will not be successful if you haven't provided substantial deposits of time, attention, advice, and assistance. That means keeping in touch, letting others know you are thinking of them, and offering genuinely felt compliments on positive developments in their personal and professional lives, as well as help when the inevitable setbacks and stumbles occur.

Read, Travel, Network, Encounter Art

The theme here is a combination of curiosity and discovery. About ideas. Places. People. The visual and performing arts.

Challenge me to predict the likelihood of an executive's success, someone I have just met, and I would respond by asking that person four questions:

- What do you read?
- Whom do you meet with at and outside of work?
- With whom do you speak most often, and with whom do you exchange e-mail most frequently?
- How do you spend your vacations, and what do you most enjoy doing in your spare time?

In my experience, the answers are leading indicators of executive success or failure. Reading widely and deeply. Listening attentively. Possessing a boundless and curious mind. Show me an executive with these attributes, and I will predict leadership of uncommon quality.

My frequent-flyer mileage cards have taken me to 47 countries and 253 cities and towns around the world. My well-stocked home library contains thousands of books and is a continuous source of intellectual sustenance. My electronic Rolodex and old-fashioned diary are crammed with new names, adventurous meetings, and fresh encounters.

These experiences and relationships allow me to benefit from the example of others, past and present. They lend authority and authenticity to my leadership at work. They are also an indispensable source of self-confidence. But the richest origin of knowledge and ideas by far is attentive, eclectic reading.

When I was nine years old, for my birthday, my dad took me on a special trip from our one-bedroom apartment in a building called the Shelbourne, at the intersection of Ocean Parkway and Brighton Beach Avenue, to Manhattan, known to all of us Brooklynites as "The City."

To go to "The City," everyone dressed appropriately, meaning for men and boys a white shirt, jacket, and tie. Somehow, Dad decided that he would encourage my early propensity to read by taking me to the original and then the only Barnes and Noble, located at 5th Avenue and 18th Street, so that I could select a book for my very own, the very first.

I roamed the shelves for several hours and came away with a paperback copy of *The Autobiography of Benjamin Franklin*. That round-trip on the D train is one I will never forget, and to this day, my precious possession sits on a shelf at home in a proud corner of its own.

Until Benjamin Franklin's work entered my life, I joined the family in believing that books could be read only by borrowing them from the Brighton Beach branch of the Brooklyn Public Library. It was there that four years later I was lucky enough to land a part-time job shelving and checking out books. My idea of wealth was not just to borrow books, but to be able to buy them too, and building a personal library at home was an aspiration I never thought could be realized.

At Abraham Lincoln High School in 1962, I discovered how thrilling it was to witness adults' exhilaration in the joy of teaching. In that freshman year, my absolute favorite was an English teacher named Miss Alice Bantecas, a short, matronly lady with a beautiful cursive handwriting, who would begin each and every class with a quotation written on the blackboard for us to discuss. And here is what greeted the students on our exciting first day of high school: "There is no frigate like a book to take us miles away." With this piece of wisdom, Emily Dickinson has been my guide ever since.

That seaworthy vessel called a book could also engender empathy, teach by example, take readers intellectually to arguments they could not otherwise imagine, to experiences they would not otherwise encounter, to role models they'd probably never meet, and to places well beyond their pocketbooks.

My fixation on reading as a source of knowledge, inspiration, and guidance was reinforced at Hobart College, where a faculty of uncommon quality and devotion to teaching united around the principle that exposure to original texts, from the Bible to Thomas Mann, was the best way to learn. Secondary sources, mere histories of the literature, however good, were derivative and superficial. They deprived one of the pleasures and the challenges of coping with original authorial meaning and intention. They glorified context, but gave short shrift to content.

Hobart's two-year required, primary-text-only, eighteen-credit Western civilization program thrust me into foreign territory, and I reveled in the intellectual journey.

Ever since, I have urged my colleagues and associates when confronting a challenge to ask: "What would others do in this situation? How has something like this been handled elsewhere? Who are the best thinkers on this subject? Let's learn from what they can teach us. Let's read up on this stuff."

Wherever your work takes you, books, periodicals, and newspapers can be extraordinarily helpful, time-saving guides. And if you wish to communicate well, orally and in writing, there is no better prescription than extensive reading to help you do both.

Staying in close touch with works that have stood the test of time, with writers who weigh their words, and with advocates who respect sound, well-developed arguments keeps your mind awake and alive. It allows you to draw from a deep well of history and insight in helping colleagues cope with the challenges of the day. It renders you a more interesting and engaging human being. It places your preoccupations in a larger and richer context, offering you the freedom to approach problems differently, buoyantly, imaginatively.

In a world of shortcuts and sound bites, where Twitter and instantaneous blogging predominate, I remain old-fashioned.

It is said on a very popular all-news radio station in New York City, WINS: "You give us twenty-two minutes, and we will give you the world."

Well, I am a long form kind of guy.

A twenty-two-minute world isn't for me.

Engaging the brightest and most creative minds you can find in any field will keep you lively and informed. It will infuse your leadership with passionate content and inspiring direction. It will broaden your frames of reference and enlarge your range of associations. It will render you a far more sophisticated, cosmopolitan, and interesting person. Leaders with well-used passports and well-thumbed books in their library; leaders comfortable in galleries and concert halls; leaders familiar with history, literature, and language are far more likely to reach sound decisions and mobilize supporters to help implement them.

Seek Work-Life Balance

Seize opportunities, personal and professional, when they present themselves. It is highly unlikely that they will come to you at convenient intervals or in accordance with your carefully drawn career plan. Instead, think of your life in phases that may require you to defer gratification and to sacrifice, at work and at home. Many people can succeed on all fronts during the course of their lives. But I know few who can do so simultaneously all of their lives.

I do recognize the need for there to be some measure of work-life balance. Lincoln Center is extremely generous to those caring for a sick child or parent; those on maternity leave; those afflicted with illness themselves; and those who must be at that important soccer game, parent-teacher conference, or fourth-grade graduation. We offer all kinds of accommodations to where employees need to be physically, and we provide them with the very best technology so that they can reach their colleagues easily wherever they may be located.

But to aspire at any given time for complete harmony between meeting the unpredictable challenges of the workplace and satisfying the often surprising needs of your children, your parents, your spouse, and your friends is an open invitation to frustration.

I know of no easy substitute for constantly juggling the pressures of work and home life. Hopefully, the help of a spouse, parents, and friends will ease the struggle. So can an empathetic employer. Lincoln Center attempts to play precisely that role.

Ask Thoughtful Questions, Listen Intently

How often have you been involved in a conversation in which those participating talk completely past one another, and pauses are not intervals for absorbing what was said, but simply a waiting period before offering one's own point of view, uninfluenced by other participants?

A key to successful leadership is learning from those closest to problems and challenges. How carefully do you pose questions? How willing are you to wait patiently for responses that may not surface as quickly or as lucidly as you'd like? How ready are you to change your mind? How observant are you of the body language of the respondent? How adept are you in reading between the lines of those you gently and enthusiastically interrogate?

When CEOs guide institutions by engaging their employees and demonstrating respect for them in the process, word spreads quickly. Permission is granted for leaders to emerge from throughout the organization. The collective energy summoned to a cause is most impressive when the entire organization is asked to contribute.

Two stories, one apocryphal, the other real, illustrate the importance of attentive listening and of framing probing questions.

Former secretary of state Henry Kissinger and his younger brother Walter are both German refugees. They have both resided in America for seventy-six years, and they are very close in age. Walter is two years younger than Henry, who celebrated his ninety-first birthday in 2014. Why is it, then, that Henry still speaks with a thick German accent, while Walter, the eighty-nine-year-old kid brother, betrays hardly any sign of his country of origin? Well, Henry's joke has it, that is because he doesn't listen.

Of course, Henry listens extremely well. His unparalleled statecraft and his accumulation of power in the Nixon administration reveal a sharp ear, one very sensitive to the forces swirling around him. His magisterial histories are the work of a distinguished diplomat, historian, and political scientist possessed of an inquisitive mind, given to few.

Jeff Immelt, the CEO of General Electric, was asked by Charlie Rose at the end of 2012 what would make for a personal good year in

2013. I was sure Immelt would reference markets to conquer, topline revenue, earnings per share, or an improvement in GE's disappointing stock price. Instead, his answer was both humbling and penetrating. My recollection is that it went something like this: "I hope that in 2013 I can pose better questions to the brilliant employees of my company and listen more intently than ever before to their answers."

Life's Compensations

In our commercial, free-enterprise society, undue emphasis is placed on money, on what one is earning. There is a widespread view that what matters most is how much an employer pays in salary and bonuses, if any, and what is offered in other terms and conditions of employment.

My experience demonstrates otherwise, especially in nonprofit, tax-exempt organizations and in government service. Those drawn to these workplaces are more concerned with making a difference than making a buck. They are moved by psychic compensation, the timely acknowledgment of a job well done, the expression of appreciation in front of their peer groups and families.

Expressing thanks takes time. It is time wisely spent. Praise well delivered buoys the spirit. It motivates, inspires, and encourages as much if not more than restricted stock options and golden parachutes do in the corridors of our nation's corporations. "I can live for two months on a good compliment," said Mark Twain.

A thank-you note for superior performance. The timely expression of appreciation for a job well done. The surprise gift of a book sent in the mail to enrich an employee's experience of her work or to expand her intellectual and professional horizons. The reference letter for an employee's child to be admitted into a nursery school, private elementary or secondary school, or college. The advocacy letter for preferential hospital admission for an employee's parent, relative, or friend. The supportive missive to a co-op board or a private club on behalf of a trustee or volunteer. All of these forms of communication matter a great deal to those who benefit from them.

Even those who work in for-profit firms are extremely responsive to the well-timed message of appreciation. By now, the propensity of Jack Welch, the former CEO of General Electric, to send handwritten notes of praise to employees located in all levels of the organization has become legendary. I suspect it is a practice not widely emulated. It should be. Communicating how much you value your colleagues is powerful.

Reward and recognition are underutilized management techniques. Repair to them frequently. What you receive in loyalty and applied energy in return is priceless.

Self-Discipline

The respect people accord to those who work hard never ceases to amaze me. Return phone calls, e-mails, and paper correspondence on the day they are received. Be available, as needed, to your fellow employees, trustees, sources of funding, and key influentials. Exhibit energy. Exude optimism. As Vince Lombardi reminds us, "The only place success precedes work is in the dictionary."

It is the CEO who should be looking to shape an institutional future beyond the next quarter or the next fiscal year. Seeing further ahead and orchestrating the staff forces around you are major responsibilities. Discharge them with care.

Paying attention. Staying alert. Recognizing that methodical and regularly scheduled business reviews will help reach better outcomes. Organizational life is itself a process of continuous improvement. It is about executing well on hundreds of little things constantly.

Each time you dial your own phone, hold meetings outside your own office where your customer or client lives and works, and respond quickly to the needs of those you serve, respect for you broadens and the willingness to help you widens.

Seek Necessary Teamwork

Beverly Sills once asked me soon after I started to work at Lincoln Center what it needed most. My quick answer caught her attention: "A chiropractor."

My observation, then and now, is that Lincoln Center is favored by many sources of strength, but it is also hobbled by weakness, apparent and undetected. If an organizational chiropractor could help employees and constituents align behind a common plan, the positive energy unleashed would be phenomenal.

It is the CEO who can most effectively bring employees together, motivate them to work cooperatively, seek common ground, and raise their aspirations. Effective leaders must spend valuable time making themselves understood. What they wish to achieve and why is not self-evident. It needs to be explained, early and often, and then be acted upon collaboratively.

Such harmonious teamwork is the stuff of uncommon institutional accomplishment. Setting inspiring objectives and then insisting on the cooperation required to achieve them is the essence of leadership.

During the early, darkest moments of my tenure at Lincoln Center, when its physical redevelopment was really threatened, no one seemed to be listening, not just to me but to anyone else. Short-term interests were espoused by constituents without much regard for their impact on others. Positions were presented in shrill, uncompromising ways. Creating conditions and articulating positions that would facilitate a meeting of the minds seemed impossible.

I remember reminding the group that we seemed to be conducting ourselves completely incorrectly:

> Go [I said], visit the Harvard rowing team.
> What you will find is that 8 people are rowing and one is shouting, not the other way around.
> Can we try that approach?

Like-mindedness and cooperation demand decisiveness. In my experience, members of the board and staff welcome an informed resolve by their leader. Drift, procrastination, and delay are the enemies of productive teamwork. As the CEO, what you are ultimately paid for is your judgment and your capacity to persuade others to join you.

Climbing a Wall of Worry

Leaders I most admire are always running scared. They are alert to threats. They constantly ask themselves what could go wrong. They do not assume that yesterday's success preordains good results tomorrow.

Quite the contrary. They most fear complacency. They never rest on their laurels. In fact, they rarely rest at all.

The propensity to look closely and regularly at the world around Lincoln Center for opportunities and threats is the stuff of leadership. There is a high correlation between lost sleep and being in charge. When you are at the top of a complex, high-quality, highly visible institution, there is always plenty to keep you up at night. Besides, sleep is highly overrated. Herb Alpert, the famous trumpeter, is quoted as saying, "While you are sleeping, someone else is practicing."

The List and the Watch: A Manager's Allies

When you are in charge of a complex organization, a constant challenge is the effective management of your scarcest resource: time.

Every high-performing chief executive I have ever encountered comes to the office each and every day determined to work through an inner-directed agenda. Outside influences like e-mail, paper correspondence, phone calls, and unplanned meetings are all expected. They go with the territory. Indeed, for a CEO, interruptions are an indispensable part of the job.

Often, sudden and unexpected demands on your time will reveal opportunities and threats that are not otherwise readily apparent. In the laudable effort to operate efficiently and effectively, do not close yourself off from those inside or outside the organization who wish to bring to your attention new ideas or courageously raise unexpected problems.

Let's concede that some portion of every day must be devoted to the unknown and the unexpected. Still, success requires a leader who is clear about what should be accomplished, works persistently on realizing priority goals, and persuades colleagues to move in the same direction.

Doing this demands discipline. Two allies can offer indispensable help: the list and the watch. Every day of the week, I write out by hand lists: of calls to place; e-mails to write; meetings to schedule; names of employees awaiting the delegation of tasks and responsibilities; and books, articles, and documents to review.

Early mornings and late evenings are devoted to reading and writing, leaving the normal business day to working telephones, conducting meetings, responding to internal and external requests, and "management by walking around."

Self-awareness is critical to management improvement. Am I spending time on matters that could be handled better by someone who reports directly to me? Is completing any given task taking up too much of my time? Are there repetitive instances in which I must resort to my own devices, revealing the inadequacy of an employee who should be handling those very tasks? Am I a victim, too often, of "upward delegation"?

Often, managers ignore or give short shrift to the opportunity cost of doing too many things themselves. They "crowd out" others from assuming responsibilities and exercising leadership. The CEO can unlock talent, unleash energy, and stimulate creativity by pausing to consider who in the organization would relish an assignment, rather than tackling the challenge at hand herself.

If the well-composed list helps to ensure that I am addressing considered priorities, then my other trustworthy friend is the watch. Time is a precious and perishable commodity. Whether and when to act is as important as the content of a decision. In my experience, the passage of time has much more often been an enemy than an ally. As time is often in short supply, how it is managed at work really matters to efficiency and effectiveness.

One of my niftiest time savers is the screen on the telephone that marks the passage of seconds as one speaks. It serves as a constant reminder that conversations needn't take long unless relaxed exchanges serve a useful purpose. Clipped telephone check-ins with staff usually do the trick.

Meetings should be handled the same way. Always start them and end them on schedule. Always be sure they have an expressed purpose, and that participants are encouraged to arrive fully prepared.

I try to think of group encounters as performances. I keep fully in mind what I hope to accomplish. I attempt to move the give and take of discussion to that end. Treating your day as a series of engagements, each of which should achieve something tangible, helps to induce discipline. Of course, if you can't figure out what you hope to realize in any given meeting or during any phone call, that is a very good indication of its not being necessary.

When I was studying for a doctorate at the University of Virginia and a law degree at Columbia University and working part-time or full-time to make ends meet, I occasionally sought appointments with important figures at school and with employers of all kinds. Often, I simply sought general advice, the kind best proffered by those blessed with an abundance of professional experience. My entreaties were advanced politely and deferentially by letter. They offered what I thought was a sound rationale for a half hour of time. More often than not, these missives and the telephone calls that followed them were turned aside pretty routinely and brusquely, even rudely. I was stunned by the lack of generosity to a young guy earnestly looking for guidance. The guardians at the gates of busy people were well armed.

In my late twenties, I promised myself that if I ever achieved a measure of success noteworthy enough for others to seek my advice, I'd see them, no questions asked.

For a couple of decades, I fully redeemed that pledge. Strangers saw me for counsel on job hunting, on a midlife crisis, and on admission to graduate school. Could I help gain access for their precocious three-year-old to the 92nd Street Y's nursery school? Could I provide some counsel on a knotty leadership or management challenge?

Nothing seemed off-limits. While this was very time-consuming, I continued to remember where I came from. There but for the passage of decades, I could still be that supplicant eager for help.

Well, my open-door policy became indistinguishable from a free-for-all. Few dentists could boast a calendar as crowded as mine. No one paid me for these counseling sessions, but I didn't administer root canals or Novocain, either! Finally, I decided, "enough."

Then an idea occurred to me. Why not ask all who wished to see me to write a simple letter or e-mail stating succinctly what was on their minds and how they thought I could be of assistance? I promised that after receiving such a message, I would reply within twenty-four hours.

What a time-saving technique that proved to be. About half of those who expressed a desire to see me didn't trouble to write at all! Others sought counseling that friends or colleagues of mine could offer more quickly or intelligently, sparing me the effort. Still others requested face-to-face advice so general that what would suit them best was basic reading, including speeches, articles, or books that I myself had written.

"Just read these, and I'll be pleased to see you subsequently," I would offer. There were very few takers.

These hardly high barriers to entry proved formidable enough to dissuade the idle and the semi-serious. Still, no small part of my working week was taken up with dispensing advice, but much, much less than had been the case before I employed my new technique.

I reported on this efficiency scheme to my wife. It met with her approval.

Then one evening, Liz asked what my next day would bring. I provided a rundown of a pretty standard schedule, but mentioned, ever so casually, that I was spending an hour with Cate Blanchett. "In whose company?" she wondered. "Just me," I allowed.

"About what are you meeting?"

"I have no idea."

"Well," Liz wondered, "whatever happened to the required e-mail or letter requesting an appointment and stating its whys and wherefores?"

"Any rule worth its salt should enjoy an exception, don't you think?"

Pick Up the Pace

I have committed many more errors through inaction or delay than through timely or even premature conduct. Mistakes by omission, not commission. Mishaps by neglect, not abuse. These are habits I have worked hard to break. Getting things "roughly right" on time or early is appreciated much more than taking a "perfect" action step too late to matter. Whether the issue is preparing a funding proposal, drafting a letter, including an item on the executive committee agenda of a board of directors meeting, or asking a poorly performing employee to resign, do it sooner is part of my credo and operating style.

Opportunities fade too quickly, and rectifiable difficulties morph into crisis rapidly, if they are left to managerial drift and inattention. A nimble, athletic style on day-to-day operational matters is devoutly to be desired. As a general rule, problems do not age well.

At Lincoln Center, speed was required, not just in adapting our programs and often altering where and when they were presented, but in every other phase of our work. Recruiting trustees. Raising funds. Influencing people.

One of my constant clarion calls to staff was always to pick up the pace. *Ahora, no mañana*. Correspondence answered on the day it was received. Phone calls welcomed with courtesy, tact, and a genuine offer of help. All of us at Lincoln Center were privileged to live in a city filled with ambition and competition. We needed to learn from what others do, especially newcomers. They are smart, savvy, hungry, eager to succeed. We had to keep moving. The race goes not to the big versus the small, but to the fast versus the slow.

Organizational Change: How Much, How Soon

On the other hand, one of the most common and misleading pieces of advice offered to new CEOs is to begin wholesale organizational change quickly. Discharge mediocre, underperforming employees or those resisting your leadership. Hire new staff who prize loyalty to you above all, preferably those who have worked at your side in the past. Announce new initiatives that signify a brisk departure from past practice.

This act first, act now, listen later approach to major institutional change rarely works. It triggers resistance. It spreads insecurity and worry throughout the organization. It leads to accusations of arbitrary and capricious behavior on the part of a novice, know-it-all CEO. It cripples morale. Who is (s)he to take that step so soon? What does (s)he really know?

Moving too quickly, except in the case of a genuine emergency, rarely works for the organization or for the fledgling CEO. Instead, become an insider. Lift expectations for individual and collective performance. Raise the metabolism of the place. Lead by example. Arrive early. Leave late. Exhibit energy, curiosity, empathy, and optimism. Emphasize steady, incremental progress and connect its achievement to employee incentives and recognition. Respect your colleagues.

Do all of that, and watch what happens. Employees who can't keep pace with activity and higher standards begin to leave of their own accord. They are replaced by more energetic and ambitious newcomers, who help to change the institutional culture. Momentum builds. Some incumbents actually change their habits and get with the program. It all can happen naturally and organically. The pace of change is deliberate. The CEO allows for time to reach decisions intelligently, to develop new information, and to course correct. Letting employees know what is expected of them and why is essential. The critical mass of the organization must be in agreement and in alignment if ambitious goals are to be realized.

Overcoming an organizational immune system accustomed to resisting innovation and change requires persistent and measured pressure. It rarely happens quickly, or dramatically, without the CEO encountering strong pushback or countervailing opposition.

At Lincoln Center, the search committee members who recommended that I be hired knew that there were many challenges to be addressed, but they were also justifiably proud of what they and their colleagues had accomplished. Indeed, two of the search committee members, Nat Leventhal, my predecessor once removed, and Beverly Sills, the first chair of the board with whom I needed to work closely, were both largely responsible for many achievements as well as for a state of affairs that called for change.

By necessity, such change occasionally meant altering what they had created and dismantling what they had built. Proceeding too quickly could easily have been viewed as a repudiation of much of their legacy. Instead, mutual trust had to be developed. Positive experiences together needed to be enjoyed. Generous acknowledgment of the achievements of predecessors would be warmly welcomed as well. Then, and only then, could recommendations for change be judged on the merits. Then, and only then, were those responsible for the status quo likely to be more receptive to change. They became allies and supporters, rather than sources of resistance.

Treat your predecessors as mentors. Ask for their advice. Consult with them as you reach critical decisions. The tendency to act as if organizational life began with your arrival is not only naive; it can be fatal. There is plenty to learn from those who came before you.

Leading from Outside In

Are we open to fresh ideas from sources outside Lincoln Center, like journalists, donors, and customers? Do we consciously look to other institutions, for-profit and nonprofit, to identify best practices that Lincoln Center would do well to emulate? The movement to demand-based pricing and yield management was probably first exploited best by Broadway theaters. The transmission of live performing arts, in the case of opera, by the Metropolitan Opera, to several thousand movie theaters. Successful examples of Internet and social media fund-raising campaigns originated with sister institutions. Best-in-class food and beverage service. Superior sales of branded merchandise. Innovative special events that draw funds and institutional attention. Where are the models of these practices worthy of emulation?

Encouragement by the CEO always to look outward, to learn from the positive experience of others, broadly construed, is indispensable. How does Disney handle long lines? Pepsico, advertising? American Express, customer service? The National Theater, subsidized-ticket pricing? Look for admired analogues. Identify how other institutions cope with challenges you are now encountering. These are the signs of a dynamic, ambitious organization, filled with professionals eager to learn.

Board members and staff colleagues are a wide-open pathway to such learning. Communication among them generates ideas and enthusiasm and should be encouraged. Too many CEOs view their boards of directors as intruders, even necessary evils, rather than as senior partners with impressive professional and social networks and storehouses of intellectual capital. In Lincoln Center's case, their associational and professional circles reach, literally, to the ends of the earth.

The inward-looking forces are strong. The tendency to compare one's own institutional performance year over year as the one and only benchmark to examine is typical. The inability to escape from the stay-at-home comfort zone is endemic among nonprofits. These are problematic tendencies at most workplaces.

Resist them. Overcome them. Dare to be open, most of all, to new ideas.

The Means and Ends of a Workplace

In the frenzy of the typical day, too many executives treat their peers and subordinates as only a means to achieve a short-term result. Beset by the pressure to complete tasks or respond to the felt needs of a boss, a client, or a customer, they lose sight of the human element at the workplace.

Driven by transactions, they neglect to nurture relationships at home or on the job, sometimes to the point of a downright lack of kindness, bordering on abuse.

Often CEOs or heads of departments are like Jekyll and Hyde figures. They "manage up" with sensitivity and concern, expressing curiosity about the lives of their superiors and sensitivity to their challenges. Little time or space seems left for those with whom they work every day. Even worse, blue-collar workers—folks like ushers, security guards, or maintenance staff—can go virtually ignored.

Try the exact opposite approach. Invest in the professional and personal lives of peers and subordinates. Support. Encourage. Teach. Assist. Greet warmly. The business you are in, more likely than not, is labor intensive. The capacity to attract and retain talent often depends more on whether workers feel truly valued, whether they are learning and growing in their jobs, and whether they are acknowledged and appreciated, than on the size of their latest salary increase or bonus. Employees want to work in a place where they are highly regarded, a place that they can call a second home, no matter their name, rank, or serial number.

The people with whom I spent most of my working and waking hours were always important to me. It was from them at every job I ever held that I drew inspiration and learned much. If they felt that I truly cared about their lives and did not see them as vehicles, like Zip Cars to be used only when needed, then productivity would zoom and the work setting could be regarded as a means to self-realization, not only to achieving organizational objectives.

In such a trusting atmosphere, when bad news occurred, I would be alerted to it immediately. No one would fear retaliation or anger. What staff could expect was, "Okay, let's roll up our sleeves and figure out how to fix this problem. There will be time enough later to determine what went wrong and how to prevent a recurrence. For now, let's correct this, all of us."

That collective approach, which focuses on "we," spreads quickly in an organization. It grows to embrace even your bosses, because they learn about how you treat others and they sense how positive people at work feel about themselves and their employer. At Lincoln Center, it was reflected in the way patrons, donors, employees, and trustees were drawn to our campus.

Do not fool yourself. If you treat a fellow employee poorly, word spreads fast. Lincoln Center is not the only organization possessed of a prison-quality grapevine. Messages about a mean or inattentive boss ricochet around organizational corridors. Mr. Jekyll, meet Mr. Hyde.

Temperament

If the secret to success begins with whom you are surrounded by, talented staff and gifted trustees, it necessarily ends with you as their leader. Maintaining an upbeat, optimistic, and energetic mood is not just essential, it is infectious.

In achieving your ambition for an organization or cause, you will encounter obstacles, active and passive resistance, conflicts, and problems. Some of your colleagues and trustees will be allies as long as good fortune prevails, but not a moment longer. Summer soldiers and sunshine patriots abound in any organization. Others can be relied on to adhere closely and consistently to the status quo they know best and from which they often benefit.

It takes stamina, fortitude, and persistence to lead in the creation of a new order of things. It demands that you possess the courage of your convictions. Those around you can easily sense any lack of confidence, any hesitations that betray weakness. How poised and self-possessed you appear, the posture you assume, really matters.

When you approach each day with vim, vigor, and determination, when you leave your doubts at home, your followers are encouraged and your detractors dwindle in number.

As a leader, you will be tested. A can-do, roll-up-your-sleeves enthusiasm; a problem-solving, consensus-oriented approach to resolving conflict; and an abiding respect for all with whom you work will tilt the odds in your favor.

Protect and Enhance the Brand

One of Lincoln Center's most treasured attributes is the strength of its brand. The power of an excellent reputation for first-class quality in discharging its multifaceted mission is a prized asset.

Worldwide, anyone who cares about the performing arts knows of Lincoln Center.

Is it possible to love orchestral music and not long to hear the New York Philharmonic?

Can you be drawn to opera as an art form and die happily without frequent trips to the Met?

If it is ballet you adore, then the home of George Balanchine and Jerome Robbins is a place where you must be a frequent guest.

Beyond affinity for particular art forms and therefore specific resident companies, the Lincoln Center brand manifests itself in "house trust."

If Lincoln Center presents a piece of art, no matter how challenging, then it must be worthy. After all, it has passed the test of cultural arbiters of impeccable taste.

Lincoln Center's imprimatur is powerful. If you wish to be anointed as a software engineering guru, then holding a degree from Stanford, Cal Tech, or MIT can hardly hurt. Doors open when one has graduated from the Harvard Business School. Got a serious knee or shoulder problem? You can't do better than the Hospital for Special Surgery. What should you see or listen to in the performing arts? Lincoln Center is your go-to institution.

Recently, the power of the Lincoln Center brand has been demonstrated not only by its attracting over five million people annually, by its award-winning ensembles and productions, and by the continued success of the now forty-year-old syndicated television program *Live from Lincoln Center*, but also by its showcase sixteen-acre campus. Hardly a week goes by when the Center is not hosting delegations from every corner of the world, whose members wish to visit the physically transformed outdoor spaces and indoor venues. These visitors include government and private dignitaries, who come prepared with dozens of questions about how Lincoln Center is governed, how it sells tickets, how it balances its budget, how it relates to its neighborhood, and how it decides what art to produce and present.

As much as anything else, it is the magnetic power of the Lincoln Center brand that generates these visits and inquiries. They led us to create a now-established institutional consulting practice, Lincoln Center Global (LCG), which is one answer to the question: How can

Lincoln Center convert the extraordinary level of interest in its operations into a new, recurring source of earned income?

Lincoln Center's reputation is outstanding. Insiders highly value it. Audiences and donors are drawn to it. Maintaining a top-flight reputation requires investment. It demands that employees do nothing to diminish or undermine the strength of Lincoln Center's brand.

The Imperative of Productivity

One of the reasons Lincoln Center could generate so many more programs and accommodate many more audience members, students, and visitors while maintaining balanced and surplus budgets is that administrative expenses grew at about the rate of inflation. The proliferation of technology, the consolidation and streamlining of workload, not automatically replacing workers who have left through the process of attrition, and constant employee training all helped foster increased productivity.

When I left Lincoln Center after an almost thirteen-year stint, serving from 2002 to 2014, its nonunion full-time workforce had dropped from 380 to 296, or by 22 percent. The compound annual growth rate (CAGR) of administrative expenses stood at only 3.1 percent per year. The overall budget had grown from $77.6 million in 2002 to $113.5 million in 2014, for a CAGR of 3.5 percent. In many ways, Lincoln Center was a lighter institution when I departed. The place had lost weight. It was fit and lithe.

The use of technology by our employees not only contributed to improved productivity, but also dramatically altered the manner in which many patrons learned about our coming attractions, purchased tickets, compared notes with one another about their experiences, and took advantage of Lincoln Center's many other offerings: reserved parking spaces, restaurant reservations, and purchasing merchandise, to cite but three examples.

Tight supplier oversight and careful expense control were also indispensable to successful budget management. The right kind of software, properly utilized, has assisted managers in containing and constraining costs. Such management information systems are simply indispensable to catalyzing productivity—doing more with fewer resources.

Of course, consolidating positions, reconfiguring what workers were assigned to accomplish, and using every vacancy as an opportunity to rethink how we approached work helped as well. So did careful control of salary increases and health-care benefits.

A great deal of the fun and much of the learning associated with the performing arts come from interacting with others who experience the same event or anticipate doing so. Modern technology links them to one another in natural communities of interest. Friendships form. Time spent at and about Lincoln Center grows. Information blossoms into knowledge. Frequency of attendance rises. So does earned revenue.

By these measures, Lincoln Center has improved its productivity markedly. But it has done so in other ways as well. It has learned how to generate more sales from fewer and better-targeted brochures, more positive responses from fewer but better-placed print and radio advertisements, more contributions from higher-end and more generous but less numerous donors. It does not take double the staff to conceive and execute ten gala events rather than five, and it takes less effort to retain and motivate high-quality, high-performing staff members than to constantly recruit and train newcomers.

When I bid Lincoln Center good-bye, it was accomplishing more with less than ever before. It was nimble. It was stronger. It moved faster.

The Persuasive Power of the Written Word

If reading helps to create the intellectual map that can guide you, writing and public speaking can contribute importantly to your success as a leader. They can embody the decisiveness and informed resolve that attract followers. As the CEO, what you are ultimately paid for is sound judgment and your capacity to persuade others. To rally them to your side, the written and spoken word are potent weapons. Use them early and often.

No matter the institutional setting and no matter the role I played, one constant I observed was the utter necessity for clear and compelling communication. Frequent. Offered in multiple forms. Carefully crafted.

When I first arrived at the 92nd Street Y, the International Rescue Committee, and Lincoln Center as the CEO and at AT&T as a junior officer of the company, I was occasionally asked what each place needed most in order to improve performance.

Curiously, my diagnosis and remedy were the same everywhere, although the organizations and their contexts varied widely. What these institutions, and no doubt many others, needed most was consensus: staff and board alignment on means and ends.

Institutional assets hiding in plain sight can be identified and put to work through timely and effective communication. To adjust the parts of an organization so that they cohere and synchronize requires constant communication about its purposes, methods, culture, and desired results. In high-performing places of business that dialogue occurs throughout the organization, from the top down, from the bottom up, and horizontally. It is expressed most powerfully through face-to-face communication among those closest to a working unit where employees spend most of their time.

But the themes struck, the language used, and the energy unleashed often begin best with written communication from the CEO.

In my professional experience, one of the most underutilized tools available to leaders is the written word. Its persuasive power, its capacity to convey meaning, and its ability to move readers to favorable action is impressive. I am mystified by how many leaders fail to deploy this tool of influence.

Professors often acknowledge that they are unsure of what they really know about a subject until they prepare to teach it and engage in dialogue with able, highly motivated students.

Lawyers observe that an oral agreement is not worth the paper it is written on.

Similarly, I am often unsure precisely of what I wish to impart and to whom until I write it down.

It is not just the subject of communication that is important, but its object.

Powerful communication is personal; its recipients must sense that what is written keeps them first and foremost in mind. The formulaic and the cliché-ridden are easily detected and readily dismissed. But the letter or memorandum crafted with the reader in mind, either as an individual or as part of a group, hits home with dramatic impact. It is memorable. It can move the recipient to think differently and to act accordingly. Its language is often repeated throughout an organization or among friends, family, and close associates.

Employees need to know directly from the CEO what are the key institutional priorities, how they can realize them, and what role each may play on that journey. Repetition to reinforce such important messages should not be avoided.

The art of the written word is worth careful development. Well-articulated prose moves, delights, surprises, flatters, amuses, and motivates. Much to my pleasure, I have found over the years that those to whom I write often keep my letters and memoranda and fondly recall them at important intervals in their lives.

The proper use of the spoken word is also a powerful and often-neglected tool. Thoughtful toasts and introductions to speakers, honorees, and employees impress the gatherings you assemble. They burnish institutional reputation and promote your organization. Audiences that Lincoln Center convenes deserve to hear remarks that are engrossing, humorous, even memorable. There is a temptation to treat such occasions as routine and mandatory. Resist it. Take the time and summon the energy to prepare for them diligently. Exploit the opportunity to thank, compliment, and communicate key messages to receptive listeners.

The Art of the Sale

As the president of Lincoln Center, it was my responsibility to persuade those with the wherewithal—talent, time, and treasure—to spend more of it on our sixteen-acre campus. And before then, on refugees and displaced people. And before then, at 92nd Street and Lexington Avenue.

Trustees, ticket buyers, volunteers, employees, public officials, donors, journalists, and foreign governments all had to spend more time at, thinking about, and offering support to institutions and causes I was privileged to lead.

Achieving this end required constant acts of persuasion. Marshaling facts. Shaping arguments. Inviting participation. Listening carefully. Responding accordingly.

It demanded a sense of purpose and an obsessive pursuit of goals. Relentlessness and persistence were invaluable allies.

Some combination of energy, discipline, optimism, and resilience will sell those tickets, recruit those trustees, impress journalists, motivate employees, attract donors, and move government officials off your back and to your side. Sustained attention to what will convert a "target of opportunity" into a partner in the enterprise is built into the makeup of a driven CEO, one possessed of a cannot-be-denied moxie.

"Most people buy, not because they believe, but because the salesman believes."

In virtually all of the high-performing organizations I am familiar with, the CEO is the salesman in chief. And that Pied Piper is usually surrounded by employees and volunteers who comprise a committed, driven sales force.

It is a source of immense satisfaction that when I bid good-bye to the Y, to the IRC, and to Lincoln Center, each enjoyed many more friends, supporters, and generous trustees. They are the leading indicators of a bright future, as are those who converted them to the status of true believer.

Supple and Resourceful Governance

One of the major distinguishing features of nonprofit institutions is their capacity to engage the intellectual energy, sweat equity, and financial support of volunteers. In this connection, I have happened upon many nonprofits that focus almost exclusively on the board of directors as their only outlet for the utilization of volunteers. The board is very important. But to concentrate on it exclusively is to think small.

Too many nonprofits keep their principal governance body pocket-sized. Their leadership is heard to claim that a board larger than, say, thirty is unmanageable, unwieldy, and unnecessary.

In the narrowest sense, this point of view has some validity. If all that is envisioned for the board is hiring, compensating, and if necessary discharging the CEO, protecting the mission and guarding against risk, then few institutions need more than that number, and perhaps even fewer than thirty will do.

But I am convinced that trustees should not be just fiduciaries. They embody a cause. As such, they are advocates, sources of expertise, and campaigners, reaching into pools of influence and affluence.

It is not by chance that the boards of the 92nd Street Y and the IRC numbered around seventy. My first recommendation to Bruce Crawford as the chair of Lincoln Center was to allow for the expansion of the board. It then numbered forty-three and has since grown to eighty.

The financial benefits of a larger board in the form of increased donations are readily apparent, as long as expectations for giving and getting are agreed to in advance as a condition of membership. Importantly, a sizable board allowed me to reach into communities of consequence—the media, advertising, high-tech, consumer goods, private equity, hedge funds, fashion, money-centered banks, entertainment—all across America and the world, to Lincoln Center's advantage.

Hardly a single important aspect of Lincoln Center's physical redevelopment or its transformed operating economic model did not benefit from the excellent advice of trustees and those they called upon in their far-flung network of colleagues and friends. A hefty board allowed me to enlarge Lincoln Center's circles of influence and to increase the impact of our place. It helped me to tap resources, not least financial, otherwise out of reach.

Those nonprofit CEOs who believe that the board of directors is the only place to properly engage volunteers should reconsider. I do not refer to the useful recruitment of volunteer ushers, tour guides, retail assistants, and candy stripers. Rather, I am raising the sights, pointing to ways in which to enhance the power of an organization by thinking imaginatively and flexibly. I am aiming to answer this question: How can we attract people of influence and means to our institution other than by membership on its board of directors?

As the board leadership at Lincoln Center joined me in energetic proselytizing for support of our cause, an opportunity repeatedly presented itself. We encountered smart, accomplished, wealthy Americans who yearned for, or could be persuaded to accept, a meaningful association with Lincoln Center that fell short of trustee financial and service commitments.

How to engage some measure of the time, treasure, and talent of such standout citizens was the challenge.

One model, already at work, is the Lincoln Center emeriti group. These volunteers, twenty-one in all, consist of former members of the board who by virtue of a change in geographic location, financial circumstance, or retirement from a full-time business life want an active association with Lincoln Center that obligates them to less than full-fledged trusteeship. Its members meet regularly. Their agendas are chock full of Lincoln Center developments and issues. When the board chair and president are wise, they consult with the emeriti group about future decisions. All members can attend any board meeting and most committee meetings, where they enjoy a voice but not a vote. All remain donors to Lincoln Center. Some are major contributors.

When the cochairs of the Lincoln Center emeriti are Bill Donaldson, the former chair of the Securities and Exchange Commission and cofounder of Donaldson, Lufkin and Jenrette, and Peter Malkin, a major civic leader and developer with substantial interests in the Empire State Building, among other properties, this is a group to be taken seriously.

A second governance model is the Lincoln Center Education (LCE) board. This body of committed volunteers, chaired by Ann Unterberg, focuses on Lincoln Center's education program for kids in the public schools and on its campus. Consisting of twenty-five members, the board's efforts to influence government policy, financially support LCE, and offer guidance to its executive director have been invaluable.

The third is a group called the Counsel's Council, chaired by Judge Judith Kaye, the former chief judge of the New York State Court of Appeals. It consists of the senior partners of some twenty-five major law firms, whose associates engaged in extremely valuable pro bono projects each year under the direction of Lesley Rosenthal, Lincoln Center's very able general counsel.[1]

Yet another is the leadership committee of the Lincoln Center Corporate Fund, chaired by Steve Swartz, the president and CEO of Hearst Corporation. These thirty-two corporate executives are critical to raising in excess of $6 million annually of unrestricted donations distributed directly to constituents. They are an important cadre of supporters.

By extension, we asked ourselves, what if we meet important figures for whom the performing arts was not a philanthropic priority, but who wanted to have some user-friendly form of sustainable involvement? Suppose they were offered an option like this: Please consider joining us for the better part of one half day a year. In a very well-prepared, four-hour session, our leading trustees and staff will present you and like-minded peers of comparable stature with the major opportunities and threats we see ahead for Lincoln Center. We will seek your advice and guidance on how best to seize and grapple with them. With your help, we may even discover that we have not entirely identified the right things to discuss! We commit to listening carefully to your views based on the briefing papers we distribute in advance and as much dialogue as you would like before, during, and after meetings. We intend to act on your recommendations. In essence, this $50,000-a-year membership on Lincoln Center's Corporate Advisory Group may well lead to expanded involvement if you are energized by the subjects and people you encounter.

Well, within nine months a very powerful group of twenty members had been assembled. Few boards of directors of nonprofit institutions would hesitate to admit these activists to their ranks.

Of all the areas in the world that might include clients of Lincoln Center Global, our consulting practice, none were as fascinating, as large, or as mysterious as performing arts centers in China, extant and new. As the extraordinarily talented managing director of the fledgling LCG practice, Kara Medoff Barnett worked her magic in tapping networks of private citizen influentials in and around China, she was aided and abetted by Katherine Farley, who was not only Lincoln Center's chair, but was also Tishman Speyer's senior managing director, with responsibility for the firm's business in that nation. Katherine is a pioneer developer in that huge country. She began her work there in the 1970s. Our contacts and meetings resulted in adding three trustees to the board. It also led to the formation of the China Advisory Council.

This council consists largely of Chinese citizens and expatriates who are drawn to the performing arts and who attend events at Lincoln Center with some regularity, often assisted by the fact that they have purchased co-ops or condominiums nearby. All were taken with the idea that Lincoln Center was willing to help broaden and deepen Chinese exposure to world-class talent and reciprocally American exposure to Chinese artists. They appreciated how much Chinese administrators could learn from Lincoln Center staff about the design, building, and operation of performing arts centers. Cochaired by Katherine Farley and a television star in China, Yang Lan, the group's prominent membership has already been able to help Lincoln Center in many ways:

client referrals to LCG, coordinating special events, offering financial contributions, and briefing us on the whys and wherefores of Chinese policies and practices in the performing arts. These thirty-one prominent corporate executives, business owners, retailers, major investors, prominent private equity and hedge fund operators, and leading artists are the latest additions to the far-ranging advisory forces Lincoln Center has assembled.

If nonprofits are prepared to be flexible and resourceful about how they engage talented volunteers—on a richly populated board of trustees, through other formal standing committees, and on advisory groups—such means of engagement will have a potent positive impact.

For Lincoln Center, the effort to stretch the meaning of governance in the direction of inclusivity and flexibility to accommodate the needs of members has worked extremely well. Taken together, including the board of directors, more than two hundred impressive individuals regard themselves rightly as important members of the Lincoln Center family. They are highly valued insiders whose reach extends far and wide.

I am acutely aware that the vast majority of nonprofits are small and do not enjoy Lincoln Center's size, longevity, well-known name, reputation, or gravitational pull. However, having an acquaintance with hundreds of nonprofits of all dimensions and types, of all ages and purposes, from all parts of the country, I am persuaded that in general they underestimate their capacity to attract more compelling figures to their boards of directors and as volunteers more generally. I know too well the cost of organizational timidity, lack of ambition, or sheer diffidence. Proportionate to the situational circumstances of the nonprofit, my advice is to be bolder and more flexible in attempting to recruit impressive adherents to your cause. They are out there. They are waiting to hear from you.

Make It Easier for Others to Help

The reporter assigned to an unfamiliar story, seeking not just content, but context. The city administrator on a new assignment needing an orientation to how Lincoln Center operates between the parent body and the resident artistic organizations. The corporation or foundation executive favorably disposed to Lincoln Center, but too busy to comb through long, prolix requests.

By identifying with the situations others find themselves in and responding quickly and directly in a form that works best for them, relationships are formed or deepened. Favorable results for Lincoln Center ensue.

If this is true of those paid to conduct business with Lincoln Center, the need to make it easy for others to help is even more imperative with volunteers.

Taking advantage of our status as a nonprofit institution in need of voluntary expertise, we have become skilled at project management of pro bono initiatives. Identify and define an institutional challenge. Gather the data needed to better understand it. Then charge a group of lawyers, or business students, or associates of trustees drawn from their firms to propose solutions to problems on a tight deadline, say 90 to 120 days. That was our method. It worked well and often.

From well-known establishments like McKinsey, IDEO, Disney, American Express, and UBS to twenty-five of New York City's major law firms, from interns drawn from every kind of professional discipline and college and university to one-off arrangements with curious and hardworking volunteers, Lincoln Center knew how to benefit from their time and sweat equity. They, in turn, came away with an insider's view of how this leading performing arts institution works and what kind of gifted professionals are drawn to it. They also attended more of our performances, struck up friendships, and enlarged their own professional networks.

The success of these task forces and commissions flowed directly from our promise to implement expeditiously sound recommendations that emerge from their work. The idea that Lincoln Center actually desired the informed opinions of outsiders and pledged to adopt them or explain why it would not or could not is a turn-on to many busy professionals.

They wish to make a positive difference to institutions or causes they care about, but they're often hampered by an inability to find a way to help. By offering a simple and direct route to assist Lincoln Center, we ignited involvement. As a result, the quality of the advice received was of a very high order.

The studies and recommendations that emerged helped to propel Lincoln Center forward and brought new ideas to a full-time staff in need of supplemental expertise and intellectual sustenance. Perhaps the most well-developed and productive partnership was Lincoln Center's multifaceted relationship with the Harvard Business School.

In a decade, 139 separate studies were conducted by some fifty HBS students and graduates. One can draw a straight line from that body of work to the following concrete examples of change at Lincoln Center, among many others:

1. The establishment of the only professional consulting practice lodged in any performing arts center in the world.
2. The siting and construction of a public television station on Lincoln Center's campus, Channel 13/WLIW, yielding handsome annual net revenue and increasing on-the-air exposure of Lincoln Center for almost all resident artistic organizations.
3. Maximizing net rental revenue from artistic spaces like the Kaplan Penthouse, the Clark Studio Theater, Alice Tully Hall, Avery Fisher Hall, and from public spaces, indoors like the David Rubenstein Atrium and outdoors like the Hearst Plaza, Josie Robertson Plaza, Tully Plaza, and even the underground concourses leading to and from subways and public parking. Superior ways and means to market these places and to price them were an important outcome of HBS studies.
4. Developing a business plan for a Dance in Cinema series that it is hoped might do for the participating companies—the New York City Ballet, San Francisco Ballet, Ballet Hispanico, and the Alvin Ailey Dance Company—and for the art form of classical dance more generally, what the Metropolitan Opera has accomplished in its successful and much-heralded movie project.
5. Studies leading to the creation of three new restaurants and the selection of Marcus Samuelsson (The American Table), Nick Valenti and Jonathan Benno (the Lincoln Ristorante), and Tom Colicchio (Wichcraft) to supervise and run them.

6. Determining criteria for the background, professional experience, and geographic locations of an expanded Lincoln Center Board of Directors.
7. Conceiving a strategy for the redevelopment of Lincoln Center, including access to the bond market and to acquiring state and federal support.
8. Documenting the case for the dramatic favorable impact of Lincoln Center and its constituents on the metropolitan area economy, for use in public policy advocacy and fund-raising proposals.
9. Studying the feasibility of creating one or more Lincoln Center international advisory councils, leading directly to the creation of the China Advisory Council.
10. Assessing the pros and cons and the ways and means of creating Lincoln Center University (LCU), a collectivity of staff that would help to provide technical training to their counterparts in countries around the world, beginning with China.

There was much else, studied but not yet implemented. Should Lincoln Center develop an alternative certification for public school arts teachers? How could Lincoln Center best modernize and upgrade its guided tour program? What tactics might work best to expand Lincoln Center's global roster of consulting clients? Could Lincoln Center's Print and Poster program, indeed retail sale of any kind, enjoy a robust future on the campus? Are there other viable new ventures Lincoln Center could pursue that will generate sustained net earned income streams, consistent with its mission? What about social media fund-raising at Lincoln Center? Is there a role for a robust spoken word program here? How can Lincoln Center best identify and train its high-potential employees and prolong their length of stay? Can the parking garage in its promotion and pricing perform measurably better? If and when the Mostly Mozart Orchestra tours or American Songbook is presented elsewhere in the United States or around the world, who are its likely corporate sponsors?

These are among the vital questions answered by the HBS teams and by other groups of skilled professionals working pro bono over the last decade.

This combination of inspiration and perspiration animated much progress at Lincoln Center, turbocharging results or giving us the courage to pursue an initiative.

There remains a huge, largely untapped reservoir of university-based talent in search of real-world opportunities and nonprofit institutions in need of analytical assistance and fresh points of view. Lincoln Center identified that source of intelligence, drive, and curiosity. By selecting volunteers carefully, preparing for their arrival rigorously, designing meaningful assignments vital to Lincoln Center's future, and either implementing their recommendations or explaining why they were not actionable, we made it easier for others to help. And not just business students. Lawyers. Accountants. Professionals of all stripes. And undergraduates.

Of course, to fully benefit from the intellectual energy and creative enthusiasm of these human resources required exposure to me, the CEO. Everyone in our organization was aware of the high regard I had for data-based studies, new ideas, and challenges to conventional wisdom. News of my visible receptivity to those who brought us such gifts spread rapidly.

Bursting the Bubble

How can all of these instrumentalities involving important figures in the life of Lincoln Center actually work?

Certainly a determined chair to help recruit and relate to these entities and their members whenever necessary is indispensable. A committed staff, able to engage trustees and many others and brief them with policy-relevant data and analysis, is critical.

But ultimately, it is the CEO to whom all would like access. In seeking it, trustees, volunteers, benefactors, government officials, activist groups, and all manner and means of the members of advisory boards pushed through my open door.

The effort to infuse fresh energy into Lincoln Center became an obsession. Doing so meant a willingness to view the place the way informed and often critical ticket buyers, donors, journalists, and civic activists might. To ward off inertia and complacency and challenge ourselves was utterly necessary. Otherwise, routine and boredom would likely set in. Otherwise, we would run the risk of living in that bubble that is said to surround not just US presidents but CEOs everywhere. Self-imposed isolation and a strong amen corner can be the ruination of a leader.

Of all the risks to Lincoln Center's artistic excellence and financial health, what I worried about most was self-inflicted pain caused by thinking about ourselves in isolation from the environment around us. Stultifying introversion is a clear and present danger to established institutions, even those thought to be at the very top of their game.

This is not advice for others. My most trusted leadership tool is a device available at any full-service drugstore. It is called a mirror.

Leadership can be lonely. Self-indulgence and self-delusion are not healthy ways to cope with that loneliness. Running institutions is not about the women and men at the top. It is about service to others. Forcing myself to experience what others think of Lincoln Center was an invaluable form of discipline.

I regularly read the work of critics, journalists, and bloggers with an open mind. I did not dismiss critical assessments breezily. I needed to take seriously those who watch our performances for a living and not, as too often had happened, allow them to be dismissed ad hominem by colleagues.

The views of our customers on the performance of our ushers, security staff, or parking lot attendants were exceedingly valuable. They helped to uncover deficiencies that either had not been detected by routine procedures and managerial supervision or were more serious than we initially believed.

I spent lots of time with more than two hundred of Lincoln Center's far-flung trustees and associated advisory body members. Their knowledge, experience, skills, and network of associations were invaluable to Lincoln Center. Asking the right questions and listening intently for the responses were essential. What I learned was invaluable.

Of course, an indispensable source of knowledge was Lincoln Center's own employees. Expectations for them were set high. By and large, my teammates delivered.

I communicated with them by telephone, by e-mail, and at departmental senior staff and ad hoc meetings. My two or three informal walk-arounds each weekday when I was in the office were very useful.

Three or four breakfast meetings were held annually for employees who had been with Lincoln Center for less than two years. Two or three all-staff meetings were also held. These methods and occasions allowed for me to convey Lincoln Center's priorities, our challenges, and our values. Just as important, they offered the opportunity for me to ask questions about whether we were doing the right things and whether we were doing things right. And then I would LISTEN. I constantly learned very useful lessons.

Lincoln Center should always be in the process of continuous improvement. It always has unfinished business on its agenda. We made our fair share of mistakes, I am sure. I am equally certain that we were aware of them and learned from them. And that is largely because no bubble surrounded our place or me. You would have searched in vain for an amen chorus. It was probably the only ensemble not welcome at Lincoln Center as long as I was there.

Heavy Lies the Head

I am not sure that there was ever a time when the CEO could rule by command and control. It is true that employees will tend to defer to authority, giving the boss the benefit of the doubt. Over time, that automatic tendency to acquiesce fades, particularly for employees who are talented and marketable. They are looking to follow the leader not by compulsion but by choice. If, by precept and example, the CEO reaches decisions that strengthen the organization, and particularly if the views of the employees closest to the issue are taken into account, then support for the CEO will be forthcoming. Not dutifully or grudgingly, but enthusiastically.

Throughout my career I viewed employees as colleagues in a common cause, not subordinates or "direct reports." The high regard I was after needed to be earned every day. Like most "bosses," CEOs tend naturally to "manage up" well. Anticipating the needs of the members of the board at whose pleasure they serve, presidents and executive directors too often give short shrift to their associates. Attention to the employee body becomes erratic and inconsistent.

The maxim that almost anything is possible to achieve in an organization as long as you do not care who receives the credit particularly applies to the CEO. Mahatma Gandhi always encouraged his followers to do the work, not hog the credit. The line to get the work done, he allowed, is always shorter! A smart CEO knows that whatever plaudits accrue to the team are hers to enjoy as well. Of course employees are especially impressed when the boss not only improves the organization, but goes out of the way to help them directly. That theme pervades this narrative, because nonprofits are labor-intensive institutions. Those who work in them trade in psychic as much as financial currency. They enjoy gratifying transactions. They appreciate the successful completion of projects. They value, most of all, building strong and enduring relationships with fellow team members.

Careful consideration of employee needs and protection of their interests win much favor. I consistently viewed my CEO job as creating and sustaining an environment in which my colleagues could do their best work and realize their professional dreams. Much of what I do for a living is identify, nurture, and reward talent. That may require raising more money to finance an idea; or protecting staff from unnecessary, unfair, or excessive trustee criticism; or assigning more resources to a problem when an employee in charge is feeling overwhelmed.

Ultimately, the values you embody as a leader and who you are as revealed to your colleagues will win the day.

Leadership can be isolating and burdensome. When you can fully share in the successes of others and helpfully intervene when crisis hits employees unexpectedly, at work or at home, that sense of being alone subsides.

But running a nonprofit is never to be confused with running for office. It is not a popularity contest. There will be occasions when tough choices are necessary. They will not always be well received. The true leader should aim neither to be feared, nor to be loved, but to be respected.

APPENDIX A

International Rescue Committee
122 East 42nd Street
New York, NY 10168–1289
Tel: (212) 551–3000
Fax: (212) 551–3180
Email: irc@intrescom.org

December 14, 1998

Dear Jim and Win:

Judging by its ability to become more self-supporting, the IRC is a 65 year old that hasn't yet come of age.

During its distinguished history, the IRC has urged and enabled refugees to become self-reliant as soon as possible and to rapidly develop the means to independence.

Ironically, the institution we all revere has refused to take the advice it proffers to others.

For reasons good or ill, solid or flimsy, the IRC has never undertaken a serious capital campaign. In fact, on more than one occasion in the past, its doors were close to shutting, irate bill collectors demanding payment for services rendered. In more recent years, annual operating deficits have threatened to become habit-forming and have undermined any chance for a substantial capital accumulation in the decade of the nineties. During that decade, thousands of non-profits improved their balance sheets significantly, taking advantage of a terrific economic environment in which to raise and invest funds.

Such sins of omission and commission are history.

Now, the IRC is well on its way to healing managerially and to redeeming its full promise programmatically.

And, now is a time for growing up, for institutional adulthood.

JAMES STRICKLER
Co-Chairman
International Rescue Committee

WINSTON LORD
Co-Chairman
International Rescue Committee

APPENDIX B

AWARDS AND RECOGNITION FOR LINCOLN CENTER REDEVELOPMENT

Alice Tully Hall
Executive Architect, Diller Scofidio + Renfro

Best Cultural Project of the Year, Greater New York
Construction User Council, 2010

American Institute of Steel Construction (AISC)
IDEAS National Award, 2010

American Institute of Architects (AIA) Honor Award
in Architecture, 2009

AIA New York Design Honor Award, 2009

AIA New York State Award of Merit, 2009

Progressive Architecture Award Citation, 2009

American Council of Engineering Companies (ACEC)
Platinum Award for Engineering Excellence, 2009

Society of American Registered Architects, Design Award of Honor, 2009

The Los Angeles Times, Top 10 Architecture Moments of 2009

The New Yorker, The Ten Most Positive Architecture Moments of 2009

The Washington Post, Best Architecture of the Decade

McGraw-Hill, Best Construction, Cultural Projects Category, 2009

The New York Construction Magazine, Best Cultural Project, 2009

The New York Times, The Arts in 2009

School of American Ballet
Executive Architect, Diller Scofidio + Renfro

International Illumination Design Award of Merit, 2008

AIA New York State Award of Excellence, 2007

International Association of Lighting Designers,
Award of Excellence, 2007

The David Rubenstein Atrium
Executive Architect, Tod Williams and Billie Tsien

LEED Gold—Official Certification

AIA Design Awards, Interiors Honor Award, 2011

Lincoln Center Hypar Pavilion
Executive Architect, Diller Scofidio + Renfro

National Award for Structural Engineering from
the American Institute of Steel Construction, 2011

AIA Design Awards, Architecture Honor Award, 2011

Elinor Bunin Munroe Film Center
Executive Architect, David Rockwell

BusinessWeek Magazine, IDEA Finalist, Environments, 2012

AIA, Citation, Interior Architecture, 2012

Interior Design Magazine, Best of the Year, Finalist, Institution, 2011

Lincoln Center Theater—Claire Tow Theater
Executive Architect, H3 Hardy Collaboration Architecture

AIA New York State Design Award of Excellence,
Institutional Category, 2013

Architect Magazine Design Review Award,
Bond Category Award Winner, 2012

Interior Design Best of Year Awards,
Institutional Category Winner, 2012

ACEC NY Chapter Engineering Excellence Diamond Award, 2012

AIA New York State Design Award, 2010

David H. Koch Theater
RC Dolner and Theometrics

CETI Fiatech Award Winner, 2009

Other Awards/Recognition

Cooper-Hewitt Design Patron Award, Reynold Levy, 2009

American Society of Civil Engineers (ASCE) Platinum Award
for Engineering Excellence, The Juilliard School, 2009

ASCE Platinum Award for Engineering Excellence,
Central Mechanical Plant Project, 2008

AIA Design Awards, Urban Design Honor Award Winner,
Lincoln Center Public Spaces, 2011

APPENDIX C

THE NEW YORK CITY OPERA: A ROAD TO RECOVERY

A WHITE PAPER WRITTEN FOR GEORGE STEEL, GENERAL MANAGER AND ARTISTIC DIRECTOR OF THE NEW YORK CITY OPERA AND SUSAN BAKER, THE CHAIRMAN OF THE BOARD

New York City is at least a two-opera town, a cultural capital that needs and deserves the creative tension between the edifice of grand opera and the productions of a far more iconoclastic opera company.

We have always admired the City Opera's artistic brio. It's going to take a lot of business brio to keep going: a commitment to living within its limited means, a return to the spirit of its modest origins as the "people's opera" and, especially, a clearer kind of thinking—artistic and managerial—than we've seen in recent years.

Editorial, *The New York Times,* June 25, 2009

THE CHALLENGE

I. FINANCIAL

The Opera's current endowment is somewhere between $10–16 million down from $57 million in December 2003. That's about 30–45% of an annual season's budget that is expected to be in the range of $30–35 million.

Moving to this desired "equilibrium" of about 10 productions annually will require an operating budget of at least this size, with commensurate levels of earned and contributed income. An endowment of the current size will generate annual income of only between $500,000–750,000.

Private and Confidential

Building back a robust paid audience in ample quantity after the house has been essentially dark for two seasons and raising annual funds at needed levels will be a major challenge. So, too, will be the elimination of any accumulated deficit, the restoration of a healthy cash reserve and the replenishment and then growth of endowment.

II. GOVERNANCE

The number of trustees and their level of involvement in terms of both service and financial support falls considerably short of what the Opera requires.

Public reports suggest that there is a $50,000 annual expectation of each trustee. While that sum is less than it needs to be, former staff allow that even it has been honored in the breach by some Directors.

In virtually every case of a nonprofit turnaround from a state of dire financial conditions, the revitalization of the board of directors has been indispensable. Mayor John Lindsay and his work as Chair of the Lincoln Center Theater. Marshall Rose at the New York Public Library. Peter May at Mt. Sinai Hospital. Helene Kaplan at the American Museum of Natural History. These institutions illustrate how "turnaround" can be catalyzed by fresh lay leadership, by able staff and by determined, energetic board recruitment.

III. REBUILDING STAFF STRENGTH AND MORALE

The New York City Opera's staff has been through six very tough years. The extensive, failed search for a new home both downtown and at the American Red Cross site. The damaging comments about hall acoustics associated with Paul Kellogg. The management interregnum that followed the announcement of his resignation. The failure to resolve outstanding issues with Gerard Mortier on mutually acceptable terms. Two seasons of darkness and before then poor box office and financial performance, generally. Media coverage filled with negative comments and forecasts.

All of these factors have weighed heavily on the few veterans who remain with the company and may well serve as barriers to the recruitment of gifted newcomers.

Creating and sustaining a committed management team will be a key to recovery.

IV. REDUCING, CONTAINING, CONTROLLING COSTS

Clearly, union negotiations on salaries, fringe benefits and work rules will be a high priority for this labor intensive arts organization. The same observation applies to bargaining for lower costs with all suppliers. The extreme financial condition of the New York City Opera demands that its historical partners join in shared sacrifice, the better to create a robust, healthy company with which to do business in their future.

V. A THREE YEAR OPERATING PLAN AND BUSINESS MODEL

The driving forces leading to the Opera's deficit are structural, not cyclical. The current recession may exacerbate the difficulties. It did not create them. And, a return to positive economic growth in the country will not of itself eliminate them.

Management must produce a credible, steady state, three year plan of artistic merit and of balanced budgets. And render explicit the financial assumptions on which it is based.

Pointing to extenuating circumstances wins no allies. Patience is running out. So is time.

Staff, working together in close partnership with an expanded and revitalized board of directors must redeem the promises of that plan and reinstate the Opera's credibility, artistically and financially.

VI. A CAMPAIGN TO REBUILD CONFIDENCE AND REPAIR DAMAGE AMONG KEY STAKEHOLDERS

The views of the New York City Opera by foundations, corporations, individual donors, media and the government of the City of New York need remedial attention. Past plans have gone awry. They were viewed as unrealistic. Deficits have grown. The attention of the audience has strayed. Management has changed.

It is therefore critical that the board of directors and staff rally around a common, realistic plan, explain and interpret it early and often, and execute it well.

Private and Confidential

THE OPPORTUNITY

To summarize, the New York City Opera needs a sound, credible operating, a fundraising strategy of real energy and heft, a marketing plan to win back its traditional audience and woo newcomers, an expanded, revitalized, generous board of directors, and a driven, determined, highly skilled management team.

VII. THE VITAL FEW KEY ELEMENTS OF RECOVERY

The New York City Opera enjoys a storied history and the respect and affection of many opera lovers. Identified with low ticket prices, promising American singers, venturesome repertoire not likely to be performed at the Metropolitan Opera and even an association with Mayor LaGuardia, the Opera can call on the goodwill of New Yorkers who wish to see it thrive. The recent editorial in the *New York Times* is illustrative of a civic pride that can be fully tapped.

a. Use the official opening of the David H. Koch Theater and the excitement and media coverage it generates to launch a seat naming and "capital" campaign.

   Formerly known as the State Theater and beloved by many, it is an oddity that virtually none of its internal spaces are named. They are of great financial value. They are assets hidden in plain sight. Waiting for a national economic recovery to capitalize on them could be a huge tactical error and, depending upon many other considerations, a campaign launched years from now may be too late for the Opera.

b. On both the revenue and expense side the efficiency and effectiveness of both the board and staff of the City Center for Music and Dance would benefit from thorough examination.

   The rental revenue of the David H. Koch Theater and its interior spaces has historically been de minimis and the manner in which common costs are handled needs a fresh look.

   CCMD has only two customers. The New York City Ballet and the New York City Opera. Is each holding its staff fully accountable for performance? Of what added value is the CCMD board? Is the kind of advanced planning utterly necessary to rent the hall and its lobby spaces being undertaken in a disciplined fashion?

Private and Confidential

Affirmative answers to these questions are required to create and sustain a healthy financial condition for the hall.

c. The magnificent $100 million pledge of David Koch can alter the view of many potential donors of the theater and its occupants. Under such circumstances, fundraising for both companies should be catalyzed and the halo effect of the gift put to best advantage.

d. Clearly, the Ballet and the Opera share a home and stresses and strains in recent years in their relationship have been abundantly clear. Susan Baker and Barry Friedberg did much to diffuse tension and to frame a workable agreement for the Theater's redevelopment.

The likelihood of a new understanding that will allow the opera to tap some $9 million it has requested as foregone earned income for its dark seasons, together with a few concessions of its own to the Ballet around scheduling and construction monitoring, will be very good news indeed. Another "green shoot" is the recent success of the Opera in securing a challenge grant to help support the 2009/2010 season. Still another, is the potential record breaking gala to open the season.

e. The identification of new board leadership for the Opera around whom veteran and new trustees can rally is imperative.

HOW LINCOLN CENTER CAN HELP

Lincoln Center is fully prepared to assist in the identification and recruitment of new members of the Board of the New York City Opera including, whenever the Opera is ready, a new Chair.

Lincoln Center is also prepared to offer its services in substituting for all or part of CCMD's current role from a management perspective. As the owners and operators of Avery Fisher and Alice Tully Halls and of all of the public spaces, the staff at Lincoln Center is fully familiar with both facility management and hall rental. There may be some significant savings associated with scale and scope should Lincoln Center play a management role at the David H. Koch Theater and substantial rental income is there for the asking provided both resident companies cooperate in date clearance, in sufficient advance planning and in acquiring the skills of attracting and delighting licensees of all kinds.

Toward exploring these possibilities, Lincoln Center is at the disposal of both the New York City Opera and the New York City Ballet.

APPENDIX D

Date: June 2, 2003
Contact: Betsy Vorce
212.875.5100
bvorce@lincolncenter.org

LINCOLN | for the
CENTER | Performing Arts

STATEMENT FROM BRUCE CRAWFORD, CHAIRMAN, AND REYNOLD LEVY, PRESIDENT, LINCOLN CENTER

Re: Looking Alteall for Avery Fisher Hall

Lincoln Center learned last Thursday afternoon, May 29, that the New York Philharmonic was engaged in serious discussions with the leadership of Carnegie Hall about the prospect of moving there permanently. We are proud to have been the home of the New York Philharmonic for over 40 years, during which time they performed before an audience of millions and reached tens of millions more through *Live From Lincoln Center* broadcasts.

Lincoln Center worked diligently to develop many alternatives that would satisfy the acoustic, programming and aesthetic needs of the New York Philharmonic, as well as of its own presentations, and was particularly flexible in offering to finance the costs of fundraising and the costs of capital planning, as well as take a leadership role in the fundraising required to realize these alternatives. Under such circumstances, and given this history, we are disappointed in the New York Philharmonic's decision.

We also are extremely enthusiastic about using Avery Fisher Hall to bring to New Yorkers, Americans and foreign tourists the world's best musicians and performers. We envision the opportunity to house this country's and the world's leading orchestras not only for three or four evenings of performance each year, but also in residence for longer periods of time.

We foresee expanding the thematic programming that has increasingly characterized our Great Performers and New Visions series. We look forward to commissioning new music, to utilizing the best of 21st century technology to enhance the audience experience and to engaging our performers with brand new audiences and with elementary, middle and high school students.

Lincoln Center's trustees and staff, as well as its constituents, feel a profound responsibility to maintain the world-class standard of performing arts for which we have become known around the globe. The forthcoming change in the use of Avery Fisher Hall allows the fulfillment of this responsibility to take on many new forms. We relish the opportunity.

70 Lincoln Center Plaza
New York, NY 10023-6583
T 212.875.5000

www.lincolncenter.org

NOTES

Chapter 1

1. This quote comes from an extensive *New York Times* story of October 11, 2001, written by Ralph Blumenthal and Robin Pogrebin. It attempts to describe a heated Lincoln Center Executive Committee meeting held on October 1, 2001. The journalists claim that two sources heard Mr. Rose complain to Beverly Sills that "you stabbed me in the back." Mr. Rose denied uttering that remark. Ms. Sills denied hearing it. Whatever the case may be about this specific comment, no one denies that the meeting and others like it were filled with contention and controversy.

2. To familiarize yourself with the *Federalist Papers* and other original documents central to America's history, see Richard Heffner, ed., *A Documentary History of the United States* (New York: Signet, 2009).

3. See Friedrich Hayek, *The Road to Serfdom* (Chicago: University of Chicago Press, 1944); Adam Smith, *The Wealth of Nations* (New York: Penguin, 1982); Milton Friedman, *Capitalism and Freedom* (Chicago: University of Chicago Press, 2002); and Alan Greenspan, *The Map and the Territory: Risk, Human Nature, and the Future of Forecasting* (New York: Penguin, 2013).

4. I recommend reading Alexis de Tocqueville, *Democracy in America* (New York: Penguin, 2003); Waldemar Nielsen, *The Endangered Sector* (New York: Columbia University Press, 1979); Lester Salamon, *The Resilient Sector: The State of Nonprofit America* (Washington, DC: Brookings Institution, 2003); and Robert D. Putnam, *Bowling Alone: The Collapse and Revival of American Community* (New York: Simon & Schuster, 2000).

5. *Gallup Poll Social Series: Mood of the Nation*, January 19, 2012.

6. 2012 *American Value Survey.*

7. 2012 *Edelman Trust Barometer.*

8. For a thorough critique of the costs of excessive law and regulation to America's economy, see Philip Howard's two books: *The Death of Commonsense: How Law Is Suffocating America* (New York: Random House, 2011) and *The Rule of Nobody: Saving America from Dead Laws and Broken Government* (New York: W.W. Norton, 2014).

9. In his landmark book *Presidential Power,* after reviewing all of the constitutional powers of the chief executive of the federal government, Richard Neustadt concludes that the capability to persuade is the most potent weapon at the president's disposal (New York: Macmillan, 1960).

Chapter 2

1. In his book *The End of Power*, Moisés Naím argues that the authoritative allocation of resources, the ability to get things done, is eroding everywhere: in companies, in US foreign policy, and in Congress. Leadership is being challenged almost wherever one looks, claims Naím. Check out the book's subtitle: *From Boardrooms to Battlefields and Churches to State, Why Being in Charge Isn't What It Used to Be* (New York: Basic Books, 2013).

2. For a classic account of the economics of nonprofit performing arts organizations, see William J. Baumol and William G. Bowen, *Performing Arts—The Economic Dilemma: A Study of Problems Common to Theater, Opera, Music and Dance* (New York: The Twentieth Century Fund, 1966).

3. The following books were published by or in association with John Wiley & Sons, Inc., and/or Lincoln Center. They are listed in alphabetical order by author: Kyle Froman, *In the Wings: Behind the Scenes at the New York City Ballet* (New York: John Wiley & Sons, 2007); James Galway, *Man with the Golden Flute* (New York: Turner Publishing, 2009); Rob Kapilow, *All You Have to Do Is Listen: Music from the Inside Out* (New York: John Wiley & Sons, 2008); Rob Kapilow, *What Makes It Great: Short Masterpieces, Great Composers* (New York: John Wiley & Sons, 2011); Reynold Levy, *Yours for the Asking: An Indispensable Guide to Fundraising and Management* (New York: John Wiley & Sons, 2008); Lincoln Center, *Poet-Linc: Poetry Slam* (London: Black Dog, 2013); John Pizzarelli and Joseph Cosgriff, *World on a Sting: A Musical Memoir* (New York: Turner Publishing, 2012); Charles A. Riley, *Art at Lincoln Center: The Public Art and List Print and Poster Collections* (New York: John Wiley & Sons, 2009); Lesley Rosenthal, *Good Counsel: Meeting the Legal Needs of Nonprofits* (New York: John Wiley & Sons, 2012); Stephen Stamas and Sharon Zane, *Lincoln Center: A Promise Realized, 1976–2006* (New York: Turner Publishing, 2006); Hao Jiang Tian, *Along the Roaring River: My Wild Ride from Mao to the Met* (New York: John Wiley & Sons, 2008); and Carl Vigeland, *The Mostly Mozart Guide to Mozart* (New York: John Wiley & Sons, 2009).

Chapter 3

1. See Willard Spiegelman's story, "Nights in Full Swing in Damrosch Park This July," *Wall Street Journal*, July 16, 2008.

2. The Lincoln Center Programming department, led by Jane Moss, Ehrenkranz artistic director, includes such talented staff as Hanako Yamaguchi, director, music programming; Jon Nakagawa, director, contemporary programming; Lisa Takemoto, production manager; Bill Bragin, director, public programming; Charles Cermele, producer, contemporary programming; Kate Monaghan, associate director, programming; Jill Sternheimer, producer, public programming; and Mauricio Lomelin, associate producer, contemporary programming.

3. Nigel Redden, the director of the Lincoln Center Festival, enjoys some very gifted colleagues. They include general manager and producer, Erica D. Zielinski; senior producer, Carmen Kovens; director of production, Paul E. King; producer, Boo Froebel; and assistant general manager, Barbara Sartore.

Chapter 4

1. By constituent, here was the breakdown for a pretty typical year: New York Philharmonic, $1.8 million; Jazz at Lincoln Center, $1 million; Chamber Music Society, $362,000; New York City Ballet, $1.9 million; Metropolitan Opera, $3.5 million; Lincoln Center Theater, $1.1 million; The Juilliard School, $1.9 million; the Film Society, $780,000; and The New York Public Library for the Performing Arts, $270,000.

2. My confidence in Lincoln Center's collective ability to climb the fund-raising mountain required by redevelopment sparked a memory. It was the end of 1988 and I had served sixteen months as the president of the IRC. If the IRC were an American, its age would have entitled it to Social Security payments. And yet institutionally, it possessed no endowment and only a minuscule cash reserve. I was convinced that an endowment drive was both necessary and possible. My cochairs needed to be persuaded. Appendix A contains the essence of the case I then advanced to the IRC's cochairs, Dr. James Strickler and Winston Lord, in an effort to convince them that it was past time to launch its first-ever capital campaign. When I left the IRC for Lincoln Center it enjoyed pledges to an endowment nearing $50 million. Today it totals $140 million. This asset has permitted the institution to act far more confidently and decisively in discharging its mission.

3. Mr. Bennack approached fund-raising with energy, purposefulness, and a sense of humor. In a long feature story by Matthew Gurewitsch, "The Maestros of Lincoln Center," *Wall Street Journal*, May 1, 2007, you will discover quintessential Frank, combining a serious point with a tongue-in-cheek warning:

> In the end a project of this size needs very broad based support from the business community—and we're getting it. Anyone whose feelings are hurt because we haven't gotten around to them yet can take heart. We will.

4. The most comprehensive analysis and description of the design and redevelopment of Lincoln Center was written by Diller Scofidio + Renfro. It is lavishly illustrated. The quote can be found on page 13 of *Lincoln Center Inside Out: An Architectural Account* (Bologna, Italy: Damiana, 2012).

5. A fuller excerpt from each of these laudatory reviews follows:

> At Last, Heavenly Acoustics Are Heard in the Hall
>
> The most remarkable and it seems to me indisputable achievement of the [Tully Hall] renovation . . . is that the Starr Theater, though not any smaller, now feels intimate and warm.
>
> —Anthony Tommasini, *New York Times*, February 23, 2009

> Rebirth of the Alice Tully concert hall
>
> Lincoln Centre embarked on an extraordinary plan to reinvent itself. And, despite being clobbered by 9/11 and the present [economic] slump, the city's great and good seemed determined to make it happen; which is remarkable when you consider that it will cost a staggering $1.2 billion.
>
> The Tully transformation is the first fruit and it's a triumph.
>
> —Richard Morrison, *The Times Online*, February 20, 2009

From Spartan to Super: New Yorkers have reason to celebrate the make-over of Lincoln Center's Tully Hall

Normally, New Yorkers never agree on anything. But everyone seems to think the new and improved Alice Tully Hall, Lincoln Center's super-sized "chamber music" venue, is swell.

—Mark Swed, *Los Angeles Times*, March 3, 2009

Now that construction huts have been removed, the exterior of the building is truly breathtaking. The entrance to Alice Tully Hall used to be concealed beneath the overhang of The Juilliard School. Now the corner of the building is all glass, curving upward like the prow of an ocean liner. The lobby is huge and inviting.

The interior of the hall seems more spacious and also more inviting. The hall now seems like a piece of sculpture. The woods used on the walls, both in their textures and the way that they are lit, convey the feeling of a kind of sacred space, which a hall of music in some ways should be.

—Howard Kissel, *Daily News*, February 29, 2009

Nip and tuck: The latest Lincoln Center refurbishment is a complex piece of urban surgery

Formerly a building that seemed to revel in its appearance as a kind of bleak service area, the architectural firm Diller and Scofidio + Renfro extended the public areas out towards Broadway, created a new sunken public plaza, opened the institution out to the city and radically remodeled both the concert hall itself and The Juilliard School, which sits awkwardly on top of it.

This is an extremely sophisticated and complex piece of urban surgery addressing a number of issues that made the old building deeply unsatisfactory.

The architects to their huge credit, have managed to achieve almost seamless transition from Belluschi's [the original architect of The Juilliard School] modernism to a sculptural theatricality.

—Edwin Heathcote, *Financial Times*, March 14–15, 2009

6. A comprehensive account of the design and development of the new Charles H. Revson Fountain was written by John Seabrook and published in the January 11, 2010, issue of the *New Yorker*.

Chapter 5

1. See Reynold Levy, *Yours for the Asking: An Indispensable Guide to Fundraising and Management* (New York: John Wiley & Sons, 2008).
2. See William Whyte, *The Social Life of Small Urban Spaces* (New York: Project for Public Spaces, 1980).

3. These included, but were hardly limited to, the New York City Department of Cultural Affairs, the New York Department of City Planning, the New York City Department of Parks and Recreation, the Public Design Commission of the City of New York, the Landmarks Preservation Commission, the New York City Department of Transportation, the Department of Buildings, the New York City Department of Environment Protection, the New York City Police Department, the New York City Fire Department, the New York City Economic Development Corporation, the Department of Citywide Administrative Services, the Office of Management and Budget, the Metropolitan Transit Authority, and the Corporation Counsel of the City of New York.

4. Diller Scofidio + Renfro, *Lincoln Center Inside Out*, 18.

5. E. B. White, *Here Is New York* (New York: Little Bookworm, 1999), 53.

6. Joseph Volpe with Charles Michener, *The Toughest Show on Earth: My Rise and Reign at the Metropolitan Opera* (New York: Alfred A. Knopf, 2006).

7. The original architects were Edward J. Matthews, Philip Johnson, Jo Mielziner, Wallace K. Harrison, Eero Saarinen, Gordon Bunshaft, Max Abramovitz, and Pietro Belluschi.

8. Philip Johnson is quoted in Diller Scofidio + Renfro, *Lincoln Center Inside Out*, 9.

9. Diller Scofidio + Renfro, *Lincoln Center Inside Out*, 25.

10. To name but a dozen such additional possibilities, none of which existed in 2002, I encourage you to try dining at Betony, Blue Ribbon Sushi, Cesca, Dovetail, Gari, Josies, Marea, Nice Matine, Ocean Grill, Quest, Sarabeth's, and Shakeshack.

11. These are the addresses of the apartment houses built by each of these developers: Zeckendorf's (15 Central Park West); Barnett's Extell (The Aldyn at 60 Riverside Blvd., The Ariel East at 2628 Broadway, The Ashley at 400 West 63rd St., One Riverside Park, 50 Riverside Blvd., The Rushmore at 80 Riverside Blvd., and The Avery at 100 Riverside Blvd.); Dan Brodsky (The Concerto at 200 West 60th St., 1 Columbus Place, South Park Tower at 129 West 60th St., South Pierre at 160 West 71st St., West End Towers at 55–75 West End Ave., and the West Pierre at 253 West 72nd St.); John Avalon (Avalon Morningside Park at 1 Morningside Dr.); Donald Trump (Trump Place on the Hudson); and Lenny Litwin (The Regent at 45 West 60th St. on Amsterdam Ave. and Hawthorn Park at 160 West 62nd St.).

Chapter 6

1. For the Mostly Mozart Festival Orchestra, Lincoln Center commissioned the firm of Fisher Dachs Associates to design a stage installation that incorporated some of these very features. It has been in use every summer since 2005. This structural innovation has been uniformly well received by musicians, audiences, and critics.

2. Our prediction came true less than seventy-two hours later and well before there was any time to organize the dignified joint announcement that Bruce Crawford and I had explicitly requested and to which Paul Guenther had agreed. The news broke through the *New York Times* on Monday, June 2, 2003, in a front-page story, "The Philharmonic Agrees to Move to Carnegie Hall," cowritten by Ralph Blumenthal and Robin Pogrebin.

3. Our joint statement, issued immediately after the leaked story in the *New York Times*, is attached in its entirety as Appendix D.

4. The quote appeared in "Philharmonic Deal, Completed Quickly, Left Some in Dark," cowritten by Ralph Blumenthal and Robin Pogrebin, *New York Times*, June 3, 2003.

5. As little is more important than the selection of an orchestra's musical leader, critics and commentators have thoroughly examined the New York Philharmonic's performance on this score. The consensus is, to put it mildly, nothing to write home about. Just the headlines or summary sentences alone provide a flavor of the consensus judgment.

For Barbara Jepson, "No Maestros in New York Philharmonic's Top Management," *Wall Street Journal*, June 22, 2004.

For Anthony Tommasini, "Local Leader Wanted: Please Apply Very Soon," *New York Times*, December 10, 2006.

Justin Davidson: "The New York Philharmonic is as reliable and consistent as a metronome—and about as dull" ("Orchestrating Change," *New York Magazine*, October 9, 2007).

Alex Ross: "For two drowsy decades, the New York Philharmonic played it safe: a pair of grand-old-man directors (Kurt Mazur, Lorin Maazel), redundant festivals of canonical composers (Brahms, Tschaikovsky), the usual parade of soloists (when in doubt, Yo-Yo Ma)" ("Waking Up: Alan Gilbert Takes Over at the New York Philharmonic," *New Yorker*, October 19, 2009).

6. *New York Times*, Quotation of the Day, page 2, from "Carnegie Hall Abandons Merger Talks with the New York Philharmonic," October 8, 2003.

7. In a *New York One* interview with Roma Torre, Guenther denied that the announcement of the New York Philharmonic's move to Carnegie Hall was a bombshell that came abruptly. "Well, first of all, it wasn't really a bombshell. This is something the board of the New York Philharmonic has been discussing since last year." Video Monitoring Services of America, July 10, 2003.

8. Here is Dicterow, violinist and concertmaster of the New York Philharmonic, on National Public Radio on June 3, 2003. "It's [Avery Fisher Hall] always very bright and shrill and it's very hard to get a balance of brass and strings and winds. It's always tough to hear one another because of the vastness of the stage."

9. Deborah Solomon, in "Orchestra for Hire: No Strings Attached," *New York Times*, October 10, 2003, wrote that during an intermission of a New York Philharmonic concert in Central Park on a Monday in July 2003, "I happened to spot Paul Guenther the chairman of the Philharmonic, who was sitting on a folding chair near the stage and appeared to be in high spirits. I asked him, only half-jokingly how he would rate the acoustics in Central Park.

"Not bad [he said without missing a beat].

Better than Avery Fisher Hall."

Chapter 7

1. A copy of the full report can be found in Appendix C.

2. The open letter was released to the *New York Times* and reported on by Daniel J. Wakin in his story of July 7, 2011.

3. Here is Ross holding forth: "Opera is the riskiest of businesses, and City Opera has landed in a precarious position. My sense is that it must finally leave Lincoln Center and escape the monopolizing shadow of the Metropolitan Opera. It should make the most of limited resources and adopt a scrappy, rebellious attitude. Instead of presenting a Broadway millionaire's adaptation of an old British film about séances, why not get an avid young composer to take on an uncomfortable political subject? I have a fantasy of City Opera setting up shop in Brooklyn and offering a crashingly atonal

opera about the life and times of David Koch" ("Flummoxed: Struggles at City Opera and Across the Country," *New Yorker*, May 9, 2011).

4. Julius Rudel, in his memoir coauthored by Rebecca Pillar, *First and Parting Impressions* (Rochester, NY: University of Rochester Press, 2013), reflects further on his frustration with the New York City Opera's decline in these memorable words:

> Now I understand completely how the actions of ill-informed Board members can destroy an [opera] company. . . . What the Board of the New York City Opera allowed to happen, or more accurately precipitated, is well-nigh criminal. I am at the stage of life where anger is not a frequently felt emotion, but when George Steel, whose knowledge of Opera is limited (to put it kindly) announced that City Opera would leave Lincoln Center, I was outraged. (174)

5. Quoted in James B. Stewart, "A Ransacked Endowment at New York City Opera," *New York Times*, October 11, 2013.

Chapter 9

1. See Allan Kozinn and Michael Cooper, "First Extended Talks at Met End Without a Labor Deal," *New York Times*, August 2, 2014, in which Tino Gagaliordi of Local 802 of the American Federation of Musicians is quoted.

2. On July 26, 2014, the Metropolitan Opera widely distributed to the press a document entitled "Corrections/Comments on Local 802 Presentation of 7/25/14: Includes Original Union Presentation with Met Comments Interlineated."

3. Peter F. Drucker, *Managing The Non-Profit Organization: Principles and Practice* (New York: HarperCollins, 1990), 128.

Chapter 10

1. There are certain culinary delicacies that Beverly and I both loved. The blintz. The knish (cabbage? cherry cheese? kasha? potato? anyone?). Chocolate babka. The perfect bagel. All are extremely difficult to prepare well. But there is nothing more challenging than making a world-class egg cream.

In Brooklyn, an egg cream is regarded as a form of high culinary art. As a service to all readers, what follows are the instructions to prepare a perfect version:

> Ingredients and implements:
>
> Use Fox's u-bet chocolate syrup. Nothing else is acceptable.
>
> Purchase an old-fashioned high-pressure seltzer bottle (a bottle of club soda or sparkling water will not suffice).
>
> For a 12-ounce glass, ladle in several tablespoons of chocolate; about half an inch will do for starters (experiment to taste).
>
> Then insert a long spoon into the glass after pouring in about one inch of whole or 2 percent milk. (Skim milk will produce too thin or "watery" a result.)
>
> Aim the seltzer bottle directly at the spoon. Mix briskly.

The result will be a perfect "white head" atop the glass of about two to four inches.

Some cognoscenti prefer vanilla egg creams. For that recipe you will need to turn to another expert. The preparation of egg creams is a highly specialized art form.

2. While there was no formal sunset provision in the donation that Herb Allen extended to Jazz at Lincoln Center, resulting in a glorious glass-cantilevered venue overlooking 59th Street and Central Park, Mr. Allen was moved to a new form of generosity. Aware that Jazz at Lincoln Center was about to embark on a capital campaign and of how few attractive naming opportunities were available to it, he voluntarily relinquished his own. Bob Appel, the chairman of the board of Jazz at Lincoln Center, offered a gift of $20 million. Now the Allen Room has been renamed the Appel Room. What Allen had done in discretionary fashion, Koch bound himself to contractually. Either way, a blessing was bestowed on both the New York City Ballet and Jazz at Lincoln Center.

Chapter 11

1. See Jeffrey Sonnenfeld, *The Hero's Farewell: What Happens When CEOs Retire* (New York: Oxford University Press, 1988), 38.

2. *BusinessWeek*, January 7, 2001.

3. See Albert O. Hirschman, *Exit, Voice, and Loyalty: Responses to Decline in Firms, Organizations and States* (Cambridge, MA: Harvard University Press, 1970).

4. An excellent memoir of two Iraq wars written in the first person by an important and involved practitioner, Richard Haass, employs the term "war of choice." See Richard Haass, *War of Necessity, War of Choice* (New York: Simon & Schuster, 2009).

Chapter 12

1. Of course, Beverly Sills also served on Lincoln Center's board of directors, and as its chair, no less. But by the time of her appointment to the board, she was no longer earning a living as an artist, having retired at the very young age of fifty.

Chapter 13

1. See Joel L. Fleishman, *The Foundation: A Great American Secret—How Private Wealth Is Changing the World* (New York: PublicAffairs, 2007), 149–155.

2. See the 1999 report entitled "To Err Is Human," published by the Institute of Medicine.

Chapter 14

1. Widely regarded as an outstanding national leader in the law of nonprofit institutions, Lesley wrote what has quickly become a standard monograph on that subject. The reader who spends time with *Good Counsel* (New York: John Wiley & Sons, 2012) will be rewarded.

SELECTED BIBLIOGRAPHY

It has always seemed to me that most bibliographies are dutifully compiled. Alphabetize the sources of your endnotes and voilà, another piece of the apparatus at the end of the book has been assembled. In fact, for reasons of cost savings and the avoidance of redundancy, fewer books contain such compilations.

My love of reading and commitment to books as sources of knowledge, inspiration, motivation, and aspiration should be readily apparent by now. What follows is a list of favorites, those I found of greatest value to an often lonely CEO on the lookout for good ideas, role models, companionship, and best practices.

When running a major institution, the pressures of the day to day can leave one without much time for thinking and planning. The books enumerated below were chosen with the reflective practitioner in mind. I am confident that any CEO, staff member, or trustee of a nonprofit or a commercial enterprise would benefit from an intellectual pause that refreshes. Take your pick.

You will find in this selection a number of thrilling first-person accounts about what it's like to run a theater, guide a dance company, manage an opera, or direct an orchestra. Actors, dancers, singers, writers, and musicians find a prominent place as well in these listings. Nurturing talent and bringing work to the stage is a fascinating act of will, an expression of admirable courage. First-rate memoirs, biographies, and autobiographies can tell such stories with uncanny accuracy and verisimilitude. The reader is taken backstage into the rehearsal hall and the boardroom, places where art meets commerce.

Lincoln Center and the resident artistic organizations that call it home are favorites of the news media. They enjoy extensive print, radio, television, Internet, and social media coverage. Much of what has assumed book form has found its way onto the list below.

The widely applauded and awarded contribution of Lincoln Center to a vibrant cityscape has received ample attention from architectural critics, urban historians, sociologists, and political scientists. The extent to which the redevelopment of Lincoln Center is both consequence and cause of broader national and local trends has been a favorite theme of a number of the authors featured here.

Of course, performing art is part and parcel of a larger economy and of leadership and management themes that operate elsewhere. As Stephen Sondheim reminds us in *Sunday in the Park with George*:

> . . . Art isn't easy
> Even when you're hot

Advancing art is easy
Financing it is not
A vision's just a vision
If it's only in your head
If no one gets to see it
It's as good as dead
It has to come to light

Bringing art to light is the stuff of raising funds, selling tickets, controlling costs, and promoting productivity. Very useful guides to all of these challenges can be found in this book selection. Leadership and management observations abound, including how best to recruit first-class talent and how best to motivate and monitor superior performance.

Part of my service at Lincoln Center coincided with America's most significant and prolonged economic downturn since the Great Depression. Americans are angry with how this deep recession came to pass and with their view of the winners and losers. They are upset at Wall Street and view its leaders as indifferent to the plight of those on Main Street. Their trust in government at all levels and in corporations hovers at all-time lows. Their perception of paralysis in politics and cronyism in the marketplace is not favorable. It is in this setting that matters of governance and accountability in the nonprofit sector assume major prominence. Very thoughtful guidance on how the third sector can retain the confidence of its donors and customers can be found among the entries below.

The role of a nonprofit university, hospital, museum, performing arts center, social service organization, think tank, or advocacy outfit is vital to the health of our democracy. These institutions and the professionals and volunteers drawn to them offer important contributions to America's economic competitiveness. In number and quality, our NGOs know no equal in the world, nor does the size and scope of American private philanthropy. In their recognition of these realities and their favorable impact on our citizens and our community, selections from this bibliography will serve the reader well.

Acocella, Joan. *Mark Morris*. New York: Farrar, Straus and Giroux, 1993.

Alexander, Jane. *Command Performance: An Actress in the Theater of Politics*. New York: PublicAffairs, 2000.

Anderson, Chris. *The Long Tail: Why the Future of Business Is Selling Less of More*. New York: Hyperion, 2006.

Anderson, Maxwell. *Scanning: The Aberrant Architectures of Diller + Scofidio*. New York: Whitney Museum of the Arts, 2003.

Andringa, Robert C., and Ted W. Engstrom. *Nonprofit Board Answer Book: Practical Guidelines for Board Members and Chief Executives*. Washington, DC: The National Center for Nonprofit Boards, 1997.

Arrillaga-Andreessen, Laura. *Giving 2.0: Transform Your Giving and Our World*. San Francisco: Jossey-Bass, 2012.

Association of Governing Boards of Universities and Colleges. *Governing in the Public Trust: External Influences on Colleges and Universities*. Washington, DC: Association of Governing Boards of Universities and Colleges, 1998.

Ballon, Hilary, and Kenneth Jackson. *Robert Moses and the Modern City: The Transformation of New York*. New York: W. W. Norton, 2007.

Banfield, Edward C. *The Democratic Muse: Visual Arts and the Public Interest*. New York: Basic Books, 1984.

Barenboim, Daniel. *Music Quickens Time*. London: Verso, 2008.

Barron, James. *Piano: The Making of a Steinway Concert Grand*. New York: Henry Holt, 2006.

Baumol, William J., and William G. Bowen. *Performing Arts—The Economic Dilemma: A Study of Problems Common to Theater, Opera, Music and Dance*. New York: The Twentieth Century Fund, 1966.

Bellah, Robert N., et al. *Habits of the Heart: Individualism and Commitment in American Life*. New York: Harper & Row, 1985.

Benedict, Stephen. *Public Money and the Muse: Essays on Government Funding for the Arts*. New York: W. W. Norton, 1991.

Bennis, Warren, and Burt Nanus. *Leaders: The Strategies for Taking Charge*. New York: Harper & Row, 1985.

Bishop, Matthew, and Michael Green. *Philanthrocapitalism: How Giving Can Save the World*. New York: The Bloomsbury Press, 2008.

Blakemore, Michael. *Arguments with England: A Memoir*. London: Faber and Faber, 2004.

———. *Stage Blood*. London: Faber and Faber, 2013.

Bloomberg, Michael. *Bloomberg by Bloomberg*. New York: John Wiley & Sons, 1997.

Bok, Derek. *Beyond the Ivory Tower: Social Responsibilities of the Modern University*. Cambridge, MA: Harvard University Press, 1982.

———. *Universities in the Marketplace: The Commercialization of Higher Education*. Princeton, NJ: Princeton University Press, 2003.

Bourscheidt, Randall, ed. *Lincoln Kirstein: Program Notes 1934–1991*. New York: Eakins Press Foundation and Alliance for the Arts, 2009.

Bowen, William G. *Inside the Boardroom: Governance by Directors and Trustees*. New York: John Wiley & Sons, 1994.

Bowen, William G. *Lessons Learned: Reflections of a University President*. Princeton, NJ: Princeton University Press, 2011.

Bremner, Robert H. *American Philanthropy*. Chicago: University of Chicago Press, 1968.

———. *Giving: Charity and Philanthropy in History*. New Brunswick, NJ: Transaction Publishers, 1994.

Brendel, Alfred. *On Music: Collected Essays*. Chicago: A Capella Books, 2009.

Breslin, Herbert, and Anne Midgette. *The King and I: The Uncensored Tale of Luciano Pavarotti's Rise to Fame by His Manager, Friend and Sometime Adversary*. New York: Random House, 2004.

Brooks, Arthur, et al. *Gifts of the Muse: Reframing the Debate About the Benefits of the Arts*. Santa Monica, CA: RAND Corporation, 2004.

Brooks, Arthur C. *Who Really Cares: The Surprising Truth about Compassionate Conservatism*. New York: Basic Books, 2006.

Broughton, Philip Delves. *Life's a Pitch: What the World's Best Sales People Can Teach Us All*. New York: Penguin, 2012.

Burlingame, Dwight F., ed. *The Responsibilities of Wealth*. Indianapolis: Indiana University Press, 1992.

Burlingame, Dwight F., and Dennis R. Young. *Corporate Philanthropy at the Crossroads*. Bloomington: Indiana University Press, 1996.

Burton, Katherine. *Hedge Hunters: Hedge Fund Masters on the Rewards, the Risk, and the Reckoning*. New York: Bloomberg News, 2007.

Callahan, David. *Fortunes of Change: The Rise of the Liberal Rich and the Remaking of America*. New York: John Wiley & Sons, 2010.

Canarina, John. *The New York Philharmonic: From Bernstein to Maazel*. New York: Amadeus Press, 2010.

Carnegie, Dale. *How to Win Friends and Influence People*. New York: Pocket Books, 1936.

Chait, Richard P. *Trustee Responsibility for Academic Affairs*. Washington, DC: Association of Governing Boards, 1984.

Chait, Richard P., Thomas P. Holland, and Barbara E. Taylor. *The Effective Board of Trustees*. New York: URJ Press, 1993.

———. *Improving the Performance of Governing Boards*. Phoenix, AZ: American Council in Education, 1996.

Cherbo, Joni M., and Margaret J. Wyszomirski. *The Public Life of the Arts in America*. New Brunswick, NJ: Rutgers University Press, 2000.

Cherbo, Joni Maya, Ruth Ann Steward, and Jane Wyszomirski. *Understanding the Arts and Creative Sector in the United States*. New Brunswick, NJ: Rutgers University Press, 2008.

Clinton, Bill. *Giving: How Each of Us Can Change the World*. New York: Alfred A. Knopf, 2007.

Clotfelter, Charles T. *Federal Tax Policy and Charitable Giving*. Chicago: University of Chicago Press, 1985.

———, ed. *Who Benefits from the Nonprofit Sector?* Chicago: University of Chicago Press, 1992.

Clotfelter, Charles T., et al. *Economic Challenges in Higher Education*. Chicago: University of Chicago Press, 1992.

Clotfelter, Charles T., and Thomas Ehrlich. *Philanthropy and the Nonprofit Sector in a Changing America*. Bloomington: Indiana University Press, 1999.

Cohan, William D. *House of Cards: A Tale of Hubris and Wretched Excess on Wall Street*. New York: Doubleday, 2009.

Cook, Philip J., and Robert H. Frank. *The Winners Take-All Society: Why the Few at the Top Get So Much More Than the Rest of Us*. New York: Penguin Books, 1996.

Coopers & Lybrand. *London: World City Moving into the 21st Century*. London: Itsmo Publications, 1991.

Crimmins, James C., and Maryh Kiel. *Enterprise in the Nonprofit Sector*. New York: Rockefeller Brothers Fund, 1983.

Croyden, Margaret. *Conversations with Peter Brook: 1970–2000*. New York: Faber & Faber, 2003.

Cullman, Lewis. *Can't Take It with You: The Art of Making and Giving Money*. New York: John Wiley & Sons, 2004.

Damon, William, and Susan Verducci. *Taking Philanthropy Seriously: Beyond Noble Intentions to Responsible Giving*. Bloomington: Indiana University Press, 2006.

David, Joshua, and Robert Hammond. *High Line: The Inside Story of New York City's Park in the Sky*. New York: Farrar, Straus and Giroux, 2011.

DiMaggio, Paul J., ed. *Nonprofit Enterprise in the Arts: Studies in Mission and Constraint*. Oxford, UK: Oxford University Press, 1986.

Donoghue, Denis. *The Arts Without Mystery*. Boston: Little, Brown, 1983.

Drucker, Peter F. *Managing a Nonprofit Organization: Principles and Practices*. New York: HarperCollins, 1990.

Endlich, Lisa. *Goldman Sachs: The Culture of Success*. New York: Touchstone, 1999.

Eyre, Richard. *National Service: Diary of a Decade at the National Theatre*. London: Bloomsbury Publications, 2003.

———. *Utopia and Other Places: Memoir of a Young Director*. London: Bloomsbury Publications, 1993.

Feld, Alan L., et al. *Patrons Despite Themselves: Taxpayers and Arts Policy—A Twentieth Century Fund Report*. New York: New York University, 1983.

Feldstein, Martin, ed. *The Economist of Art Museums*. Chicago: University of Chicago Press, 1991.

Fiedler, Johanna. *Molto Agitato: The Mayhem Behind the Music at the Metropolitan Opera*. New York: Doubleday, 2001.

Findlater, Richard, ed. *At the Royal Court: 25 Years of the English Stage Company*. New York: Grove Press, 1981.

Fisher, Roger, and William Ury. *Getting to Yes: Negotiating Agreement Without Giving In*. New York: Penguin Books, 1991.

Fleishman, Joel L. *The Foundation: Great American Secret*. New York: PublicAffairs, 2007.

Fleming, Renee. *The Inner Voice: The Making of a Singer*. New York: Penguin Books, 1991.

Florida, Richard. *Cities and the Creative Class*. New York: Routledge, 2005.

———. *The Flight of the Creative Class: The New Global Competition for Talent*. New York: HarperCollins, 2007.

———. *The Great Reset*. New York: Harper, 2010.

———. *The Rise of the Creative Class*. New York: Perseus Books, 2002.

———. *Who's Your City?* New York: Basic Books, 2008.

Fram, Eugene H., and Robert F. Pearse. *The High-Performance Nonprofit: A Management Guide for Boards and Executives*. Milwaukee, WI: Family Service America, 1992.

Freund, Gerald. *Narcissism and Philanthropy: Ideas and Talent Denied*. New York: Viking, 1996.

Friedman, Carolyn S., and Karen B. Hopkins. *Successful Fundraising for Arts and Cultural Organizations*. Westport, CT: Oryx Press, 1997.

Frohnmayer, John. *Leaving Town Alive: Confessions of an Arts Warrior*. New York: Houghton Mifflin, 1993.

Froman, Kyle. *In the Wings: Behind the Scenes at the New York City Ballet*. New York: John Wiley & Sons, 2007.

Gale, Robert L. *The Committee on Trustees*. Washington, DC: Association of Governing Boards of Universities and Colleges, 1996.

Galway, Sir James. *The Man with the Golden Flute*. New York: John Wiley & Sons, 2009.

Gardner, Deborah S. *The Nathan Cummings Foundation: Looking to the Future, Honoring the Past*. n.p.: privately printed, 1997.

Gardner, John. *Excellence*. New York: W. W. Norton, 1961.

———. *On Leadership*. New York: Free Press, 1990.

———. *Self-Renewal: The Individual and the Innovative Society*. New York: W. W. Norton, 1981.

Gardner, John W. *Living, Leading and the American Dream*. San Francisco: Jossey-Bass, 2003.

Garment, Leonard. *Crazy Rhythm*. New York: Random House, 1997.

Gaudiani, Claire. *The Greater Good: How Philanthropy Drives the American Economy and Can Save Capitalism*. New York: Henry Holt, 2003.

Gay, Peter. *Mozart*. New York: Viking, 1999.

Gaylin, Willard, Ira Glasser, Steven Marcus, and David J. Rothman. *Doing Good: The Limits of Benevolence*. New York: Pantheon Books, 1975.

Gelb, Arthur. *City Room*. New York: Berkley Books, 2003.

Giamatti, A. Bartlett. *The University and the Public Interest.* New York: Athenaeum Press, 1981.

Gladwell, Malcolm. *The Tipping Point: How Little Things Can Make a Big Difference.* New York: Little, Brown, 2000.

Glaeser, Edward. *Triumph of the City.* Penguin Press, New York, 2001.

Glaser, John S. *An Insider's Account of the United Way Scandal: What Went Wrong and Why.* New York: John Wiley & Sons, 1994.

Goldberger, Paul. *Building Up and Tearing Down: Reflections on the Age of Architecture.* New York: Random House, 2009.

———. *The City Observed: New York; A Guide to the Architecture of Manhatten.* New York: Random House, 1979.

———. *Why Architecture Matters.* New Haven, CT: Yale University Press, 2009.

Gottlieb, Robert. *George Balanchine: The Ballet Maker.* New York: HarperCollins, 2004.

Grace, Kay Sprinkel, and Alan L. Wendroff. *High Impact Philanthropy: How Donors, Boards, and Nonprofit Organizations Can Transform Communities.* New York: John Wiley & Sons, 2001.

Gradenwitz, Peter. *Leonard Bernstein: The Infinite Variety of a Musician.* New York: Berg Publishers, 1987.

Gregorian, Vartan. *The Road to Home: My Life and Times.* New York: Simon & Schuster, 2003.

Gross, Michael. *Rogues' Gallery: The Secret Story of the Lust, Lies, Greed, and Betrayals That Made the Metropolitan Museum of Art.* New York: Random House, 2009.

Grossman, Allen, Christine W. Letts, and William P. Ryan. *High Performance Nonprofit Organizations: Managing Upstream for Greater Impact.* New York: John Wiley & Sons, 1999.

Grove, Andrew S. *Only the Paranoid Survive: How to Exploit the Crisis Points That Challenge Every Company and Career.* New York: Doubleday, 1996.

Hall, Donald. *Life Word.* Boston: Beacon Press, 1993.

Hall, Peter Dobkin. *Inventing the Nonprofit Sector.* Baltimore, MD: Johns Hopkins University Press, 1992.

Harman, Oren. *The Price of Altruism: George Price and the Search for the Origins of Kindness.* New York: W. W. Norton, 2010.

Harrison, Lawrence E., and Samuel P. Huntington. *Culture Matters: How Values Shape Human Progress.* New York: Basic Books, 2000.

Harvard Business Review. *On Finding and Keeping the Best People.* Boston: Harvard Business School Press, 1994.

———. *On Leadership.* Boston: Harvard Business School Press, 1998.

———. *On Managing People.* Cambridge, MA: Harvard Business School Press, 1999.

———. *On Nonprofits.* Cambridge, MA: Harvard Business School Press, 1994.

Harwood, John, and Gerald F. Seib. *Pennsylvania Avenue: Profiles in Backroom Power.* New York: Random House, 2008.

Heilbrun, James, and Charles M. Grey. *The Economics of Arts and Culture.* 2nd ed. Cambridge, MA: Cambridge University Press, 2008.

Himmelstein, Jerome L. *Looking Good and Doing Good: Corporate Philanthropy and Corporate Power.* Indianapolis: Indiana University Press, 1997.

Hodgkinson, Virginia A., Richard W. Lyman, and Associates. *The Future of the Nonprofit Sector: Challenges, Changes, and Policy Considerations.* San Francisco: Jossey-Bass, 1989.

Homans, Jennifer. *Apollo's Angels: A History of Ballet.* New York: Random House, 2010.

Horowitz, Joseph. *Artists in Exile: How Refugees from Twentieth-Century War and Revolution Transformed the American Performing Arts*. New York: HarperCollins, 2008.

———. *Classical Music in America: A History of Its Rise and Fall*. New York: W. W. Norton, 2005.

Houle, Cyril O. *Governing Boards: Their Nature and Nurture*. San Francisco: Jossey-Bass, 1989.

Howe, Fisher. *The Board Member's Guide to Fundraising*. San Francisco: Jossey-Bass, 1991.

Ignatieff, Michael. *The Needs of Strangers: An Essay on Privacy, Solidarity, and the Politics of Being Human*. New York: Penguin, 1984.

Ingram, Richard T. *Effective Trusteeship: A Guide for Board Members of Independent Colleges and Universities*. Washington, DC: Association of Governing Boards of Universities and Colleges, 1995.

———. *Governing Independent Colleges and Universities: A Handbook for Trustees, Chief Executives, and Other Campus Leaders*. Washington, DC: Association of Governing Boards of Universities and Colleges, 1993.

Ivey, Bill, and Steven J. Tepper. *Engaging Art: The Next Great Transformation of America's Cultural Life*. New York: Routledge, 2008.

Jackson, Peggy M. *Nonprofit Strategic Planning: Leveraging Sarbanes-Oxley Best Practices*. New York: John Wiley & Sons, 2007.

Jacobs, Jane. *The Death and Life of Great American Cities*. New York: Random House, 1961.

Jazz at Lincoln Center. "House of Swing." Frederick P. Rose Hall, October 18, 2004.

Jeffri, Joan. *The Emerging Arts: Management, Survival and Growth*. New York: Praeger, 1980.

Johnson, Simon, and James Kwak. *13 Bankers: The Wall Street Takeover and the Next Financial Meltdown*. New York: Pantheon Books, 2010.

Jowitt, Deborah. *Jerome Robbins: His Life, His Theater, His Dance*. New York: Simon & Schuster, 2004.

Kaiser, Michael M. *The Art of the Turnaround: Creating and Maintaining Healthy Arts Organizations*. Waltham, MA: Brandeis University Press, 2008.

Kasparov, Garry. *How Life Imitates Chess: Making the Right Moves, from the Board to the Board Room*. New York: Bloomsbury, 2008.

Katzenbach, Jon R., and Douglas K. Smith. *The Wisdom of Teams: Creating the High-Performance Organization*. Boston: Harvard Business School Press, 1993.

Kayden, Jerold S. *Privately Owned Public Space: The New York City Experience*. New York: John Wiley & Sons, 2000.

Kenney, Charles. *No Ordinary Life: The Biography of Elizabeth J. McCormack*. New York: PublicAffairs, 2012.

Kenyon, Nicholas. *Simon Rattle: From Birmingham to Berlin*. London: Faber and Faber, 2001.

Kerr, Clark. *Presidents Make a Difference: Strengthening Leadership in Colleges and Universities*. New York: Carnegie Corporation, 1984.

Kerr, Clark, and Marion L. Gade. *The Many Lives of Academic Presidents: Time, Place & Character*. Washington, DC: Association of Governing Boards of Universities and Colleges, 1986.

Koch, Frank. *The New Corporate Philanthropy: How Society and Business Can Profit*. New York: Plenum Press, 1979.

Koolhaas, Rem. *Delirious New York*. New York: Monacelli Press, 1994.

Kopp, Wendy. *One Day, All Children: The Unlikely Triumph of Teach for America and What I Learned Along the Way.* New York: PublicAffairs, 2001.

Kotler, Phillip. *Corporate Social Responsibility: Doing the Most Good for Your Company and for Your Cause.* Hoboken, NJ: John Wiley & Sons, 2005.

Kramer, Lawrence. *Why Classical Music Still Matters.* Berkeley: University of California Press, 2007.

Kravsilovsky, M. William, and Sidney Shemel. *This Business of Music.* New York: Billboard Books, 1990.

Kuhn, Thomas S. *The Structure of Scientific Revolutions.* 3rd ed. Chicago: University of Chicago Press, 1996.

Kushner, Harold S. *Living a Life That Matters: Resolving the Conflict Between Conscience and Success.* New York: Alfred A. Knopf, 2001.

Lagemann, Ellen Condliffe. *Philanthropic Foundations: New Scholarships, New Possibilities.* Bloomington: Indiana University Press, 1999.

Lebrecht, Norman. *The Maestro Myth: Great Conductors in Pursuit of Power.* New York: Pocket Books, 1997.

———. *Managers, Maestros and the Corporate Murder of Classical Music: When the Music Stops.* New York: Simon & Schuster, 1996.

———. *Who Killed Classical Music? Maestros, Managers, and Corporate Politics.* London: Carol Publishing Group Edition, 1997.

———. *Why Mahler? How One Man and Ten Symphonies Changed Our World.* New York: Pantheon Books, 2010.

Legon, Richard D. *The Board's Role in Fundraising.* Washington, DC: Association of Governing Boards of Universities and Colleges, 1997.

Leondar, Barbara, and Charles B. Neff. *Presidential Search.* Washington, DC: Association of Governing Boards of Universities and Colleges, 1992.

Lewis, Michael. *The Big Short: Inside the Doomsday Machine.* New York: W. W. Norton, 2010.

Lincoln Center, Inc. "Report on the Yujiapu Arts Center, Part I and Part II." Unpublished manuscript, n.d.

Lipman, Samuel. *Music after Modernism.* New York: Basic Books, 1979.

Lithgow, John. *Drama: An Actor's Education.* New York: Harper, 2011.

Liu, Eric, and Scott Noppe-Brandon. *Imagination First: Unlocking the Power of Possibility.* San Francisco: Jossey-Bass, 2009.

Lopate, Phillip. *Writing New York: A Literary Anthology.* New York: Washington Square Press, 1998.

Lorsch, Jay W. *Pawns or Potentates: The Reality of America's Corporate Boards.* Boston: Harvard Business School Press, 1989.

Lowenstein, Roger. *The End of Wall Street.* New York: Penguin Press, 2010.

Lupone, Patti. *Patti Lupone: A Memoir.* New York: Crown Publishing, 2010.

Mace, Myles L. *Directors: Myth and Reality.* Cambridge, MA: Harvard Business School Classics, 1971.

Machlis, Joseph. *The Enjoyment of Music.* New York: W. W. Norton, 1977.

Magat, Richard. *An Agile Servant: Community Leadership by Community Foundations.* New York: The Foundation Center, 1989.

———. *Philanthropic Giving: Studies in Varieties and Goals.* New York: Oxford University Press, 1989.

Mandelbaum, Michael. *The Frugal Superpower: America's Global Leadership in a Cash-Strapped Era.* New York: PublicAffairs, 2010.

Marsalis, Wynton. *Moving to Higher Ground: How Jazz Can Change Your Life*. New York: Random House, 2008.

———. *To a Young Jazz Musician: Letters from the Road*. New York: Random House, 2004.

Martins, Peter. *Far from Denmark*. Boston: Little, Brown, 1982.

———. *In the Wings: Behind the Scenes at the New York City Ballet*. New York: John Wiley & Sons, 2007.

McCarthy, Kathleen D. *Philanthropy and Culture: The International Foundation Perspective*. Philadelphia: University of Pennsylvania, 1984.

McCormick, Malcolm, and Nancy Reynolds. *No Fixed Points: Dance in the Twentieth Century*. New Haven, CT: Yale University Press, 2003.

Menand, Louis. *The Marketplace of Ideas: Reform and Resistance in the American University*. New York: W. W. Norton, 2010.

Mokwa, Michael P., William M. Dawson, and E. Arther Prieve. *Marketing the Arts*. New York: Praeger Publishers, 1980.

Morgenson, Gretchen, and Joshua Rosner. *Reckless Endangerment: How Outsized Ambition, Greed, and Corruption Led to Economic Armageddon*. New York: Henry Holt, 2011.

Morris, Edmund. *Beethoven: The Universal Composer*. New York: HarperCollins, 2005.

Morrison, Richard. *Orchestra—The LSO: A Century of Triumph and Turbulence*. London: Faber & Faber, 2004.

Mueller, Robert K. *Board Life: Realities of Being a Corporate Director*. New York: Amacom, 1974.

Muller, Jerry Z. *Adam Smith in His Time and Ours*. Princeton, NJ: Princeton University Press, 1993.

Naïm, Moisés. *The End of Power*. New York: Basic Books, 2013.

Nason, John W. *Foundation Trusteeship: Service in the Public Interest*. New York: The Foundation Center, 1989.

———. *The Nature of Trusteeship: The Role and Responsibilities of College and University Boards*. Washington, DC: The Association of Governing Boards of Universities and Colleges, 1982.

———. *Trustees and the Future of Foundations*. New York: Council on Foundations, 1977.

Newhouse, Victoria. *Site and Sound: The Architecture and Acoustics of New Opera Houses and Concert Halls*. New York: Monacelli Press, 2012.

Nielsen, Waldemar A. *The Big Foundations*. New York: Columbia University, 1972.

———. *The Endangered Sector*. New York: Columbia University Press, 1979.

———. *The Golden Donors: A New Anatomy of the Great Foundations*. New York: E. P. Dutton, 1985.

———. *Inside American Philanthropy: The Dramas of Donorship*. London: University of Oklahoma Press, 1996.

Novak, Michael. *Business as a Calling: Work and the Examined Life*. New York: Free Press, 1996.

O'Clery, Conor. *The Billionaire Who Wasn't: How Chuck Feeney Made and Gave Away a Fortune Without Anyone Knowing*. New York: PublicAffairs, 2007.

O'Connell, Brian. *America's Voluntary Spirit: A Book of Readings*. New York: The Foundation Center, 1983.

———. *Fifty Years in Public Causes: Stories from a Road Less Traveled*. Hanover, MA: Tuft University Press, 2005.

Odendahl, Teresa, ed. *America's Wealthy and the Future of Foundations*. New York: The Foundation Center, 1987.

———. *Charity Begins at Home: Generosity and Self Interest Among the Philanthropic Elite*. New York: Basic Books, 1990.

Olson, Mancur. *The Rise and Decline of Nations: Economic Growth, Stagflation and Social Rigidities*. New Haven, CT: Yale University Press, 1982.

Ostrower, Francie. *Why the Wealthy Give: The Culture of Elite Philanthropy*. Princeton, NJ: Princeton University Press, 1995.

Panas, Jerold. *Mega Gifts: Who Gives Them, Who Gets Them*. Chicago: Bonus Books, 1984.

Papp, Joseph, and Kenneth Turan. *Free for All: Joe Papp, the Public, and the Greatest Theater Story Ever Told*. New York: Doubleday, 2009.

Payton, Robert L. *Philanthropy: Voluntary Action for the Public Good*. New York: Collier-Macmillan, 1988.

Peale, Norman Vincent. *The Power of Positive Thinking*. New York: Fawcett Crest, 1956.

Peyser, Joan. *Bernstein: A Biography*. New York: Simon & Schuster, 1987.

Phifer, Joan Parker. *Public Art: New York*. New York: W. W. Norton, 2009.

Pifer, Alan. *Philanthropy in an Age of Transition: The Essays of Alan Pifer*. New York: The Foundation Center, 1984.

Pogrebin, Abigail. *One and the Same*. New York: Doubleday, 2009.

Polisi, Joseph W. *American Muse: The Life and Times of William Schuman*. New York: Amadeus Press, 2008.

———. *The Artist as Citizen*. New York: Amadeus Press, 2005.

Purnick, Joyce. *Mike Bloomberg: Money, Power, Politics*. New York: PublicAffairs, 2009.

Putnam, Robert D. *Bowling Alone: The Collapse and Revival of American Community*. New York: Simon & Schuster, 2000.

Randel, Don Michael. *The Harvard Dictionary of Music*. Cambridge, MA: Harvard University Press, 2003.

Rich, Frank. *Ghost Light: A Memoir*. New York: Random House, 2000.

Rockefeller, David. *Memoirs*. New York: Random House, 2002.

Rockwell, John. *All American Music: Composition in the Late Twentieth Century*. New York: Alfred A. Knopf, 1983.

Rosenberg, Claude, Jr. *Wealthy and Wise: How You and America Can Get the Most Out of Your Giving*. Boston: Little, Brown, 1994.

Rosenthal, Lesley. *Good Counsel: Meeting the Legal Needs of Nonprofit*. New York: John Wiley & Sons, 2012.

Rosovsky, Henry. *The University: An Owner's Manual*. New York: W. W. Norton, 1990.

Ross, Alex. *Listen to This*. New York: Farrar, Straus, and Giroux, 2010.

———. *The Rest Is Noise: Listening to the Twentieth Century*. New York: Farrar, Straus, and Giroux, 2007.

Rosso, Henry A. *Rosso on Fund Raising: Lessons from a Master's Lifetime Experience*. San Francisco: Jossey-Bass, 1996.

Rubin, Robert E., and Jacob Weisberg. *In an Uncertain World*. New York: Random House, 2003.

Salamon, Julie. *Rambam's Ladder: A Meditation on Generosity and Why It Is Necessary to Give*. New York: Workman Publishing, 2003.

Salamon, Lester M. *America's Nonprofit Sector: A Primer*. New York: The Foundation Center, 2012.

———, ed. *Global Civil Society: Dimensions of the Nonprofit Sector*. Baltimore, MD: Johns Hopkins Center for Civil Society Studies, 1999.

———, et al. *Government and the Third Sector: Emerging Relationships in Welfare States*. San Francisco: Jossey-Bass, 1992.

———. *Holding the Center: America's Nonprofit Sector at a Crossroads*. New York: A Report for the Nathan Cummings Foundation, 1997.

———. *The Resilient Sector: The State of Nonprofit America*. Washington, DC: Brookings Institution Press, 2003.

Salamon, Lester M., and Helmut K. Anheier. *The Emerging Nonprofit Sector: An Overview*. New York: Manchester University Press, 1996.

Sandel, Michael J. *What Money Can't Buy: The Moral Limits of Markets*. New York: Farrar, Straus and Giroux, 2012.

Schroeder, Alice. *The Snowball: Warren Buffett and the Business of Life*. New York: Bantam Books, 2009.

Scott, Katherine Tyler. *Creating Caring and Capable Boards: Reclaiming the Passion of Active Trusteeship*. San Francisco: Jossey-Bass, 2000.

Seltzer, Michael. *Securing Your Organization's Future: A Complete Guide to Fundraising Strategies*. New York: The Foundation Center, 1987.

Shannon, James P., ed. *The Corporate Contributions Handbook: Devoting Private Means to Public Needs*. San Francisco: Jossey-Bass, 1991.

Shore, Bill. *The Cathedral Within*. New York: Random House, 1999.

Siblin, Eric. *The Cello Suites: J. S. Bach, Pablo Casals, and the Search for a Baroque Masterpiece*. New York: Atlantic Monthly Press, 2009.

Silber, John. *Architecture of the Absurd: How "Genius" Disfigured a Practical Art*. New York: Quantuck Lane Press, 2007.

Sills, Beverly. *Bubbles: A Self-Portrait*. New York: Warner Books, 1976.

Smith, David H. *Entrusted: The Moral Responsibilities of Trusteeship*. Bloomington: Indiana University, 1995.

Smith, James A. *The Idea Brokers: Think Tanks and the Rise of the New Policy Elite*. New York: Free Press, 1991.

Sokol, Martin L. *The New York City Opera: An American Adventure*. New York: Collier Macmillan, 1989.

Sondheim, Stephen. *Finishing the Hat: Collected Lyrics (1954–1981) with Attendant Comments, Principles, Heresies, Grudges, Whines and Anecdotes*. New York: Alfred A. Knopf, 2010.

———. *Look, I Made a Hat: Collected Lyrics (1981–2011) with Attendant Comments, Amplifications, Dogmas, Harangues, Digressions, Anecdotes and Miscellany*. New York: Alfred A. Knopf, 2011.

Sonnenfeld, Jeffrey. *The Hero's Farewell: What Happens When CEOs Retire*. New York: Oxford University Press, 1998.

Sorkin, Andrew Ross. *Too Big to Fail*. New York: Viking, 2009.

Soros, George. *Soros on Soros: Staying Ahead of the Curve*. New York: John Wiley & Sons, 1995.

Stamas, Stephen, and Zane Sharon. *Lincoln Center: Promise Realized*. New York: John Wiley & Sons, 2007.

Stanton, Ronald P. *Recollections & Reflections: A Trader's Life: A Memoir*. New York: privately printed, 2010.

Steckel, Richard, and Robin Simons. *Doing Best by Doing Good*. New York: Penguin Books, 1992.

Stein, Tobie S. *Workforce Transitions from the Profit to the Nonprofit Sector*. New York: Plenum Press, 2002.

Steinhardt, Arnold. *Indivisible by Four: A String Quartet in Pursuit of Harmony*. New York: Farrar, Straus and Giroux, 1998.

———. *Violin Dreams*. New York: Houghton Mifflin, 2006.

Steinhardt, Michael. *No Bull: My Life In and Out of Markets*. New York: John Wiley & Sons, 2001.

Taylor, Paul. *Private Domain*. New York: Alfred A. Knopf, 1987.

Tharp, Twyla. *Push Comes to Shove: An Autobiography*. New York: Bantam Books, 1992.

Trachtenberg, Stephen Joel. *Big Man on Campus: A University President Speaks Out on Higher Education*. New York: Simon & Schuster, 2008.

Tusa, John. *Engaged with the Arts: Writings from the Frontline*. London: I. B. Tauris, 2007.

Vanguard Public Foundation. *Robin Hood Was Right: A Guide to Giving Your Money for Social Change*. New York: Vanguard Public Foundation, 1977.

Vogel, Harold L. *Entertainment Industry Economics: A Guide for Financial Analysis*. Cambridge, UK: Cambridge University Press, 2001.

Volpe, Joseph. *The Toughest Show on Earth: My Rise and Reign at the Metropolitan Opera*. New York: Alfred A. Knopf, 2006.

Warner, Irving R. *The Art of Fund Raising*. New York: Harper & Row, 1975.

Weeden, Curt. *Corporate Social Investing*. San Francisco: Berrett-Koehler, 1998.

Weill, Sandy. *The Real Deal: My Life in Business and Philanthropy*. New York: Warner Business Books, 2006.

Weisberger, Lauren. *The Devil Wears Prada: A Novel*. New York: Doubleday, 2003.

Weisbord, Burton A. *The Nonprofit Economy*. Cambridge, MA: Harvard University Press, 1988.

Wessel, David. *In Fed We Trust: Ben Bernanke's War on the Great Panic*. New York: Crown, 2009.

White, E. B. *Here Is New York*. New York: Little Book Worm, 1949.

White, Virginia P. *Grants for the Arts*. New York: Plenum Press, 1980.

Whitehead, John C. *A Life in Leadership: From D. Day to Ground Zero, an Autobiography*. New York: Perseus Books, 2005.

Willensky, Elliot, and Norval White. *AIA Guide to New York City*. New York: Harcourt Brace Jovanovich, 1988.

Wolf, Thomas. *Managing a Nonprofit Organization in the Twenty-First Century*. New York: Simon & Schuster, 1999.

Wolf, Thomas, Dr., and Nancy Glaze. *And the Band Stopped Playing: The Rise and Fall of the San Jose Symphony*. Cambridge, MA: Wolf, Keens, 2005.

Wolfensohn, James D. *A Global Life*. New York: PublicAffairs, 2010.

Wood, Miriam M., ed. *Nonprofit Boards and Leadership: Cases on Governance, Change and Board-Staff Dynamics*. San Francisco: Jossey-Bass, 1996.

Wuthnow, Robert. *Acts of Compassion: Caring for Others and Helping Ourselves*. Princeton, NJ: Princeton University Press, 1999.

———. *Learning to Care: Elementary Kindness in an Age of Indifference*. New York: Oxford University Press, 1995.

Wuthnow, Robert, and Virginia A. Hodgkinson. *Faith and Philanthropy in America*. San Francisco: Jossey-Bass, 1990.

Young, Edgar. *Lincoln Center: The Building of an Institution*. New York: New York University Press, 1980.

Zabel, William D. *The Rich Die Richer and You Can Too*. New York: William Morrow, 1995.

Zander, Alvin. *Making Boards Effective*. San Francisco: Jossey-Bass, 1993.

INDEX

ABOUT THE AUTHOR

Reynold Levy was most recently the president of Lincoln Center for the Performing Arts, from March 1, 2002 to January 31, 2014. Before that he was president of the International Rescue Committee, a senior officer at AT&T and the president of the AT&T Foundation, executive director of the 92nd Street Y, and staff director of the Task Force on the New York City Fiscal Crisis.

A frequent recipient of awards and honorary degrees, Levy maintains a busy schedule of public speaking, university teaching, and consulting. Currently he is an adjunct professor at Columbia University's School of International Public Affairs and a special advisor to the private equity firm General Atlantic.

Levy is a member of the Council on Foreign Relations, the chairman of the Charles H. Revson Foundation, a fellow of the American Academy of Arts and Sciences, and a member of the Tony Awards Nominating Committee. He also serves as a director of First Republic Bank.

A graduate of Hobart College, Phi Beta Kappa, Levy earned a PhD in government and foreign affairs from the University of Virginia and a law degree from Columbia University.

They Told Me Not to Take That Job is his fourth book.

PublicAffairs is a publishing house founded in 1997. It is a tribute to the standards, values, and flair of three persons who have served as mentors to countless reporters, writers, editors, and book people of all kinds, including me.

I. F. Stone, proprietor of *I. F. Stone's Weekly*, combined a commitment to the First Amendment with entrepreneurial zeal and reporting skill and became one of the great independent journalists in American history. At the age of eighty, Izzy published *The Trial of Socrates*, which was a national bestseller. He wrote the book after he taught himself ancient Greek.

Benjamin C. Bradlee was for nearly thirty years the charismatic editorial leader of *The Washington Post*. It was Ben who gave the *Post* the range and courage to pursue such historic issues as Watergate. He supported his reporters with a tenacity that made them fearless and it is no accident that so many became authors of influential, best-selling books.

Robert L. Bernstein, the chief executive of Random House for more than a quarter century, guided one of the nation's premier publishing houses. Bob was personally responsible for many books of political dissent and argument that challenged tyranny around the globe. He is also the founder and longtime chair of Human Rights Watch, one of the most respected human rights organizations in the world.

·   ·   ·

For fifty years, the banner of Public Affairs Press was carried by its owner Morris B. Schnapper, who published Gandhi, Nasser, Toynbee, Truman, and about 1,500 other authors. In 1983, Schnapper was described by *The Washington Post* as "a redoubtable gadfly." His legacy will endure in the books to come.

Peter Osnos, *Founder and Editor-at-Large*